ADVANCED ALGORITHMS
FOR NEURAL NETWORKS
A C++ SOURCEBOOK

ADVANCED ALGORITHMS
FOR NEURAL NETWORKS
A C++ SOURCEBOOK

Timothy Masters

WILEY
JOHN WILEY & SONS, INC.
New York • Chichester • Brisbane • Toronto • Singapore

Publisher: Katherine Schowalter
Editor: Diane D. Cerra
Managing Editor: Micheline Frederick

Designations used by companies to distinguish their products are often claimed as trademarks. In all instances where John Wiley & Sons, Inc. is aware of a claim, the product names appear in initial capital or all capital letters. Readers, however, should contact the appropriate companies for more complete information regarding trademarks and registration.

This text is printed on acid-free paper.

Copyright © 1995 by John Wiley & Sons, Inc.

All rights reserved. Published simultaneously in Canada.

This publication is designed to provide accurate and authoritative information in regard to the subject matter covered. It is sold with the understanding that the publisher is not engaged in rendering legal, accounting, or other professional service. If legal advice or other expert assistance is required, the services of a competant professional person should be sought.

The algorithms and programs in this book have been prepared with care and tested extensively. The publisher and author make no warranty of any kind, expressed or implied, of their suitability for any particular purpose. In no event will the publisher or author be liable for any consequential, incidental, or indirect damages (including damages for loss of business profits, business interruption, loss of business information, and the like) arising from the use or inability to use the programs and algorithms in this book, even if the publisher or author has been advised of the possibility of such damages.

Portions of the source code were originally published in *Practical Neural Network Recipes in C++* by Timothy Masters.
Copyright © 1993 by Academic Press, Inc.

Reproduction or translation of any part of this work beyond that permitted by section 107 or 108 of the 1976 United States Copyright Act without the permission of the copyright owner is unlawful. Requests for permission or further information should be addressed to the Permissions Department, John Wiley & Sons, Inc.

Library of Congress Cataloging-in-Publication Data:

Masters, Timothy.
    Advanced algorithms for neural networks : a C++ sourcebook /
    Timothy Masters.
        p.   cm.
    Includes index.
    ISBN 0-471-10588-0 (paper/disk)
    1. Neural networks (Computer science)   2. Computer algorithms
    3. C++ (Computer program language) I. Title.
    QA76.87.M367 1995   94-43390
    006.3—dc20   CIP

Printed in the United States of America
10 9 8 7 6 5 4 3 2 1

This book is dedicated to the two people who are primarily responsible for my love of statistics. Robert Schell introduced me to statistics and showed me the beauty and joy that lie beyond means and standard deviations. Eugene Klimko expertly guided me through the nuances and subtleties of mathematical statistics. I hope that this text serves as yet another clear demonstration of the close connection between neural networks and statistics and so increases the beauty of both of these fields.

Preface

As neural networks become accepted in the mainstream defense and industrial communities, there is an ever-increasing need to advance the state of the art to keep up with expectations. When neural networks were an interesting intellectual curiosity, a unique blend of biology and technology, there was much leeway in the design of algorithms. A training method that required a weekend to produce a neural network that worked surprisingly well was acceptable. But when neural networks are expected to make real-time decisions on the trading floor, weekend training algorithms are not exactly hot commodities. And when neural networks assist in medical diagnosis, taking part in life-or-death decisions, thorough validation of their performance would seem to be important. This book addresses some of these issues.

The title *Advanced Algorithms for Neural Networks* could easily apply to a twenty-volume set. New architectures are appearing daily, and rigorous theoretical results are finally lending respectability to what many have long seen as arcane technology. So how does one choose topics from this vast universe of possibilities? My criteria are straightforward. Build on whatever strong foundations already exist, and always strive for practicality. Every algorithm in this book is one that has known value and immediate functionality. This leaves open the possibility that some powerful new technique may be ignored. That's a risk worth taking, as whatever is truly worthwhile will survive and make its way into future works. The fact of the matter is that the neural network field is highly isolated from other related fields. Mathematical and statistical techniques that are in widespread use in some circles have been woefully neglected in the neural network community. Thus, I have set two goals for this text. The first is to introduce to the reader a variety of standard algorithms that are useful in neural network applications but that have not yet seen widespread acceptance among neural network professionals. The second goal is to choose some of the most powerful neural network architectures and advance the state of their development. This text makes contributions in both of these areas.

The most widespread neural network model in use today is the multiple-layer feedforward network (MLFN). The primary disadvantage of this model is that its training time can be monstrous. Three chapters are devoted to this problem. The first chapter works at improving the speed with which the algorithm crawls to the bottom of the nearest local minimum. Traditional backpropagation is an abomination. So the popular and effective conjugate gradient algorithm is presented in detail. An unusual variation in which second derivative information can be used to speed the line search is also shown. Finally, the Levenberg-Marquardt algorithm, which is often very fast in small, well-behaved problems, is presented in detail.

The second chapter surveys stochastic training algorithms. These are necessary to cope with the multitude of poor local minima that plague MLFNs. An algorithm of my own design that seems to work very well for neural networks is shown first. Then a generic version of traditional simulated annealing is given. This highly adaptable algorithm can be easily customized by the reader. Finally, the unusual but often effective method of stochastic smoothing is shown.

The third chapter integrates the material of the preceding two chapters into exceptionally effective training algorithms. Alternating stochastic methods with direct descent combines the speed of deterministic descent with the reliability of random search. And the efficiency of stochastic smoothing can be greatly increased by using the gradient to supply hints.

My favorite neural network is the probabilistic neural net (PNN). Its training speed is often orders of magnitude faster than that of the MLFN. Its performance is usually superb, and it intrinsically provides mathematically sound confidence levels for its decisions. This neural network model is examined in detail. Two immensely valuable generalizations of the basic form are presented, and new methods of training this modified PNN are supplied.

The generalized regression neural network (GRNN), a variation of the PNN that is capable of function mapping, has been taking the neural network community by storm. It is described in detail here, and PNN training algorithms are generalized to encompass this model. The same extensions that I applied to the PNN are applied to the GRNN to produce a neural network that has immense power in general function mapping applications.

Several years ago, Dr. Moon Kim showed how a decades-old statistical technique could be recast as a neural network. The Gram-Charlier neural net (GCNN) does not have the broad applicability of the PNN and the MLFN, but in some situations it is superb. It is one of those rare best-of-all-worlds models that combine extremely fast training with extremely fast execution. This model, along with some recent improvements, is presented in detail.

A common problem in neural network applications is an overabundance of measured variables. The sheer quantity of data can overwhelm training algorithms. Moreover, some neural network models are intolerant of redundancy in the variables. Methods for both reducing the number of variables and simultaneously decreasing their redundancy are discussed.

Perhaps the most important part of a neural network solution is validation. Does the model really perform as it should? This question does not generally receive the attention that it merits. One of the reasons for avoiding the validation issue is that known data for training and testing is often rare or expensive (or both). An entire chapter is devoted to validation. The first half of the chapter shows how the researcher can test the reliability of the test results. Too often a neural network is tested, and the only product of the validation process is an error measure. No effort is made to test the validity of the error measure itself. This important subject is treated in depth. The second half of the chapter shows how precious data can be used with maximum efficiency. It is not widely known that a dataset can often be legitimately used for both training *and* validation. The performance assessments of these methods are as good as or even better than the results obtained by splitting the dataset into training and testing parts. The most popular and reliable methods for accomplishing this seemingly magical feat are shown.

The final chapter is a user's manual for the PNN program that is included on the accompanying code disk. This program implements all of the PNN, GRNN, and GCNN algorithms discussed in the text. Complete source and an executable are provided, and the chapter includes a test suite to help the reader verify correct operation of the program.

The code disk also includes source and an executable for a program called MLFN2. This is an updated version of the MLFN program that I supplied with my earlier *Signal and Image Processing with Neural Networks*. Complete backward compatibility is maintained. Several small bugs in the original program are fixed, and the training algorithms presented in the first three chapters of this text are implemented.

All of the program code in this book is in C++, as this language combines high-level, object-oriented structure with nearly the speed and compactness of assembler. An attempt has been made to use designs unique to C++ only when they are vital. Thus, much of the code can be easily adapted to C compilers. Vector and Matrix classes, as well as operator overloading, have been deliberately avoided. Such specialized constructs contribute little or nothing to program efficiency and complicate the lives of programmers who wish to use these algorithms in other languages. Strictly C++ techniques have been used only when they significantly improve program readability or efficiency. Because the operation of all programs is thoroughly discussed in the accompanying text, translation to other languages should not be difficult.

All of the C++ code in this book and on the accompanying disk has been tested for strict ANSI compatibility. No special proprietary libraries are ever referenced. The author uses Symantec C++ version 6.1. The code has also been compiled with Borland C++ Professional. It is anticipated that any ANSI C++ compiler should be able to compile the code correctly.

Contents

1. Deterministic Optimization 1
    Traditional Backpropagation 2
        An Advantage of Steepest Descent 8
    Line Minimization 8
        Refining the Interval 18
        Incorporating Derivative Information 26
    Conjugate Gradient Methods 31
    Levenberg-Marquardt Learning 47
        Code for Levenberg-Marquardt Learning 57

2. Stochastic Optimization 73
    Overview of Simulated Annealing 74
    Primitive Simulated Annealing 76
        Refinements 77
        Code for Primitive Annealing 79
    Conventional and Advanced Simulated Annealing 83
        The Details 92
        Code for General Simulated Annealing 96
        Usage Guidelines 101
    Stochastic Smoothing 103
    Random Perturbation 112
        Code for Perturbing a Point 113
        Generating Uniform Random Numbers 116
        Chopping, Stacking, and Shuffling 118
        Normally Distributed Random Numbers 125
        Cauchy Random Vectors 127
        A Final Thought 133

3. Hybrid Training Algorithms 135
    Simple Alternation 136
    Stochastic Smoothing with Gradient Hints 144

4. Probabilistic Neural Networks I: Introduction 157
Foundations of the PNN 158
PNN versus MLFN versus Traditional Statistics 161
Bayes Classification 162
Parzen's Method of Density Estimation 163
Multivariate Extension of Parzen's Method 170
The Original PNN 171
Computation in the PNN 173
Code for Computing PNN Classification 176
Optimizing Sigma 177
Accelerating the Basic PNN 190
Bayesian Confidence Measures 192

5. Probabilistic Neural Networks II: Advanced Techniques 193
Different Variables Rate Different Sigmas 194
A Continuous Error Criterion 197
Derivatives of the Error Function 201
Incorporating Prior Probabilities 204
Efficient Computation 205
Classes May Deserve Their Own Sigmas, Too 212
Optimizing Multiple-Sigma Models 220

6. Generalized Regression 223
Review of Ordinary Regression 224
Simple Linear Regression 226
Multiple Regression 227
Polynomial Regression 230
The General Regression Neural Network 234
An Intuitive Approach 237
Donald Specht's GRNN Architecture 239
Computing the Gradient 240
The GRNN in Action 246

Contents

7. The Gram-Charlier Neural Network **251**
    Structure and Overview of Functionality 253
    Motivation 256
    Series Expansions of Densities and Distributions 258
        Hermite Polynomials and Normal Density Derivatives 259
        An Alternative Representation of the Density 262
        Computing Hermite Polynomials 263
        Computing the Coefficients 263
        Finding the Coefficients from a Sample 266
    What's Wrong with this Picture? 270
        Other Problems 272
    Edgeworth's Expansion 273
        Mathematics of the Edgeworth Expansion 275
        Code for a GCNN with Edgeworth's Modification 279
    Comparing the Models 282
    Multivariate Versions of the GCNN 289

8. Dimension Reduction and Orthogonalization **293**
    Principal Components 295
        Scaling and Computation Issues 300
        Code for Principal Components 303
    Principal Components of Group Centroids 316
    Discriminant Functions 319

9. Assessing Generalization Ability **335**
    Bias and Variance in Statistical Estimators 337
        Notation 338
        What Good Are They? 340
        Bias and Variance of the Sample Mean 341
    The Jackknife and the Bootstrap 343
        The Jackknife 343
        Code for the Jackknife 349
        The Bootstrap 351

Code for the Bootstrap	355
Final Comments on the Jackknife and the Bootstrap	356
Economical Error Estimation	359
Population Error, Apparent Error, and Excess Error	360
Overview of Efficient Error Estimation	364
Cross Validation	365
Code for Cross Validation	367
The Bootstrap Estimate of Excess Error	369
Code for the Bootstrap Method	371
Efron's E0 Estimator	373
Code for the E0 Estimator	374
The E632 Estimator	376

10. Using the PNN Program ... 379

Output Mode	381
Network Model	382
Kernel Functions	383
Building the Training Set	384
Learning	386
Confusion Matrices	387
Testing in AUTOASSOCIATION and MAPPING Modes	389
Saving Weights and Execution Results	389
Alphabetical Glossary of Commands	390
Verification of Program Operation	394

Appendix ... 403

Disk Contents	403
Hardware and Software Requirements	405
Making a Backup Copy	405
Installing the Disk	405

Bibliography ... 407

Index ... 427

ADVANCED ALGORITHMS
FOR NEURAL NETWORKS
A C++ SOURCEBOOK

1
Deterministic Optimization

- Traditional backpropagation

- Line minimization

- Conjugate gradient learning

- Levenberg-Marquardt learning

Many neural network models are trained by finding a set of weights or other parameters that minimizes some measure of the network's error. There are two broad categories of algorithms for finding optimal values. In this chapter we will discuss *deterministic* algorithms. This family is characterized by the fact that at each step of the optimization process the actions taken are completely determined by explicit formulas. In general, the march toward the nearest valley in the error function is relentlessly downhill. The implication is that deterministic algorithms are usually quite efficient, requiring relatively few expensive function evaluations in order to find a minimum. Their main problem is that they will usually gravitate to whatever local minimum happens to be nearest the starting point. If the function has a large number of minima, many of which are inferior to some global minimum, then deterministic algorithms can be dangerously misleading in their results. In the next chapter, we will discuss an alternative family called *stochastic* algorithms. This family relies to a great extent on random searches. Thus, stochastic algorithms are relatively slow but more likely to find the global minimum. Further discussion of this topic will be postponed until the next chapter.

This text will not attempt to provide anything approaching a complete presentation of the topic of function optimization. Neither will it adequately serve as a sourcebook for general-purpose optimization algorithms. Books like Press *et al.* (1992) are far more suitable for that task. The focus in this text will be on those particular algorithms that are known to be effective for training common neural network models.

Traditional Backpropagation

No discussion of neural network training would be complete without at least a polite acknowledgment of that old workhorse known as *backpropagation*. This is unfortunate, as both the name and the associated algorithm are poorly chosen. Nevertheless, when David Rumelhart, Geoffrey Hinton, and Ronald Williams developed this algorithm in the late 1980's (along with several other people working independently), they made a truly monumental contribution to the field of neural networks. I would not dare to disparage their brilliant and valuable work. Any disparagement put forth here is instead directed at the mass of researchers who, for too many subsequent years, blindly accepted that method, never attempting to improve its performance.

That is changing at last, with powerful new training algorithms being published monthly, and some of these actually appearing in commercial products. In this first section, we will present a brief historical perspective, show why the method is both misnamed and often ineffective, and end by showing one way in which it may actually be somewhat superior to many other training methods.

First, let's tackle the name. In the early days of neural networks, a serious impediment to the widespread use of many models was the fact that provably effective training algorithms were not known. In particular, this was true of the multiple-layer feedforward network that has come into such widespread use. When it was first shown how the gradient of the error function for this model could be computed and then used to train the network, a major step forward was taken. We will not detail the mathematics of gradient computation here. The original derivation is in the classic Rumelhart *et al.* (1986). Another derivation, along with source code, can be found in Masters (1993). A detailed generalization of the gradient computation to the complex domain is in Masters (1994). All that we need to know right now is that backpropagation involves a two-step process. The first step is the ordinary forward pass, in which the effect of the inputs is propagated forward through the network to reach the output layer. When the gradient is computed, a second pass, this time *backward* through the network, is taken. The errors at the output layer are propagated backward toward the input layer, with the partial derivatives of the total error with respect to the weights in each layer appearing along the way. Thus, it is perfectly reasonable to use the term backpropagation to describe this method of computing the gradient.

This is where an unfortunate circumstance steps in. Although the pioneers who developed this technique were brilliant in their field, they apparently were not very experienced in sophisticated optimization algorithms. They chose to apply a relatively primitive minimization method to train the network. Their classic paper linked the backpropagation method of computing the gradient with direct gradient descent as a means of training the multiple-layer feedforward network. Somehow the two have become inextricably entwined. Consequently, when the term backpropagation is used, direct gradient descent is implied. I will make an attempt to distinguish between these two concepts, but the task is probably hopeless due to its deep entrenchment in tradition.

Let us examine the direct gradient descent algorithm that has miraculously survived for so long as a standard method of training neural networks. It has a powerful property: It can be mathematically proven that this algorithm will always converge to a local minimum in the error function. The fact that an immense number of iterations are often necessary is beside the point. It *will* converge.

The philosophy driving this method, often also called *steepest descent*, is simple. From the current point, determine which direction points downward most steeply, and go that way. The direction of steepest descent is always along the (negative) gradient. So all we do is compute the gradient and move in the opposite direction. We are guaranteed to reduce the function value, at least in the neighborhood of the current point. And there lies the rub. How far do we move? Although a little step might take us down into the valley, a bigger step might just as easily take us back up the other side, to our detriment. There are several ways of determining the step size. We will start with one that is very safe, but is only rarely used.

The most conservative way of moving downward along the gradient direction is to use a line minimization algorithm and go to the bottom of the valley in that direction. Line minimization will be discussed in detail on page 8. For now, just imagine that we take a step out in the negative gradient direction. If the function increases, we have gone too far, so back up. If the function decreases, we are on the right track. Step again. Repeat this forward and backward motion at ever-decreasing step sizes until we cannot decrease the function any more. This is our new point, and we compute the gradient here and minimize in that new direction. This algorithm makes a lot of intuitive sense. But it turns out to be extremely inefficient. The line minimization requires a lot of function evaluations that are wasted. Figure 1.1 shows a typical path taken by this method. The points at the bottoms of the valleys follow a zig-zag path. Each line minimization moves to a tangent of the function's level curve, from which it then sets out in a direction perpendicular to the previous direction. This is an extremely expensive way to find a minimum. On the other hand, it is close to a very powerful method. We will return to this topic on page 31 when conjugate gradient algorithms are discussed.

Gradient descent minimization can be both simplified and generally speeded up by avoiding the line minimization. Simply take a step whose length is preordained to be some fixed size and hope for the best. As long as the step is reasonably small, the function will decrease. Even though we will almost surely fail to descend as much as we would if we used line minimization to find the true bottom along the gradient line, we will most likely more than make up for that by the economy of having taken a single step instead of a long sequence of steps along the gradient. This, in fact, is the original training algorithm described in Rumelhart *et al.* (1986).

As can be imagined, there are a lot of risks associated with the use of a fixed step size. It is crucial that we not jump too far from the current point at which the gradient was calculated. Thus, the steps must be small. They must not be tiny, though, or our path may resemble that shown in Figure 1.2. We will make it to the bottom eventually, but not until a ridiculous number of steps have been taken. On the other hand, that may be better than stepping too far. Figure 1.3 shows how we may oscillate wildly if the step size is too large. The step-size parameter is a vital choice that must be made whenever this algorithm is employed.

Figures 1.1 and 1.3 illustrate a problem that is common with naive steepest descent. Even when the step size is carefully chosen, the path taken crosses back and forth throughout the weight space unless the step size is set to an unrealistically small value. It would be nice if we could take advantage of the overall momentum toward the minimum to propel the steps more strongly in that direction. In fact, Rumelhart *et al.* (1986) shows how this can be easily accomplished. After computing the gradient at the current point, add to that vector a moderate fraction of the previous search vector. The effect is essentially that of an IIR low-pass filter. The high-frequency zig-zag motion is attenuated, while the low-frequency trend toward the minimum is strengthened. Figure 1.4 shows a typical path when momentum is imposed. Notice that the search directions are stretched out, and the total path length is reduced.

Judicious use of momentum can profoundly speed convergence of naive steepest descent. This is an extremely valuable modification to the basic algorithm. However, it is not a perfect solution to the problem. Even in ideal circumstances, zig-zagging still occurs. And choosing the fraction of the previous search direction to add to the current gradient is not easy. If the fraction is too small, little benefit will be obtained. If it is too large, convergence will be slowed or even prevented entirely. It was bad enough that this algorithm already required that the fixed step size be specified. Now we have another important parameter to choose. That's no fun at all.

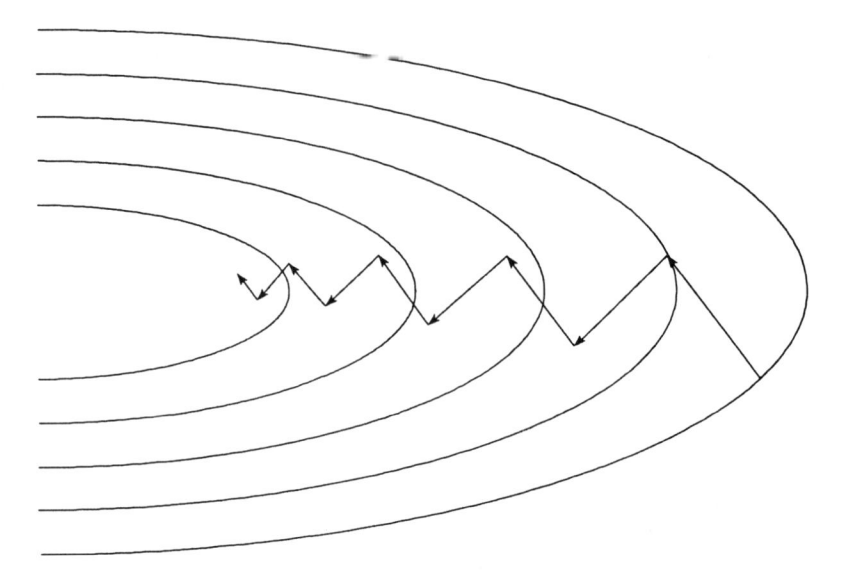

Figure 1.1 Steepest descent with line minimization.

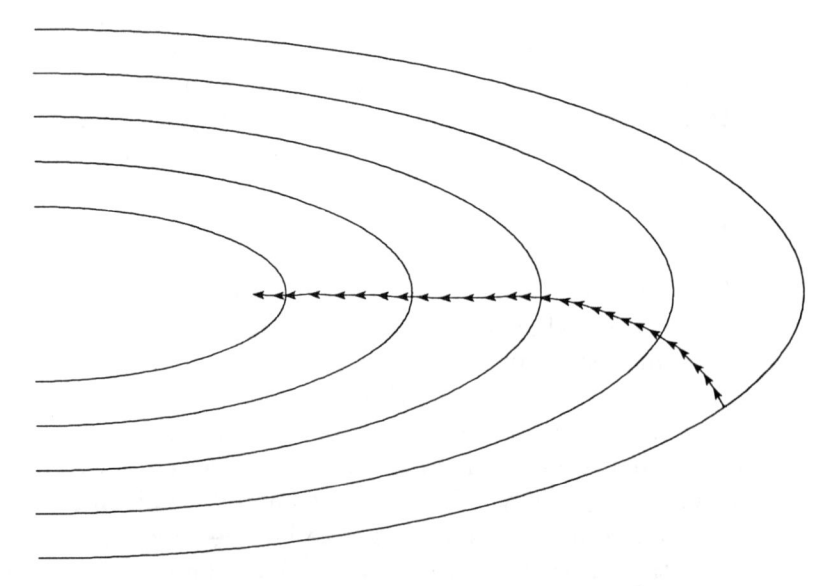

Figure 1.2 Fixed step size too small.

Traditional Backpropagation

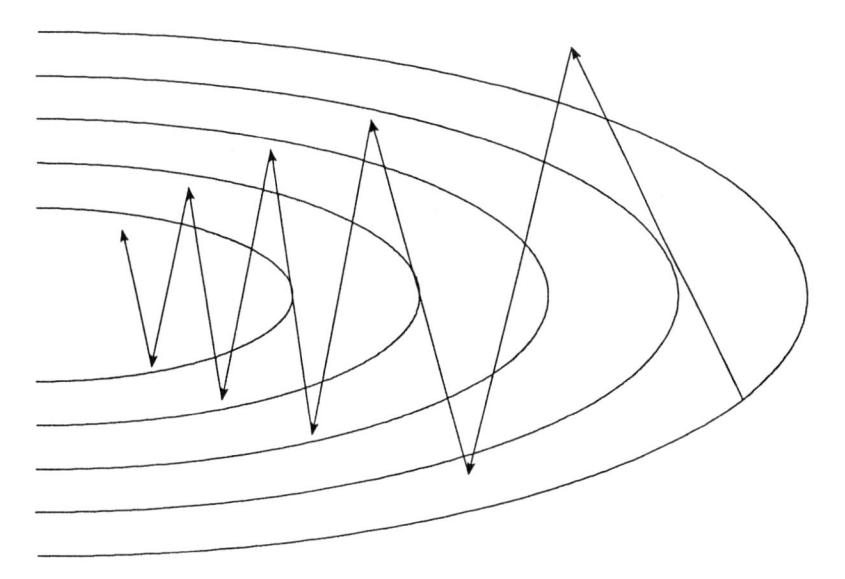

Figure 1.3 Fixed step size too large.

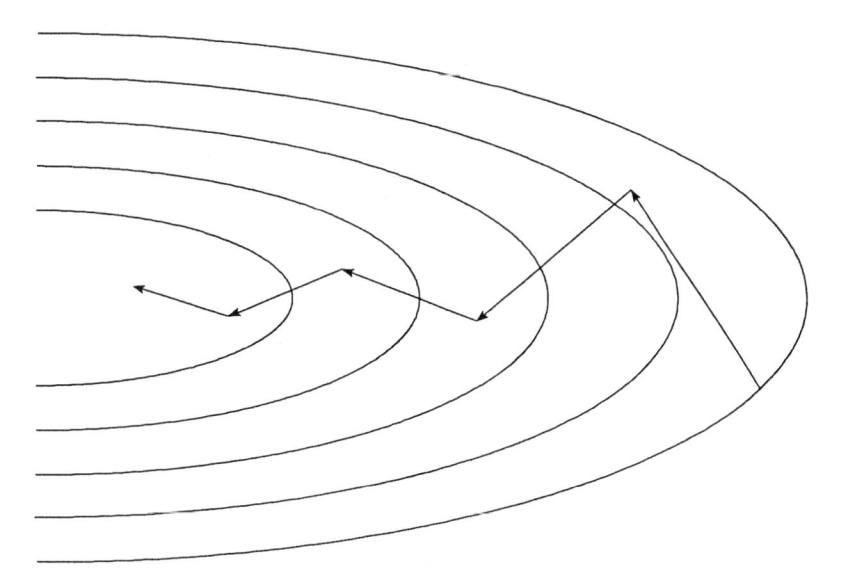

Figure 1.4 Using momentum.

An Advantage of Steepest Descent

We have seen that naive steepest descent along the gradient is not a particularly good training algorithm. Not only is it inelegant and slow, but it requires that the poor user set one or two important parameters. Even with momentum, the method has little to recommend it. However, there does seem to be one backhanded way in which the crudeness of the algorithm sometimes works to its advantage. Understand that this one advantage does not outweigh the many disadvantages of the method. But it should be mentioned for academic interest.

One of the most serious problems in neural network training is the existence of multiple local minima that are inferior to the global minima. Methodical optimization algorithms can easily become trapped in these false minima. Chapter 2 will discuss stochastic techniques for avoiding this problem, but they can impose significant expense and complication. It would be better if the optimization algorithm itself could somehow avoid the local minima. But that is an unrealistic expectation. The best deterministic minimization algorithms will quickly and efficiently gravitate to the nearest local minimum.

This is where the simple expedient of jumping around in fixed step sizes can actually be an advantage. This method does *not* strongly gravitate to the nearest local minimum. It just takes a blind hop in that direction. When there is a series of small local minima on the way down to the ultimate bottom (a common occurrence), fixed steps will often jump right over these local minima and land in the vicinity of a global minimum. I have often seen problems in which intelligent deterministic minimization algorithms land with high probability in poor local minima, while the "stupid" method known as backpropagation manages to somehow avoid them. This doesn't happen often, mind you; certainly not often enough to discourage use of good modern methods. But it is a consideration that at least merits mention on academic grounds.

Line Minimization

The optimization algorithm to be discussed in this section is only rarely used alone as a primary learning algorithm. Rather, it is a workhorse subroutine for more advanced procedures. Nevertheless, it is extremely important. In most cases, line minimization accounts for nearly 100 percent of the time taken by the overall optimization process! The sophisticated algorithm that typically surrounds line minimization usually involves nothing more than fancy but fast bookkeeping for calculation of which direction to search next. Therefore, it is vitally important that we make the line optimization subroutine as efficient as possible.

Most readers know what is meant by the term *line minimization*. But for the sake of those who are not sure, we will define it. This operation is generally performed in the context of multivariate optimization. At the outermost level, we must adjust two or more variables to minimize a function of those variables. Attacked blindly, this is an extremely difficult problem. Thus, most multivariate optimization methods introduce a subproblem. They simultaneously adjust all of the variables, with the values of those variables being a linear parametric function of a single parameter variable. In other words, the ultimate goal is to find values of x_1, x_2, ..., such that the function $f(x_1, x_2, ...)$ is minimized. In vector notation, we want to find a vector **x** that minimizes $f(\mathbf{x})$. A subgoal is encountered when we specify a starting point **p** and a direction **d**, and we attempt to find a value for the scalar t that minimizes the univariate function $f(\mathbf{p}+t\mathbf{d})$. Since we are minimizing along the line determined by the point **p** and the direction **d**, we call this line minimization.

At first glance this does not seem to be a particularly difficult problem. There is, after all, only one variable involved. It should not be too hard to find the value of the parameter t that minimizes this function. The catch comes when we realize that speed is of the essence. The author regularly works with problems in which a single evaluation of the function can take nearly an hour on a fast computer. We obviously must locate the minimum in as few function evaluations as possible.

Most line minimization algorithms involve two steps. The first step is to bound a minimum. We locate three points such that the function value at the middle point is less than the values at the two outer points. We thereby are assured that a minimum lies between the outer points. The possibility that a better minimum may lie elsewhere is ignored. Deterministic algorithms are always happy with what they've got at the moment.

The second step is to successively narrow the interval determined by the outer points. New points inside the interval are tried, and the endpoints are adjusted according to the function value of each new point. Responsible algorithms will use as much intelligence as possible in selecting the new trial points, and they will also keep the minimum bounded at all times.

There are two ways of approaching the initial bounding step. The most common method is to start with a point that has been given and go from there. If we are lucky, we already know which way is downhill, so we just merrily step along in that direction until the function turns up. If we are not so lucky, we simply reverse ourselves if the first step goes uphill. That approach is typically used when optimizing the weights in a multiple-layer feedforward network. We have a current point, and we know the gradient at that point. Since this method is so common, and since we will not have any significant need for it in this text, no more will be said on the issue. Press *et al.* (1992) provides an excellent implementation. Masters (1993) gives a version that is specifically designed for neural network training and provides an intuitive explanation of its operation as well.

The second approach to initial minimum bounding is used when we do not have a starting point. All we have is a wide interval in which we *think* the minimum will lie, and we are not even positive about that. This is the case for sigma optimization in probabilistic and generalized regression neural networks. In many applications we do not have a clue as to what the ideal sigma weight(s) may be. The possible range is large. Worse still is the fact that multiple minima are not unusual. Since the problem of multiple minima is relatively easy to handle in one dimension, it is necessary that we do our best to find the global minimum. And even when line minimization is used as part of the conjugate gradient algorithm for sigma optimization, we will see a little later that the bounding method about to be discussed is usually superior to the initial-point method that is traditionally used in conjunction with conjugate gradients.

Finding the global minimum inside an interval is actually easy. Since by definition we are avoiding the use of local information for the sake of getting the global picture, there are no sophisticated operations to consider. We simply divide the grand interval into equal parts and evaluate the function throughout. Pick the point having the smallest function value, and we are there. The only small trick is that we must be prepared for the possibility that the function may be at its minimum at one of the two endpoints. When this happens we need to continue stepping out in that direction until the function turns up. But that is trivial.

Line Minimization

There are several small special points to consider. Different problems are best served by different methods of spacing the points at which the function is evaluated. Most traditional implementations of line minimization algorithms assume that the effect of the parameter is additive, so the interval is divided in a linear sense. The differences between adjacent points are equal. However, when the variables are sigma weights, their effect is multiplicative. (If that is not clear now, it will become clear in Chapter 4 when actual applications of this algorithm are discussed.) Therefore, we make provision for logarithmic spacing. The *ratios* of adjacent points are equal. This makes a lot more sense for many of the uses of this routine.

Another important consideration is that we must make every effort possible to economize on function evaluations. As we will see later, it will often be the case that the function value at the lower endpoint of the grand interval is already known when this subroutine is called. It would be a small but callous waste to evaluate it again. So we include the option of skipping the first function evaluation, getting it instead from the parameter list. This is flagged by specifying the number of points to be the negative of what is actually desired.

Operation of this bounding routine is straightforward. Code for accomplishing this primitive task is now listed. An explanation of its operation will follow.

```
int glob_min (
    double low ,                    // Lower limit for search
    double high ,                   // Upper limit
    int npts ,                      // Number of points to try
    int log_space ,                 // Space by log?
    double critlim ,                // Quit global if crit drops this low
    double (*criter) (double) ,     // Criterion function
    double *x1,
    double *y1 ,                    // Lower X value and function there
    double *x2,
    double *y2 ,                    // Middle (best)
    double *x3,
    double *y3                      // And upper
    )
{
    int i, ibest, turned_up, know_first_point, user_quit ;
    double x, y, rate, previous ;
```

```
if (npts < 0) {
  npts = -npts ;
  know_first_point = 1 ;
  }
else
  know_first_point = 0 ;

if (log_space)
  rate = exp ( log (high / low) / (npts - 1) ) ;
else
  rate = (high - low) / (npts - 1) ;

x = low ;

previous = 0.0 ;              // Avoids "use before set" compiler warnings
ibest = -1 ;                  // For proper critlim escape
turned_up = 0 ;               // Must know if function increased after min

for (i=0 ; i<npts ; i++) {

  if (i  ||  ! know_first_point)
    y = criter ( x ) ;
  else
    y = *y2 ;

  if ((user_quit = (y < 0.0))  !=  0) {
    if (! turned_up)
      return 1 ;
    y = -y ;
    }

  if ((i == 0)  ||  (y < *y2)) {          // Keep track of best here
    ibest = i ;
    *x2 = x ;
    *y2 = y ;
    *y1 = previous ;                      // Function value to its left
    turned_up = 0 ;                       // Flag that min is not yet bounded
    }
```

Line Minimization

```
      else if (i == (ibest+1)) {          // Didn't improve so this point may
        *y3 = y ;                         // be the right neighbor of the best
        turned_up = 1 ;                   // Flag that min is bounded
        }

      previous = y ;                      // Keep track for left neighbor of best

      if (! user_quit)
        user_quit = user_pressed_escape () ;

      if ((user_quit || (*y2 <= critlim))  &&  (ibest > 0)  &&  turned_up)
        break ; // Done if (abort or good enough) and both neighbors found

      if (user_quit)                      // Alas, both neighbors not found
        return 1 ;                        // Flag that the other 2 pts not there

      if (log_space)
        x *= rate ;
      else
        x += rate ;
      }


/*
   At this point we have a minimum (within low,high) at (x2,y2).
   Compute x1 and x3, its neighbors.
   We already know y1 and y3 (unless the minimum is at an endpoint!).
*/


   if (log_space) {
     *x1 = *x2 / rate ;
     *x3 = *x2 * rate ;
     }
   else {
     *x1 = *x2 - rate ;
     *x3 = *x2 + rate ;
     }
```

```
/*
   Normally we would now be done.  However, the careless user may have
   given us a bad x range (low,high) for the global search.
   If the function was still decreasing at an endpoint, bail out the
   user by continuing the search.
*/

   if (! turned_up) {                          // Must extend to the right (larger x)
     for (;;) {                                // Endless loop goes as long as necessary

       user_quit = user_pressed_escape () ;
       if (user_quit)                          // Alas, both neighbors not found
         return 1 ;                            // Flag that the other 2 pts not there

       *y3 = criter ( *x3 ) ;

       if (*y3 < 0.0)
         return 1 ;

       if (*y3 > *y2)                          // If function increased we are done
         break ;

       if ((*y1 == *y2)  &&  (*y2 == *y3))     // Give up if flat
         break ;

       *x1 = *x2 ;                             // Shift all points
       *y1 = *y2 ;
       *x2 = *x3 ;
       *y2 = *y3 ;

       rate *= 3.0 ;                           // Step further each time
       if (log_space)                          // And advance to new frontier
         *x3 *= rate ;
       else
         *x3 += rate ;
       }
     }

   else if (ibest == 0) {                      // Must extend to the left (smaller x)
     for (;;) {                                // Endless loop as long as necessary
```

Line Minimization

```
         user_quit = user_pressed_escape () ;
         if (user_quit)                         // Alas, both neighbors not found
            return 1 ;                          // Flag that the other 2 pts not there

         *y1 = criter ( *x1 ) ;

         if (*y1 < 0.0)
            return 1 ;

         if (*y1 > *y2)                         // If function increased we are done
            break ;

         if ((*y1 == *y2)  &&  (*y2 == *y3))    // Give up if flat
            break ;

         *x3 = *x2 ;                            // Shift all points
         *y3 = *y2 ;
         *x2 = *x1 ;
         *y2 = *y1 ;

         rate *= 3.0 ;                          // Step further each time
         if (log_space)                         // And advance to new frontier
            *x1 /= rate ;
         else
            *x1 -= rate ;
         }
      }
   return 0 ;
}
```

The parameter list is long but straightforward. The lower and upper limits that hopefully bound the global minimum are specified. In case the function is still decreasing at one of the endpoints, the search interval will be automatically extended. The number of function evaluations is specified next. This should be large enough that the global minimum is likely to be found, yet small enough that search time is not excessive. The user sets log_space equal to any nonzero value to indicate that logarithmic (rather than linear) spacing is to be used across the interval. The final input in the list is the address of the criterion function that will be minimized.

The other members of the parameter list (with one possible exception noted later) are all output values. These are three points, with the x variables being the location within the interval, and the y variables being the corresponding function values. The first point is the lower bound of the interval that contains the minimum. The last point is the upper bound. The point in the middle has a function value less than its two neighbors.

There is one situation in which one of these last parameters may be used for input. If, at the time this subroutine is called, the function value at the lower endpoint is known, then the user sets npts equal to the negative of its desired value. Then, the function value at the lower endpoint is input in y2.

The first action taken depends upon whether or not the user is supplying the function value at the leftmost end of the interval. If so, the user flagged that fact by making npts negative. We check for that, then set our own flag. Next, the difference or factor that separates each point from the next is computed. The variable previous is initialized so that zealous compilers do not complain that it is used before being set. Technically, it is used that way, but the logic of the program guarantees that there is no problem. The compiler doesn't know that, though. The variable ibest keeps track of the location of the best (smallest function) point. It must be initialized to a negative number so that in case the very first point satisfies the user's critlim, proper subsequent action will be taken. (See the complex if statement later in the loop.) Finally, the flag turned_up indicates whether or not a local minimum has been located.

We now loop through the points spanning the interval. The variable x, which was initialized to the leftmost endpoint, will always be the current point being evaluated. If the user specified the function value at the left endpoint, get it on the first pass. Otherwise, evaluate the function.

It is expected that the user-supplied criterion subroutine will return a negative number if and only if the user pressed ESCape during function evaluation. We set a local flag accordingly. If no local minimum has yet been found, abort immediately and return 1 as a flag to the caller that there was complete failure. On the other hand, if the function has turned up, then just flip the sign of the function back to what it should be, and we will do a graceful return very soon.

The next if statement handles the housekeeping involved with setting a new record for low function value. Note that the first point automatically falls into that category. We keep track of its location, save the point, and reset turned_up as a flag that a local minimum has not been bounded. Note that it is possible for this flag to flip several times during traversal of the interval if there are multiple local minima. We also set y1 to be the function value at the previous point.

If a new record wasn't set, and if the current point happens to be the point just past the best so far, then we have bounded the minimum. Flag that fact, and save the function value of that upper bound. We ignore the possibility of an exact tie.

The rest of this loop is mostly trivial busywork. Keep track of the previous point so that when a new record is set, we know its left neighbor. See if an impatient user has pressed ESCape. The if statement for an early but normal exit is a little tricky. In order to do a normal return, three things must be true. First, either the user must have pressed ESCape, or the user's minimum criterion must have been satisfied. Second, the minimum must not be at the left endpoint. Third, the minimum must not be at the right endpoint. If any of those conditions are not met, we keep trying for a rigorous bound.

The next if statement handles an abnormal return. If the user pressed ESCape, and the other conditions preclude a normal return, then we immediately return 1 as an error flag for the caller.

The last step in the traversal loop is to advance to the next point. This is done either additively or multiplicatively, according to the user's desire. Unless a premature end is forced by the user pressing ESCape or by the critlim being reached, all points will be tested. We do not stop at the first local minimum, but search the entire interval for the global minimum.

When we have found the minimum and exit the loop, we need to return to the user not only the minimum point, but its neighbors as well. The function values have been preserved in y1 and y3, but we did not bother keeping track of x1 and x3. We compute them after the loop is completed.

Under normal circumstances we would now be done. However, the interval specified by the user may not have been wide enough. If turned_up is zero, the function was still decreasing as of the rightmost endpoint. So we march on. If ibest is zero, the function was at its minimum at the leftmost endpoint, so we go back to the left. The only slightly unusual part of this code is that we increase the step size each time we advance. This is crucial to avoiding huge amounts of wasted time. Nobody knows just how far we may need to go. By increasing the jump size with each step, we rapidly cover more territory.

Refining the Interval

We just discussed a global method for locating a trio of points such that a minimum lies between the outermost pair of points. The second step of line minimization is to refine this interval. There is little dispute over the best way of accomplishing this task. Although several competing methods exist, the competition is not fierce. Brent's method [Brent, 1973] is widely accepted as the best. It is largely based on the hope (and fact, in most cases) that when one is near a minimum, the function behaves roughly like a parabola. As the interval is refined, this algorithm keeps track not only of the bounding trio, but also the three points having the smallest function value. (Note that these two trios may or may not be exactly the same set of points.) It fits a parabola to the three best points and computes the location of the minimum of that parabola. Provided that certain criteria are met by that new point, it is chosen as the next point at which the function is evaluated, under the assumption that it will be very near the minimum. If the criteria are not met, then the larger of the two intervals defined by the bounding trio is split with the golden ratio, and a new trio is defined according to the function value there. This process repeats until several convergence criteria are satisfied.

Brent's algorithm is an unusual mix of simplicity and sophistication. It contains no advanced mathematics. There are only a few decisions to be made during its execution. Superficially, it all seems easy. The catch is that there are a great many subtle difficulties to prevent. We will not go into any depth here. Press *et al.* (1992) contains a good discussion, and Brent (1973) is the ultimate authority. The program description at the end of the listing will devote a little space to the problems and their solutions. For now, we only state that a numerically stable way of computing the minimum (or maximum!) of a parabola through three points is given by Equation (1.1). Also, Figure 1.5 illustrates a typical stage of the algorithm. The bounding interval is shown enclosed by a bracket. A parabola (dotted line) is fitted through the three best points, and its minimum, which will be the next point evaluated, appears as a hollow circle. The labels in that figure correspond to variables in the program. Note that the distance separating the point at the lower end of the bounding interval from the fitted parabola is indicative of the problems this method can have when derivatives are changing so rapidly that a second-order fit is inappropriate. That's why we are always ready to punt via the golden section.

Line Minimization

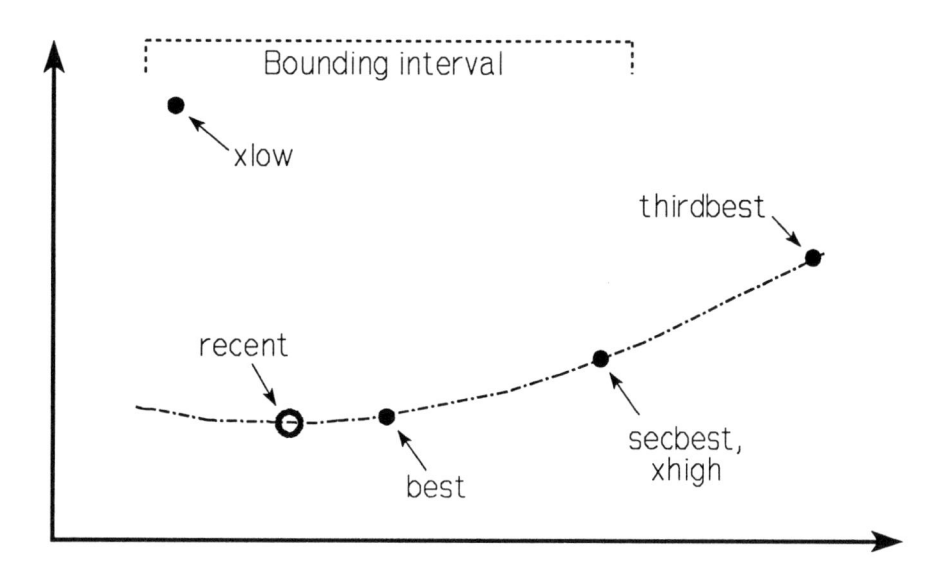

Figure 1.5 Brent's method.

$$a = (x_2 - x_1)(y_2 - y_3)$$
$$b = (x_2 - x_3)(y_2 - y_1)$$
$$\hat{x} = \frac{b(x_2 - x_3) - a(x_2 - x_1)}{2(a - b)} \tag{1.1}$$

```
double brentmin (
  int itmax ,                    // Iteration limit
  double critlim ,               // Quit if crit drops this low
  double eps ,                   // Small, but greater than machine precision
  double tol ,                   // Brent's tolerance (>= sqrt machine precision)
  double (*criter) (double) ,    // Criterion function
  double *x1 ,                   // Lower X value, input and output
  double *x2 ,                   // Middle (best), input and output
  double *x3 ,                   // And upper, input and output
  double y                       // Function value at x2
  )
```

```
{
  int iter, user_quit ;
  double prevdist, step, xlow, xmid, xhigh, tol1, tol2 ;
  double xbest, xsecbest, xthirdbest, fbest, fsecbest, fthirdbest ;
  double numer, denom, testdist, xrecent, frecent, t1, t2 ;

  user_quit = 0 ;

/*
   Initialize prevdist, the distance moved on the previous step, to 0 so that the
   'if (fabs ( prevdist ) > tol1)' encountered on the first iteration below will fail, forcing
   a golden section the first time.  Also initialize step to 0 to avoid a zealous compiler
   from pointing out that it was referenced before being set.
*/

  prevdist = step = 0.0 ;

/*
   We always keep the minimum bracketed between xlow and xhigh.
   xbest has the min function ordinate so far (or latest if tie).
   xsecbest and xthirdbest are the second and third best.
*/

  xbest = xsecbest = xthirdbest = *x2 ;
  xlow = *x1 ;
  xhigh = *x3 ;

  fbest = fsecbest = fthirdbest = y ;

/*
   Main loop.  For safety we impose a limit on iterations.
*/

  for (iter=0 ; iter<itmax ; iter++) {

    if ((user_quit = user_pressed_escape ()) != 0)
      break ;

    if (fbest < critlim)    // Do we satisfy user yet?
      break ;
```

Line Minimization

```
            xmid = 0.5 * (xlow + xhigh) ;
            tol1 = tol * (fabs ( xbest ) + eps) ;
            tol2 = 2. * tol1 ;

/*
   The following convergence test simultaneously makes sure xhigh and xlow are
   close relative to tol2, and that xbest is near the midpoint.
*/
            if (fabs ( xbest - xmid )  <=  (tol2 - 0.5 * (xhigh - xlow)))
               break ;

/*
   Avoid refining function to limits of precision
*/
            if ((iter >= 2)  &&  ((fthirdbest - fbest) < eps))
               break ;

            if (fabs ( prevdist ) > tol1) { // If we moved far enough try parabolic fit
               t1 = (xbest - xsecbest) * (fbest - fthirdbest) ;   // Temps for the
               t2 = (xbest - xthirdbest) * (fbest - fsecbest) ;   // parabolic estimate
               numer = (xbest - xthirdbest) * t2  -  (xbest - xsecbest) * t1 ;
               denom = 2. * (t1 - t2) ;                 // Estimate will be numer / denom
               testdist = prevdist ;                    // Will soon verify interval is shrinking
               prevdist = step ;                        // Save for next iteration
               if (denom != 0.0)                        // Avoid dividing by zero
                  step = numer / denom ;                // This is the parabolic estimate to min
               else
                  step = 1.e30 ;                        // Assures failure of next test

               if ((fabs ( step ) < fabs ( 0.5 * testdist ))  // If shrinking
                && (step + xbest > xlow)                 // and within known bounds
                && (step + xbest < xhigh)) {             // then we can use the
                  xrecent = xbest + step ;              // parabolic estimate
                  if ((xrecent - xlow  <  tol2) ||      // If we are very close
                     (xhigh - xrecent  <  tol2)) {      // to known bounds
                     if (xbest < xmid)                  // then stabilize
                        step = tol1 ;
                     else
                        step = -tol1 ;
                  }
               }
            }
```

```
      else { // Parabolic estimate poor, so use golden section
        prevdist = (xbest >= xmid) ?  xlow - xbest  :  xhigh - xbest ;
        step = .3819660 * prevdist ;
        }
      }

    else { // prevdist did not exceed tol1: we did not move far enough
           // to justify a parabolic fit.  Use golden section.
      prevdist = (xbest >= xmid) ?  xlow - xbest  :  xhigh - xbest ;
      step = .3819660 * prevdist ;
      }

    if (fabs (step)  >=  tol1)       // In order to numerically justify
      xrecent = xbest + step ;       // another trial we must move a
    else {                           // decent distance.
      if (step > 0.)
        xrecent = xbest + tol1 ;
      else
        xrecent = xbest - tol1 ;
      }

/*
   At long last we have a trial point 'xrecent'.  Evaluate the function.
*/

    frecent = criter ( xrecent ) ;

    if (frecent < 0.0) {
      user_quit = 1 ;
      break ;
      }

    if (frecent <= fbest) {          // If we improved...
      if (xrecent >= xbest)          // Shrink the (xlow,xhigh) interval by
        xlow = xbest ;               // replacing the appropriate endpoint
      else
        xhigh = xbest ;
      xthirdbest = xsecbest ;        // Update x and f values for best,
      xsecbest = xbest ;             // second and third best
      xbest = xrecent ;
      fthirdbest = fsecbest ;
```

Line Minimization

```
          fsecbest = fbest ;
          fbest = frecent ;
        }

      else {                          // We did not improve
        if (xrecent < xbest)          // Shrink the (xlow,xhigh) interval by
          xlow = xrecent ;            // replacing the appropriate endpoint
        else
          xhigh = xrecent ;

        if ((frecent <= fsecbest)     // If we at least beat the second best
         || (xsecbest == xbest)) {    // or we had a duplication
          xthirdbest = xsecbest ;     // we can update the second and third
          xsecbest = xrecent ;        // best, though not the best.
          fthirdbest = fsecbest ;     // Recall that we started iters with
          fsecbest = frecent ;        // best, sec and third all equal.
        }
        else if ((frecent <= fthirdbest) // Oh well.  Maybe at least we can
         || (xthirdbest == xbest)     // beat the third best or rid
         || (xthirdbest == xsecbest)) { // ourselves of a duplication
          xthirdbest = xrecent ;      // (which is how we start the
          fthirdbest = frecent ;      // iterations)
        }
      }
    }

  *x1 = xlow ;
  *x2 = xbest ;
  *x3 = xhigh ;

  if (user_quit)
    return -fbest ;
  else
    return fbest ;
}
```

The first two parameters passed to this subroutine control its termination under what may be termed abnormal conditions. For safety purposes it is good to be able to set an upper limit on the number of iterations. Also, we may want to specify a function value that is acceptable. If this goal is attained, no further minimization is attempted. The eps parameter is used to facilitate portability. It should be set to a very small value that is greater than the smallest difference that can be computed in the precision of the computer on which this routine is used. I typically set this equal to 1.e-12 for machines using 8-byte doubles. The tol parameter is the usual method for controlling termination. Roughly speaking, it determines the precision (in x) to which the minimum is located. The remaining parameters specify the address of the criterion function and the three bounding points. The user must supply the value of the function at the middle (best) point. This routine will supply new interior points at which the function is evaluated.

After some trivial initializations, the main loop commences. The first actions are to see if we are exiting at the user's direction, either by pressing ESCape or by the function dropping to a small enough value. Then a clever convergence test is performed. A test value is computed in such a way that if the function is large, the test value will be relative; while if the function is tiny, the test value will be absolute and in terms of the machine precision. The convergence test simultaneously makes sure that the bounding interval is small compared to the user's requirement (otherwise the right-hand side will be negative), and also verifies that the best point is near the center of the bounding interval. It is hoped that the reader sees the beauty in this simple but elegant logic.

One more convergence test is performed. Some users of this program may wish to remove it, but I find it important in neural network training. The difference between the current best (smallest) function value and the third best is compared with the approximate machine precision as supplied by the user. If the function improvement is that small, we ignore the fact that the location of the exact minimum has not yet been determined to the user's accuracy limit. We decide that it's just not worth the effort of continuing and quit trying. In some applications we may want to locate the true minimum as accurately as possible. But in most neural network applications we do not care where the minimum is, as long as the error has been reduced to nearly the minimum possible.

We now come to a major decision point. We need to pick a new point inside the bounding interval at which the function will be evaluated. Since, in practice, that function evaluation will be done at great cost, it behooves us to pick the new point with great care. We have two choices. We can take the easy route and split the larger of the two intervals defined by the bounding trio. That will provide a point that is widely separated from the other points and hence guarantee that we split off a pretty big chunk of the total interval. On the other hand, that *guaranteed minimum return* approach also guarantees that only the wildest coincidence will cause the new point to be a significant improvement. There is no sophistication here. An intelligent alternative is to fit the three best points to a parabola and locate its minimum using Equation (1.1). This will quite likely give us a new point that is close to the true minimum. This is surely the way to go. Or is it? What if on the last iteration we only moved a tiny distance? In that case the definition of the parabolic minimum will be numerically unstable. It would thus be better simply to split the larger interval as mentioned earlier. This is the motivation for the decision. If prevdist, the distance previously moved, is large compared with the user-specified tolerance, we are justified in doing a parabolic fit. Otherwise, take the safe route. The else part many lines below finds the larger interval and splits it by the golden section.

Now let's investigate the parabolic fit. We do a straightforward implementation of Equation (1.1). But we are still not quite home free on the use of a parabola. We need to verify two more things. One is obvious: We never, ever, want to slip outside the bounding interval. That is our comfort and a major component of our convergence insurance. If the denominator of Equation (1.1) is zero, not only will we commit the cardinal sin of division by zero, but we will also jump to infinity, clearly a violation of the bounding interval. These related problems are solved by forcing a huge step size if the denominator is zero. The other thing to verify is more subtle but nonetheless important in pathological situations. It can occasionally happen that the parabolic method will go into oscillation, generating points that bounce back and forth in terribly slowly decreasing cycles around the best point. To prevent this from happening, we make sure that the step size is decreasing at a reasonable rate. We follow the heuristic given in Press *et al.* (1992) of comparing the step size to the one *two* iterations back, rather than the most recent.

We are just about ready to choose the new point based on the parabolic fit. There is one more small issue to be dealt with. Remember that our first major decision involved using the parabolic fit only if we had just moved at least toll from the previous point. For similar reasons of numerical efficiency, we want to avoid choosing a new point that is close to one of the two bounding points. We check its distance from both ends, and if it is too close, we instead place the new point close to the best on whichever side contains the larger interval.

At this time we have just about completed this quite complex choice of a new point. We either have used a parabolic fit, or else we have used a golden-section split of the larger interval. We apply that same old numerical efficiency test one last time. We want to move a reasonable distance from the best so far, in order to justify the cost of a function evaluation. If the step size is at least equal to tol1, we go ahead and do it. But if not, we only use the step to determine the direction to move away from the best point. The actual distance moved is tol1.

Wow. It's been a struggle, but we at last have the point at which the precious function evaluation is performed. It's easy from now on. See if we improved; if so, shrink the bounding interval and update the record of the first, second, and third best points. If we did not improve, we still can shrink the bounding interval. But now the job of updating the three best points is a little more complicated. See where the new function value fits in and act accordingly.

Incorporating Derivative Information

If it is economical to compute the first derivative (and perhaps even the second derivative) of the function, there are ways that this information may be used in the line minimization. Press *et al.* (1992) discusses this topic. That reference correctly points out that extrapolation to the minimum via a derivative can be dangerous and must be used with the greatest caution. The safest use of the derivative is as an indicator of which side of the best point the minimum lies on. For most neural network applications, the cost of computing the gradient is more expensive than it is worth in line minimization, so we will not pursue the subject of refinement based on derivative information. It is best to do the interval refinement using only the function values. In other applications in which it may be cheap to compute the gradient along with the function, incorporation of the derivative would probably be beneficial.

There is, however, one way in which derivative information may be efficiently used in line minimization for neural network training. Although it is too expensive to compute derivatives for all of the points tested during refinement, we do have to compute the gradient once, just to get the search direction. When we study probabilistic and generalized regression neural network training in Chapters 5 and 6, we will see that it is relatively easy to compute the vector of *second* derivatives of the error along with the gradient. This is the diagonal of the Hessian matrix. We can put this information to excellent use in the first step of line minimization, bounding the minimum. Let us see how.

Superficially, it may seem that the slow part of line minimization is the refinement stage. There are all those function evaluations as the minimum is chased. But the fact of the matter is that in many or most applications in which we must approach minimization blindly, it is actually the initial bounding that is the slowest. This section has focused on a global search strategy. But in practice the heaviest use of line minimization will involve stepping out from a known point in a known direction. The global algorithm given earlier can be viewed as a special case of this general problem. If we choose an initial step size that is too large, we will overburden the refinement stage. So we usually choose a fairly small step size. But if it is too small, we must step out many times, incurring great expense evaluating the function until it turns upward. The ideal situation would be if we could use the global bounding algorithm presented above to step out from the known point, but step exactly the right distance the first time: Take one step that puts us almost exactly at the line minimum, then take one more step at which the function turns up. We would thereby have our bounding trio immediately, with the least possible number of function evaluations, and the center point would be near the minimum. There is a way we can use derivative information to help us achieve that goal.

Remember that at the minimum of a function, its first derivative is zero. So what we do is use (one step of) Newton's method to approximate the root of the derivative. Suppose that at some point x the function and its first and second derivatives are $f(x)$, $f'(x)$, and $f''(x)$, respectively. Given this information, Newton's method tells us that the best guess for the location of the minimum (the root of the derivative) is given by Equation (1.2).

$$x_{min} = x - \frac{f'(x)}{f''(x)} \qquad (1.2)$$

There is one little detail that should be kept in mind. This formula is just as happy leading to a maximum as to a minimum. All we are doing is finding the root of the derivative, and the derivative is zero in both cases. So to keep covered, we should check the sign of the second derivative. It is positive in the vicinity of a minimum.

Line minimization is, in general, used as a component of multivariate optimization. It is assumed (in this section) that we can compute both the gradient and the diagonal of the Hessian matrix. But what we need here is the first and second derivatives of the function *along the line of travel*. In other words, we need the derivatives with respect to the parameter that determines location along the line, not with respect to any of the raw variables. These are easily obtained. The (scalar) directional first derivative in some direction is simply the length of the projection of the gradient vector on the direction vector. In other words, we compute the dot product of the gradient vector with the unit length search direction vector. If the search direction vector is not unit length, we must compensate by dividing by its length. The directional second derivative is the quadratic form of the (unit length) search direction over the Hessian. These methods of computing the directional derivatives are expressed in Equation (1.3). In that equation, **g** is the gradient vector, **s** is the search direction vector, and **H** is the Hessian matrix.

$$d_1 = \frac{\mathbf{g} \cdot \mathbf{s}}{\|\mathbf{s}\|}$$

$$d_2 = \frac{\mathbf{s}'\mathbf{H}\mathbf{s}}{\|\mathbf{s}\|^2}$$

(1.3)

When we divide the directional first derivative by the directional second derivative to effect Newton's method as shown in Equation (1.2), the length of the search direction vector partially cancels. That step size is, of course, in terms of absolute distance in the space of the raw variables. Hence we must parameterize the line search in terms of a unit length direction vector. If we do not, the computed step size must be divided by the length of the search direction vector. Since the bookkeeping of the conjugate gradient algorithm would be significantly increased by normalizing the search direction, we choose to leave its length alone and instead scale the line search. So now when we divide the step length by the search vector length to compensate for the fact that it is not normalized, the latter disappears entirely.

It's time to be specific about this procedure. We have a point **p** and a search direction **s** whose length is not necessarily normalized to unity. We traverse the line determined by that point and direction using a parameter t. We seek a minimum of $f(\mathbf{p} + t\mathbf{s})$. Without loss of generality, assume that we are currently sitting at **p**, so that $t = 0$ at the starting point. Let **g** be the gradient vector here, and let **H** be the Hessian matrix. In practice we will make that a diagonal matrix. The vector of second derivatives will comprise its diagonal, and all other entries will be zero. Such an approximation can spell disaster for full multidimensional Newton methods, but it is quite good for this particular application. The value of t that will hopefully place us at the minimum is given by Equation (1.4).

$$t_{min} = -\frac{\mathbf{g} \cdot \mathbf{s}}{\mathbf{s}' \mathbf{H} \mathbf{s}} \qquad (1.4)$$

It can sometimes happen that Equation (1.4) may provide a poor step distance. This happens mainly when the diagonal approximation to the Hessian is poor and the search direction happens to be such that the inadequacy of the diagonal Hessian is emphasized. This leads to a heuristic insurance policy that I find works well. Scan the diagonal of the Hessian, looking for the largest positive second derivative. The negative of its reciprocal, or a value slightly larger in magnitude, is a reasonably good step length to take. (Reader exercise: Why?) In the majority of cases, Newton's estimate is much better. But we cannot always totally rely on Newton. What if the directional second derivative, the denominator of Equation (1.4), is negative? Then Newton is useless. I always compute the heuristic shown in Equation (1.5). If Newton's step from Equation (1.4) is not in the ballpark of the heuristic, the latter is used instead. This insurance policy is not needed very often, but it is good to have around.

$$t_{min} = \frac{-1.5}{\text{MAX DIAG}(\mathbf{H})} \qquad (1.5)$$

At the end of the next section, we will see a complete conjugate gradient subroutine that implements the methods just discussed. However, some readers may wish to incorporate these techniques into other programs. The few lines of code from the conjugate gradient program that concern use of derivatives for optimizing the initial bounding search will now be listed. This fragment appears in its full context in the next section.

```
dot1 = dot2 = 0.0 ;                         // For finding directional derivatives
high = 1.e-4 ;                              // For heuristic scaling
for (i=0 ; i<n ; i++) {                     // For all variables
  if (deriv2[i] > high)                     // Search diagonal of Hessian
    high = deriv2[i] ;                      // For heuristic insurance
  dot1 += direc[i] * g[i] ;                 // For directional first derivative
  dot2 += direc[i] * direc[i] * deriv2[i] ; // and second
}

scale = dot1 / dot2 ;                       // Newton's ideal but unstable scale
high = 1.5 / high ;                         // Less ideal but more stable heuristic

if (high < 1.e-4)                           // Subjectively keep it realistic
  high = 1.e-4 ;

if (scale < 0.0)                            // This is truly pathological
  scale = high ;                            // So stick with old reliable
else if (scale < 0.1 * high)                // Bound the Newton scale
  scale = 0.1 * high ;                      // To be close to the stable scale
else if (scale > 10.0 * high)               // Bound it both above and below
  scale = 10.0 * high ;

user_quit = glob_min ( 0.0 , 2.0 * scale , -3 , 0 , critlim ,
       univar_crit , &t1 , &y1 , &t2 , &y2 , &t3 , &y3 ) ;
```

The above code cumulates the numerator of Equation (1.4) in dot1 and the denominator in dot2. The variable high keeps track of the maximum diagonal of the Hessian. It is initialized to a small positive number as insurance against dividing by zero later, as well as to keep it in reasonable bounds. The same thing is done after computing its reciprocal. This constant may be problem dependent, but I find it to be widely applicable.

Normally, the ideal Newton step will be used. However, if it implies a step away from the direction we want to search, we use the heuristic step instead. Also, we bound the Newton step to be within a modest range of the heuristic step. The choice of the factors for that bounding is very arbitrary, and readers are encouraged to experiment.

The last line of that code shows how the computed step size is ultimately used. The global interval runs from zero, the current point, to twice the optimal step size. Three points are specified, so that causes the center point to appear right in the middle of the interval, exactly at the hopeful location of the minimum. If all goes well, the bounding trio will be had on the first shot. Since we needed to compute the gradient anyway, to find the search direction, this is an extremely effective use of second derivative information if it is available.

Some readers may be so enamored of this technique that they will be tempted to incorporate it into the refinement stage of line minimization. Instead of locating the supposed minimum by fitting a parabola through three points, these readers may try to use Newton's method as just described. Certainly, the number of iterations required will be reduced. On the other hand, I am of the opinion that the price paid for computing the derivatives is too high. But who knows? It may be worth a try for some ambitious souls.

Conjugate Gradient Methods

This section will present one of the most popular and effective families of multivariate optimization algorithms. There is an almost magical beauty in conjugate gradient methods. They have nearly (or entirely) the power and convergence speed of full second-order methods. Yet they require neither the computation nor even the storage of any second-order information. That is a matter of no small importance. When there are more than a handful of variables to be optimized, storage and manipulation of an n^2 Hessian matrix can be a heavy burden. And computing all those second derivatives rapidly becomes prohibitively expensive. An algorithm that behaves as if it were based on second-order information, yet which neither explicitly computes nor stores anything having to do with second derivatives, is one step this side of a miracle.

The full mathematics of conjugate gradients is not overly complicated, but it is rather long and tedious. Therefore, our presentation will be cursory and will feature an intuitive approach. Readers who want the complete story should start by carefully studying the excellent general discussion of multivariate minimization in Acton (1970), then graduate to the detailed discussion of conjugate gradients in Press *et al.* (1992). Even more mathematical details can be found in Gill, Murray, and Wright (1981) and the classic Golub and Van Loan (1989).

Before proceeding, it would be good to review the material on steepest descent starting on page 2. In particular, study Figure 1.1. A major goal of intelligent algorithms is elimination of the bouncing off the walls that plagues naive algorithms. We saw that introducing a momentum term helped but did not solve the problem entirely. Explicit second-order methods solve the problem by using second derivatives (or their approximations) to rotate the gradient so that it points toward the minimum. Unfortunately, in many or most practical situations, those methods are so uneconomical that they simply cannot be used, no matter how good their theoretical performance might be.

The root cause of the difficulties associated with naive gradient descent is that every time we descend to the minimum in some direction, we lose a sizable amount of our hard-earned progress from previous descents. Look again at Figure 1.1. We compute the gradient at the starting point and find the minimum in that direction. The gradient at that new point is perpendicular to the first search direction. We then locate the minimum in that new direction. Unfortunately, when we get there, we are dismayed to find that the gradient is not much different from what it was at the starting point. We already put a tremendous amount of effort into minimizing along nearly that same direction not too long ago, and now we must do it again. Ouch! Wouldn't it be nice if we could instead minimize along a direction that had the property of not taking back progress already made? We can: All we do is minimize in a direction that is *conjugate* to the previous direction(s).

Most readers know what it means for two directions (vectors) to be perpendicular (orthogonal). In words, it means that motion along one of them does not generate any motion along the other. In mathematics, it means that their dot product is zero. So what does it mean for a pair of vectors to be conjugate? The concepts are not entirely different. A major difference is that the concept of orthogonality involves only the pair of vectors in question. The concept of conjugacy additionally involves a quadratic function (a multivariate polynomial having no terms higher than the second order). In other words, we cannot really say that two vectors are simply conjugate. To be precise we must say that two vectors are conjugate *with respect to* some quadratic function. In practice, the quadratic function is assumed to be known, so we usually omit any mention of it. But the reader must understand that its presence is crucial. We can now state what is implied by two vectors, say **r** and **s**, being conjugate. It means that when we move along one of them, say **r**, the change in the gradient of the function is perpendicular to the other vector, **s** in this case. An equivalent mathematical formulation of this condition is shown without proof in Equation (1.6). See any of the previously cited references for proof. In that equation, **H** is the Hessian matrix of second derivatives of the function.

$$\mathbf{r'Hs} = 0 \qquad (1.6)$$

What are the implications of this to function minimization? First, it should be emphasized that the definition of conjugacy depended on the function being quadratic, which implies a constant Hessian matrix. In real life we will never be blessed in this way, so everything we are about to say will be compromised to the degree that the function is not quadratic. On the other hand, many practical functions have a fairly constant Hessian, especially in the neighborhood of a minimum. So we generally are quite safe in our assumption.

With that warning taken, let us think about minimization. We start at a point, compute the gradient there, and descend to the minimum along that line. The naive approach would be to compute the gradient again, noting that it will be perpendicular to the previous search direction and descend once more. But what if we instead computed a direction that is conjugate to the first search direction, and minimized along that line? By the definition of conjugacy, any change in the gradient resulting from that minimization motion will be orthogonal to the previous search direction. In other words, if we were already at a minimum in that previous search direction, we will remain at a minimum in that direction. This new minimization does not cost us any of our winnings in the previous minimization. That is in sharp contrast to the situation with naive steepest descent. It's time for an example: Look at Figure 1.6 and Equation (1.7). A specific example involving explicit points and search directions is illustrated there.

This example is primitive in that it involves only two independent variables, and the function being minimized is a perfect quadratic. However, it is instructive to study its geometry and actually work through some steps. The reader will then hopefully better appreciate the power of the conjugate gradient method. Observe that Equation (1.7) tells us not only the form of the function, but also shows us how to compute the gradient at any point. It is also seen that the Hessian is constant, with the value 2.0 at both diagonals and −1.5 in the off-diagonal positions. The following discussion is terse, but most readers should be able to verify each step. In fact, that is recommended.

34 *Deterministic Optimization*

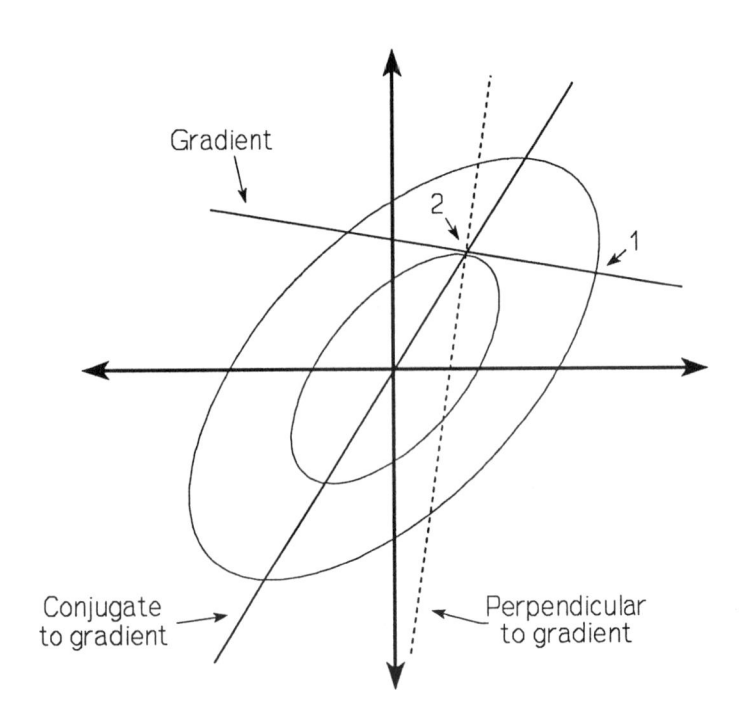

Figure 1.6 Conjugate directions.

$$f(x, y) = x^2 + y^2 - 1.5xy$$
$$\frac{\partial f}{\partial x} = 2x - 1.5y$$
$$\frac{\partial f}{\partial y} = 2y - 1.5x$$
$$\frac{\partial^2 f}{\partial x^2} = \frac{\partial^2 f}{\partial y^2} = 2 \qquad (1.7)$$
$$\frac{\partial^2 f}{\partial x \, \partial y} = -1.5$$

We have a simple quadratic function for which we seek the minimum. The search starts at point 1 whose location happens to be (6, 4), an arbitrarily chosen point. The gradient at that point is (6, −1). A line in that direction through point 1 passes through one of the two level ellipses that are shown. Note that, as expected, the gradient is perpendicular to the ellipse at the point of tangency. If we parameterize that line as point 1 plus t times the gradient, the derivative of the parameterized function with respect to t is $92\,t + 37$. Set that equal to zero to find the location of the function's minimum along the gradient line. The solution, $t = -0.4022$, gives us a location of approximately (3.587, 4.402). That line minimum is labeled as point 2.

Everything has been straightforward so far. Here is the important part: If we simply compute the gradient at this new point and naively minimize along that direction, we would be following the dotted line. That's not terrible, but it's not very good either. Let's compute a conjugate direction instead. (Since we have only two variables, there is only one direction that is conjugate here. In higher dimensions there will be more.) We compute the conjugate direction using Equation (1.6). Let **r** be the gradient direction and **H** be the Hessian. If **s** = (x, y) then we get $13.5x + 11y = 0$. Notice in Figure 1.6 that the line through point 2 in this direction passes directly through the minimum of the function! Not bad.

Actually, that observation is not unexpected. In fact, it can be proved that if we are minimizing a perfect quadratic in n variables, then n line minimizations in directions that are mutually conjugate are all that are needed to find the minimum. This should agree with intuition if we recall what it means for directions to be conjugate. Every time we minimize along one of these directions, previous minimizations are preserved. After we have done this n times, we are at a minimum in all directions. As long as the directions span the entire space, which is easily proved, we can do no better.

This is all very nice, but so far we have really done nothing special. When we computed the direction that is conjugate to the previous search direction, we casually glossed over the role that the Hessian played. Since this was a simple contrived example, we knew the Hessian. Unfortunately, in real-life problems, the Hessian will be difficult or impossible to compute. In those rare cases in which it can be economically computed, we might as well use Newton's method or a relative. Here is where the magic enters.

Let $\mathbf{g}_i$ be the *negative* gradient at point i in our search for the minimum. Let $\mathbf{h}_i$ be the direction that we will search from this point.

To initialize the algorithm, set $\mathbf{g}_0$ and $\mathbf{h}_0$ both equal to the negative gradient at the starting point. At each step we must keep track of the gradient and the search direction at the previous step (but *only* that one previous step). Compute the search direction for the current step using Equation (1.8).

$$\gamma = \frac{(\mathbf{g}_i - \mathbf{g}_{i-1}) \cdot \mathbf{g}_i}{\mathbf{g}_{i-1} \cdot \mathbf{g}_{i-1}} \qquad (1.8)$$

$$\mathbf{h}_i = \mathbf{g}_i + \gamma \, \mathbf{h}_{i-1}$$

It can be shown that as long as we are careful to locate the minimum in each successive search direction, the sequence of $\mathbf{h}_i$ search directions will be mutually conjugate to the extent that the Hessian is constant. The remarkability of this result cannot be overstated. We have attained that holy grail of multivariate optimization, a set of mutually conjugate search directions, *with no explicit knowledge of the Hessian*. In fact, unlike some other methods that also avoid computing the Hessian, we don't even have to store any approximation to it. The only extra storage space that we need is a few vectors to preserve the gradient and the search direction from the previous step, a mere pittance. I consider this algorithm to be one of the seven wonders of modern mathematics.

Astute readers will immediately notice the similarity of this algorithm to traditional backpropagation with momentum. The second line in Equation (1.8) tells us that the new search direction is the gradient at this point plus a scalar times the previous search direction. There are only two differences: In traditional backpropagation, the step size is fixed, while in the conjugate gradient algorithm, the step size is carefully chosen to be the line minimum along the search direction. Also, in backpropagation the momentum term is (usually) fixed. In the conjugate gradient algorithm, the momentum is optimally adjusted for each new step. These are actually two quite significant differences, and they account for the typically huge difference in performance. However, the similarities should be noted out of academic interest.

In the beginning of this section, we spoke of the *family* of conjugate gradient algorithms, yet we have just presented a single specific algorithm. The explanation of this seeming contradiction is that there is indeed a family, but the differences are generally small, and the family member shown here is fairly universally accepted as the best. See Press *et al.* (1992) for more details on this topic. Another difference among family members has to do with what action is taken when the method starts to fail. In many cases the Hessian will change so much from step to step that the property of mutual conjugacy will be lost, and the computed search direction will not be very good. Some implementations take the simple expedient of restarting with the gradient as the search direction every n steps. That approach is not so silly as it may seem and can be recommended in many applications. The author chooses a more gentle approach that will be discussed when the program is listed and analyzed. In fact, it is time to do just that. Here is a subroutine for implementing the conjugate gradient algorithm. A discussion will follow. It is vital to note that this version is specifically designed for training probabilistic and generalized regression neural networks. For this reason, there are several places where the variables are explicitly forced to remain positive. Readers who wish to use this program for more general purposes should remove those few lines of code.

```
static double gamma ( int n , double *g , double *grad ) ;      // Forward declarations
static void find_new_dir ( int n , double gam , double *g ,
             double *h , double *grad ) ;

/*
   This routine uses the general univariate minimizers 'glob_min' and
   'brentmin' to minimize along the gradient line.  So, just like we do in
   the various class' 'learn' routines, we must have a local function for
   them to call, and it must have access to the relevant data.
   These statics handle that.
*/

static double univar_crit ( double t ) ;          // Local univariate criterion
static double *local_x, *local_base, *local_direc ;   // It uses these
static int local_n ;
static double (*local_criter) (double * , double * , double * , int ) ;


double dermin (
   int itmax ,             // Iteration limit
   double critlim ,        // Quit if crit drops this low
   double eps ,            // Small, but greater than machine precision
   double tol ,            // Convergence tolerance
```

```
   double (*criter) (double * , double * , double * , int ) , // Criterion func
   int n ,                        // Number of variables
   double *x ,                    // In/out of independent variable
   double ystart ,                // Input of starting function value
   double *base ,                 // Work vector n long
   double *direc ,                // Work vector n long
   double *g ,                    // Work vector n long
   double *h ,                    // Work vector n long
   double *deriv2                 // Work vector n long
   )
{
   int i, iter, user_quit, convergence_counter, poor_cj_counter ;
   double fval, fbest, high, scale, t1, t2, t3, y1, y2, y3, dlen, dot1, dot2 ;
   double prev_best, old_fbest, toler, gam, improvement ;

/*
   Initialize for the local univariate criterion which may be called by
   'glob_min' and 'brentmin' to minimize along the search direction.
*/


   local_x = x ;
   local_base = base ;
   local_direc = direc ;
   local_n = n ;
   local_criter = criter ;

/*
   Initialize that the user has not pressed ESCape.
   Evaluate the function and, more importantly, its derivatives, at the
   starting point.  This call to criter puts the gradient into direc, but
   we flip its sign to get the downhill search direction.
   Also initialize the CJ algorithm by putting that vector in g and h.
*/

   user_quit = 0 ;
   fbest = criter ( x , direc , deriv2 , 1 ) ;      // Grad in direc, and 2'nd derivs
   prev_best = 1.e30 ;
   for (i=0 ; i<n ; i++)                             // Flip sign of gradient
      direc[i] = -direc[i] ;
```

Conjugate Gradient Methods 39

```
   memcpy ( g , direc , n * sizeof(double) ) ;     // Init CJ algorithm by putting
   memcpy ( h , direc , n * sizeof(double) ) ;     // neg grad in g and h

if (fbest < 0.0) {   // If user pressed ESCape during criter call
   fbest = ystart ;
   user_quit = 1 ;
   goto FINISH ;
   }
```

/*
   Main loop. For safety we impose a limit on iterations. There are two counters that
   have somewhat similar purposes. The first, convergence_counter, counts how
   many times an iteration failed to reduce the function value to the user's tolerance
   level. We require failure several times in a row before termination.

   The second, poor_cj_counter, has a (generally) higher threshold.
   It keeps track of poor improvement, and imposes successively small limits on
   gamma, thus forcing the algorithm back to steepest descent if CJ is doing poorly.
*/

```
convergence_counter = 0 ;
poor_cj_counter = 0 ;

for (iter=0 ; iter<itmax ; iter++) {

   if (fbest < critlim)                         // Do we satisfy user yet?
      break ;
```

/*
   Convergence check
*/

```
   if (prev_best <= 1.0)                        // If the function is small
      toler = tol ;                             // Work on absolutes
   else                                         // But if it is large
      toler = tol * prev_best ;                 // Keep things relative

   if ((prev_best - fbest)  <=  toler) {        // If little improvement
      if (++convergence_counter >= 3)           // Then count how many
         break ;                                // And quit if too many
      }
```

```
      else                                  // But a good iteration
         convergence_counter = 0 ;          // Resets this counter

/*
   Does the user want to quit?
*/

      if ((user_quit = user_pressed_escape ()) != 0)
         break ;

/*
   Here we do a few quick things for housekeeping.  We save the base for the linear
   search in 'base', which lets us parameterize from t=0.  We find the greatest second
   derivative.  This makes an excellent scaling factor for the search direction so that
   the initial global search for a trio containing the minimum is fast.  Because this is so
   stable, we use it to bound the generally better but unstable Newton scale.  We also
   compute the length of the search vector and its dot product with the gradient vector,
   as well as the directional second derivative.  That lets us use a sort of Newton's
   method to help us scale the initial global search to be as fast as possible.  In the
   ideal case, the 't' parameter will be exactly equal to 'scale', the center point of the
   call to glob_min.
*/

      dot1 = dot2 = dlen = 0.0 ;      // For finding directional derivatives
      high = 1.e-4 ;                  // For scaling glob_min
      for (i=0 ; i<n ; i++) {
         base[i] = x[i] ;             // We step out from here
         if (deriv2[i] > high)        // Keep track of second derivatives
            high = deriv2[i] ;        // For linear search via glob_min
         dot1 += direc[i] * g[i] ;    // Directional first derivative
         dot2 += direc[i] * direc[i] * deriv2[i] ; // and second
         dlen += direc[i] * direc[i] ;  // Length of search vector
         }

      dlen = sqrt ( dlen ) ;          // Actual length

/*
   The search direction is in 'direc' and the maximum second derivative is in 'high'.
   That stable value makes a good approximate scaling factor.  The ideal Newton
   scaling factor is unstable.  So compute the Newton ideal, then bound it to be near
```

the less ideal but far more stable maximum second derivative. Pass the first function value, corresponding to t=0, to the routine in *y2 and flag this by using a negative npts.
*/

```
scale = dot1 / dot2 ;            // Newton's ideal but unstable scale
high = 1.5 / high ;              // Less ideal but more stable heuristic
if (high < 1.e-4)                // Subjectively keep it realistic
   high = 1.e-4 ;

if (scale < 0.0)                 // This is truly pathological
   scale = high ;                // So stick with old reliable
else if (scale < 0.1 * high)     // Bound the Newton scale
   scale = 0.1 * high ;          // To be close to the stable scale
else if (scale > 10.0 * high)    // Bound it both above and below
   scale = 10.0 * high ;

y2 = prev_best = fbest ;

user_quit = glob_min ( 0.0 , 2.0 * scale , -3 , 0 , critlim ,
         univar_crit , &t1 , &y1 , &t2 , &y2 , &t3 , &y3 ) ;

if (user_quit || (y2 < critlim)) { // ESCape or good enough already?

   if (y2 < fbest) {             // If global caused improvement
      for (i=0 ; i<n ; i++) {    // Implement that improvement
         x[i] = base[i] + t2 * direc[i] ;
         if (x[i] < 1.e-10)      // Limit it away from zero
            x[i] = 1.e-10 ;      // Fairly arbitrary constant
         }
      fbest = y2 ;
      }

   else {                        // Else revert to starting point
      for (i=0 ; i<n ; i++)
         x[i] = base[i] ;
      }

   break ;
   }
```

```
/*
   We just used a crude global strategy to find three points that bracket the minimum.
   Refine using Brent's method.  If we are possibly near the end, as indicated by the
   convergence_counter being nonzero, then try extra hard.
*/

   if (convergence_counter)
      fbest = brentmin ( 20 , critlim , eps , 1.e-7 ,
                   univar_crit , &t1 , &t2 , &t3 , y2 ) ;
   else
      fbest = brentmin ( 10 , critlim , 1.e-6 , 1.e-5 ,
                   univar_crit , &t1 , &t2 , &t3 , y2 ) ;

/*
   We just completed the global and refined search.  Update the current point to
   reflect the minimum obtained.  Then evaluate the error and its derivatives there.
   (The linear optimizers only evaluated the error, not its derivatives.)  If the user
   pressed ESCape during dermin, fbest will be returned negative.
*/

   for (i=0 ; i<n ; i++) {
      x[i] = base[i] + t2 * direc[i] ;
      if (x[i] < 1.e-10)              // Limit it away from zero
         x[i] = 1.e-10 ;               // Fairly arbitrary constant
      }

   if (fbest < 0.0) {                  // If user pressed ESCape
      fbest = -fbest ;
      user_quit = 1 ;
      break ;
      }

   improvement = (prev_best - fbest) / prev_best ;

   if (fbest < critlim)                // Do we satisfy user yet?
      break ;

   fval = criter ( x , direc , deriv2 , 1 ) ; // Need derivs now
   for (i=0 ; i<n ; i++)               // Flip sign to get
      direc[i] = -direc[i] ;            // negative gradient
```

```
      if (fval < 0.0) {                // If user pressed ESCape
        user_quit = 1 ;
        break ;
        }

      gam = gamma ( n , g , direc ) ;

      if (gam < 0.0)
        gam = 0.0 ;

      if (gam > 10.0)                  // limit gamma
        gam = 10.0 ;

      if (improvement < 0.001)         // Count how many times we
         ++poor_cj_counter ;           // got poor improvement
      else                             // in a row
         poor_cj_counter = 0 ;

      if (poor_cj_counter >= 2) {      // If several times
        if (gam > 1.0)                 // limit gamma
          gam = 1.0 ;
        }

      if (poor_cj_counter >= 6) {      // If too many times
        poor_cj_counter = 0 ;          // set gamma to 0
        gam = 0.0 ;                    // to use steepest descent (gradient)
        }

      find_new_dir ( n , gam , g , h , direc ) ; // Compute search direction


      } // Main loop

FINISH:

   if (user_quit)
      return -fbest ;
   else
      return fbest ;
}
```

The first parameter list entry is nothing more than a safety factor. The user can limit the number of iterations. In the vast majority of situations, this should be set to a large number, relying on the fact that normal convergence is extremely likely within a reasonable time period. The second parameter should be viewed the same way. If the value of the function being minimized ever drops this low, iteration will cease. However, I usually set this equal to zero and let normal convergence rule. The eps parameter is passed to the brentmin subroutine (see page 19). The tol parameter is what really determines convergence. The routine quits when improvement this small or smaller is all that could be obtained for several successive iterations.

The remainder of the parameter list is straightforward. The caller specifies the address of the function to be minimized, along with the number of variables. The x vector serves as both the input of the starting point and the output of the location of the minimum. The user must also provide the value of the function at the starting point. Several work vectors are needed as well.

The first few lines are just drudgery. This subroutine will call glob_min and brentmin, which are both written for general-purpose minimization. They call a local criterion function that needs access to some information. We must initialize a few static variables to provide this information. Then we set a flag to indicate that the user has not pressed ESCape, evaluate the function and its first and second derivatives, and flip the sign of the gradient. We copy the negative gradient into g and h as is required for the first iteration of the conjugate gradient algorithm. In case the user pressed ESCape during the call to the criterion function, that function will return a negative number. We check for that fact and gracefully exit if so. Finally, we zero two counters that are used for convergence heuristics. One counts how many times the user's tolerance has not been satisfied so that we know when to quit. The other counts how many times a less stringent criterion has not been met. This lets us move away from the conjugate gradient algorithm into steepest descent, a move that is sometimes needed to get the algorithm back on track.

At the beginning of the iteration loop, we perform three checks for exiting. If the user's criterion limit has been attained, we are done. If the user's tolerance limit for function improvement has failed to be met several times in a row, quit. This is the normal means of terminating. Note how we accommodate both very small (near zero) and very large function values. Finally, we quickly abort if the user pressed ESCape.

Conjugate Gradient Methods 45

The next block of code was discussed in the previous section. We compute the heuristic step size and the directional derivatives so that we can use Equation (1.4) to find the optimal step size for the bounding routine glob_min. We do two other things in this same loop. We copy the current point to base, which is the point from which the line search will commence. We also compute the length of the search vector. That length is not actually needed for the algorithm. But it is quick and easy to compute, and printing it can yield some valuable information to the user who wants to trace the operation in detail. Then we compute the step size (putting it in scale) and limit the Newton ideal to be near the more stable heuristic.

The global bounding algorithm is told to start with three points, the middle point being at the theoretical minimum. If all goes well, that is all that will be needed to find a bounding trio. After the bounding is done, we see if we are done. This is indicated either by the user having pressed ESCape or by the user's criterion being met. If the global minimization improved the function, get that new point; otherwise, stick with the starting point.

Now we must refine the bounding interval. If the convergence counter is nonzero, we are probably near the end of our travail. In that case it pays to be thorough in our search for the line minimum. Otherwise, we can afford to be a little sloppy to save time. (But we must never be too sloppy. The conjugate gradient algorithm relies on fairly accurate location of the minimum.) After refinement is complete, the parametric location is converted to the true location of the new improved point. We also check to see if the user pressed ESCape during refinement, and exit if so. Note that this version of the algorithm is intended for training probabilistic and generalized regression networks. Since their parameters must always be positive, we arbitrarily enforce that limitation here. Readers who use this program for other purposes should remove these limits if necessary.

We are nearing the end of the loop. Check to see if the user's criterion has been met, and quit if so. Also compute the fraction of improvement. That will be used for evaluating the performance of the conjugate gradient algorithm.

The last step is to evaluate the function and its derivatives, then compute the search direction for the next iteration. This function evaluation is a small waste in that we already know what it is from the refinement algorithm. But we need to make this call anyway, as we need the gradient for the conjugate gradient algorithm, and we need the second derivatives as well if we want to use Newton's method to estimate the optimal step size. Recall that the global and refinement routines only evaluated the function, not its derivatives, to save time.

We impose a few heuristics at this time. The gamma parameter is arbitrarily limited to a restricted range. I have found this conducive to good performance for neural network training, though I know of no solid reason why this is so. Also, we keep count of how many times in a row the function performance is poor. That is usually nothing more than a sign of immanent convergence, but it can signal the fact that the conjugate gradient algorithm is pooping out and needs a shove back toward the direction of steepest descent. If poor performance has happened only a few times in a row, limit gamma moderately. If that does not help, set gamma equal to zero to force strict descent.

At the end of this loop we call two subroutines. One computes gamma according to the first line in Equation (1.8), and the other computes the new search direction by means of the second line in that equation. Since these are both straightforward, they are listed here with no further explanation. We also list the trivial local routine that computes the function when called by glob_min or brentmin.

```
double gamma ( int n , double *g , double *grad )
{
  int i ;
  double denom, numer ;

  numer = denom = 0.0 ;

  for (i=0 ; i<n ; i++) {
    denom += g[i] * g[i] ;
    numer += (grad[i] - g[i]) * grad[i] ;   // Grad is neg gradient
    }

  if (denom == 0.0)   // Should never happen (means gradient is zero!)
    return 0.0 ;
  else
    return numer / denom ;
}

void find_new_dir ( int n , double gam , double *g , double *h , double *grad )
{
  int i ;
```

```
    for (i=0 ; i<n ; i++) {
      g[i] = grad[i] ;
      grad[i] = h[i] = g[i] + gam * h[i] ;
      }
  }


  static double univar_crit ( double t )
  {
    int i ;
    for (i=0 ; i<local_n ; i++) {
      local_x[i] = local_base[i] + t * local_direc[i] ;
      if (local_x[i] < 1.e-10)
        local_x[i] = 1.e-10 ;
      }
    return local_criter ( local_x , (double *) NULL , (double *) NULL , 0 ) ;
  }
```

Levenberg-Marquardt Learning

In the previous section, we presented an optimization algorithm that has nearly the convergence speed of second-order methods, while avoiding the need to compute and store the potentially huge Hessian matrix. In many or most neural network applications, it is practically impossible to compute the second partial derivatives that comprise the Hessian. Algorithms exist, but they are simply too slow to be of much use. And hundreds of weights are not unusual, so even storing the matrix is difficult. Thus, the conjugate gradient algorithm is the method of choice for general-purpose use.

In the interest of fairness and completeness, an excellent alternative to the method of conjugate gradients is now shown. It is called the Levenberg-Marquardt (LM) algorithm in honor of its inventors. The problem of computing the vast number of second derivatives in the Hessian is alleviated by using instead an approximation to the Hessian that can be quickly found during the backpropagation that produces the gradient. However, the Hessian must still be stored, along with a scratch matrix of the same order. Furthermore, a large system of linear equations must be solved for each iteration. This algorithm is useless when there is a large number of weights to learn. But for small problems, the method of this section will frequently execute considerably faster than the conjugate gradient algorithm. It is a tool worthy of any well-equipped, professional workshop.

There is one other minor limitation of the LM algorithm. It cannot be used for general-purpose function minimization. It is specifically designed to minimize the mean squared error. Since this error measure is widely applicable and generally excellent, this limitation is of no real import.

Many or most minimization algorithms work primarily with the network error itself, adjusting the weights in such a way that the error is repeatedly reduced. The gradient of the error is used as a tool to point the way toward a more promising region. The LM algorithm is somewhat unusual in that the error is used only as an insurance policy to guarantee convergence to a minimum. The tactic of Levenberg and Marquardt is to reduce the gradient to a vector of all zeros. It is well known that the gradient is zero at local minima, maxima, and saddle points only. Thus, if one takes reasonable precautions to eliminate the latter two possibilities, zeroing the gradient is equivalent to finding a local minimum. This focus on the gradient rather than on the error itself is a feature of all Newton methods and their relatives.

How does one reduce the gradient to zero? We already saw Newton's method in one dimension on page 27 when Equation (1.2) was used to estimate the location of a line minimum. That equation generalizes to multiple dimensions as shown in Equation (1.9).

$$\mathbf{w}_{min} = \mathbf{w}_0 - \mathbf{H}^{-1}\mathbf{g} \qquad (1.9)$$

In that equation, $\mathbf{w}_0$ is some point (weight set) and $\mathbf{w}_{min}$ is the point at which the gradient is hopefully zero. Note that the subscript *min* is used because it is assumed that the surrounding algorithm is intelligently leading toward a minimum. Newton's method used alone is just as happy finding a local maximum or saddle point. In that same equation, $\mathbf{H}$ is the Hessian matrix of second partial derivatives and $\mathbf{g}$ is the gradient vector. If the function happens to be purely quadratic, Equation (1.9) will jump directly to a point at which the gradient is zero. Otherwise, the quality of the new point will depend entirely on the degree to which the Hessian is constant along the way.

What can go wrong with this approach to closing in on the point of zero gradient? The big danger is that the Hessian at $\mathbf{w}_0$ is wildly incorrect. When that happens, the computed $\mathbf{w}_{min}$ will end up somewhere out in deep left field, and the network error will be monstrous.

Even if the Hessian is computed exactly, it is often the case that it changes so rapidly that $\mathbf{H}$ at $\mathbf{w}_0$ is not at all representative of $\mathbf{H}$ at the minimum. And the method of this section will not even use an exact computation: $\mathbf{H}$ will only be estimated. This is double trouble. We need a *plan B* in case of difficulty.

Luckily for us all, there is a simple alternative that is absolutely foolproof, even if it is a little inefficient. Recall the definition of the gradient. It points in the direction of maximum function increase over a very short distance. So we know that if we move away from $\mathbf{w}_0$ for a very small distance in the direction of the negative gradient, we are guaranteed to see a decrease in the error. This inspires an elementary scheme. First try the efficient but dangerous Equation (1.9). If it works, fantastic. If not, multiply the gradient $\mathbf{g}$ by a tiny number and subtract that vector from $\mathbf{w}_0$. As long as the multiplier is tiny enough, this will give us a better point. Then try again from there. Eventually, we will be so close to the local minimum that the quadratic term in Taylor's expansion will dominate, and Newton will prevail.

The beauty of the LM algorithm is that it does not limit itself to the two extremes of the pure Newton method on one hand and primitive steepest descent on the other hand. Instead, it smoothly blends the two methods into a single formula for estimating $\mathbf{w}_{min}$. This formula lies on a continuum between the foolproof but slow descent down the gradient and the fast but risky Equation (1.9). The position of this formula along the risk–reward continuum is dynamically adjusted as the algorithm progresses. When things are going well, Newton is favored. When things go badly, retreat to steepest descent is allowed. The elegantly simple way to achieve this is shown in Equation (1.10).

$$\mathbf{w}_{min} = \mathbf{w}_0 - (\mathbf{H} + \lambda \mathbf{I})^{-1} \mathbf{g} \qquad (1.10)$$

In that equation, $\mathbf{I}$ is the identity matrix (zero, except for ones along the diagonal). Observe that if λ is zero, Equation (1.10) reduces to the pure Newton's method of Equation (1.9). Conversely, if λ is large, the computed Hessian $\mathbf{H}$ will be swamped out, and the result will be a small step in the direction of the negative gradient. The value of λ determines the position of Equation (1.10) along the risk–reward continuum.

The gradient and Hessian of the error are easily computed by repeated application of the chain rule for differentiation. For the sake of simplicity, the development here will be for a single real-domain output neuron. Differentiation is a linear operation. The derivative of a sum is the sum of the derivatives. Therefore, multiple output neurons are accommodated by handling each separately and summing. Similarly, extension to the complex domain is had by treating the real and imaginary parts separately and summing. We will also take advantage of linearity by computing the derivatives based on a single training case. The derivatives for the entire training epoch are computed by summing the derivatives within the epoch. This will all be illustrated in the code that appears later.

We start by laying out some notation. Let the input vector be **x** and let its associated correct output response (a real scalar) be t. (The letter t is traditional because the correct response is sometimes called the *target*.) Suppose that the neural network produces an actual response of y. The squared error, which is what we seek to minimize, is then $e = (y-t)^2$. The gradient vector is composed of the partial derivatives of that error with respect to each network weight, w_i. The (i, j) element of the Hessian matrix is the second partial derivative of e with respect to the pair of weights w_i and w_j. Straightforward application of the chain rule and the multiplication rule gives us Equations (1.11) and (1.12), which show how to compute those derivatives.

$$\frac{\partial e}{\partial w_i} = 2(y-t)\frac{\partial y}{\partial w_i} \qquad (1.11)$$

$$\frac{\partial^2 e}{\partial w_i \partial w_j} = 2\left[\frac{\partial y}{\partial w_i}\frac{\partial y}{\partial w_j} + (y-t)\frac{\partial^2 y}{\partial w_i \partial w_j}\right] \qquad (1.12)$$

The key to quickly estimating the Hessian is found in Equation (1.12). The first term in brackets is the product of two factors, each of which is a component of the gradient. These factors, the partial derivatives of the output activation with respect to the weights, are produced by the ordinary backpropagation algorithm. So this first component of the Hessian can be obtained as a trivial byproduct of gradient computation.

It is the second component, the one involving the second partial derivatives, that appears to be the problem. The second derivatives of the output activation with respect to pairs of weights could certainly be computed. But it would not be easy, especially considering how many of them there might be. How important is this component? A little thought tells us that it may not be very important at all in the grand scheme. For any *individual* training case, the second partial derivative might be quite significant. However, notice that it is multiplied by the error of this case, $y-t$. It is usually reasonable to assume that the errors in the training set are fairly independent and identically distributed around a mean of zero. Sometimes the error will be positive, and sometimes it will be negative. And they will typically balance out. So when this second component of the Hessian is summed across the entire training set, there will usually be a strong tendency for these terms to cancel, leaving a grand sum of approximately zero for the second component. In other words, it can be ignored!

Some readers will undoubtedly grumble a little at such callous reliance on tenuous assumptions. Strictly speaking, their concern is justified. A lot of things can go wrong. The errors may have a heavy-tailed and skewed distribution that thwarts cancellation. Or the model may fit badly, so the errors are unavoidably unbalanced. These are distinct possibilities. But the truth of the matter is that in practice, this approximation almost always is very good. And please remember that errors in the Hessian will not affect the accuracy of the results, nor will they prevent convergence. Errors will simply slow convergence by forcing more reliance on gradient descent. We have an effective insurance policy in place.

To complete the discussion on computing the gradient and Hessian, we need to show how to find the partial derivative of the output activation, y, with respect to a given weight. This is treated thoroughly in just about every neural network text ever written, so we will not dwell on the subject here. The only difference between other derivations and the one here is that they invariably are finding the partial derivative of the *total error*, while we need the partial derivative of the *output activation* of a single neuron. Thus, other derivations will start right out by multiplying by $y-t$ as a consequence of the chain rule. We delay that until later, as shown in Equation (1.11). We have the further simplification of having to deal with only one output, while most other derivations must handle the general case of any number of outputs. Otherwise, the two cases are identical.

Briefly, differentiation goes like this: Suppose that w is a weight leading to an output neuron. Let the activation function of the output neuron be $f(a)$. The net input to the output neuron, a, is the sum across all connections of the source activation times the weight connecting that source to the output neuron. Right now we are concerned with only one source, the one whose output passes through the weight w that is the object of this differentiation. Let that source's activation be o. Since

$a = ow$ plus similar terms for the other sources that do not involve this particular weight, the derivative of a with respect to w is equal to o. The output of the output neuron is $f(a)$, so the derivative of the output with respect to w, which is what we seek, is $of'(a)$.

When the weight w connects the input to the hidden layer, things are a little trickier. Suppose for the moment that we have exactly one hidden layer. Let $g(h)$ be the activation function of the hidden neuron, and let i be the input that passes through w to this hidden neuron. Then by exactly the same argument as was used for the output neuron, we find that the derivative of the hidden neuron's activation with respect to the input weight w is $ig'(h)$. Let w_o be the weight connecting this hidden neuron to the output neuron. The input to the output neuron is then $w_o g$ plus terms from other hidden neurons that are not affected by this weight w. The multiplication rule and chain rule tell us that the derivative of the output activation with respect to w is the product of the derivative of the hidden neuron's output with respect to w, times w_o, times the derivative of the output activation. This is expressed in Equation (1.13). In that equation, remember that h is the net input to the hidden neuron, and a is the net input to the output neuron.

$$\frac{\partial y}{\partial w} = i g'(h) w_o f'(a) \quad (1.13)$$

If there are two or more hidden layers, things get considerably more complicated. Suppose, for now, that there are exactly two hidden layers. We need to find the partial derivative of the final output with respect to a weight, w, connecting the input layer to the first hidden layer. The problem is that the output is affected by all of the neurons in the second hidden layer. We must invoke the generalized chain rule and sum across that layer. It helps to introduce an intermediate term. Let δ_k be defined as the partial derivative of the final output with respect to the input to neuron k in the second hidden layer. Neuron k in the second hidden layer, whose activation is h_k, is connected to the output neuron by a weight w_k. The argument used in the previous paragraph tells us that δ_k may be found as shown in Equation (1.14).

$$\delta_k = g'(h_k) w_k f'(a) \quad (1.14)$$

Let us now compute the partial derivative of the final output with respect to the input to a neuron in the first hidden layer. Call this quantity δ (as opposed to the already computed δ_k's of the second hidden layer). Variation in the activation of this neuron in the first hidden layer will affect the activations of all neurons in the second hidden layer. In particular, let this neuron be connected to neuron k in the second hidden layer by weight v_k. The generalized chain rule tells us that δ is computed by Equation (1.15). In that equation, h is the activation of this neuron in the first hidden layer. Note that Equation (1.15) is identical to Equation (1.14), except that in accordance with the generalized chain rule we sum across all terms that contribute to output variation.

$$\delta = g'(h) \sum_k v_k \delta_k \qquad (1.15)$$

We are nearly there! We have just found δ, the partial derivative of the final output with respect to the input of this neuron in the first hidden layer. Let w be a weight connecting an input whose value is i to this neuron through w. Then Equation (1.16) tells us what we need. By the way, compare that to Equation (1.13), thinking about what δ is for the output layer.

$$\frac{\partial y}{\partial w} = i\delta \qquad (1.16)$$

In the unlikely event that the reader needs more than two hidden layers, this algorithm is easily extended recursively. For every layer that has a preceding hidden layer, save its δ values in a vector. This will not often be needed.

We have strayed far enough from the meat of this section, the Levenberg-Marquardt algorithm. Let us now return. In the last few paragraphs, we learned how to compute $\partial y/\partial w_i$ for any weight w_i. We have also seen how these quantities can be used in Equation (1.11) to compute the gradient, **g**. We have stated that these same quantities can be used in Equation (1.12) to estimate the Hessian, **H**, as long as we are willing to ignore the second component in that equation. Finally, we know that Equation (1.10) can be used to advance to a (hopefully) better location. All that lacks is a method for choosing λ in that equation.

There are two aspects to the problem of choosing λ. We must choose an initial value, and we must adjust the value during iterations as needed. Some authorities suggest choosing a fixed initial value, such as $\lambda = 0.001$. I vehemently disagree with this approach. Any fixed constant may be gigantic for some applications and tiny for others. A better way is to adapt the initial value to the problem at hand. A good method is to search the diagonal of **H** at the starting point and find the largest value. If that value is used for λ, the result will be a nice compromise of risk versus reward. The estimated Hessian will exert some influence, but there will also be a tendency toward simple descent along the negative gradient.

How do we update λ as iteration progresses? The LM algorithm keeps it simple. If Equation (1.10) produces improvement, reduce λ to attempt more efficiency. If that equation results in deterioration, retreat to a larger λ. Press *et al.* (1992) suggest multiplying or dividing λ by a factor of ten. I use a factor of two instead, as that value seems more appropriate for the rigors of neural network learning. Higher factors are probably better for more well-behaved functions.

The most difficult part of the LM algorithm is knowing when to quit. A poor iteration, one in which the error decreased very little, may be due to being near the minimum. Or it might just be the result of instability or inaccuracy of the Hessian. Therefore, it is potentially dangerous simply to quit when the improvement on an iteration is tiny. Naturally, we do not want to waste time wandering aimlessly around some nearly flat rolling dunes at the bottom of a valley. So it is prudent to quit if a fair number of poor iterations in a row are experienced. However, neural networks are famous for vast expanses of nearly flat areas, with a delightful cliff waiting just over the horizon. Do not be anxious to quit too soon; patience often pays a handsome reward when training neural networks.

A good quitting criterion is the size of the gradient. It will drop to a very tiny value in the vicinity of the true minimum. Many times, when the algorithm is wandering far and wide but significant improvement may be just around the corner, the gradient will still be significant. Thus, I always check on the maximum magnitude of the gradient's components. If even one of them is not tiny, it is probably good to continue.

One more small but important point should be made: Equation (1.10) implies that we invert the modified Hessian matrix and multiply by the gradient to get the increment vector that will be subtracted from the current weight vector. This is shown in the first line of Equation (1.17). But as anyone who has passed Numerical Analysis 101 knows, that would actually be both slow and numerically unstable. The correct method is to compute the singular value decomposition of the modified

Hessian, then use back-substitution to solve the linear system shown in the second line of Equation (1.17). Under ideal conditions, those two lines are mathematically equivalent. In practice, they can be the difference between failure and success.

$$\Delta = (\mathbf{H} + \lambda I)^{-1} \mathbf{g}$$
$$(H + \lambda I) \Delta = \mathbf{g}$$
(1.17)

The overall flowchart of my version of the Levenberg-Marquardt algorithm is shown in Figure 1.7. A few details concerning convergence are omitted. Those will be discussed when the source code is analyzed. The basic algorithm works in the following way: A pass through the training set is made, and the error, *negative* gradient, and Hessian are computed. The latter two quantities are saved in "latest and best" work areas. Then λ is initialized as the largest diagonal element of the Hessian, and the *reset* flag is set to TRUE. We now enter into the first step of the main loop.

The first step of each iteration is to check the *reset* flag. If it is TRUE, the Hessian and gradient are retrieved from the areas where the latest, best values have been saved. Then Equation (1.10) is used to compute the next weight set. This involves three steps: The diagonal of **H** is increased by λ, the linear system is solved for Δ, and that quantity is added to the current weight vector. (We add because we actually computed the negative gradient.) The training epoch is performed, and the error, negative gradient, and Hessian are computed at this latest point. If the error decreased, we are happy. Check for convergence, copy the Hessian and gradient into the preservation areas, turn off the *reset* flag to avoid wasting time retrieving them, and reduce λ to favor Newton's method. If, on the other hand, the error got worse, we must punt. Subtract Δ from the weight vector to get back to where we were before this step. Turn on the *reset* flag so that the previous gradient and Hessian will be retrieved from their saved areas. And last but certainly not least, increase λ so that we tend more toward a simple descent along the negative gradient.

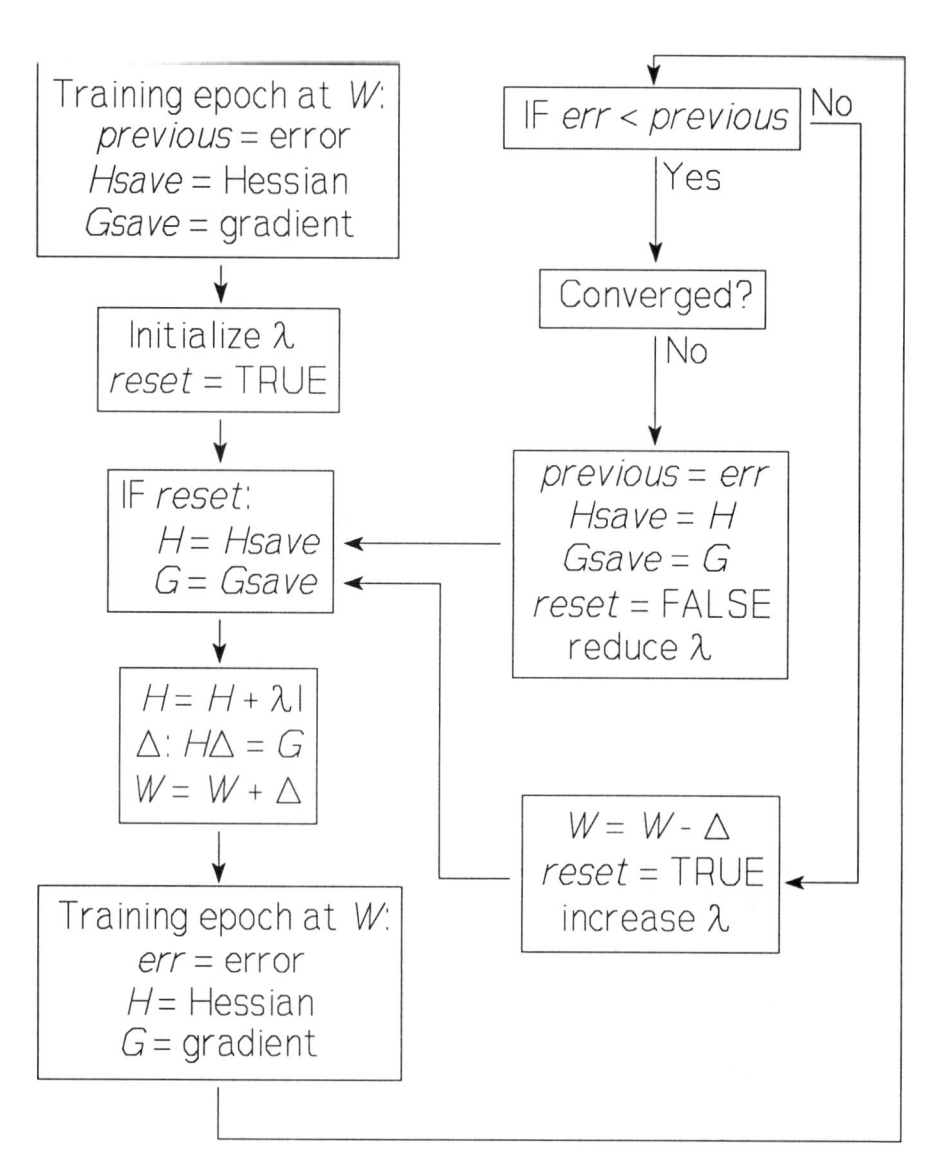

Figure 1.7 Levenberg-Marquardt algorithm.

Code for Levenberg-Marquardt Learning

Source code for my version of the Levenberg-Marquardt algorithm is now given. It largely follows the flowchart of Figure 1.7. However, there are several subtleties included in the code that would have unnecessarily cluttered the flowchart. These are related to checking for and enhancing convergence. They will now be discussed.

It has already been stated that λ is initialized to the largest diagonal element of **H**. This technique need not be limited to initialization. The primary cause of poor performance of the LM algorithm is instability or inaccuracy of the estimated **H**. When the Hessian changes rapidly in the neighborhood of the current point, a not uncommon event, Newton's method is worthless. It may be that numerous marginal improvements in the error have resulted in λ being reduced to a value that is smaller than is really justified. If several bad iterations happen in a row, or if a run of improvements is entirely marginal, then it is time to back up and try again. Search the diagonal of the Hessian and make sure that λ is at least as large as them all.

The other modification not shown in the flowchart relates to the convergence check. A lot happens in that one box labeled *Converged?*. First, it should be emphasized that one should check for convergence *only when there was improvement*, never after failure. Failure is invariably due to problems with the Hessian, rather than due to being near the minimum. I admit to having an exit in place in the failure section of the code. If failure happens many times in a row, exit is taken. However, that is emergency insurance only. In practice, that exit will never be taken.

The convergence check I use has two components: First, if the error decreased significantly, all is well and we continue iterating. Only if there was marginal improvement do we check further. The main check involves examination of the gradient. If all of its components are tiny, we are satisfied and quit. This is the main exit point and is the one almost always taken in practice. As a backup to avoid hours of endless wandering, we count the number of times we had marginal improvement with no intervening good results. If that gets to be too many, we quit. Please note that this is a dangerous escape route, especially in neural network learning. When numerous marginal improvements are had but the gradient is not yet tiny, it is likely that just a few more iterations will pay off handsomely in a drop off a cliff. Be wary of taking this escape too soon.

The code that was promised many paragraphs ago now appears. Some explanations of its trickier parts will follow. Keep in mind that this is not a complete subroutine. Superfluous details like memory allocation, class variable declarations, and error checks have been eliminated for clarity. The entire subroutine can be found in the routine LEV_MARQ.CPP on the accompanying code disk.

```
double LayerNet::lev_marq (
    TrainingSet *tptr ,         // Training set to use
    int maxits ,                // Maximum iterations allowed, 0 if no limit
    double reltol ,             // Relative error change tolerance
    double errtol               // Quit if error drops this low
    )
{
    int i, n, nvars, iter, key, bad_cnt, trivial_cnt, reset_ab ;
    double *work1, *work2, *hessian, *grad, *delta ;
    double error, maxgrad, lambda ;
    double prev_err, improvement ;
    SingularValueDecomp *sptr ;

    if (nhid1 == 0)             // No hidden layer
        nvars = nout * nin_n ;  // _n version includes bias, so nin_n=nin+1
    else if (nhid2 == 0)        // One hidden layer
        nvars = nhid1 * nin_n + nout * nhid1_n ;
    else                        // Two hidden layers
        nvars = nhid1 * nin_n + nhid2 * nhid1_n + nout * nhid2_n ;

/*
    Compute the error, Hessian, and error gradient at the starting point.
*/

    error = lm_core ( tptr , work1 , work2 , hessian , grad ) ;
    prev_err = error ;          // Will be 'previous iteration' error
    reset_ab = 1 ;              // Flag to use most recent good hessian and grad

/*
    Every time an iteration results in increased error, increment bad_cnt
    so that remedial action or total escape can be taken.
    Do a similar thing for improvements that are tiny via trivial_cnt.
*/
```

Levenberg-Marquardt Learning

```
      bad_cnt = 0 ;                    // Counts bad iterations for restart or exit
      trivial_cnt = 0 ;                // Counts trivial improvements for restart or exit

   /*
      Initialize lambda to slightly exceed the largest magnitude diagonal of the Hessian.
   */

      lambda = 0.0 ;
      for (i=0 ; i<nvars ; i++) {
        if (hessian[i*nvars+i] > lambda)
          lambda = hessian[i*nvars+i] ;
        }

      lambda += 1.e-20 ;


   /*
      Main iteration loop is here
   */

      iter = 0 ;
      for (;;) {                       // Each iter is an epoch

        if ((maxits > 0)  &&  (iter++ >= maxits))
          break ;

   /*
      Check current error against user's max.
   */

        if (error <= errtol)           // If our error is within user's limit
          break ;                      // then we are done.

        if (error <= reltol)           // Generally not necessary: reltol<errtol in
          break ;                      // practice, but help silly users

        if (reset_ab) {                // Revert to latest good Hessian and gradient?
          memcpy ( sptr->a , hessian , nvars * nvars * sizeof(double) ) ;
          memcpy ( sptr->b , grad , nvars * sizeof(double) ) ;
          }
```

/*
   Add lambda times the unit diagonal matrix to the Hessian.
   Solve the linear system for the correction, add that correction to the
   current point, and compute the error, Hessian, and gradient there.
*/

```
      for (i=0 ; i<nvars ; i++)                   // Shift diagonal for stability
        sptr->a[i*nvars+i] += lambda ;

      sptr->svdcmp () ;                           // Singular value decomposition
      sptr->backsub ( 1.e-8 , delta ) ;           // Back substitution solves system

      step_out_lm ( 1.0 , delta ) ;               // Jump to new point
      error = lm_core ( tptr , work1 , work2 , sptr->a , sptr->b ) ;

      improvement = (prev_err - error) / prev_err ;
      if (improvement > 0.0) {
```

/*
   This correction resulted in improvement. If only a trivial amount, check the gradient
   (relative to the error). If also small, quit. Otherwise count these trivial improvements. If there were a few, the Hessian may be bad, so retreat toward steepest
   descent. If there were a lot, give up.
*/

```
        prev_err = error ;                        // Keep best error here

        if (improvement < reltol) {               // Marginal improvement?
          maxgrad = 0.0 ;                         // Check the size of the gradient
          for (i=0 ; i<nvars ; i++) {
            if (fabs ( sptr->b[i] ) > maxgrad)
              maxgrad = fabs ( sptr->b[i] ) ;
            }

          if (error > 1.0)                        // Relative to function value
            maxgrad /= error ;

          if (maxgrad <= reltol)                  // Normal convergence exit is here
            break ;
```

```
                if (trivial_cnt++ == 4) {              // Revitalize
                    for (i=0 ; i<nvars ; i++) {       // By retreating toward descent
                        if (hessian[i*nvars+i] > lambda)
                            lambda = hessian[i*nvars+i] ;
                        }
                    }
                else if (trivial_cnt == 10)            // Alternate normal escape from loop
                    break ;
                }
            else
                trivial_cnt = 0 ;                      // Reset counter whenever good improvement
```

/*
   Since this step was good, update everything: the Hessian, the gradient, and the 'previous iteration' error. Zero reset_ab so that we do not waste time copying the Hessian and gradient into sptr, as they are already there. Cut lambda so that we approach Newton's method.
*/

```
            memcpy ( hessian , sptr->a , nvars * nvars * sizeof(double) ) ;
            memcpy ( grad , sptr->b , nvars * sizeof(double) ) ;
            reset_ab = 0 ;
            bad_cnt = 0 ;
            lambda *= 0.5 ;
            }

        else {
```

/*
   This step caused an increase in error, so undo the step and set reset_ab to cause the previous Hessian and gradient to be used. Increase lambda to revert closer to steepest descent (slower but more stable). If we had several bad iterations in a row, the Hessian may be bad, so increase lambda per the diagonal. In the very unlikely event that a lot of bad iterations happened in a row, quit. This should be extremely rare.
*/

```
            step_out_lm ( -1.0 , delta ) ;             // Back to original point
            reset_ab = 1 ;                             // Fetch old Hessian and gradient
            lambda *= 2.0 ;                            // Less Newton
```

```
         if (bad_cnt++ == 4) {                  // If several bad in a row
           for (i=0 ; i<nvars ; i++) {          // Make sure very un-Newton
             if (hessian[i*nvars+i] > lambda)
               lambda = hessian[i*nvars+i] ;
             }
           }
         if (bad_cnt == 10)                     // Pathological escape from loop
           break ;                              // Should almost never happen
         }
       } // This is the end of the main iteration loop

    return prev_err ;  // This is the best error
}

/*
--------------------------------------------------------------------------

   Local routine to add correction vector to weight vector

--------------------------------------------------------------------------
*/

void LayerNet::step_out_lm ( double step , double *direc )
{
   int i, n ;

   if (nhid1 == 0) {                   // No hidden layer
     n = nout * nin_n ;
     for (i=0 ; i<n ; i++)
       out_coefs[i] += *(direc++) * step ;
     }

   else if (nhid2 == 0) {              // One hidden layer
     n = nhid1 * nin_n ;
     for (i=0 ; i<n ; i++)
       hid1_coefs[i] += *(direc++) * step ;
     n = nout * nhid1_n ;
     for (i=0 ; i<n ; i++)
       out_coefs[i] += *(direc++) * step ;
     }
```

```
    else {                          // Two hidden layers
      n = nhid1 * nin_n ;
      for (i=0 ; i<n ; i++)
        hid1_coefs[i] += *(direc++) * step ;
      n = nhid2 * nhid1_n ;
      for (i=0 ; i<n ; i++)
        hid2_coefs[i] += *(direc++) * step ;
      n = nout * nhid2_n ;
      for (i=0 ; i<n ; i++)
        out_coefs[i] += *(direc++) * step ;
      }
    }
```

The basic philosophy of this implementation has already been explained, so repetition will be avoided. We now take a quick jog through the code, pausing only at areas of special interest.

The normal convergence criterion is specified by the user via rel_tol. This quantity is used for both the gradient check and the improvement check. Two other special escape mechanisms are also available. In case satisfaction may be obtained by nothing more than the error falling to a certain level, err_tol is provided. Finally, to avoid the possibility of endless iterations, maxits imposes an upper limit.

The total number of weights to be optimized, nvars, is computed based on the number of layers and the number of neurons in each layer. Initialization continues by making a pass through the training set, calling lm_core to compute the error, the Hessian, and the negative gradient. The previous iteration's error, prev_err, is set equal to the starting point error. The flag reset_ab is set so that on the first iteration, the Hessian and gradient that were just computed will be retrieved. Two convergence counters, trivial_cnt and bad_cnt, are set to zero. These will count the number of trivial improvements and outright failures, respectively. Finally, λ is initialized to be equal to the largest diagonal element of the Hessian, plus a tiny amount for cheap insurance against the extraordinarily unlikely event of severe degeneracy.

We now embark on the main iteration loop. The first step is to check for escape by counting iterations and comparing the error to the user's criterion. If we are to go on, as is the usual case, we retrieve the Hessian and gradient from the areas where the latest and best have been saved. This is done only if they are needed, as specified by the reset_ab flag. Then the main action takes place. The diagonal of the

Hessian is incremented by λ, the linear system is solved for Δ, that quantity is added to the current weights via a call to step_out_lm, and the error, Hessian, and gradient are computed at that new point. The improvement is computed, and we act accordingly.

If this iteration was successful, we set prev_err equal to the error here so that it is ready for the next iteration or possible return to the caller. Then we check for convergence. If there was significant improvement, we check no further. Otherwise, examine the gradient. Base the convergence decision on the maximum element. As a concession to general-purpose use of this algorithm, the gradient size is divided by the function value if that value is large. This keeps the check fair by making it relative.

If the gradient is still too large, we count the number of trivial improvements. When a few in a row are reached, the Hessian is blamed and λ is pushed up if it is small relative to the diagonal. Finally, as a last resort, we quit if a large number of trivial improvements occurred in a row. Do not be hasty here if the task is neural network learning.

If convergence is not obtained, we prepare for the next iteration. Preserve the Hessian and gradient in case we later need to retreat to this known good quantity. Turn off the reset_ab flag to avoid wasting time retrieving them when we already have them in place. Reset the counter of bad iterations, and optimistically decrease λ to head toward Newton's method.

If this iteration resulted in an increase in the error, we must try again with a more conservative approach. Subtract Δ from the weight vector to get back to the point from which this bad step was taken. Turn on the reset_ab flag so that the previous Hessian and gradient are retrieved. Increase λ to back off from Newton's method. If several bad iterations have happened in a row, mistrust the Hessian. Increase λ if needed to get it up large enough to overcome a bad Hessian. Finally, employ a little disaster insurance. If numerous bad iterations have occurred in a row, something mighty peculiar is going on. Get out. This should virtually never happen, as the negative gradient always points downhill, but why take chances?

The Levenberg-Marquardt algorithm has been quite thoroughly discussed. There is one more loose end to tie up. The code shown above called lm_core to compute the error, Hessian, and gradient for a training epoch. Many readers will already have the code or the knowledge required to write the code for that routine. One simply uses traditional backpropagation to compute the derivatives of the outputs

Levenberg-Marquardt Learning

with respect to the weights. Then Equations (1.11) and (1.12) provide **g** and **H**, respectively. However, for the sake of completeness, code fragments will now be shown to illustrate these computations. This first listing is the overall coordinator of the effort. It passes through the training set, calling a worker routine to do the hard part.

```
double LayerNet::lm_core_real (
   TrainingSet *tptr ,
   double *hid2delta ,
   double *grad ,
   double *alpha ,
   double *beta
   )
{
   int i, j, tset, n ;
   double err, error, *dptr, targ, factor ;

/*
   Compute length of grad vector (number of parameters).
*/

   if (nhid1 == 0)                          // No hidden layer
      n = nout * (nin+1) ;
   else if (nhid2 == 0)                     // One hidden layer
      n = nhid1 * (nin+1) + nout * (nhid1+1) ;
   else                                     // Two hidden layers
      n = nhid1 * (nin+1) + nhid2 * (nhid1+1) + nout * (nhid2+1) ;

   for (i=0 ; i<n ; i++) {                  // Zero alpha and beta for summing
      beta[i] = 0.0 ;
      for (j=0 ; j<=i ; j++)                // Symmetric, so only cumulate half
         alpha[i*n+j] = 0.0 ;
      }

   error = 0.0 ;                            // Will cumulate total error here
   for (tset=0 ; tset<ntrain ; tset++) {    // Do all samples

      dptr = ... ;                          // Point to this sample
      trial ( dptr ) ;                      // Evaluate network for it
      err = 0.0 ;                           // Cumulates for this presentation
```

```
    for (i=0 ; i<nout ; i++)                    // Sum for all outputs
      process_real ( dptr , i , target[i] , &err ,
                     alpha , beta , hid2delta, grad ) ;

    error += err ;
    } // for all tsets

/*
    Fill in the other half of alpha via symmetry.  Find the mean per case and output.
*/

  for (i=1 ; i<n ; i++) {
    for (j=0 ; j<i ; j++)
      alpha[j*n+i] = alpha[i*n+j] ;
    }

  factor = 1.0 / ((double) ntrain  *  (double) nout) ;
  return factor * error ;
}
```

The code listed above starts by computing the number of variables according to the number of layers and the number of neurons in each layer. Then it zeros alpha (where the Hessian will be cumulated) and beta (where the gradient will be cumulated). Those names are chosen in deference to traditional use in the literature. Such standardization may help the reader compare this implementation to others.

The main loop passes through the entire training set. For each case, dptr is set to point to that case, and the usual forward pass is made to compute the activation of each neuron in the network. Then each output neuron is processed separately. The error, alpha, and beta are summed across all output neurons by calling process_real for each.

After the epoch is complete, there is a little cleaning up to do. The work routine only computed half of Alpha, as the Hessian is always symmetric. We must fill in the other half. Finally, divide the error by the number of training cases and the number of outputs to get an average.

We now come to the tricky part. The process_real routine cumulates the error, the gradient, and the Hessian for a single output variable of a single training case. The full text of this routine can be found in LM_CORE.CPP on the accompanying code disk. Here is a summary.

Levenberg-Marquardt Learning

```
void LayerNet::process_real (
  double *input ,
  int idep ,
  double target ,
  double *err ,
  double *alpha ,
  double *beta ,
  double *hid2delta ,
  double *grad
  )
{
  int i, j, n, nprev ;
  double delta, *hid1grad, *hid2grad, *outgrad, outdelta ;
  double *outprev, *prevact, *gradptr, diff, *aptr ;

/*
   Compute length of grad vector and gradient positions in it.  Also point to layer
   previous to output and its size.  Ditto for layer after hid1.
*/

  if (nhid1 == 0) {                    // No hidden layer
    n = nout * (nin+1) ;
    outgrad = grad ;
    nprev = nin ;
    }
  else if (nhid2 == 0) {               // One hidden layer
    n = nhid1 * (nin+1) + nout * (nhid1+1) ;
    hid1grad = grad ;
    outgrad = grad + nhid1 * (nin+1) ;
    outprev = hid1 ;
    nprev = nhid1 ;
    }
  else {                               // Two hidden layers
    n = nhid1 * (nin+1) + nhid2 * (nhid1+1) + nout * (nhid2+1) ;
    hid1grad = grad ;
    hid2grad = grad + nhid1 * (nin+1) ;
    outgrad = hid2grad + nhid2 * (nhid1+1) ;
    outprev = hid2 ;
    nprev = nhid2 ;
    }
```

```
/*
   Save the derivative of this output activation with respect to net input
*/

   if (outlin)
      outdelta = 1.0 ;
   else
      outdelta = actderiv ( out[idep] ) ;

/*
   Compute output gradient.  Prevact is the activity in the layer prior to the output layer.
*/

   if (nhid1 == 0)                  // If no hidden layer
      prevact = input ;             // Then direct connection to inputs
   else
      prevact = outprev ;           // Point to previous layer

   gradptr = outgrad ;
   for (i=0 ; i<nout ; i++) {
      if (i == idep) {
         for (j=0 ; j<nprev ; j++)
            *gradptr++ = outdelta * prevact ;
         *gradptr++ = outdelta ;    // Bias activation is always 1
         }
      else {
         for (j=0 ; j<nprev ; j++)
            *gradptr++ = 0.0 ;
         *gradptr++ = 0.0 ;
         }
      }

/*
   Cumulate hid2 gradient (if it exists)
*/

   if (nhid2) {
      gradptr = hid2grad ;
      for (i=0 ; i<nhid2 ; i++) {
         delta = outdelta * out_coefs[idep*(nhid2+1)+i] ;
         delta *= actderiv ( hid2[i] ) ;
```

```
          hid2delta[i] = delta ;
          for (j=0 ; j<nhid1 ; j++)
            *gradptr++ = delta * hid1[j] ;
          *gradptr++ = delta ;          // Bias activation is always 1
          }
        }

/*
   Cumulate hid1 gradient (if it exists).
   If there is hid2 layer, we must use the generalized chain rule to sum across those
   neurons.  If not, then we only do the 'idep' output neuron.
*/

      if (nhid1) {
        prevact = input ;
        gradptr = hid1grad ;
        for (i=0 ; i<nhid1 ; i++) {
          if (nhid2) {
            delta = 0.0 ;
            for (j=0 ; j<nhid2 ; j++)
              delta += hid2delta[j] * hid2_coefs[j*(nhid1+1)+i] ;
            }
          else
            delta = outdelta * out_coefs[idep*(nhid1+1)+i] ;
          delta *= actderiv ( hid1[i] ) ;
          for (j=0 ; j<nin ; j++)
            *gradptr++ = delta * prevact[j] ;
          *gradptr++ = delta ;          // Bias activation is always 1
          }
        }

      diff = target - out[idep] ;       // Target minus attained output
      *err += diff * diff ;

      for (i=0 ; i<n ; i++) {
        beta[i] += diff * grad[i] ;
        aptr = alpha + i*n ;
        for (j=0 ; j<=i ; j++)
          aptr[j] += grad[i] * grad[j] ;
        }
      }
```

The parameter list starts with three inputs: the input data vector, the ordinal number of the output neuron (dependent variable), and the target activation of that output neuron. The next three parameters are combined input/output, as they are cumulated. They are the error, the Hessian, and the (negative) error gradient, respectively. This gradient, beta, must be distinguished from the *grad* gradient that also appears here. The latter is a work vector that holds the gradient of the output activation, as opposed to the gradient of the total error. The last two variables in the parameter list are work vectors.

The first step looks more complicated than it really is. All that is done is to consider how many layers exist, and how many neurons are in each layer. Based on this information, the number of elements in the output gradient is computed. Also, we compute the position of each layer's gradient component in the grand gradient vector. Finally, we point to the layer just previous to the output layer. This may be the input, the first (and only) hidden layer, or the second hidden layer, depending on the number of layers.

The variable *outdelta* is used to hold the derivative of this output neuron's activation with respect to its net input. If the output is linear (the identity function in the author's implementation), the derivative is one. Otherwise, it must be computed.

Some readers may wish to review the material starting on page 51 at this time. As the term *backpropagation* implies, we start with the output layer and work backwards. The previous layer's activation vector is in *prevact*. Initialize a scratch pointer to point to the position of the output gradient in the grand gradient vector. Then do each output neuron. For the current output neuron, *idep*, the partial derivative of the output with respect to the weight is the product of the derivative of the output with respect to the input, *outdelta*, multiplied by the derivative of the input with respect to the weight. That, of course, is just the value of the activation that is coming through that weight. The activation of the bias term is always one. For output neurons other than the current one, changing their weights will not affect this particular neuron, as there is no connection. So their gradient is zero.

If there are two hidden layers, we move back to the second hidden layer. Again following standard practice, we start by computing delta for this layer's neurons (Equation (1.14)). For each hidden neuron, this is the partial derivative of the final output activation with respect to the input to this hidden neuron. This is just the product of the output delta, times the weight connecting the hidden neuron to the output neuron, times the derivative of the hidden neuron's activation function. We need to save these deltas, as they will be needed when processing the first hidden layer. Experienced readers may be a little confused at this point, because other algorithms sum across *all* outputs in this step. The difference is simple. Other implementations are computing the derivative with respect to the *total error*, which involves all output neurons. We, on the other hand, are just interested in the output activation of the single idep neuron.

Once we have each hidden neuron's delta, finding the derivative with respect to a weight is easy. It is just the delta times the value of the activation passing through that weight (Equation (1.13) or (1.16), which are equivalent). We do that calculation for each of the nhid1 connections to the first hidden layer. Again, the value of the bias activation is one.

Last of all we do the first hidden layer. As always, we start by computing each neuron's delta, the derivative of the final output activation with respect to this neuron's input. If there is no second hidden layer, this is easy. It is just the product of the output delta times the connection weight times the derivative of this neuron's activation function. But if there is a second hidden layer, it is more complicated. The output activation is affected by every neuron in the second hidden layer, and this first hidden layer neuron affects every second hidden layer neuron. Thus, we must invoke the generalized chain rule and sum across all neurons in the second hidden layer (Equation (1.15)). The contribution of each second hidden layer neuron is its delta (already saved) times the connection weight. Multiply that sum by the derivative of the activation function, and we get the delta for this neuron. For each weight connecting to the input, the derivative of the neuron's input with respect to that weight is just the value of the input passing through that weight. So use Equation (1.16) for every input connection, including the unit bias.

The final step in this core processing routine is to use the gradient of the output activation to compute the Hessian and the gradient of the error. This is just Equations (1.12) and (1.11), respectively. While we are at it, we cumulate the total error.

One last small point should be made. If storage space is at a premium, one can take advantage of the symmetry of the Hessian and save only half of it. Since the entire matrix needs to be present for the singular value decomposition, the savings will not be tremendous. In virtually all implementations, the LM algorithm will be rendered useless by time constraints long before space becomes an issue.

2

Stochastic Optimization

- Motivation for random methods

- A primitive algorithm

- Conventional and advanced techniques

- Stochastic smoothing

- Uniform, normal, and Cauchy random numbers

The previous chapter dealt with deterministic optimization. Those methods are extremely efficient in that they locate the nearest local minimum using relatively few function evaluations. Their weakness is that they gravitate to any convenient minimum, no matter what its quality may be. This chapter deals with optimization methods that rely more on random numbers than on exact equations. They trade away efficiency in order to gain a more global view. These stochastic algorithms generally require more function evaluations than their deterministic cousins; usually a *lot* more. In return, they are far more likely to locate a global minimum, or at least a minimum that is relatively good. Note, by the way, that we often refer to *a* global minimum, as opposed to *the* global minimum. The reason is simple. In many or most neural networks, there will be many global minima, all providing identical performance. This is due to the symmetries inherent in many neural network architectures.

It should be emphasized that virtually all of the algorithms presented in this chapter are rarely, if ever, used alone as a single training method. They are simply too inefficient to be practical; usually they form part of a hybrid training procedure. Some of these hybrids will be discussed in the next chapter. However, every stochastic optimization algorithm given here is theoretically capable of standalone performance, and each will be treated as such.

Overview of Simulated Annealing

Annealing is a metallurgical term. When the atoms in a piece of metal are laid out in a wildly helter-skelter arrangement, the metal is (usually) hard and brittle. Sometimes we want metal to be hard, while other times we want it to be soft so that it can be bent and shaped easily without breaking. Many centuries ago it was discovered that this property could be changed at will. To harden metal, it is heated to a high temperature, then cooled suddenly by plunging it into a cold liquid. To soften metal and make it pliable, it is heated as before, but the cooling is done very slowly. Modern science has discovered the internal mechanism behind this ancient technology. When the metal is heated the atoms shake violently, so that at any given moment their orientation is highly random. If the metal is plunged into a cold liquid, the motion stops almost immediately and the atoms remain locked into whatever random orientation they happened to be in at the time of the

Overview of Simulated Annealing

plunge. However, if the cooling is done slowly, the motion abates in a more regular fashion. As the temperature decreases, the average position of each atom has a tendency to be such that they line up in a way that is characteristic of the particular metal. As long as the temperature is above absolute zero, the motion continues, but it becomes less and less as cooling progresses. The key is that at *any* temperature there is some tendency for the atoms to prefer an organized structure. It is just that at high temperatures the motion is so violent that the tendency toward organization is overwhelmed. As the motion diminishes, though, the atoms spend more and more time lined up with each other, with the departures from this stable state becoming less profound all the time. If the metal worker is careless and lets the temperature drop too suddenly at some stage of the process, the atoms will become locked in orientations that are only partially lined up. Subsequent motion will be centered about this less-than-optimal layout, and further cooling, no matter how slow, will be futile. But if the cooling is done slowly until room temperature is reached, the atoms will lie in a well-organized array, and the metal will be soft and workable.

This same principle can be applied to function optimization. Suppose we want to find the global minimum of a function that is fraught with a multitude of local minima. We choose some starting point, then violently toss the point around, evaluating the function at each new random location. Establish some criterion that will cause the position of the point at any given time to favor areas at which the function value is relatively low. This corresponds to the atoms of a metal favoring an organized arrangement, even while randomly departing from that arrangement. Then slowly decrease the degree to which the point is randomly tossed about. At any stage of this process, the position of the point will tend to focus on areas at which the function is relatively low. When the perturbations eventually become small, with any luck at all the point will be hopping about in the vicinity of the global minimum.

It must be emphasized that there is no real definition of what simulated annealing really is. There is no algorithm that can be called the archetypical simulated annealing process. The only requirements are that sufficient randomness must be inherent in the point selection process so that a wide field can be covered; more optimal points must be somewhat favored over less optimal points; and the degree of randomness must slowly decrease. Within those extremely broad constraints, anything is possible.

Primitive Simulated Annealing

We will start out by presenting a primitive but perfectly acceptable algorithm. It is almost inappropriate to attach the modern term *simulated annealing* to it, as this algorithm really has been around for many years as a crude optimization method. It is sometimes taught to students as the *wrong* way to minimize a multivariate function, since for well-behaved applications it is grossly inefficient. But with the surge in interest in stochastic methods, largely due to the surge in interest in neural networks, this old method has some new appeal. For functions that have multiple minima, it often works quite well at locating the global minimum.

The concept is simple: You are sitting at some point, and you want to move to a more optimal point. So you search the neighborhood of the current point, looking for a better spot. After examining a great number of candidates, pick the one whose function value was the best (minimum in our applications). If it is better than the current point, move to this new improved point and make it the center for the next random search. If the average search distance from the center point is gradually reduced, you have an algorithm than can justifiably be called simulated annealing. This is illustrated for three temperatures in Figure 2.1.

The algorithm starts out with a very broad search area, delineated with the bottom bracket shown in that figure. The leftmost dotted line marks the spot that turned out to be the lowest of all the random points in that interval that were tried. Not enough points were tested to find the global minimum, but at least the best point is down pretty low. That point becomes the center of the search at the next temperature.

The distance searched at this new medium temperature is less than it was at the high temperature. This is illustrated with the second bracket up from the bottom. The center dotted line is the point that happened to be the best within this medium-temperature random search. It is not much lower than the previous best, but at least it is an improvement. It becomes the center of the final, low-temperature search area.

That last search area is the smallest of all. If it does not include the global minimum, it may be futile. That sad situation would correspond to a metallurgist erring by letting the metal cool too quickly at some stage. Overly rapid cooling causes the process to become

Primitive Simulated Annealing

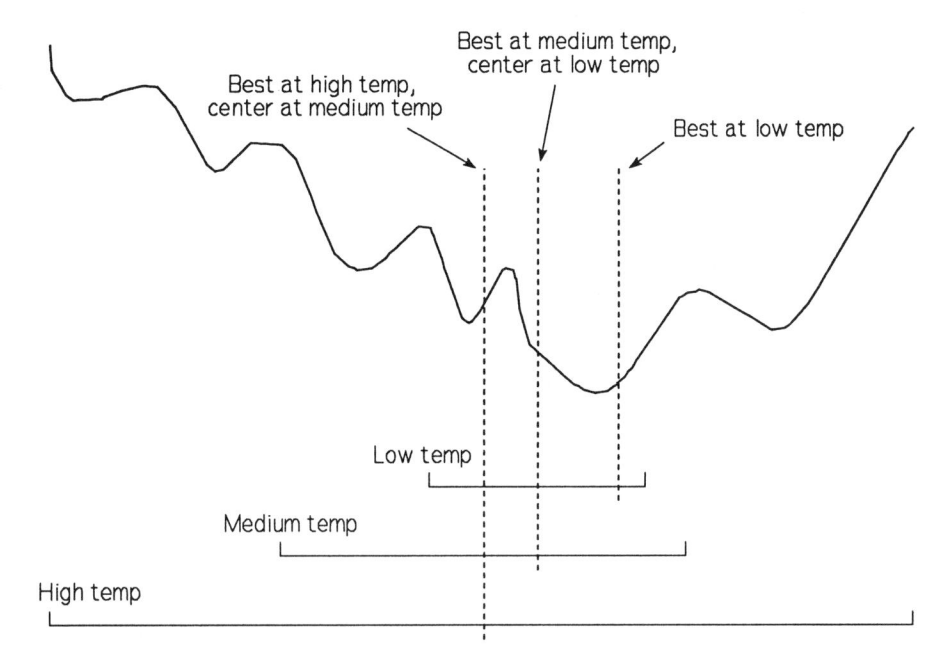

[Figure: curve with annotations "Best at high temp, center at medium temp", "Best at medium temp, center at low temp", "Best at low temp", and brackets labeled "Low temp", "Medium temp", "High temp"]

Figure 2.1 Primitive simulated annealing.

hopelessly locked in an unprofitable area. This presents us with the worst dilemma of simulated annealing. How quickly do we lower the temperature relative to the number of function evaluations? If we drop it too slowly, an excessive amount of time may be required. But if we drop it too quickly, we may end up wasting even more time by fruitless searches in an area that does not contain the minimum that we seek. Unfortunately, this remains a major unsolved problem. Doctoral candidates looking for a thesis topic need look no further. Any contributions to this area would be gratefully accepted.

Refinements

There are several subtle points to consider when implementing this algorithm. We will mention a few of them here. Since the entire field of simulated annealing is relatively new and unexplored, readers are highly encouraged to experiment.

    The temperatures used, and the nature of the search at each temperature, are critically important. There are many difficult issues to resolve, and the issues are complicated by the fact that these quantities interact strongly. For example, we know that the temperature should drop slowly. This implies the rule that the wider the temperature range covered, the more temperatures are needed. That, in turn, implies that to keep the number of function evaluations reasonable, the number of iterations at each temperature should be decreased as the number of temperatures increases. But it is the search at each given temperature that determines the center about which the next search will be conducted, so limiting this search will compromise the global nature of the algorithm. It is obvious that there are many tradeoffs to be made, and these must be done intelligently. Here is a list of guidelines that may be of some help.

- Make the starting temperature as small as possible, as long as it is large enough that the global minimum can be encountered. Don't waste time searching wildly far from the most profitable area.

- Make the stopping temperature as large as possible, as long as it is small enough that the final point will likely lie in the basin of attraction of the global minimum. Don't use expensive simulated annealing for refinement when the true minimum can be more efficiently located with a deterministic algorithm later.

- Decide on a rate at which the temperature will be lowered, and choose the number of temperatures accordingly. Reducing the temperature about 10 to 20 percent each time is reasonable. Faster reduction may be too confining, making it impossible to escape from the basin of attraction of a poor local minimum once inside that basin. Slower reduction necessitates fewer iterations at each temperature, compromising the global search.

- It is usually profitable to continue iterating at a given temperature as long as the function is still decreasing. A long string of tries with no improvement indicates that we may be near the bottom. This is implemented with the setback parameter in the code given in the next section.

Primitive Simulated Annealing

- Choose the probability distribution of the random perturbations according to the nature of the problem. In the vast majority of cases, an ordinary Gaussian (normal) distribution is appropriate. However, in some cases, we may suspect that the global minimum is in far-left field somewhere. If that is unlikely but possible, using a Gaussian distribution with a large variance would probably be a waste of time. We would be better off using a heavy-tailed distribution like the Cauchy. That will focus most effort on the local area, just like the Gaussian, but will still occasionally venture far away.

Code for Primitive Annealing

We now present a code fragment that implements this primitive simulated annealing algorithm. This code is not a strictly complete subroutine in that it has been pulled directly from the MLFN2 neural network training program, and many superfluous lines have been removed. Also, some variables are parts of the class to which the routine belongs, so they are not declared. However, every effort has been made to present this code in such a way that the algorithm itself is clear. Readers should have no trouble adapting it to their own applications.

```
int LayerNet::anneal1 (
   int itry                          // Passed by caller for more randomization
  )
{
  int ntemps, niters, setback ;
  int i, iter, improved, itemp ;
  long seed, bestseed ;
  double tempmult, temp, fval, bestfval, starttemp, stoptemp, fquit ;

  ntemps = ...                       // Number of temperatures
  niters = ...                       // Iterations at each temperature
  setback =                          // Keeps iterating if improving
  starttemp = ...                    // Starting temperature
  stoptemp = ...                     // Stopping temperature
  density = ...                      // Probability density
  fquit = ...                        // Quit if error drops this low
```

```
/*
    The best point so far is kept in 'bestnet' so initialize it to be the current point.  That
    will also be the center around which perturbations are done.  Find and preserve the
    function value there so we can keep track of the best.
*/

   copy_weights ( bestnet , this ) ;    // Current weights are best so far
   bestfval = trial_error ( ) ;         // Evaluate network error

/*
    This is the outer, temperature reduction loop.  The current temperature is in 'temp'
    and we regularly reduce it by the factor 'tempmult'.
*/

   temp = starttemp ;
   tempmult = exp( log( stoptemp / starttemp ) / (ntemps-1)) ;

   for (itemp=0 ; itemp<ntemps ; itemp++) {        // Temp reduction loop

      improved = 0 ;                               // Flags if this temp improved

      for (iter=0 ; iter<niters ; iter++) {        // Iters per temp loop

         seed = flrand () ;                        // Get a random seed
         sflrand ( seed ) ;                        // Brute force set it
         for (i=itry ; i ; i--)                    // Peel off a few
            flrand() ;                             // To avoid reps across tries
         perturb ( bestnet , this , temp , density ) ;  // Randomly perturb about best

         fval = trial_error () ;                   // Compute network error

         if (fval < bestfval) {                    // If this iteration improved
            bestfval = fval ;                      // then update the best so far
            bestseed = seed ;                      // and save seed to recreate it
            improved = 1 ;                         // Flag that we improved

            if (bestfval <= fquit)                 // If we reached the user's
               break ;                             // limit, we can quit

            iter -= setback ;                      // It often pays to keep going
```

```
         if (iter < 0)                              // at this temperature if we
            iter = 0 ;                              // are still improving
         }

      if (improved) {                               // If this temp saw improvement
         sflrand ( bestseed ) ;                     // set seed to what caused it
         for (i=itry ; i ; i--)                     // Peel off a few
            key = flrand() ;                        // To avoid reps across tries
         perturb ( bestnet , this , temp , density ) ;  // Recreate best
         copy_weights ( bestnet , this ) ;          // which will become next center
         sflrand ( bestseed / 2L + 999L ) ;         // Jog seed away from best

      if (bestfval <= fquit)                        // If we reached the user's
         break ;                                    // limit, we can quit

      temp *= tempmult ;                            // Reduce temp for next pass
      }                                             // through this temperature loop

   copy_weights ( this , bestnet ) ;                // Return best weights in this net
   neterr = bestfval ;                              // Trials destroyed weights, err
}
```

The only variable shown in the parameter list here is *itry*. If this routine is called more than once to effect independent trials, this parameter should be set to a different number each time. Something simple like the trial number (0, 1, 2, ...) is excellent. Later in this description we will see how the *itry* parameter is used to increase randomization across trials. The remaining annealing parameters are shown being set at the beginning of the code.

The best point (weight set) will be preserved at all times and used as the center about which perturbation will take place at each temperature. So before starting to anneal, we must copy the user's current weights into the work area in which the best will be preserved. We also evaluate the network error there. A subtle point should be considered at this time: It will often be the case that the user is commencing the annealing process around a center of zero. The network error at zero may be moderately small. This is especially true if the network is being used to classify a large number of categories. The usual technique is to train in such a way that exactly one output will be nonzero, that corresponding to the correct class. A totally zero weight set will produce zero for all outputs, which is not too far from the correct response! Most users would be annoyed if it happened that all annealing trials produced higher error than this, so the final optimal network had all zero weights. That scenario is not as uncommon as might be thought. And it gets worse. Suppose that simulated annealing is being used to provide good starting weights for a directed descent algorithm. Then the gradient will be zero, and directed descent will go nowhere! Therefore, a simple bit of insurance is called for. If the initial weights are all zero, it may be preferable to set bestfval to some huge number rather than the actual error. That way it is guaranteed that *something* other than zero will be output at the end of the process. Of course, if the user is restarting training with a set of currently good weights, then we must use the true error. Be warned. This is a potentially serious problem that crops up uncomfortably often.

At the beginning of the temperature loop we initialize the improved flag that will tell us whether or not any improvement was had at that temperature. Then the iteration loop begins.

The obvious way to save an improved weight set is simply to copy it to a holding area. But if the network is large, that involves a lot of effort, not to mention the sometimes significant amount of memory required. A better way is to preserve the random number generator's seed just before the perturbation is done. That way we can always recreate the weight set at a later time by setting the seed to that preserved value. There are two subtle dangers with this approach though. If the random number generator is of the shuffling type, or anything more sophisticated than a simple linear congruential algorithm, a given number will not always be followed by the same number at different times. That is the whole point of shuffling. Thus it is not sufficient to just save the seed. We must also explicitly reset the seed before perturbing in order to reset the shuffling generator. But the act of resetting the seed introduces yet another subtle problem. By doing so we have partially thwarted the purpose of shuffling. We have just guaranteed that each time a perturbation commences by setting the seed to some value, the exact same random sequence will be generated each time that value is used. Within a given annealing operation, this is of no consequence. But if multiple tries are done, we are at the mercy of chance repetition of the same seed. That is not good. So we employ a trivial but effective remedy. After setting the seed, we peel off a few random numbers. The precise quantity removed is determined by the caller of the annealing routine, and it must be set to a different value for each try. That way, even if fate conspires against us and happens to deal us exactly the same random number across several tries, the ensuing random sequence will be different. Readers of Masters (1993) should note that this technique was not employed in the annealing algorithm presented in that book. Those who are using that code would do well to implement this simple enhancement. In most cases it makes no difference. But there are some pathological network architectures that can create inefficiencies due to this problem.

After trying a newly perturbed point, its function value is compared to the best so far. If there was improvement, the seed is saved so that the point can be recreated later. Also, we employ the heuristic that as long as improvement is happening, we might as well keep looking around at this center point and temperature. We set back the iteration counter, but we do not let it become negative, which would invite excessive looping. The philosophy behind setting back the counter after improvement is that once we land near the minimum, we will only have a slight chance of further improvement at this temperature, so we might as well stop trying and lower the temperature. But as long as we keep improving, we are probably not yet near the minimum.

After all iterations at a given temperature are completed, the flag *improved* indicates whether or not improvement was had at that temperature. If so, the best point is recreated by setting the random seed, peeling off a few random numbers according to the trial number, and perturbing from the same center that was used throughout the loop. This best point is copied into *bestnet* for preservation as well as to serve as the center for the next temperature. Then the temperature is reduced and we start again. After all temperatures have been done, the best weights and their associated error are retrieved into this network.

Conventional and Advanced Simulated Annealing

Let us be clear from the outset: Even when the modifier *conventional* is employed, there is no real definition of what simulated annealing is. The rough guidelines stated at the beginning of this chapter are all that are agreed upon. Thus, this chapter will not pretend to set forth the quintessential simulated annealing algorithm. No such animal exists. Rather, it will lay out a broad foundation upon which a variety of techniques can be constructed. Several common versions of simulated annealing can be put together with the tools presented in this section. Other types that are not discussed in the literature can be built as well. The reader should think of this section as a tool chest instead of as a final product. On the other hand, several final products that have known effectiveness will be illustrated.

The cornerstone of the style of simulated annealing presented in this section is *travel*. The primitive annealing discussed in the previous section searched the neighborhood of a point, then moved to the best new point. Searches were wide, but actual motion was rarely great. The algorithm gradually closed in on the minimum in a series of relatively few jumps across relatively short distances. The method now discussed is very different from the primitive method. There is a *lot* of travel involved. The point (weight set) is in almost continuous motion. In its random walk looking for a good minimum, a tremendous expanse of the problem domain may be covered. Also in contrast to the previous method is the fact that this method can wander uphill nearly as easily as downhill. The primitive method had a degree of tenacity. At the conclusion of each temperature pass, the function value at the final point would, at worst, be the same as when it started. In this method it is possible for the point to find itself in a wonderful locality, then stupidly wander off to a terrible region, perhaps never to return. Superficially, this may seen like a terrible waste. And during debugging sessions, it is heartbreaking to see it happen. Nonetheless, that behavior is an important part of the algorithm, and one must endure the bad that sometimes accompanies the good.

The basic algorithm works roughly like this: We start out at some point (often zero, the origin) and take a big trial jump in a random direction. The value of the function at that trial point is compared with the value at the current point. We then make a random decision as to whether we move to the trial point or stay at the current point. The probability of accepting the new point and moving to it is based on the value of the function at the new point relative to that at the current point. The acceptance rule is defined in such a way that improvements are more likely to be accepted than are worsenings. The net effect is that we wander about, sometimes getting worse, but more often improving. A lot of territory is covered, but the tendency is to stay near good areas. This is illustrated in Figure 2.2. Note how the motion is quite random and often is in a direction away from the minimum (at the center of the ellipses). But also notice that the neighborhood of the minimum is a favorite locality. The wanderings of the point keep taking it back in that direction more than anywhere else.

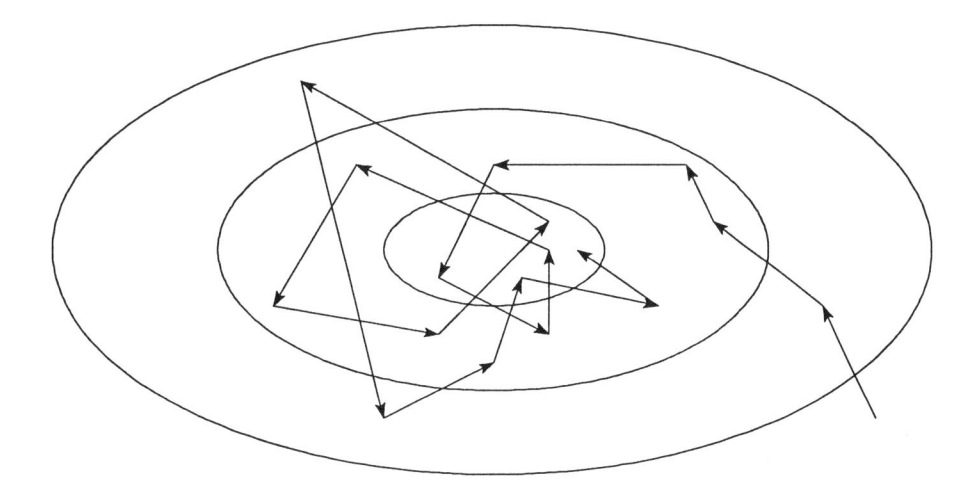

Conventional and Advanced Simulated Annealing

Figure 2.2 Random jumps favoring the minimum.

At any given time, the point is more likely to be near the minimum than far from it. This is not guaranteed, of course; disaster may strike. It's all in the probabilities, but the probabilities are on our side.

As time passes, the temperature is lowered. In most implementations of simulated annealing, there is at least one implication of a lowered temperature, and usually two. The most important and quite universal effect of a lowered temperature is on the means by which we compute the probability of accepting a new point. At high temperatures even a relatively large increase in function value gives a high probability of accepting the new, inferior point. This facilitates a lot of motion early in the process so that a great deal of territory is covered in long series of jumps. As the temperature drops, the acceptance criterion becomes stiffer. The hope is that by the time fairly low temperatures are reached, the point is already in the vicinity of the global minimum. It would be counterproductive to let the point wander too far away. Thus, at low temperatures, even a modest function increase for the trial point will result in it being rejected with high probability.

The second effect of a temperature decrease is commonly employed (including in this text) but is not universal. It is generally good to decrease the degree of perturbation as the temperature decreases. This should seem perfectly reasonable, especially to those who have studied the primitive annealing of the previous section. As the minimum is approached, smaller steps are appropriate. Not all simulated annealing methods do this. In a sense, it is not truly needed.

The increasing strictness of the acceptance criterion will strongly tend to enforce this effect whether or not we do it explicitly. Once near the minimum, large jumps will almost invariably cause a large function increase, resulting in essentially zero probability of moving. Only small jumps have a chance of being accepted. But the intuition rightly complains that a lot of expensive function evaluations are wasted this way. It seems that the best response to lowering the temperature is to close in on the minimum with both mechanisms: Strengthen the acceptance criterion and lessen the vigor of the jumps. Most algorithms in the literature do this, and we will too.

When the perturbation distance is decreased concomitantly with the temperature, something happens that at first glance may seem peculiar, but that is really quite natural. Readers should carefully ponder the points raised in the next few paragraphs. While understanding them is not a prerequisite to successfully using simulated annealing, they will explain away what might otherwise be mysteries to those who watch the operation in progress solving real problems.

Let us start by reviewing the primary role of temperature in the traditional version of simulated annealing presented in this section. Whenever a new point is tried, the function value there is compared with that at the current point. The probability of accepting the new point and moving to it depends on the relative function values. If the new point has a higher (worse) value, then the acceptance probability will be smaller than if the new point saw improvement. The temperature is a parameter that affects the strictness of this criterion. When the temperature is high, significant worsening is tolerated. At low temperatures, even moderate worsening will result in nearly zero probability of acceptance. If the perturbation distance were kept constant as the temperature is dropped, the steadily strengthening criterion would result in fewer and fewer transitions to new points. However, think about the effect of simultaneously decreasing the perturbations. At a low temperature, each new point is closer to the current point than was the case at higher temperatures. Therefore, the function value at each new point will also be closer to the function value at the current point. Significant differences in function values will be rare. This will work in direct opposition to the increasing strictness of the acceptance criterion. By decreasing the perturbations along with the temperature, we will somewhat stabilize the acceptance rate. It will not strongly drop to zero as would happen with constant perturbation.

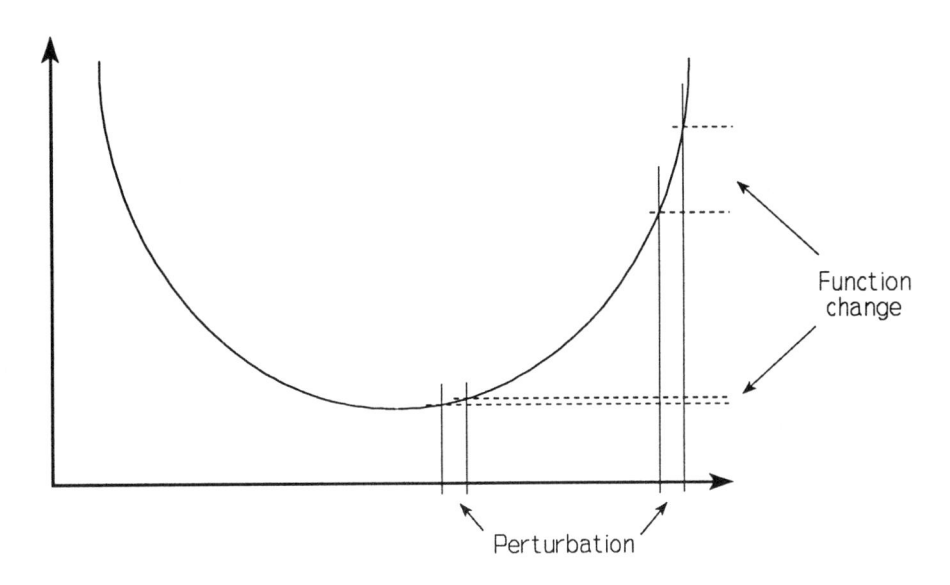

Figure 2.3 Minima are usually parabolic.

We are still not at the bottom of things. There are two more effects that come into play as the endgame approaches. One obvious effect is that the nearer we are to the global minimum, the less likely we are to randomly choose a new point that is an improvement. When we start, we may be near the top of a hill where almost every way is down. When we are in the bottom of the global minimum, every way is up. Thus, there is a natural tendency for the acceptance rate to drop toward the end *as long as we are near a good minimum*. But there is another *bottom-of-the-valley* effect that works in just the opposite way. Look at Figure 2.3.

In all but the most pathological situations, the bottom of a minimum will resemble the curve shown in this figure. Near the center we see the function evaluated at two points. The difference in the associated function values is small. At the far right we see the function evaluated at another two points separated by the same distance as the first pair. Yet look at the difference in function values. It is many times greater than was the case near the bottom. So for any given jump distance, the resulting function difference will decrease as the minimum is approached. As a result, all other things being equal, transitions near the minimum are more likely to be accepted than transitions further from the minimum. This is a self-limiting process, though. As soon as the point wanders away from the minimum, the function differences will grow, and further departure from the vicinity of the minimum will be discouraged.

How do we choose the degree of perturbation and the acceptance criterion function? Obviously, they are both problem dependent. The initial perturbation should be large enough that the domain in which the global minimum lies is thoroughly searched, yet small enough that few expensive function evaluations are wasted off in distant lands that hold no promise. Also, the acceptance criterion should match the scale of the function variation if we are to avoid nearly universal acceptance or rejection. Determining the degree of perturbation is usually easy, as it is closely related to the application. In most neural network training situations, one can easily come up with rough estimates on the range of possible weights, as long as the data is scaled intelligently.

Scaling the acceptance criterion is usually not too difficult, either. Many papers have been written on this subject, some of them employing highly sophisticated probabilistic models for analyzing the surface of the error function. I prefer a method that is simple, yet seems to work well. Just bounce around the domain for a while using the perturbation that was chosen for the starting temperature. Compute the standard deviation of the function at a representative collection of points, and use that to scale the criterion. As a side bonus of this method, we get an initial idea of the lay of the land. It is not unreasonable to keep track of the minimum point visited and use that as the starting point for annealing!

Even though the standard deviation of the function allows for automated scaling of the acceptance criterion, it is important to provide the user with some degree of secondary control. Some users may feel that their problem calls for a great deal of initial wandering in order to find a hidden global minimum. Other users may be confident that the global minimum is nearby and has a broad basin of attraction, so they may prefer a more conservative approach in which trial points with even moderately worse function values are rejected with high probability. This sort of versatility can be provided by means of what we shall call (for lack of a better term) a *user-scale* parameter. Assuming that some sort of automatic scaling has already been provided by the standard deviation of the function, a large value of this user-scale parameter would cause the acceptance criterion to be very loose. Quite large deteriorations would be accepted with high probability, so the journey would be far and wide. Similarly, a small value of the user scale would create a strict criterion, with the result that any but the smallest deteriorations would be rejected with high probability. We will get to a minimum relatively quickly, but it may not be very good from a global perspective.

How does one choose a good value for this user scale? Many excellent dissertations could be written on this topic. Therefore, it is with great fear and trepidation that I dare to make some generalizations. After carefully considering all of the unusual effects and interactions that take place during simulated annealing, and after observing a fair number of real-life problems being solved, the following general guidelines appear reasonable:

- The acceptance rate should be high at first. Many experts recommend about 80 percent of trial points be accepted in the early stages. Choose the user scale accordingly.

- After annealing has progressed for a while, the acceptance rate should have dropped to a fairly low value. Failure to do so often indicates a problem. The user scale may be too high, the temperature may be dropping too quickly, or the perturbations may be inappropriately scaled.

- When annealing has progressed to the point of diminishing returns, the acceptance rate will usually stabilize around some moderate asymptote. If it is still dropping, progress is being made.

It must be emphasized that these guidelines are extremely broad, and they are definitely not to be interpreted as universal. Simulated annealing is currently as much an art as a science. Experience and intuition seem to be as important as sophisticated mathematics in many cases. That said, Figures 2.4 through 2.6 illustrate some common situations. Figure 2.4 shows the acceptance rate during a simulated annealing process in which the parameters are chosen well, and the problem is well behaved. The rate starts out somewhere around 80 percent. This is a good compromise, allowing a lot of wandering in search of a global minimum, yet encouraging some economization of function evaluation. Then we get a good indication of progress being made by the fact that the acceptance rate drops to a fairly small value. This is due to the current point hovering in a low (good) area, from which most trial points are inferior. Finally, as the temperature drops more and the location of the minimum is refined, the

Acceptance rate
1.0

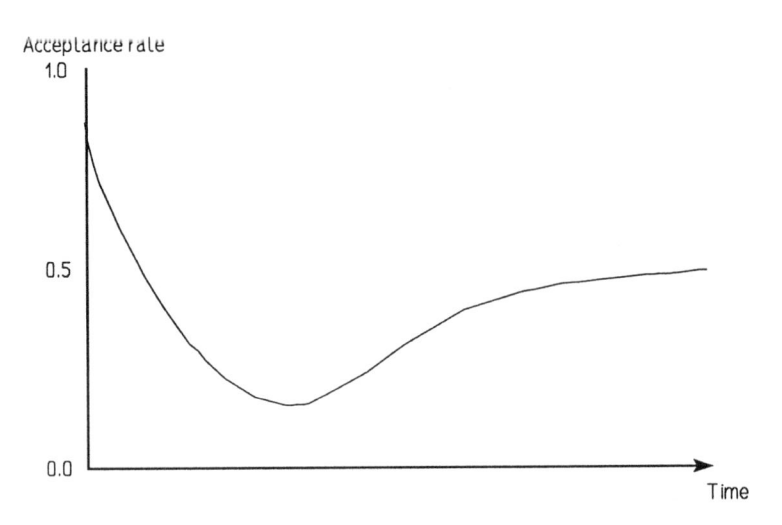

0.5

0.0
Time

Figure 2.4 Good annealing.

quadratic effect shown in Figure 2.3 starts to take over. Between the fact that the jumps are short at a low temperature, and the corresponding function changes are tiny, the acceptance rate pushes up until it hits an approximate asymptote created by the now strict acceptance criterion and the low position of the current point. Unless computer time is cheap, this would be a good time to quit.

Figure 2.5 shows what typically happens when the user scale is set too high. When annealing starts, the acceptance rate is nearly 100 percent. That, of course, defeats the whole philosophy of simulated annealing. Granted, a broad domain will be traversed; but so what? If nearly all trial points are accepted, there will be no incentive for the current point to favor good areas. It will just wander aimlessly, while the CPU clock ticks away the dollars. As the temperature drops and the criterion gets stricter, the rate will drop off and some progress will be made. But by then the perturbation will probably be too small to be worth much anyway. Therein lies a fiasco.

Finally, Figure 2.6 shows what happens when the user scale is too small. The acceptance rate will be small at first. There may be a short dip to an even lower level as the point rapidly gravitates to the nearest local minimum. It will bounce around there until the perturbation becomes small enough that the bottom is approached closely and the quadratic effect kicks in. This is a good way to get to a bottom fast, but if the user cares so little about finding the global minimum, a deterministic algorithm might as well be used.

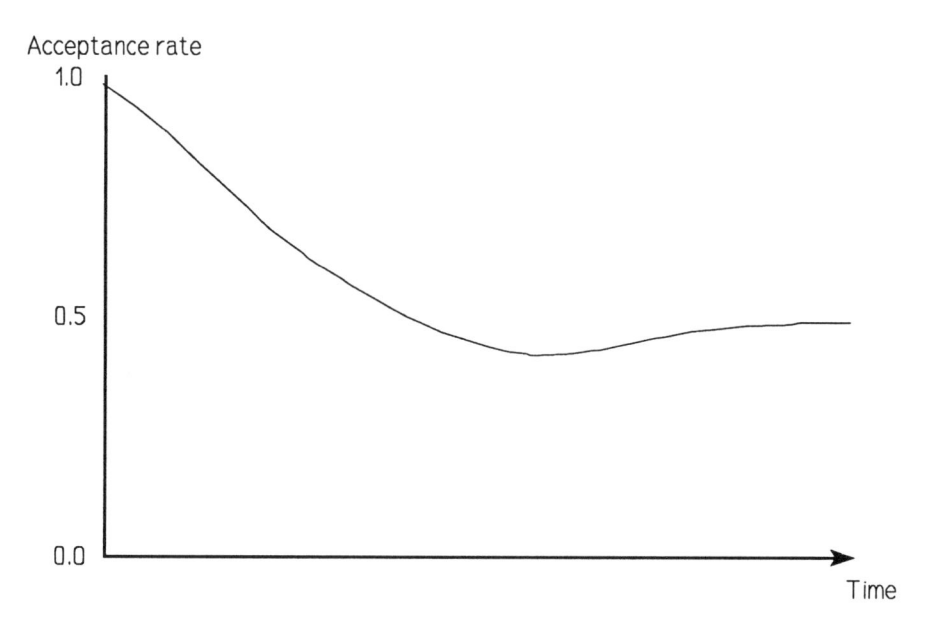

Figure 2.5 User scale is too large.

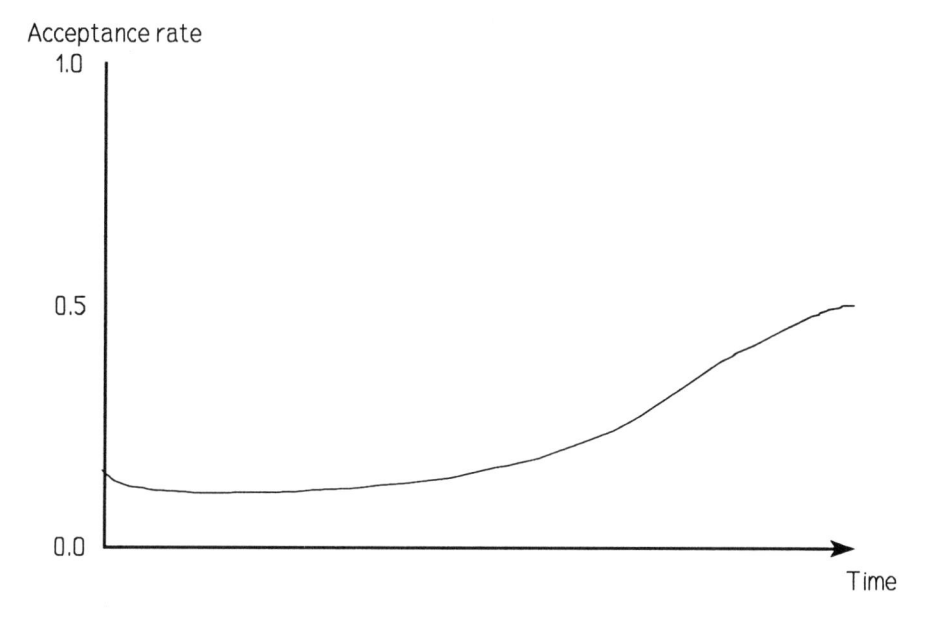

Figure 2.6 User scale is too small.

The Details

Thus far, simulated annealing has been discussed only in broad generalities. It is time to lay out some specifics. What do we mean by *random perturbation* of a point? How is the temperature reduced? And just what is this mysterious temperature-dependent *acceptance criterion* that determines a probability based on the difference of two function values? These questions will be answered in this and other upcoming sections.

Let us start with the subject of random perturbation, as this topic will be quickly dismissed by deferring to a later, more detailed treatment. Basically, all that we are doing is adding a random vector to the vector that defines the current point. The sum of these two vectors is a new trial point. Call the basic perturbation vector $\Delta = (\delta_1, \delta_2, ...)$. Random samples of this vector are generated by means of a random number generator that has unit scale. For normal distributions, this is taken to be unit variance. If the reader employs more exotic distributions, the standard scale for the random number generator should be reasonable in some sense, so that the user can easily choose starting and stopping temperatures.

The simplest way to let the temperature determine the degree of perturbation is just to multiply the random vector by the temperature. If the temperature is T, then we generate a random value of Δ and add $T\Delta$ to the current point. More exotic methods are possible, but their supposed justification often brings us dangerously close to Voodoo annealing. This direct approach seems to work well. It is also good for the user, as the interpretation of temperature is straightforward. For example, if normally distributed random vectors are used, the temperature is the standard deviation of the perturbations. Such simplicity is an admirable goal throughout life.

Nothing more will be said here about generation of random perturbations. This surprisingly complex subject will be treated in detail on page 112.

What about lowering the temperature? It turns out that if one examines the literature on simulated annealing, this is the most frequently discussed and least understood subject. Experts agree on only a few points: The reduction schedule is critical to efficient and effective operation; every problem requires a different schedule; and changing the schedule dynamically, as annealing progresses, is the best approach. Unfortunately, there is little known about how to use information gleaned during the annealing process to optimize the temperature reduction schedule. About all that is known is that some commonly used schedules are generally better than other commonly used schedules. There is an evolution going on right now—not a revolution, mind you; a painfully slow evolution. The two most prevalent schedules will be presented here, and some references will be made to forward the reader to more advanced information.

By far the most commonly used temperature reduction method is a straightforward geometric progression. A fixed factor that is less than 1.0 is specified. Each time the temperature is to be reduced, the current temperature is multiplied by this factor. The factor is based on the starting and stopping temperatures and the number of temperatures desired. Equation (2.1) shows how to compute and use the factor.

$$f = (\text{STOP} / \text{START})^{1/(\text{NTEMPS}-1)}$$
$$T_{i+1} = fT_i$$
(2.1)

Some of the most important pioneering work on the use of simulated annealing for function optimization, especially in the context of neural networks, has been done by Harold Szu. In the classics Szu (1986) and (1987), he proposes an alternative that he calls a *fast* cooling schedule. It is characterized by an unusually rapid temperature drop at the beginning, and a very slow dropoff rate later on. This method is defined in Equation (2.2).

$$f = \frac{\text{START} - \text{STOP}}{\text{STOP}\,(\text{NTEMPS} - 1)}$$
$$T_k = \frac{\text{START}}{1 + kf}$$
(2.2)

It must be emphasized that the fast reduction defined in Equation (2.2) is highly specialized. Harold Szu uses it in combination with a very heavy-tailed distribution, the Cauchy. It is likely that poor results will be obtained if this schedule is used with lighter-tailed distributions. On the other hand, experimentation is encouraged.

The two temperature reduction schedules shown in Equations (2.1) and (2.2) are graphed in Figure 2.7 with a starting temperature of 5, a stopping temperature of 0.1, and 50 temperatures. Note how rapidly the fast reduction method drops off.

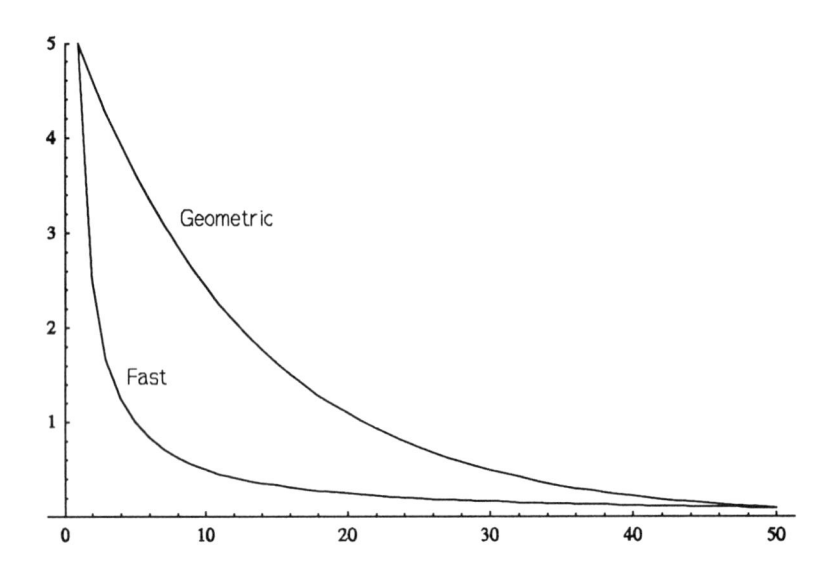

Figure 2.7 Temperature reduction schedules.

The acceptance criterion is not so widely debated as the temperature reduction schedule. There are only two principal contenders. The most common way of computing an acceptance probability is based on the Boltzmann distribution. This is the actual distribution that physicists know governs the energy distribution of a solid in thermal equilibrium. The *Metropolis criterion* exploits this physics by using Equation (2.3) to determine the acceptance probability in terms of the function value at the current point, f_i, the value at the new trial point, f_j, the temperature, T, and a user-defined scale factor, c.

$$P_{ACCEPT} = \text{MIN}\,(1,\, e^{\frac{f_i - f_j}{cT}}) \tag{2.3}$$

As one would intuitively hope, this equation implies that an improvement is always accepted. In fact, just staying the same is accepted with probability one. The key is that deterioration may also be accepted. The probability of accepting a bad move is determined by how bad the deterioration is, relative to the temperature. Note that a scaling factor c is included in the calculation to compensate for problem-dependent scaling of the function's range.

Since Equation (2.3) is very closely tied in with the physics of real annealing, it has been used for many years. It continues to be popular. However, Szu (1986) introduced an alternative that is intended to accompany his fast algorithm (fast temperature reduction per Equation (2.2), and Cauchy random perturbations). This acceptance criterion behaves quite differently from the usual Metropolis criterion. Trial points are much less likely to be accepted under the Szu criterion. In fact, even a slight improvement is accepted with only somewhat greater than 50 percent probability. This is in marked contrast to the Metropolis criterion that accepts anything from status quo or better. Equation (2.4) is Szu's acceptance criterion, and Figure 2.8 illustrates the contrast between the two criteria.

$$P_{ACCEPT} = \frac{1}{1 + \exp\left(\frac{f_j - f_i}{cT}\right)} \qquad (2.4)$$

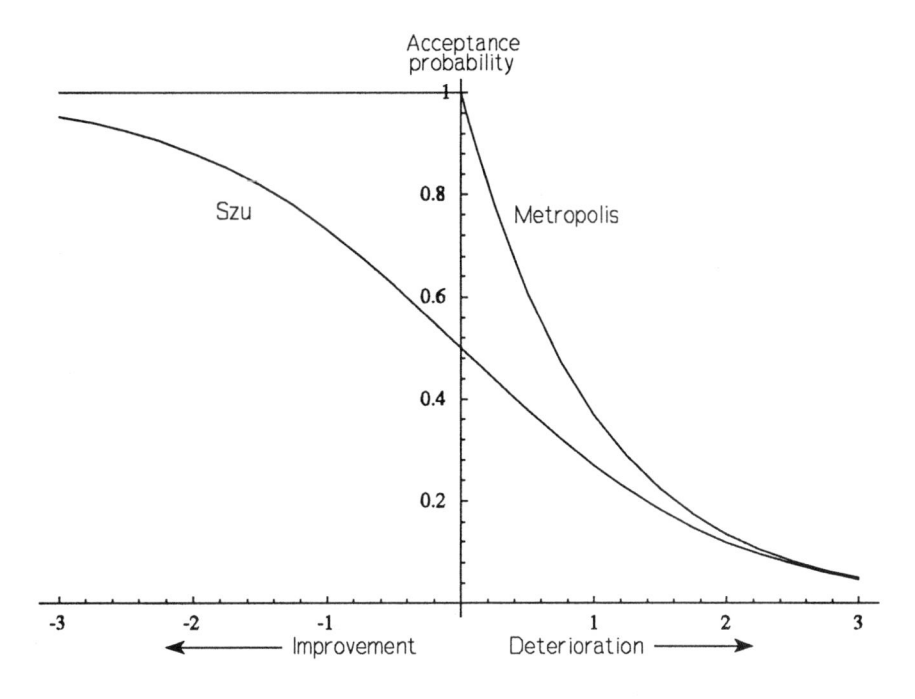

Figure 2.8 Acceptance criteria.

Code for General Simulated Annealing

We now present foundation code for implementing a variety of simulated annealing techniques based on the methods just described. This is not an absolutely complete subroutine. It has been extracted from the MLFN2 source code. However, only the superfluous aspects of the code have been removed so as to enhance the clarity of the algorithm. Readers should have no trouble performing the slight modifications needed to integrate it with their own applications.

```
int LayerNet::anneal2 ()
{
   int ntemps, niters, setback, nvars ;
   int i, iter, itemp, climb, reduction, n ;
   long seed, bestseed ;
   double tempmult, temp, fval, bestfval, starttemp, stoptemp, fquit ;
   double current_fval, prob, ratio, fsum, fsqsum ;

   ntemps = ...              // Number of temperatures
   niters = ...              // Iterations at each temperature
   setback =                 // Keeps iterating if improving
   starttemp = ...           // Starting temperature
   stoptemp = ...            // Stopping temperature
   density = ...             // Probability density
   fquit = ...               // Quit if error drops this low
   ratio = ...               // User scale for acceptance criterion
   climb = ...               // Metropolis vs. Szu acceptance
   reduction = ...           // Temperature reduction schedule

/*
   The best point so far is kept in 'bestnet', so initialize it to the user's starting estimate. Also, initialize 'bestfval', the best function value so far, to be the function value at that starting point. The current net is in 'worknet', so similarly copy this net to it.
*/

   copy_weights ( bestnet , this ) ; // Current weights are best so far
   copy_weights ( worknet , this ) ;
   bestfval = current_fval = trial_error () ;
```

Conventional and Advanced Simulated Annealing

```
/*
    Compute the starting temperature and the factor that will be needed
    to reduce it later.
*/

   temp = starttemp ;
   if (reduction == ANNEAL_REDUCE_GEOMETRIC)
      tempmult = exp ( log ( stoptemp / starttemp ) / (ntemps-1)) ;
   else if (reduction == ANNEAL_REDUCE_FAST)
      tempmult = (starttemp - stoptemp) / (stoptemp * (ntemps-1)) ;


/*
    We use a heuristic method to estimate the ratio by which the temperature
    (standard deviation of perturbations) is multiplied to get the scale factor for convert-
    ing the function change to an acceptance probability.
    This is the user-specified ratio times the standard deviation. Simultaneously take
    this opportunity to look for a good starting point.
*/


      n = 0 ;                                        // Samples going into estimate
      fsum = fsqsum = 0.0 ;                          // Sum of f and its square

      for (iter=0 ; iter<(niters*ntemps/10+1) ; iter++) { // Dedicate 10%

         perturb ( worknet , this , temp , density ) ; // Randomly perturb
         fval = trial_error () ;                     // Compute error here

         ++n ;                                       // Count points
         fsum += fval ;                              // For finding mean
         fsqsum += fval * fval ;                     // And standard deviation

         if (fval < bestfval) {                      // If this iteration improved
            copy_weights ( bestnet , this ) ;        // Maintain record of best
            bestfval = fval ;                        // then update the best so far

            if (bestfval <= fquit)                   // If we reached the user's
               goto FINISH ;                         // limit, we can quit

            iter -= setback ;                        // It often pays to keep going
```

```
            if (iter < 0)                      // at this temperature if we
               iter = 0 ;                      // are still improving
            }
         }                                     // Loop: for all initial iters

      fsum /= n ;                              // Mean function
      fsqsum /= n ;                            // Mean square
      fsqsum = sqrt ( fsqsum - fsum * fsum ) ; // Standard deviation
      ratio *= fsqsum / starttemp ;            // Scaling ratio

      copy_weights ( worknet , bestnet ) ;     // The best above becomes current
      current_fval = bestfval ;

/*
      Simulated annealing starts here
*/

      for (itemp=0 ; itemp<ntemps ; itemp++) { // Temp reduction loop

         for (iter=0 ; iter<niters ; iter++) { // Iters per temp loop

            perturb ( worknet , this , temp , density ) ; // Randomly perturb
            fval = trial_error () ;

            if (fval < bestfval) {             // If this iteration improved
               copy_weights ( bestnet , this ) ; // Maintain record of best
               bestfval = fval ;               // then update the best so far

               if (bestfval <= fquit)          // If we reached the user's
                  break ;                      // limit, we can quit

               iter -= setback ;               // It often pays to keep going
               if (iter < 0)                   // at this temperature if we
                  iter = 0 ;                   // are still improving
               }

            prob = exp ( (current_fval - fval) / (ratio * temp) ) ; // Metropolis

            if (! climb)                       // Szu
               prob = 1.0 / (1.0 + 1.0 / prob) ;
```

```
            if (unifrand() < prob) {              // Accept this trial point?
               copy_weights ( worknet , this ) ;
               current_fval = fval ;
               }
            }

         if (bestfval <= fquit)                   // If we reached the user's
            break ;                               // limit, we can quit

         if (reduction == ANNEAL_REDUCE_GEOMETRIC)
            temp *= tempmult ;
         else if (reduction == ANNEAL_REDUCE_FAST)
            temp = starttemp / (1.0 + tempmult * (itemp+1)) ;

         } // Temperature reduction loop

/*
   The trials left this weight set and neterr in random condition.
   Make them equal to the best, which will be the original
   if we never improved.
*/

FINISH:
   copy_weights ( this , bestnet ) ;              // Return best weights in this net
   neterr = bestfval ;
}
```

The reader should be familiar with the code for primitive annealing listed on page 79, as many of the parameters in this code are similar to the earlier code. The overall program structure has many similarities also. Annealing parameters that they have in common include the number of temperatures and iterations per temperature, starting and stopping temperature, setback count, random density, and user's stopping value. Parameters unique to this routine are *ratio* for scaling according to the function's scale; *climb*, which determines whether the Metropolis or Szu acceptance criterion is used; and *reduction*, which specifies the temperature reduction schedule. The function scale factor cT in the denominator of Equations (2.3) and (2.4) is the product of two numbers: the standard deviation of the function, as determined by some initial skipping about, and the *ratio* parameter.

This usually lets the user easily influence the initial acceptance rate. The climb parameter is so named because the Metropolis criterion can be said to climb down, since it always accepts improvement. This parameter acts as a flag. If it is nonzero, the Metropolis criterion (Equation (2.3)) is used; while if it is zero, the Szu criterion (Equation (2.4)) is used. Finally, the reduction parameter is set to one of the global constant values seen later in the code to specify whether geometric or fast temperature reduction is employed.

Two working areas for holding network weight sets are required. The current point will always be in worknet, and the best point found during the entire annealing process will be preserved in bestnet. The starting weight set is copied to these areas, and the function (network error) is evaluated there.

The current temperature will be in temp, so initialize this variable to the starting temperature. Both geometric reduction (Equation (2.1)) and fast reduction (Equation (2.2)) require that a constant be computed, so do that.

We now use a heuristic technique to help accommodate the infinitude of possibilities for the scaling of the range of the function being minimized. Some error functions may be tiny and have little variation, while others may vary over a wide range. The acceptance criteria (Equations (2.3) and (2.4)) are obviously sensitive to the function's variation, so it is nice to relieve the user of the responsibility for compensating for this effect. The easiest approach is to find some measure of the function's variation. We choose to do a bit of jumping around at the starting temperature, computing the standard deviation of the function values. The choice of using 10 percent of the total number of trials, plus any due to setback, is arbitrary. Also, it is not vital that the counter be set back each time improvement is had. The main reason for doing so is that we take advantage of this initial search to locate a good starting point for the annealing that soon follows. The setback action improves the quality of the starting point. A second reason is that setback causes the area of the rough minimum to receive extra attention in the computation of the standard deviation. That is probably a little more fair, since we will be starting there. Finally, we compute the scale factor ratio as the product of the user-specified value, times the standard deviation, divided by the starting temperature. During annealing, this factor will be multiplied by the temperature, so the net result will be that the function is scaled correctly.

We now start the two nested loops, temperature reduction and iterations within each temperature. The lack of any code between these two loops should tell the reader that the significance of looping within a constant temperature is much less for this method of annealing than for the primitive method discussed at the start of this chapter.

The current point in worknet is randomly perturbed, and this new trial point is tested. If the function value is less than the best so far, we preserve the trial point and the new record value. Also, the iteration counter is set back.

Now we come to the cornerstone of this method of simulated annealing. The acceptance criterion is computed. The function difference is weighted, and Equation (2.3) is used to find the acceptance probability. If the user has instead chosen to use Szu's criterion, Equation (2.4), then only a slight modification is needed. A uniform random number is generated, and it is compared with the probability that was just computed. If chance dictates, the new trial point is accepted by being copied into the current point, worknet. So ends the iteration-within-temperature loop.

We are about to finish the temperature loop. All that needs to be done is to reduce the temperature for the next pass. This is a straightforward application of either Equation (2.1) or (2.2), according to the user's specification. When the temperature loop is complete, we retrieve the best weight set to return to the caller.

Usage Guidelines

We have discussed the philosophy and mathematics of traditional simulated annealing, including some recent alternatives and modifications. A comprehensive code fragment illustrating the algorithms has also been given. We complete this presentation by listing some general guidelines for using these algorithms. The guidelines shown here should not be taken as immutable, and experimentation is encouraged. However, inexperienced users should take them as a starting point.

- The starting temperature should be as low as possible for economy, as long as it is large enough to cover the domain in which the global minimum may lie. In general, one should use a somewhat lower temperature than that used for the previously described primitive annealing. That version is locked into a center around which perturbation is done, while this version wanders more freely.

- The stopping temperature should not be any lower than is needed to be reasonably sure of ending up in the basin of attraction of the global minimum. Once there, more efficient deterministic algorithms can be used.

- This version of simulated annealing seems to require smaller temperature decrements than the primitive version. Therefore, use many temperatures and relatively few iterations at each temperature. For geometric reduction, enough temperatures should be used that the drop is no more than a few percent.

- Fast temperature reduction almost definitely requires that a Cauchy (or another heavy-tailed) distribution be used. The climb parameter should probably also be zero in this case, so that Szu's acceptance criterion is used.

- If there is a significant possibility that the global minimum lies very far from the starting point, a heavy-tailed distribution like the Cauchy, in conjunction with a moderate starting temperature, may be more efficient than a light-tailed distribution (like the normal) in conjunction with a high starting temperature.

- The ratio parameter should be set so that approximately 80 percent of all trial points are accepted early in the annealing process. In practice, this often corresponds to a value in the range 2 to 5. Slightly larger acceptance rates cause a larger area to be searched, while much smaller rates use fewer function evaluations but encourage falling into a poor local minimum. The optimum choice depends on how many local minima are expected.

- If the acceptance rate does not eventually drop significantly from where it started, ideally to well under 50 percent, suspect problems.

- If the acceptance rate rises and stabilizes after dropping to a low value, the point of diminishing returns has probably been reached. More progress can certainly be made, but at relatively high cost.

Stochastic Smoothing

And now for something completely different. In this section we look at minimization from a statistical perspective. We act as if the *underlying* function to be minimized is actually nice, being well-behaved in its true form. However, the function *that we see* is the true function after corruption by noise. It is not the function itself that causes problems for us; rather, it is the noise that has been added to the function. In many neural network applications, this is a valid point of view, and stochastic smoothing will work well. In other applications this is not a valid perspective at all, and stochastic smoothing will not be particularly great. This algorithm is a method of extremes. Either it will perform very well, or it will perform very poorly. There is rarely a middle ground. Neural network experts will eventually get a feel for when this method should be used and when it should not be used.

A rough rule of thumb for determining whether or not stochastic smoothing is appropriate is based on the nature of the data and the difficulty of the problem. If there are plenty of neurons, so that the network is very likely large enough to handle the problem, and if multiple minima are likely to be caused by inconsistent and noisy data, stochastic smoothing is probably a good approach. On the other hand, if the data is clean and the problem is expected to be difficult because a minimum number of neurons are being used for the sake of good generalization or other economy, then this method should not be used. As a classic example, the exclusive-or problem gives this method tremendous difficulty, while many straightforward industrial control problems trained with noisy data usually are solved well with stochastic smoothing.

Another consideration in the choice of optimization algorithms is that like the algorithms previously presented in this chapter, stochastic smoothing is rarely good enough to be used alone. It is best combined with a deterministic algorithm so that the strengths of the two approaches can act synergistically. In the next chapter, we will see how the gradient of the error function can provide useful hints to the basic stochastic smoothing algorithm. But for now we will restrict our attention to the pure stochastic version.

If we were lucky, we would be able to gather repeated samples of the objective function, all taken at the same point in the domain, and average those samples to arrive at an estimate of the function value there. In practice, we will almost never have that option. The problem will be defined in such a way that if we evaluate the function at the same point twice, we will get the same value both times. So we take the next best route. We estimate the value of the underlying function at a particular point by randomly sampling the function in the neighborhood of that point and computing the average of those function values. Statisticians will immediately scream that all sorts of confounding effects may easily survive this procedure and invalidate the results. Our only reply is that we must hope for the best, as the nature of the problem has forced us into this corner. In a broad class of problems, this random sampling method works well.

It's time to be specific. Let Δ be an n-dimensional random vector whose probability density function is given by Equation (2.5). The parameter T is a scale factor. We also expect that h is piecewise differentiable, and that as T goes to zero, the density $h(\Delta, T)$ approaches the Dirac delta function.

$$h(\Delta, T) = \frac{1}{T^n} h\left(\frac{\Delta}{T}\right) \qquad (2.5)$$

Let $f(\mathbf{x})$ be the function we are trying to minimize. For some value of $\mathbf{x}$, sample this function at many random points centered at $\mathbf{x}$ and perturbed by a random vector having the density function given by Equation (2.5). In other words, repeatedly evaluate $f(\mathbf{x}+\Delta)$ for many random values of Δ. We can now define a new function, $\psi(\mathbf{x}, T)$, as the expected value of $f(\mathbf{x}+\Delta)$. The mathematical definition of this expectation is shown in Equation (2.6).

$$\psi(\mathbf{x}, T) = \int_{\mathbf{R}^n} f(\mathbf{x}+\Delta) \, h(\Delta, T) \, d\Delta \qquad (2.6)$$

It might be theoretically possible to numerically evaluate Equation (2.6) at any point using standard integration algorithms. However, it should be obvious that in practice, this would be essentially impossible. Even if the dimensionality were low, the number of function evaluations required would be prohibitively large. This leads us to the reason for including this algorithm in a chapter on stochastic optimization. We use a random number generator to control the computation of $\psi(\mathbf{x}, T)$. Instead of deterministically evaluating the expected value of $f(\mathbf{x}+\Delta)$ using Equation (2.6), we stochastically approximate that expected value by randomly sampling Δ with the density $h(\Delta, T)$ and averaging.

Many readers will not be able to follow the mathematical explanation just given. That is no problem. Let us now explore the process from a more intuitive point of view. We are computing the convolution of the observed objective function, $f(\mathbf{x})$, with a smoothing function, $h(\Delta, T)$. A frequent choice for the smoothing function is the ordinary Gaussian, with T being the standard deviation common to all variables. The random values of Δ will be centered around the origin, so most of the samples that go into the average used to estimate $\psi(\mathbf{x}, T)$ will cluster near $\mathbf{x}$. If T is very small, then all of the samples will be very near $\mathbf{x}$, so the mean value that estimates $\psi(\mathbf{x}, T)$ will be very near $f(\mathbf{x})$. In other words, for small T, $\psi(\mathbf{x}, T) \approx f(\mathbf{x})$. In fact, given the conditions on h specified earlier, it is not difficult to show that equality is approached in the limit as T goes to zero. Conversely, if T is large, it is unlikely that equality will be approached. Samples that are quite far from $\mathbf{x}$ will be a part of the ensemble that determines the average. A great deal of local variation in $f(\mathbf{x})$ will be smoothed out by the inclusion of these distant points.

The smoothing process is illustrated in Figures 2.9 through 2.12. Figure 2.9 shows a function that would be practically impossible to minimize with a deterministic algorithm. Figure 2.10 is a Gaussian smoothing function. When the functions illustrated in these two figures are convolved, the result is shown in Figure 2.11. The process of averaging across a relatively wide distance has totally eliminated the multiple valleys, leaving only a nice smooth function that can easily be minimized. Finally, if the scale, T, is of moderate size, then moderate smoothing will be obtained. This is shown in Figure 2.12.

It may be that all we are interested in is the minimum of a highly smoothed version of the objective function. However, that is not usually the case. We almost always want to find the exact global minimum of the objective function. Then, the only purpose of the smoothing operation is to remove the valleys that cause trouble during minimization. Understand that the location of the minimum of the smoothed function will not, in general, be the same as that of the objective function itself. Naturally, we are operating on the assumption that the minima will be close. If not, this entire algorithm is useless for finding the global minimum of the objective function. But when they are reasonably close, as will usually happen, the overall procedure is straightforward.

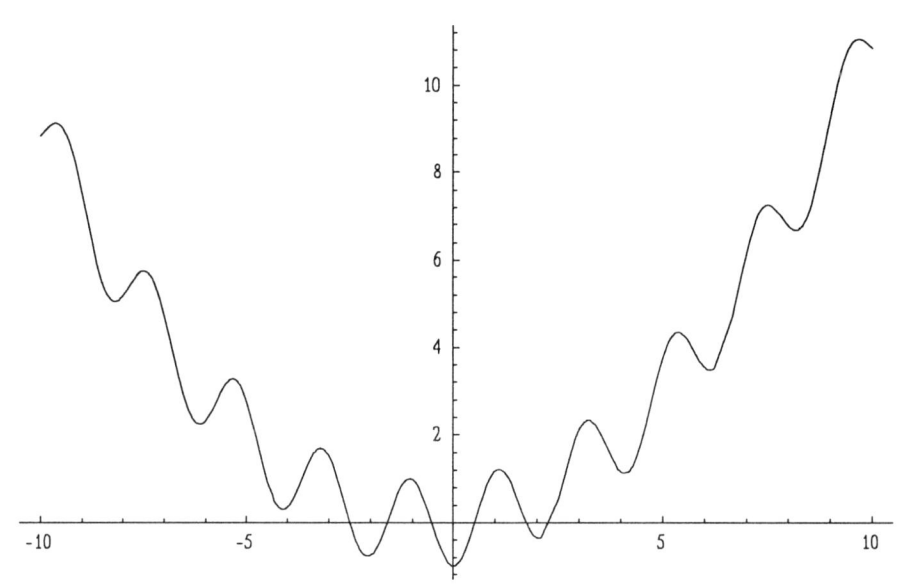

Figure 2.9 Objective function to be minimized.

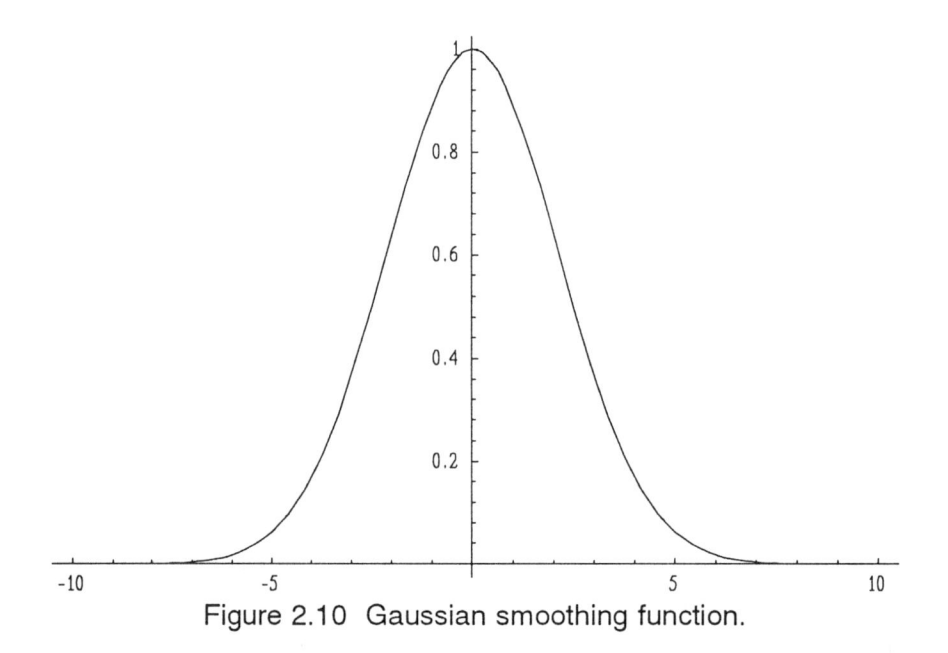

Figure 2.10 Gaussian smoothing function.

Stochastic Smoothing

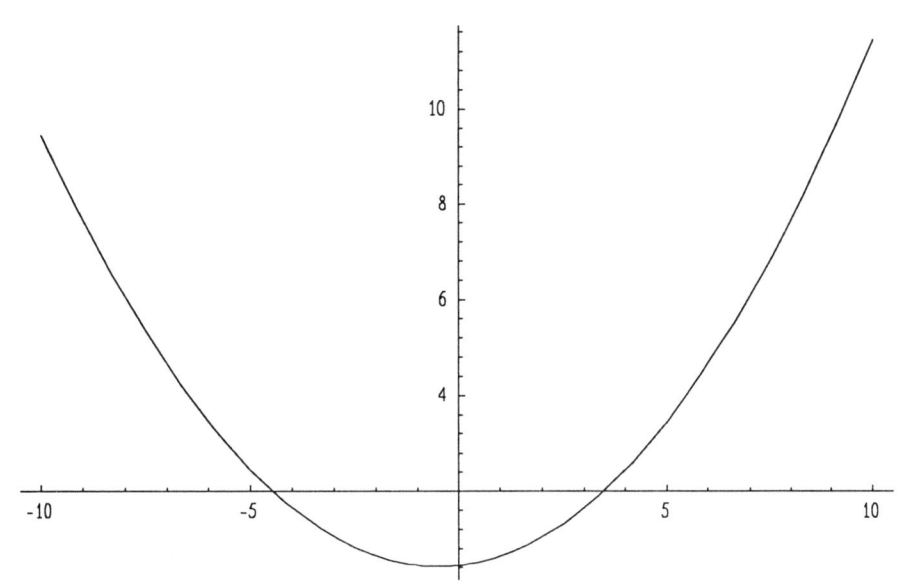

Figure 2.11 Heavy smoothing using very large scale.

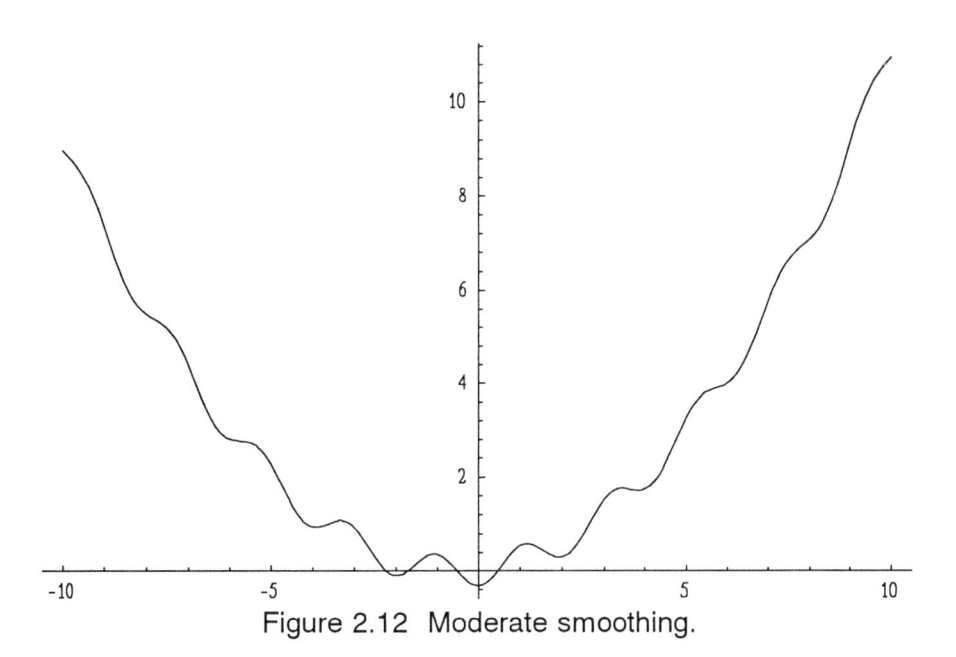

Figure 2.12 Moderate smoothing.

To use stochastic smoothing to minimize a function, start at a very high temperature. (Aha! Why else would the letter T have been chosen to represent the scale—standard deviation in the Gaussian case—of the random vector?) Find the approximate minimum of this highly smoothed version of the objective function. Then lower the temperature a little and gravitate toward the minimum of this slightly different function. Keep doing that until the temperature is very small. At that time, the smoothed function, $\psi(\mathbf{x}, T)$, will almost exactly equal the objective function, $f(\mathbf{x})$. With any luck at all, we will now be sitting near the global minimum of that function, having gently slid there in one continuous process.

It's useful to think about how this algorithm is different from the versions of simulated annealing presented earlier in this chapter. In those methods, we worked only with the exact objective function. It was evaluated at many specific points. In the primitive version of annealing, the algorithm was always centered around a particular point that had a relatively low function value. In the more traditional version, the location of the current point fluctuated wildly, but it was always more likely to be near a good spot than a bad spot. In stochastic smoothing, we are not so concerned with the value of the function itself as we are concerned with values of a closely related smoothed function. This is good when the minimum of this smoothed function is reasonably close to the global minimum of the objective function, because then we can gently slide from one to the other as the temperature is lowered. However, that may not always happen. Look at Figure 2.13.

The error function graphed as a solid line in that figure is typical of what happens when a neural network is trained on data that is not linearly separable, and when the number of hidden neurons is close to the minimum number required to learn the data. Groups of local minima abound, and many of these minima have approximately equal function values. When the primitive annealing algorithm is applied to an error function like the one shown in Figure 2.13, the center point will very likely land in one or the other of the two basins early in the process, and subsequent annealing will cause descent into the bottom. In the more conventional annealing algorithm, the point will, at first, spend about half its time bouncing around one local minimum, and half around the other. Eventually, as the temperature drops low enough, it will become trapped in one basin and favor that area from then on. In other words, either of these two algorithms will probably be effective for functions like the one shown.

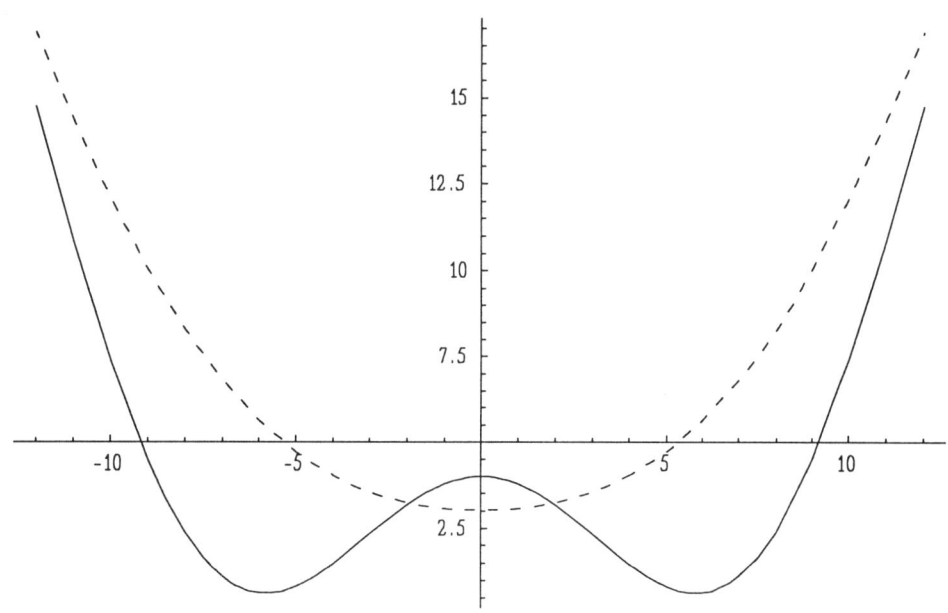

Figure 2.13 Smoothing can cause distortion.

Now consider the shape of the smoothed version of the function, shown as a dashed line in that figure. Its minimum will be right in the middle of the two local minima! When the algorithm gravitates toward the minimum of the smoothed function, it will actually be pulling away from where it should be. The result will be rather like the donkey who starved to death standing between two hay stacks because he couldn't decide which was closer. By the time the temperature gets low enough for the two local minima to appear, it may be too late to travel far enough to get to either one of them. The algorithm will be stuck in the middle, just starting to descend, when the bell rings and the time is up.

In the next chapter, we will show how gradient information can be used to provide the stochastic smoothing algorithm with powerful hints. At that time a detailed code fragment will illustrate the technique. For now, let us be satisfied with a simple statement of a basic algorithm. As was the case for simulated annealing, there is no universal agreement as to just how stochastic smoothing is to be done. The algorithm given here is modest in complexity, yet I have found that it performs well. When the gradient can be computed, as is usually the case for neural networks, the gradient should be used as shown in the next chapter. Therefore, the algorithm shown here is primarily for educational purposes. However, readers should study it carefully, as the details relating to basic stochastic smoothing will be glossed over in the next chapter when we return to this procedure.

There are two major operations performed. The first is initialization. We have been given a starting point, typically the origin. In order to approximate the value of the smoothed function at the starting point, we generate random vectors for perturbing the starting point, and average the function at these random points. Assume that the user has requested that ntemps temperatures be used, with the temperatures running from starttemp to stoptemp, and that niters iterations are to be done at each temperature. The trivial initialization operation is performed as shown here.

```
        avg_x ← (0, 0, ...)
        avg_f ← 0
        iter ← 0
L1:     Δ ← random ( starttemp )
        x ← avg_x + Δ
        f ← func ( x )
        avg_f ← avg_f + f
        iter ← iter + 1
        if (iter < niters)
              go to L1
        avg_f ← avg_f / niters
```

We have just stochastically estimated the value of the smoothed function at the origin (or around whatever starting point was used). Now we need to move avg_x in such a way that the smoothed function decreases. A reasonable method is to check the value of the objective function in a randomly selected point nearby. If it exceeds the value of the smoothed function, we probably do not want to move that way, so try another random point. Keep looking until we find a point whose function value is less than the smoothed function. This is most likely a good direction in which to move, and by including that point in the average, we will lower the value of the smoothed function.

So how do we incorporate a new point in the current ensemble? A moving average is a good, intuitive method. Weight the new point in proportion to what its contribution to the set of niters points would be, and reduce the influence of the current set accordingly. In other words, compute the adjusted location and smoothed function value as 1 / niters times the new point, plus (1 − 1 / niters) times the old ensemble value. Many readers will be worried that such low weighting of new points, commensurate with the number of trials being done per temperature, will result in a time lag that interferes with fast convergence to a minimum. These readers are partially correct, and there may be some reason for increasing the weight a bit. However, that is dangerous. If the weight is increased much, there will be a significantly increased tendency to gravitate toward the nearest local minimum, instead of performing a more thorough global search. Also, keep in mind that many temperatures are being done. Over the grand procedure, the time lag will not be significant. Finally, in the next chapter, we will see how a modification involving the same setback that was used for simulated annealing provides the algorithm with time to catch up with itself.

The ideas just presented are now expressed as a formal algorithm. The initialization operation shown several paragraphs ago has been performed. We have computed the average function value in the vicinity of the starting point. The smoothed function will now be minimized. Keep in mind that several simplifications to a truly effective algorithm have been made for the sake of clarity. More details will be given in the next chapter when actual code is presented.

```
        fac ← 1.0 / niters
        T ← starttemp
        tempmult ← (stoptemp / starttemp) ^ (1 / (ntemps-1))
        itemp ← 0
L2:     ngood ← nbad ← 0
        iter ← 0
L3:         Δ ← random ( T )
            x ← avg_x + Δ
            f ← func ( x )
            if ( f < avg_f)
                ngood ← ngood + 1
                avg_x ← fac * x  +  (1-fac) * avg_x
                avg_f ← fac * f  +  (1-fac) * avg_f
            else
                nbad ← nbad + 1
            iter ← iter + 1
            if ( iter < niters )
                go to L3
        itemp ← itemp + 1
        if ( itemp < ntemps )
            T ← T * tempmult
            go to L2
```

Why do we keep the counters ngood and nbad in this algorithm? They play no direct role in the computation. Nevertheless, they are good to have around. Their relative values are an indication of how close to convergence we have come. In general, at the very beginning of the process, these two counters will run about even. A randomly selected point will stand about a 50–50 chance of being better than the average function value centered at the origin (or at any other randomly selected starting point). As the minimum of the smoothed function is approached, improvements will become increasingly difficult to obtain. Finally, after spending some time in the vicinity of the minimum, improvements will become almost impossible. This is because the averaged function values will no longer be representative of the true value of the smoothed function there. The act of keeping only improved points will bias the average downward, so that avg_f will grow smaller and smaller as time passes. This effect will not be a significant consideration as long as avg_x is moving along toward the smoothed minimum. But as soon as its gets there and motion slows, the bias will become more and more pronounced until it seriously impedes further improvement. Therefore, implementors of this algorithm would do well to print the improvement rate for the user. If the rate becomes tiny, the user may wish to decrease the temperature faster to reduce the number of expensive function evaluations. On the other hand, there is certainly no harm in a low improvement rate if time is cheap. Although the estimate of the smoothed function value will be biased downward, it will never drop below the nearest local minimum. As long as the temperature is high enough, escape to a better minimum is still possible. The main problem is that efficiency suffers. This may or may not be serious.

Random Perturbation

This chapter has thus far dismissed the random perturbation aspect of simulated annealing as just something that we do in a black box. All of the code given so far has done the perturbation by calling a subroutine named perturb. Even when the theory of annealing was discussed, about all that was said about the random numbers is that their variation should be something reasonable for the sake of the user. It is time to get down to specifics.

Random Perturbation

This topic merits its own section because the correct generation of random numbers is far more complicated than most people believe. It is extremely easy to use some technique that intuitively seems perfectly reasonable, yet actually is abominable in an obscure but important way. The random number generator supplied with the FORTRAN compiler of a major manufacturer's mainframe computer had a serious flaw that invalidated many research projects over a period of years before the problem was discovered! Therefore, we will treat this issue from the bottom up. Uniform random numbers are the foundation on which all other random distributions are built, so that will be the first major topic discussed. From there we will gradually progress all the way to the multivariate Cauchy distribution, a surprisingly sophisticated problem. Several intermediate distributions and techniques will appear along the way.

Code for Perturbing a Point

Before digging into the nitty-gritty of random number generation, let us dispense with a picky detail. Some readers may wonder about the perturb routine that is regularly called in the code seen earlier in this chapter. It is mostly straightforward, but as long as it is short, we may as well list it so that there is no confusion. This is directly extracted from the MLFN2 program with only slight modification for clarity. The first parameter is the input weight set that is the current point, and the second parameter is the output of the new trial point. The other two parameters are the temperature (already scaled appropriately) and the probability density function desired. This subroutine just takes care of the busywork of locating the individual weight vectors and then calling the shake subroutine to do the perturbation. Also, the limit subroutine is called to force the weights to lie within a reasonable range. This is not vital, but it helps in neural network applications by preventing the wandering from taking the point extremely far from the most promising area. The sigmoid activation functions commonly employed strongly limit the maximum error, which, in turn, can sometimes allow very large and very bad jumps to be taken. Applications in which the error is not so limited may benefit from removing the weight limits.

```
void LayerNet::perturb (
    LayerNet *cent ,                // Input: current point
    LayerNet *perturbed ,           // Output: new trial point
```

```
      double temp ,                            // Degree of perturbation
      enum RandomDensity dens                  // Probability density to use
      )
   {
      int n ;

      if (nhid1 == 0) {                        // No hidden layer
         n = nout * (nin+1) ;
         shake ( n , cent->out_coefs , perturbed->out_coefs , temp , dens ) ;
         limit ( n , perturbed->out_coefs , 20.0 ) ;
         }

      else if (nhid2 == 0) {                   // One hidden layer
         n = nhid1 * (nin+1) ;
         shake ( n , cent->hid1_coefs , perturbed->hid1_coefs , temp , dens ) ;
         limit ( n , perturbed->hid1_coefs , 20.0 ) ;
         n = nout * (nhid1+1) ;
         shake ( n , cent->out_coefs , perturbed->out_coefs , temp , dens ) ;
         limit ( n , perturbed->out_coefs , 20.0 ) ;
         }

      else {                                   // Two hidden layers
         n = nhid1 * (nin+1) ;
         shake ( n , cent->hid1_coefs , perturbed->hid1_coefs , temp , dens ) ;
         limit ( n , perturbed->hid1_coefs , 20.0 ) ;
         n = nhid2 * (nhid1+1) ;
         shake ( n , cent->hid2_coefs , perturbed->hid2_coefs , temp , dens ) ;
         limit ( n , perturbed->hid2_coefs , 20.0 ) ;
         n = nout * (nhid2+1) ;
         shake ( n , cent->out_coefs , perturbed->out_coefs , temp , dens ) ;
         limit ( n , perturbed->out_coefs , 20.0 ) ;
         }
   }
```

The shake subroutine that perturb calls to individually perturb each weight vector illustrates a subtle but important aspect of random number usage. It also illustrates the fact that I do not strictly follow the letter of the law in this regard, although this is done purposely and probably with justification. But first let us look at the shake routine. It is given the number of variables, the current coordinate vector, the

Random Perturbation

output area for the new vector, the degree of perturbation, and the probability density desired.

```
void shake (
  int nvars ,                           // Number of variables
  double *center ,                      // Input: current point
  double *x ,                           // Output: new trial point
  double temp ,                         // Scale of random numbers
  enum RandomDensity dens               // Probability density desired
  )
{
  switch (dens) {
    case NormalDensity:
      while (nvars--)
        *x++ = *center++ + temp * normal () ;
      break ;
    case CauchyDensity:
      cauchy ( nvars , temp , x ) ;
      while (nvars--)
        *x++ += *center++ ;
      break ;
    }
}
```

When generating random vectors, it is important to distinguish between two possibilities. The multivariate probability density function may be the product of the individual marginal densities of each scalar variable, as is the case for the uncorrelated normal distribution. In this situation we can take the expedient of generating each component of the random vector individually. This is seen in the NormalDensity case of the switch statement above. The normal subroutine is called once for each variable, each time generating a single scalar random number. But in general, this is not possible. For example, the multivariate Cauchy distribution is not the product of the marginal densities. The entire vector must be generated in one shot. This is illustrated above in the CauchyDensity case. An nvars vector, x, is generated in one subroutine call, then each component is added to the current point. If all this is unclear, don't worry. It will be treated in more detail later. If it is still not clear then, don't worry anyway. Just use the subroutines as shown.

Now that the importance of generating certain multivariate random vectors as an entity has been stated, let it be pointed out that the code shown above does not strictly do this for neural networks when the Cauchy density is employed. Each layer's weight vector follows a true multivariate Cauchy distribution, but the grand weight set for the entire neural network does not. Its density function is the product of the individual multivariate kernels. I have not conducted any rigorous scientific comparison studies, but am of the considered opinion that this is the correct approach for multiple-layer feedforward networks. The unique structure of these networks, in which the effect of each weight vector is buffered by the neuron's activation functions, would seem to call for this separation. Also, use of a single grand multivariate distribution would create an all-or-nothing effect. Most of the time, the entire weight set would lie close to home, while occasionally the entire set would be out in left field in an almost definitely worthless locale. (The mechanism by which that occurs will be discussed later.) By separating the distributions onto each layer's weight vector, the wild components are distributed better. Perhaps I am wrong here; rigorous testing would be nice. But the intuition is good, and this method appears to work well in practice.

Generating Uniform Random Numbers

Nearly all random number generators, scalar or multivariate, simple or complex, rely on a source of uniform random numbers as their foundation. They use one or more uniform random numbers to construct another specialized random number or vector. What is a *uniform random number*? It is a random number each of whose possible values is equally likely. (Purists who take exception to the term *possible values* must remember that we are dealing with computers that have a finite resolution.) Virtually all practical random number algorithms generate an integer whose range is from zero to some fixed maximum value. If the algorithm is good, each of the integers in that range will be equally likely, and the value generated at any given time will have no statistical relationship to those numbers that were generated previously. Naturally, there will be a relationship of some sort. We are, after all, dealing with a deterministic algorithm here. The next random number in a series is computed by means of an explicit formula, so in a sense, strict randomness is out of the question. But that is not the point. In fact, for many applications, repeatability is an asset that allows us to carefully study events. All that we really care about is *statistical* randomness. We want our definitely non-random random numbers to behave as if they were really random. This text is not an appropriate forum for a detailed discussion of what this means. Knuth (1981) is an excellent reference for those who want more information. Press *et al.* (1992) is also a great source for practical advice and algorithms. We will simply present some random number generators whose statistical performance is known to be good and hope that the reader is trusting.

The most common uniform random number generator, and the one that we will use here, is called the *linear congruential algorithm*. It generates a sequence of random numbers using Equation (2.7).

$$r_{i+1} = (ar_i + c) \bmod m \qquad (2.7)$$

If the three constants, a, c, and m, are chosen carefully, the performance of this quick and simple technique is surprisingly good. It is vital to understand, though, that the choice of constants is critical. One does not dare to guess. There are very few good choices. Press *et al.* (1992) supplies a list that probably includes all of the good ones.

Sometimes I find it hard to believe that sets of constants exist such that every number from 0 through $m-1$ will appear from Equation (2.7) before repetition sets in. That seems almost too much to expect from a perverse world order, but it is true nonetheless. On the other hand, this exhaustive generation, and the uniform probability distribution that it implies, are not enough for a random number generator to be usable. What if the selected constants produced a random sequence that alternated even-odd-even-odd and so forth. Not many people would be willing to call that a random number generator! Such an effect is called *serial correlation*. If the generated sequence alternated parity, that would be easily seen. The problem with linear congruential generators is that serial correlation is guaranteed by the algorithm. It is just not always so obvious as alternating parity. The goal is to choose the constants so that the inevitable serial correlation is minimized.

It is worth taking a moment to expand on the meaning of serial correlation. This is a very general term that has implications beyond the simple lagged covariance familiar to statisticians. It refers to *any* regular relationship among the random numbers produced. There is one type of serial correlation that is particularly troublesome to linear congruential generators. Suppose that we peel off random numbers in sets of k at a time. Each of those k-tuples defines a point in k-dimensional space. What we ideally hope is that the points will randomly fill that space. Unfortunately, we do not get what we hope for in this case. Instead, all of the points will lie on planes of dimension $k-1$. There will be at most about $m^{1/k}$ such planes, and perhaps a lot fewer than that. If m is small, that is not a lot of planes. If the process that we are simulating with our random number generator expects the points to be uniformly distributed throughout some k-space, we may be in big trouble. Luckily, this is a problem that is easily remedied, and we will soon see how to use shuffling as an effective solution.

Before leaving the linear congruential algorithm, one more of its weaknesses should be mentioned. Its low-order bits have a strong tendency to be less random than its high-order bits. Suppose that we have a 16-bit linear congruential random number generator, and we want to produce random numbers having the values 0–3 with equal probability. We should generate them from the 16-bit random number r by means of $(r>>14)\&3$ rather than $r\%4$. Note that *and*ing the shifted number with 3 is necessary because some C++ compilers propagate the high-order bit (and some don't).

Chopping, Stacking, and Shuffling

The linear congruential algorithm is easy to implement, fast to execute, and adequate for many applications. However, it suffers from several problems that preclude its use in highly sophisticated applications. The most serious problem is usually that it repeats itself after $m-1$ numbers have been generated. Serial correlation may be a problem also. We will now discuss how these difficulties may be avoided with only a moderate amount of additional work.

One tool that we will need is the ability to generate a random number having a specified number of bits. If we could simply pick m to be the correct power of two, all would be well. For example, if we need 16 bits, it would be nice to let $m = 2^{16} = 65536$. Alas, we are not so lucky. None of the few good values of m are obliging. We must choose a larger value and process the result to get it down to the required number of bits. But how?

Therein lies a deadly trap for the unwary. The obvious method is simply to select the number of bits we want by means of a mask. But let's see if that works. Suppose we want a two-bit random number. Letting $m = 4$ would do the trick, but that is a bad value for m. Let us say that $m = 5$ gives a good random sequence, which we will call the random source. We generate our two-bit random number by taking the two lower bits of the random source. That source produces each of the numbers 0–4 with equal probability. But the two lower bits of both 0 and 4 are 0. This means our two-bit random number will have the value 0 twice as often as it has the values 1, 2, or 3. The obvious method is an obvious flop.

The correct method is to examine the random number produced by the source generator and ignore it if it exceeds the maximum desired output. In the simple example just presented, each time the number 4 is returned by the source generator, we would pass it by and ask the generator for another value. One implication of this algorithm is that we want m to be as small as possible. Otherwise, we will waste a lot of time generating random numbers that just get thrown away. By the way, there is no reason to limit this technique to generating random numbers that are defined by a certain number of bits. We can generate random numbers within any range by using a source generator that is uniform in a wider range and discarding values outside the desired range. Just beware of discarding so many that economy suffers.

Another warning about this rejection method is in order. If the source is a simple linear congruential algorithm, the period of the final random numbers, after discarding, will be equal to its number of possible values. In the example above, the source generator has a period of five, but the masked outputs after rejection have a period of four. As will be seen soon, this has enormous consequences in some situations. However, there is a very easy way to reduce this problem to some degree. Use a value of m that is many times larger than needed, so that the period of the source is relatively long, and reject based on an interval that is an integer multiple of the final desired interval. Then divide to get the ultimate random number. Consider our little example once more. We want a random number in the range 0–3. We could let $m = 10$ and reject source random numbers that exceed 7. Divide the source by two to get the desired result. The period will be 8.

To illustrate these principles, we present some code. Here is a subroutine that produces 16-bit random numbers. By using a much larger value of m than the largest ultimate random number, the period is extended to 10 times 2^{16}. It wastes less than 10 percent of the generated numbers.

```
#define IM 714025L              // These constants are from Press et. al.
#define IA 1366I                // "Numerical Recipes in C"
#define IC 150889L              // Do not tamper with them unless you are an expert

static long seed = 797L ;       // Keep the current seed here

static long mult = IM / 65536L  // Period (interval) multiplier, 10 here
static long max = mult * 65536L ; // Large source interval

long rand16 ()                  // This is the random generator
{
   for (;;) {                   // Loop until in range

      seed = (IA * seed + IC) % IM ; // Linear congruential source

      if (seed < max )          // Reject per large source interval
         return seed / mult ;   // Return in desired interval
      }
}
```

    The expanded rejection interval method just illustrated is a fast and simple way of generating random numbers in a specified interval that have a period significantly longer than the interval. However, that period may still be too short for many applications. Also, serial correlation, the bane of pure linear congruential methods, is still present. Both of these problems may be almost totally eliminated by shuffling the random numbers produced by the linear congruential algorithm. It works this way. Initialize by filling a table with random values. Then use the simple linear congruential generator to randomly select an entry from the table. The selected value is returned to the user, and its place in the table is refilled with a new random number. The effect is to randomly reorder the outputs of the simple generator. Its effective period is raised to a gigantic number. And since the serial placement of the outputs is scattered all about, serial correlation is reduced to almost nothing. Figure 2.14 illustrates shuffling, and the subroutine rand1s produces shuffled random numbers. Also, the simple routine rand16_1 extracts 16-bit random numbers from the sequence produced by rand1s.

Random Perturbation

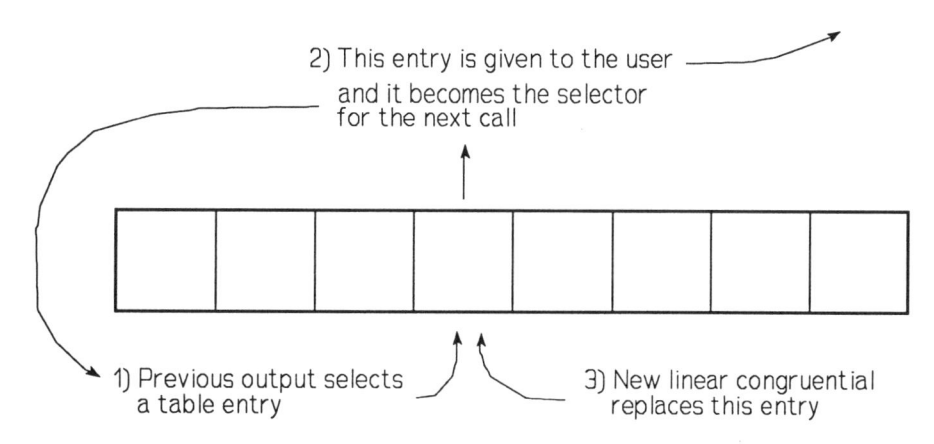

Figure 2.14 Shuffling a random sequence.

1) Previous output selects a table entry
2) This entry is given to the user and it becomes the selector for the next call
3) New linear congruential replaces this entry

```
#define TABLE_LENGTH_1 103
#define IM1 714025L              // These constants are from Press et. al.
#define IA1 1366L                // "Numerical Recipes in C"
#define IC1 150889L              // Do not tamper with them unless you are an expert

static long seed1 = 797L ;                   // Keep the current seed here
static long table1[TABLE_LENGTH_1] ;         // Keep shuffle table here
static int table_initialized1 = 0 ;          // Has it been initialized?
static long randout1 ;                       // Shuffled outputs kept here

void srand1s ( long iseed )                  // Set the random seed
{
  seed1 = iseed ;
  table_initialized1 = 0 ;                   // Must also rebuild table!
}

long rand1s ()                               // Random number generator
{
  int i ;

  if (! table_initialized1) {                // Initialize shuffle table before use
    table_initialized1 = 1 ;                 // Flag to avoid more inits
```

```
    for (i=0 ; i<TABLE_LENGTH_1 ; i++) {      // Fill entire table
      seed1 = (IA1 * seed1 + IC1) % IM1 ;     // Linear congruential generator
      table1[i] = seed1 ;                     // Fill table
      }
    seed1 = (IA1 * seed1 + IC1) % IM1 ;
    randout1 = seed1 ;                        // One more for first use
    }

  i = (int) ((double) TABLE_LENGTH_1 * (double) randout1 / (double) IM1) ;
  randout1 = table1[i] ;                      // This output comes from table
  seed1 = (IA1 * seed1 + IC1) % IM1 ;         // Generate new random number
  table1[i] = seed1 ;                         // to replace used entry
  return randout1 ;                           // then return old entry
}

long rand16_1 ()                              // Produce 16-bit random numbers
{
  long k ;
  long mult = IM1 / 65536L ;                  // Maximize use of the
  long max = mult * 65536L ;                  // source range

  for (;;) {                                  // Wait until in range
    k = rand1s () ;                           // Shuffled random number
    if (k < max )                             // If it is in reduced range
      return k / mult ;                       // Produce output number
    }
}
```

    Nowadays, 32-bit computers are the norm. The ANSI standard only requires 16-bit random numbers, and that is a real pity. It's just not enough, even for many small applications. There is a real need for 32-bit random number generators. Alas, it is difficult to directly use the linear congruential algorithm to generate 32-bit random numbers in C. The power of assembler is really needed to deal with overflow problems. If C code is mandatory, the best bet is to generate two 16-bit random numbers and paste them together. But this must be done carefully. There must be no relationship between the two 16-bit generators. For example, suppose that we use a straight linear congruential algorithm to generate a sequence with a period somewhat longer than 2^{16}, and use rejection to produce a 16-bit sequence from it. Then we employ different constants with the same method for the other

16-bit sequence. It's easy to think that we have two independent random sequences. But they both have a period of 2^{16}, so only that many different 32-bit numbers will be generated, and the period of the 32-bit numbers will also be 2^{16}. That is a disaster.

The easiest way to produce two independent sources of 16-bit random numbers is to shuffle each independently. As an additional safety factor, different linear congruential constants should be used so that different sequences are produced if the same seed happened to be used for each. I use the following constants for the second random number generator:

```
#define TABLE_LENGTH_2 97
#define IM2 312500L
#define IA2 741L
#define IC2 66037L
```

The code for the second generator will not be listed. It is identical to the code for the first generator except that the constants shown above are used, and an independent seed and shuffle table are kept. Complete source code is provided in the routine FLRAND.CPP on the accompanying disk.

As long as both 16-bit generators are shuffled, there is little need to shuffle the 32-bit output. However, except for table initialization, shuffling is not terribly expensive compared with the operations that will be performed on the random numbers in most applications. So for the sake of thoroughness, the 32-bit code now supplied shuffles the result. Some readers may want to remove the shuffling. I am of the (unproven) opinion that the period of this random generator is close enough to infinity for all applications currently envisioned.

```
#define TABLE_LENGTH 113
static long table[TABLE_LENGTH] ;         // Keep shuffle table here
static int table_initialized = 0 ;        // Has it been initialized?

/*
   Set the random seed
*/

void sflrand ( long iseed )
{
   srand1s ( (iseed >> 16 ) & 65535L ) ;
```

```c
      srand2s ( iseed & 65535L ) ;         // Set the individual seeds
      table_initialized = 0 ;              // Must also rebuild table!
}

/*
   This is the actual random number generator
*/

static long randout ;
long flrand ()
{
   int i ;

   if (! table_initialized) {              // Initialize shuffle table before use
      table_initialized = 1 ;              // Flag to avoid more inits
      for (i=0 ; i<TABLE_LENGTH ; i++)     // Fill entire table
         table[i] = (rand16_1() << 16)  |  rand16_2() ; // Put it in the table
      randout = (rand16_1() << 16)  |  rand16_2() ; // One more for first use
      }

   i = (int) ((double) TABLE_LENGTH * (double) (randout & 0x7FFFFFFFL) /
      ((double) 0x7FFFFFFFL + 1.0)) ;      // Avoid cast problems with hi bit
   randout = table[i] ;                    // This output comes from table
   table[i] = (rand16_1() << 16)  |  rand16_2() ; // Replace used entry
   return randout ;                        // then return old entry
}
```

There is only one subtle part of the above code that should be noted. When the location in the table is calculated in the fourth line from the end, the high-order bit of randout is removed by masking, and the corresponding limit is employed for the denominator. This avoids problems with the (double) cast interpreting a value with the high bit set as a negative number.

Before leaving the topic of uniform random numbers, let us be able to supply floating point uniforms in the range [0, 1). Note that the tradition is to allow true zero, but not true one. This sort of random number will be needed frequently. They can be generated easily by dividing an integer random number by its maximum plus one. We can take nearly full advantage of 8-byte double precision by using two 32-bit random numbers. Mathematically precise random doubles can be generated only by means of implementation-specific routines, generally written in assembler. However, the following code is more than adequate for virtually all applications. Note that on many hardware platforms it is possible (though highly unlikely) for this code to generate a value of exactly 1.0. In case the target application would be harmed by this, suitable precautions should be taken.

```
double unifrand ()
{
   double denom = 0x7FFFFFFFL + 1.0 ;
   double r1 = flrand () & 0x7FFFFFFFL ;
   double r2 = flrand () & 0x7FFFFFFFL ;
   return (r1 + r2 / denom) / denom ;
}
```

Normally Distributed Random Numbers

After the uniform distribution, which is the foundation for nearly all other random number generators, the most frequently needed random distribution is the Gaussian or normal distribution. Because the central limit theorem says (loosely) that sums of independent random variables tend to have a normal distribution, this distribution is fundamental to many or most standard statistical procedures. Moreover, normal random numbers are used to build random numbers having many other useful distributions. Therefore, we need a ready source of them.

If it is not important that the random numbers exactly follow a normal distribution, there is an extremely quick and easy way to generate approximately normal random deviates. We simply take advantage of the central limit theorem and sum a few uniform random numbers. It is amazing how quickly the sum approaches normality.

Standardized normal deviates are produced by remembering that the mean of a uniform random number in [0, 1) is 0.5, and its variance is 1/12. In particular, Equation (2.8) can be used to produce a fairly normal random deviate X from n uniform deviates U_i.

$$X = \sqrt{\frac{12}{n}} \left(\sum_{i=1}^{n} U_i - \frac{n}{2} \right) \quad (2.8)$$

I sometimes do random perturbation for simulated annealing using the sum of only four uniform deviates. By subtracting two of them from the other two, centering is obtained automatically. The resulting random number is only moderately normal, but exact normality is not required. In fact, the relatively light tails may be beneficial by preventing moves over great distances in one jump.

When exact normality is not important, a few quickly generated uniform deviates may be all that are needed to do the job. The following code fragment appears in many of my programs:

```
temp *= 3.464101615 / (2.0 * ((double) 0x7FFFFFFFL + 1.0)) ;  // SQRT(12)=3.464...

while (nvars--) {
  r = (double) (flrand() & 0x7FFFFFFFL) +
      (double) (flrand() & 0x7FFFFFFFL) -
      (double) (flrand() & 0x7FFFFFFFL) -
      (double) (flrand() & 0x7FFFFFFFL) ;
  *x++ = *center++ + temp * r ;
}
```

This method is obviously quick and simple. However, it is not much more difficult to compute random variables having an exactly normal distribution. The most popular general portable method is the *Box-Muller* algorithm. It actually computes two independent random deviates simultaneously. It starts with two uniform random numbers, U_1 and U_2. The variables X_1 and X_2 shown in Equation (2.9) are (surprisingly, to some) independent and follow a normal distribution with mean zero and unit variance.

$$\begin{aligned} X_1 &= \sqrt{-2 \ln U_1} \sin 2\pi U_2 \\ X_2 &= \sqrt{-2 \ln U_1} \cos 2\pi U_2 \end{aligned} \quad (2.9)$$

Since transcendental functions are relatively slow to compute, it is always good programming practice to use both X_1 and X_2 if possible. For neural network applications, the time taken to generate random numbers is generally insignificant compared to what will be done with those random numbers, so speed is no great concern here. Readers who want exactly normal random numbers and who require the best possible speed have several alternatives. Press *et al.* (1992) shows a clever way to avoid computing the sin and cos functions. However, there is a price to pay in that, on the average, about 27 percent more random deviates (and a little other arithmetic) will be needed than in the direct application of Equation (2.9). For modern computers with extremely fast transcendental functions built in, these two alternatives may be nearly equivalent in speed. Readers who have fanatic speed requirements, or who simply have a thirst for unusual algorithms, are highly encouraged to see Knuth (1981). That book contains a variety of some truly fascinating normal random number generation algorithms. I sincerely wish that speed were more important to neural network applications so that I would have an excuse for including some of those wonderfully exotic algorithms in this text. Sadly, I must settle for the rather mundane code that implements the Box-Muller method of generating normal random deviates.

```
void normal_pair ( double *x1 , double *x2 )
{
   double u1, u2 ;

   for (;;) {
      u1 = unifrand () ;
      if (u1 <= 0.0)      // Safety: log(0) is undefined
         continue ;
      u1 = sqrt ( -2.0 * log ( u1 )) ;
      u2 = 2.0 * PI * unifrand () ;
      *x1 = u1 * sin ( u2 ) ;
      *x2 = u1 * cos ( u2 ) ;
      return ;
      }
}
```

Cauchy Random Vectors

The Cauchy distribution is interesting and unusual. It has exceptionally heavy tails. Very wild outliers happen regularly. This can be illustrated with a physical example. Suppose that you are facing a wall, standing a few feet away from it, and holding a flashlight in your hand. Imagine a point on the wall directly in front of you. We will call that point the origin. If you were to point the flashlight directly left or right, parallel to the wall, the beam of light would not touch the wall. But if it were even the tiniest bit pointed in toward the wall, a spot would be illuminated. Now suppose that you randomly point it somewhere in the 180-degree range from left to right, with the angle following a uniform distribution. The location of the spot of light on the wall relative to the origin follows a Cauchy distribution. It should be obvious that extremely large values of this random variable will be common. The density function of a Cauchy random variable is plotted in Figure 2.15 along with a normal density.

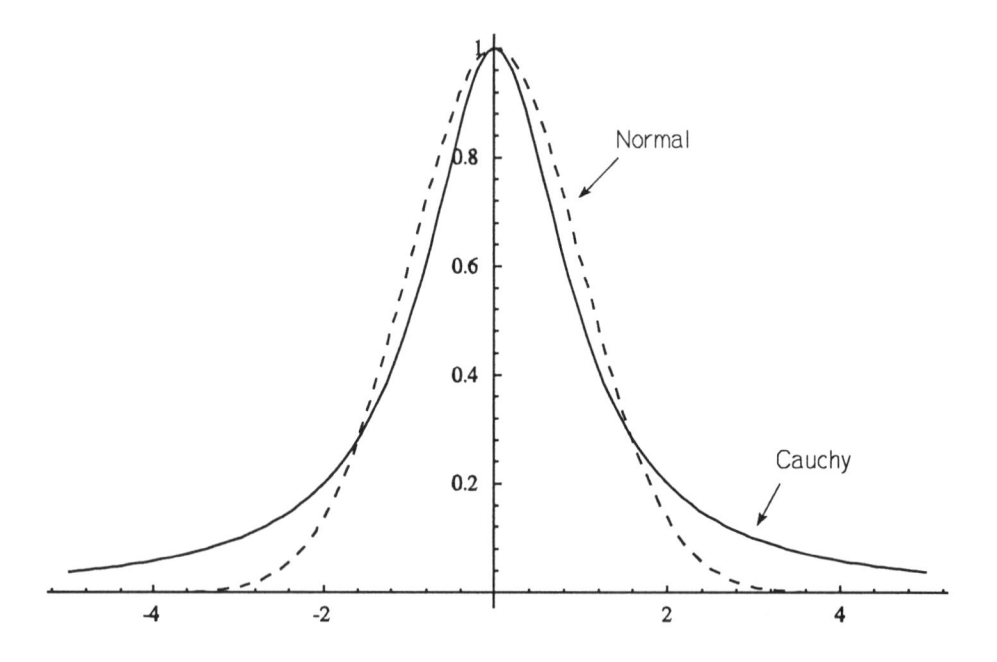

Figure 2.15 Cauchy and normal densities.

For the sake of mathematically inclined readers, a curious property of the Cauchy distribution will be mentioned. The tails are so heavy that neither its mean nor its variance is defined. This implies that the Strong Law of Large Numbers does not apply. The mean of a large number of Cauchy random variables does not tend toward zero. In fact, let $X_1, ..., X_n$ be a collection of n independent random variables following the same Cauchy distribution. Then their mean, $(X_1 + ... + X_n) / n$ follows the Cauchy distribution!

It is a little tricky generating random vectors having a multivariate Cauchy distribution. One difficulty is that the density function, shown in Equation (2.10), cannot be expressed as the product of the individual marginal densities. Therefore, we cannot simply generate a set of individual scalar random variables to make up the components of the vector. The entire vector must be generated in one shot.

$$f(x_1, \ldots, x_n) = \frac{\beta\, \Gamma[(n+1)/2]}{\pi^{(n+1)/2} \left(\beta^2 + \sum_{i=1}^{n} x_i^2 \right)^{(n+1)/2}} \qquad (2.10)$$

Observe that the random vector occurs in the density function only in terms of its squared length. This tells the statisticians in the audience that the direction of the vector will be uniformly distributed on an n-sphere. Alas, the distribution of the length of the vector is not so easily divined. Devroye (1986), as cited in Styblinsky and Tang (1990), provide the following method. Generate a random variable, B, having the Beta distribution with parameters $n/2$ and $1/2$. Then the new random variable $R = $ sqrt $(B/(1-B))$ has the same distribution as the length of a Cauchy random vector with unit scale ($\beta = 1$). Vectors having arbitrary scale are produced by multiplying unit-scale vectors by β. Let us now tackle these subproblems one at a time.

Recall that the parameters of the required beta distribution are $n/2$ and $1/2$. Significant simplification can be had if we provide only the capability of parameters of the form $k/2$, where k is an integer. Readers who need the generality of arbitrary real parameters should consult Knuth (1981).

Generating beta random variables is easy if one has access to a source of gamma random variables. Let X_1 and X_2 be random variables following gamma distributions with positive real parameters v_1 and v_2, respectively. Then the new random variable $B = X_1 / (X_1 + X_2)$ follows a beta distribution with parameters v_1 and v_2. This fact inspires the following trivial code for generating a beta random variable.

```
double beta ( int v1 , int v2 )
{
  int i ;
  double x1, x2 ;

  x1 = gamma ( v1 ) ;
  x2 = gamma ( v2 ) ;
  return x1 / (x1 + x2) ;
}
```

One implementation detail about that code should be clarified. Recall that we are working with parameters of the form $k/2$. This routine will be used to generate beta random variables whose parameters are really $v_1/2$ and $v_2/2$. Thus, the gamma(k) subroutine must generate random deviates with parameter $k/2$. The routines have been deliberately coded this way to prevent the user from accidentally violating assumptions by calling it with a more general real parameter. Also note that as far as generating beta random variables goes, arbitrary positive real parameters are theoretically legal in the above algorithm. The problem arises with the gamma distribution.

We now need the ability to generate gamma random variables with parameter $k/2$. This is a little tricky, but not too bad. We can make some use of the fact that a gamma random variable with parameter $k/2$ is 0.5 times a chi-square random variable with k degrees of freedom. As long as k is small, we can easily generate a chi-square random variable with k degrees of freedom by summing the squares of k standard normal random deviates. However, that method quickly becomes expensive as k grows; we shall use it only for $k = 1$. We can also take advantage of the fact that a gamma distribution with a parameter of 1.0 is just an exponential distribution. A general method that works as long as the parameter strictly exceeds 1.0 is given in Knuth (1981). Here is a subroutine the generates gamma random variables having parameter $v/2$.

```
double gamma ( int v )
{
  int i ;
  double x, y, z, vm1, root ;

  switch (v) {

    case 1:                      // Chi-square with 1 df is 2 gamma(.5)
      x = normal () ;
      return 0.5 * x * x ;

    case 2:                      // Gamma(1) is exponential(1)
      for (;;) {
        x = unifrand () ;
        if (x > 0.0)
          return -log ( x ) ;
      }
```

```
         default:                    // Valid for all real a>1 (a=v/2)
            vm1 = 0.5 * v - 1.0 ;
            root = sqrt ( v - 1.0 ) ;

            for (;;) {
               y = tan ( PI * unifrand () ) ;
               x = root * y + vm1 ;
               if (x <= 0.0)
                  continue ;
               z = (1.0 + y * y) * exp ( vm1 * log(x/vm1) - root * y ) ;
               if (unifrand () <= z)
                  return x ;
            }
      }
}
```

For those few readers who might want to generalize this subroutine to handle arbitrary positive real parameters, the following may be helpful. The hitch comes in the algorithm in the default section. It is legal for arbitrary real values of the gamma parameter, not just for the multiples of 1 / 2 as shown here. However, it is valid only when the parameter exceeds 1.0. We handle the situation of the parameter being less than or equal to 1.0 by making use of two special cases. Readers will have to consult Knuth (1981) for a somewhat more complex general algorithm.

The final subproblem in Cauchy random number generation is that of producing random deviates that are uniformly distributed on the surface of a unit sphere. When $n = 2$, one can simply generate a uniform angle in the range 0–2π and compute its sine and cosine. When $n = 3$ it (surprisingly) turns out that all three components of the random vector have a uniform distribution over $[-1, 1]$. Thus, one simply generates a uniform deviate in this interval for one of the components, and then one uses the case of $n = 2$ to find the other two coordinates along the circular cross-section. There is an amazingly simple general method, though. One generates each component of the vector as a normal random deviate, then one normalizes the vector to unit length. Like the Cauchy distribution itself, the multivariate distribution for that random vector has a density that involves only the length of the vector. This implies a uniform distribution of its direction. We now provide code for generating a random vector that is uniformly distributed on the surface of a unit sphere. Note how it takes advantage of the Box-Muller method for providing independent random pairs.

```
void rand_sphere ( int nvars , double *x )
{
  int i ;
  double length ;

  length = 0.0 ;
  for (i=0 ; i<nvars/2 ; i++) {      // Efficiently generate pairs
    normal_pair ( &x[2*i] , &x[2*i+1] ) ;
    length += x[2*i] * x[2*i]  +  x[2*i+1] * x[2*i+1] ;
    }

  if (nvars % 2) {                 // If odd, get the last one
    x[nvars-1] = normal () ;
    length += x[nvars-1] * x[nvars-1] ;
    }

  length = 1.0 / sqrt ( length ) ;
  while (nvars--)
    x[nvars] *= length ;
}
```

Everything is ready. We can now put it all together to generate Cauchy random vectors. The special case of $n = 1$ is handled separately. Remember that at the beginning of this section we gave the example of shining a flashlight on a wall. The distance of the spot from the origin is proportional to the tangent of the uniformly distributed angle. Note how values approaching infinity are avoided here. For n greater than one, we use the algorithm already described. A random vector uniformly distributed on a sphere is generated to determine the direction of the Cauchy vector. Then a beta random variable is generated and transformed to determine the length of the Cauchy vector. Care is taken to disallow division by zero. Finally, the vector is scaled to its correct length.

```
void cauchy ( int n , double scale , double *x )
{
  double temp ;
```

```
if (n == 1) {
   temp = PI * unifrand () - 0.5 * PI ;
   x[0] = scale * tan ( 0.99999999 * temp ) ;
   return ;
   }

rand_sphere ( n , x ) ;

temp = beta ( n , 1 ) ;

if (temp < 1.0)
   temp = scale * sqrt ( temp / (1.0 - temp) ) ;
else
   temp = 1.e10 ;

while (n--)
   x[n] *= temp ;
}
```

A Final Thought

By now there may well be a few readers who are annoyed that so many pages of a neural network text have been wasted on the subject of random number generation. Let those readers be assured that those pages are definitely not wasted. The most important neural network training algorithms rely heavily on stochastic methods for at least part of their operation. Without a good source of random numbers, the most sophisticated stochastic algorithm in the world is worthless. If any reader takes one of the stochastic algorithms given in this text, or any other for that matter, and feeds it with the ANSI rand() generator supplied with their compiler, disaster is almost guaranteed. Furthermore, erroneous substitutes abound. In order to perform as expected, a stochastic algorithm must be fed with random numbers that have a large number of possible values, have an effectively infinite period, and have minimal serial correlation. If even one of these requirements is not fulfilled, performance will suffer, and total failure is a distinct possibility. Be warned.

3

Hybrid Training Algorithms

- Simple deterministic/stochastic alternation
- Stochastic smoothing with gradient hinting

The previous chapters have discussed fast but risky deterministic training algorithms, as well as slow but reliable stochastic training algorithms. It should come as no surprise that the very best training algorithms combine those two methods. A truly effective neural network training algorithm will make use of stochastic elements, so that locating a good minimum is likely; yet it also will contain enough deterministic elements for reasonable economy. This chapter will present two of the most popular hybrids.

Simple Alternation

The most basic way of hybridizing stochastic and deterministic algorithms is to alternate them. Anneal for a while, then efficiently descend for a while, then anneal some more, and so forth. If the alternation is done intelligently, this simple method can be extremely effective. What do we mean by the alternation being done intelligently? Here are a few reasonable guidelines:

- Start the process with a stochastic algorithm to take maximum advantage of its global nature. If deterministic descent is used first, the point may end up so far down in a local minimum that even a good random method may have trouble escaping.

- Know when to give up and start all over. It is generally accepted that several independent parallel runs of simulated annealing are more effective (in terms of results relative to cost) than one long run. Be prepared to completely retry the algorithm a fair number of times with different random sequences, as opposed to sinking all resources into one enormous effort.

- Conclude that a minimum has been reached, and it is time for a brand new try, when the deterministic algorithm has converged *and* a subsequent stochastic algorithm has failed to escape from that minimum. Neural network error functions often have saddle points and small local minima all along the downward path, so we should always try to escape from what may be a small pocket of trouble.

- Never use a stochastic algorithm to descend to the bitter end. Use this expensive procedure to find the neighborhood of a minimum, then switch to a deterministic algorithm.

- It can be important to persevere with deterministic descent even when the slope is almost flat, as sudden dropoffs to better territory are not uncommon. However, that is a very expensive process. Save it for the most promising candidates. Most of the time, be liberal about quitting. A good approach is to build up a modest collection of candidates found with a cheap, low-accuracy method. Then use an expensive method on only the best one in the collection.

- It often happens that gentle annealing after convergence of a deterministic algorithm will produce a little progress. Pursue that a few times, but be ready to give up if it happens several times in a row. We may be abandoning a potentially big payoff, but it is a high-stakes gamble that is rarely worth taking.

I have put those ideas together into an algorithm that appears to work well. It is implemented in the MLFN2 program as the AN1_CJ and AN2_CJ learning methods. The stochastic component is either the primitive annealing (AN1) or the general annealing (AN2) described in Chapter 2. The conjugate gradient algorithm is used for the deterministic component. A rough flowchart of the procedure is shown in Figure 3.1. A code fragment that illustrates the details of the algorithm now appears. This code is extracted from the MLFN2 program, so many declarations, memory allocations, and so on, have been omitted for clarity.

```
void LayerNet::anx_cj ()
{
  int i, itry, n_escape, n_retry, bad_count, new_record, refined ;
  long seed ;
  double err, prev_err, best_err, start_of_loop_error, best_inner_error ;
  double initial_accuracy, final_accuracy ;
  LayerNet *worknet, *worknet2, *bestnet ;

  n_escape = n_retry = 0 ;
```

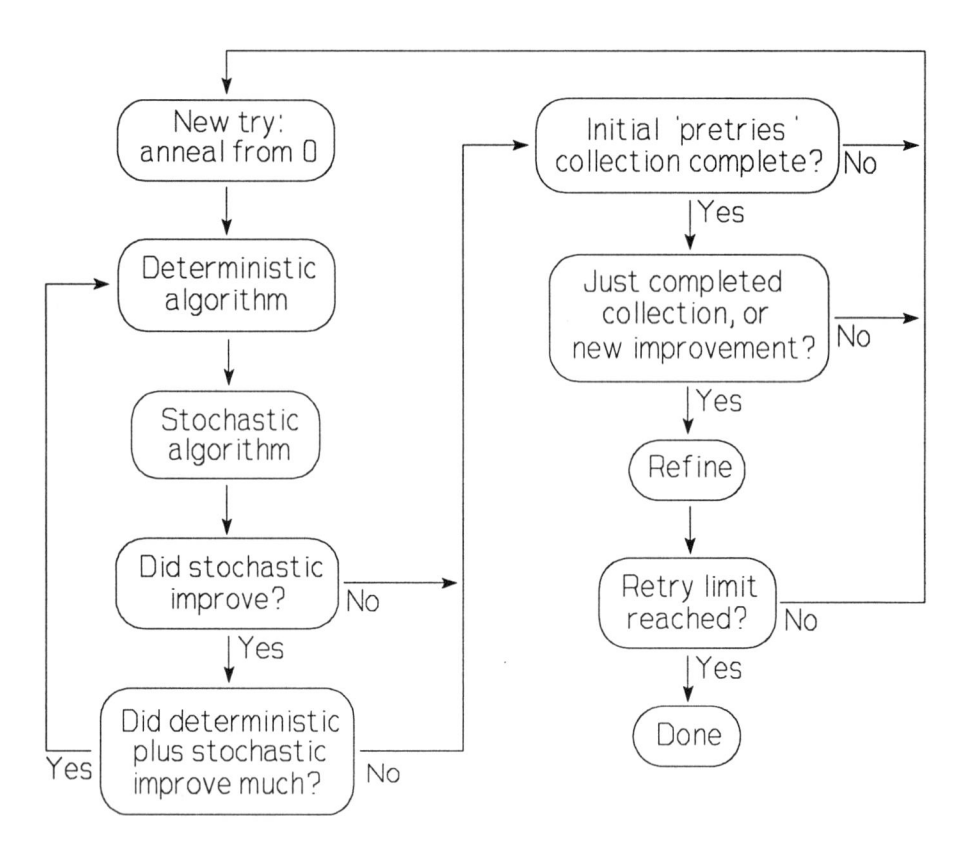

Figure 3.1 Alternating stochastic/deterministic methods.

```
/*
   Start by annealing around the starting weights.  These will be zero if the net was
   just created.  If it was partially trained already, they will be meaningful.  Anneal1
   guarantees that it will not return all zero weights if there is a hidden layer, even if
   that means that the error exceeds the amount that could be attained by all zeros.
*/

   best_err = best_inner_error = 1.e30 ;
   anneal1 ( tptr , lptr , worknet , 1 , 0 ) ;

/*
   Do conjugate gradient optimization, finding a local minimum.  Then anneal to break
   out of it.  If successful, loop back up to do conjugate gradient again.  Otherwise
   restart totally random.
*/
```

Simple Alternation

```
    bad_count = 0 ;                                  // Handles flat local mins
    refined = 0 ;                                    // Ever refine to high res?  Not yet.
    new_record = 0 ;                                 // Refine when new inner err record set
    initial_accuracy = pow ( 10.0 , -lptr->cj_acc ) ;
    final_accuracy = initial_accuracy * pow ( 10.0 , -lptr->cj_refine ) ;

    for (itry=1 ; ; itry++) {                        // Outer loop retries

      if (neterr < best_err) {                       // Keep track of best
        copy_weights ( bestnet , this ) ;
        best_err = neterr ;
        }

      if (neterr <= lptr->quit_err)
        break ;

      start_of_loop_error = neterr ;
      err = conjgrad ( tptr , 32767 , initial_accuracy ,
              lptr->quit_err , lptr->cj_progress ) ;
      neterr = fabs ( err ) ;                        // err<0 if user pressed ESCape

      if (neterr < best_err) {                       // Keep track of best
        copy_weights ( bestnet , this ) ;
        best_err = neterr ;
        }

      if (err <= lptr->quit_err)                     // err<0 if user pressed ESCape
        break ;

      seed = flrand() - (long) (itry * 97) ;         // Insure new seed for anneal
      sflrand ( seed ) ;

      prev_err = neterr ;                            // So we can see if anneal helped

      anneal1 ( tptr , lptr , worknet , 0 , itry ) ;

      if (neterr < best_err) {                       // Keep track of best
        copy_weights ( bestnet , this ) ;
        best_err = neterr ;
        }
```

```
      if (best_err <= lptr->quit_err)
        break ;

      if (neterr < best_inner_error) {            // Keep track of best inner for refine
        best_inner_error = neterr ;
        new_record = 1 ;                          // Tells us to refine
        }

      if ((prev_err - neterr) > 1.e-7) {          // Did we break out of local min?
        if ((start_of_loop_error - neterr) < 1.e-3)
          ++bad_count ;                           // Avoid many unprofitable iters
        else
          bad_count = 0 ;
        if (bad_count < 4) {
          ++n_escape ;                            // Count escapes from local min
          continue ;                              // Escaped, so gradient learn again
          }
        }

/*
   After first few tries, and after each improvement thereafter, refine to high resolution
*/

      if ((itry-n_escape >= lptr->cj_pretries)  &&  (new_record || ! refined)) {
        if (! refined) {                          // If refining the best of the pretries
          copy_weights ( this , bestnet ) ;       // Get that net
          neterr = best_err ;
          }
        refined = 1 ;                             // Only force refine once
        new_record = 0 ;                          // Reset new inner error record flag
        err = conjgrad ( tptr , 0 , final_accuracy ,
                lptr->quit_err , lptr->cj_progress ) ;
        neterr = fabs ( err ) ;                   // err<0 if user pressed ESCape
        if (neterr < best_err) {                  // Keep track of best
          copy_weights ( bestnet , this ) ;
          best_err = neterr ;
          }
        }

      if (++n_retry > lptr->retries)
        break ;
```

```
    zero_weights () ;                              // Failed to break out, so retry random
    seed = flrand() - (long) (itry * 773) ;        // Insure new seed for anneal
    sflrand ( seed ) ;
    anneal1 ( tptr , lptr , worknet , 1 , itry ) ;
    }

  copy_weights ( this , bestnet ) ;
  neterr = best_err ;
  return ;
}
```

This algorithm is quite complex, and it deserves close study. I have used it as my workhorse training method for several years, and its track record is generally excellent.

If one examines the flowchart shown in Figure 3.1, it can be seen that stochastic optimization is used in two different ways. It is used at the start of each main outer retry loop, where annealing commences from a center at the origin. This provides a good starting point for the deterministic algorithm. Then it is used after the deterministic algorithm has converged, where its purpose is to break out of what may be a small local minimum or even perhaps a saddle point. We will count how many times the former happens using the variable n_retry, while occurrences of the latter are counted in n_escape. These two variables are initialized to zero.

Two different *best* error records will be kept. One of these, best_err, is the error of the grand best network found so far. That network is preserved in bestnet. The other error record is kept in best_inner_error. This is the best error ever found *before* refinement. Whenever this record is broken by the main deterministic/stochastic loop, the lucky network will be deemed worthy of the expensive refinement operation. We initialize these two variables to a huge value so that something will be accepted as having broken the records. Then anneal to find a good starting point for the conjugate gradient algorithm.

Sometimes a learning algorithm will become trapped in the midst of a broad, flat plain. Progress out of this area can be excruciatingly slow. Therefore, we count how many times the deterministic/stochastic loop has been traversed with only trivial improvement each time. If we do it too many times, give up. That count is kept in bad_count, which we initialize to zero.

One of the most difficult to understand yet important concepts in this algorithm is that of *pretries*. There is often a tremendous payoff in pushing a deterministic algorithm to the limit of accuracy. If one has the patience to diligently plod along a seemingly endless path of nearly zero gradient, one is frequently rewarded with a sudden drop into a narrow chasm in the error surface. On the other hand, that journey can be terribly expensive. One does not want to make it often. Thus, it behooves us to perform several inexpensive tries first. Anneal from zero to find a good starting point, then deterministically descend, but quit the descent before it gets too expensive. Then anneal from zero again, and descend. Repeat this a few times, keeping track of the best network. When a reasonable number of these pretries has been done, recover the best and pick up the deterministic descent from where it left off. But this time refine it to relatively high accuracy. This collection process is done only once during execution of the algorithm. Thereafter, refinement is done only when the record best error is broken. The refined flag is initialized to zero now to indicate that refinement has not yet been done. After the first time it is done, this flag will be set to one.

After the best of the pretry collection has been refined, we will refine again only when the network produced by a particular outer loop retry is better than the best so far at that point. Only those record breaking nets are deemed worthy of expensive refinement. The new_record flag is used to indicate whether or not the current network has broken that record and hence deserves refinement. Initialize it to zero.

The accuracy of the initial and the refinement stages of deterministic descent are now set. Note that the user specifies a number of decimal digits, and we convert that into a relative number. Note also that the user's refinement specification is in terms of *additional* digits above and beyond the usual, rather than an actual number of digits.

The main, outer retry loop now begins. The structure of the program here is slightly different from the flowchart. The flowchart shows annealing at the top, whereas this code starts the loop with the deterministic step and does the annealing at the bottom. The reason is that we already did the initial annealing. This structure makes it easier to deal with issues of initialization methods. The net effect is obviously the same either way.

We start out with two housekeeping matters. Keep track of the best network so far, and see if the user's quitting criterion has been attained. Then we record the error at this time and execute the conjugate gradient algorithm at the low initial accuracy. The conjgrad algorithm returns the negative of the actual error if the user pressed ESCape, so we take that into account when saving the network error. And once again we keep track of the best net so far and check on the quitting criterion.

Now that the deterministic algorithm has apparently converged, it is time to anneal around that point to see if it can escape from what may be a small local minimum or a saddle point. We set the random seed to a number that depends on the try so as to encourage a different sequence for each try. Then we record the error before annealing so that we will know if progress was made. After annealing, we again perform that same old pair of tasks: keep track of the best network and check on the stopping criterion. We also keep tabs on the best performance of the unrefined retries. If this one sets a new record, update the record and flag this fact so that refinement will be done (if other conditions are also right).

We now come to a slightly tricky section that is partly omitted from the flowchart for the sake of its clarity. First we see if the annealing helped to even a tiny degree. If not, we conclude that the local minimum has been found acceptably well for now, and we just drop down to the potential refinement step. But if annealing helped even a little, there may still be hope for this try. Compare the current error to start_of_loop_error, which was the error before the conjugate gradient step was done. If the improvement due to the deterministic/stochastic pair was insignificant, increment the counter that concerns slow creeping along a plain. But if there was significant improvement, reset that counter. We have patience for a while. As long as the counter is small, count this escape from a local minimum and try deterministic descent again. But if the counter is not small, it is probably not worth wasting any more time on this region. Decide that we have located the local minimum as well as we reasonably can.

At this time, we have presumably found the bottom of a local minimum, at least to the rough initial accuracy. We now consider refinement to higher accuracy. First of all, we do not refine until after the user-specified number of pretries have been done. Also remember that escape from a local minimum should not count as a real try. Only those that started from scratch by annealing from zero are valid tries. If that condition is met, then we refine if either a new record was just set, or we have just completed the collection of pretries (which is indicated by refinement never having been done).

If refinement is indicated, we need the network that is to be refined. If refinement has not yet been done, due to the fact that the pretry collection was just now completed, then the network that we will refine is the best so far, so retrieve it from bestnet. Otherwise, we are already in possession of the one to be refined, as this is the one that just broke the old record. Set the refined flag so that from now on only record-breakers will be refined. Reset the new_record flag in preparation for the next try. Refine to the final accuracy, preserve the network error, and keep track of the best so far.

The main outer loop is almost done. Count the number of retries and quit if the user's limit has been reached. Otherwise, reset the weights to zero, set the random seed to a number that depends on the try to avoid useless replication, and anneal to find a new starting point. This anneal step is at the top of the flowchart in Figure 3.1. After final exit from the outer loop, retrieve the best network for the caller.

Stochastic Smoothing with Gradient Hints

In Chapter 2 we presented an algorithm that stochastically smooths a function and finds the minimum of the smoothed function. By gradually decreasing the amount of smoothing, we were able to gently slide to the global minimum of the original function. A major drawback of that algorithm is that it is entirely stochastic. Points at which the function is evaluated are selected totally randomly. That is good in that total randomness encourages location of the global minimum. But it is bad in that a large, frequently excessive number of function evaluations are required. Wouldn't it be nice if we could preserve the random nature of the search, yet slip the algorithm little hints concerning where especially promising areas might be located? These areas could be somewhat favored. By design, there would be a higher probability of a randomly chosen point lying in the vicinity of a promising area than in an area that is likely to be a poor prospect. There is a way to do this. Remember that differentiation is a linear process. The derivative of a sum is the sum of the derivatives. When we approximate the value of the smoothed function by averaging the objective function values at randomly selected points, we can simultaneously approximate the gradient of the smoothed function by averaging the gradients at each random point. At least on a local scale, the smoothed function will decrease faster in the direction of the negative gradient than in any other direction. Thus, the algorithm would do well to favor that direction.

What is the best way to favor the gradient direction while still preserving the global nature of the search? There are numerous approaches. Styblinski and Tang (1990) provides an exotic algorithm along with a good historical bibliography. Chin (1994) presents a related algorithm that he claims is superior. Both of these algorithms employ strong deterministic descent tightly interwoven with the stochastic component, which makes me a little nervous with regard to finding the global minimum. They are undoubtedly very efficient for moderately easy problems, but their effectiveness at difficult problems involving many local minima is questionable. Also, these algorithms require that the user must set a relatively large number of critical parameters. Although careful tailoring of the method to particular problems is thereby facilitated, I prefer the KISS (Keep It Simple, Stupid) principle. No disparagement of these excellent algorithms is intended; they quite probably execute several times faster than the primitive method espoused in this text when they are correctly tuned to the problem at hand. However, when an easy-to-use general-purpose algorithm is needed, and the problem may be plagued with many local minima, this algorithm is good. Remember that there is *always* a tradeoff in probability of locating the global minimum versus number of function evaluations. When slick tricks make heavy use of the gradient, fewer function evaluations will be needed, but attraction to the nearest local minimum will increase. You pay your money and you take your choice.

The most straightforward way of biasing the random process in favor of the (negative) gradient direction is simply to add some multiple of the gradient to the point. In other words, generate a random perturbation exactly as in the pure stochastic version, and add that to the current point. Then multiply the gradient of the smoothed function by a constant and add that as well. The result is that the effective center about which perturbation takes place is shifted in the direction of maximum decrease of the smoothed function. Early in the process, when a thorough global search is most important, the gradient shift must be small relative to the purely random deviation. Later, as it becomes more likely that the center point is already in or near the basin of attraction of the global minimum, the gradient may safely exert more influence on the point selection process. This gradient shift is illustrated in Figures 3.2 and 3.3.

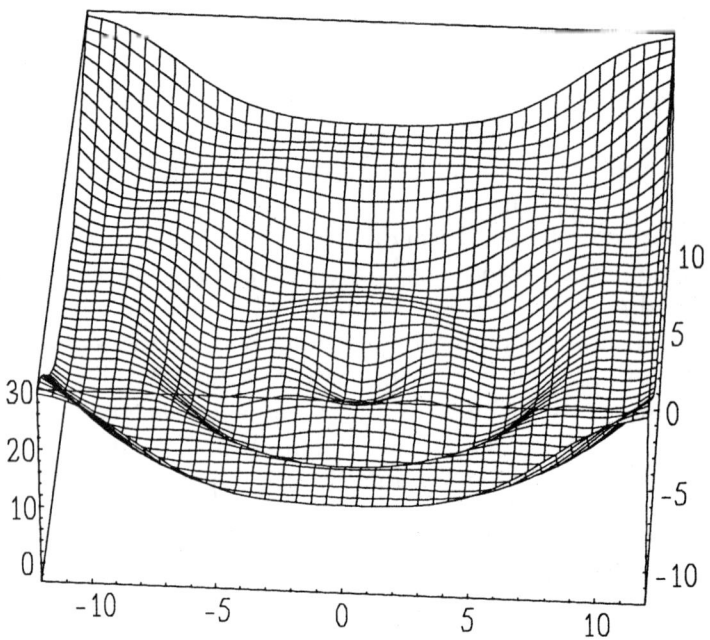

Figure 3.2 A difficult function to minimize.

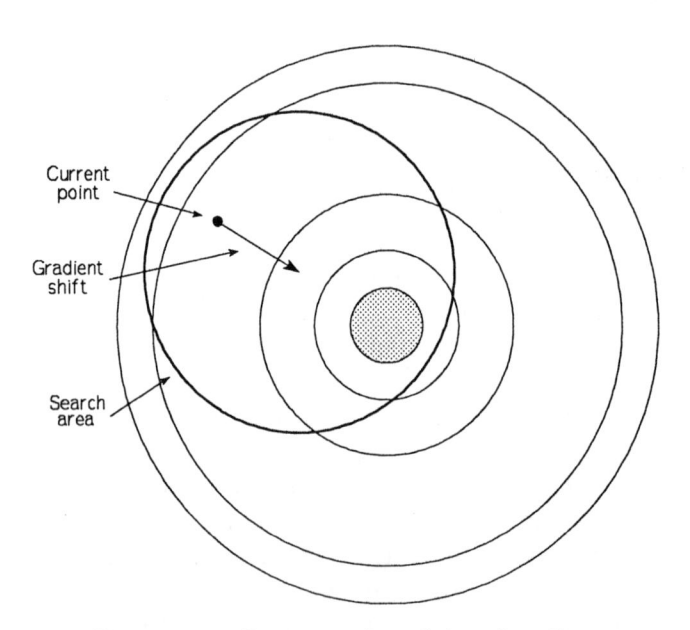

Figure 3.3 Contour plot of that function.

Figure 3.2 portrays a bivariate function whose global minimum is surrounded by a circular valley that would trap deterministic algorithms. Figure 3.3 shows some equal-height contours of the function. In that figure, the current point appears as a small solid circle. The pure stochastic algorithm would center the random vector generator at this point. But if we estimate the smoothed gradient and shift the center in the negative gradient direction, the effective area encompassed by the random vector generator will focus on the more promising area shown as a large, darker circle centered at the end of the gradient shift arrow.

How do we choose the weight used to multiply the gradient before adding it to the point? For general problems, and in the usual absence of explicit second derivative information, this is a tough question to answer. It depends strongly on the nature of the minimum that is being approached. Luckily, for most neural network applications, there is a rough rule of thumb that can reliably get us in the right ballpark. It turns out that a multiple in the range 0.2–1.0 seems to work for about 99.9% of all problems that I have seen. This is a fairly surprising observation, and I lack a ready explanation for the universality of this constant. But it is amazingly dependable. As long as the random perturbation dominates the net change, use of any fixed constant in that range will nearly always be acceptable.

There is an even better approach, though. We can easily devise a means for dynamically adjusting the degree of gradient use, optimizing it for the shape of the smoothed function at any time. Doing so will also increase the rigor of the algorithm, as errors in the initial setting of the constant are corrected automatically before they become a problem. It works like this: Instead of fixing a constant gradient weight, let the weight be a random number. Keep track of the performance of the randomly generated points, and adjust the distribution of the random gradient weight accordingly. If unusually large random weights are found to be more likely to provide an objective function decrease, then raise the mean of the random weight generator so as to favor larger weights. Conversely, if unusually small random weights give the best results, lower the mean. This method will track the smoothed function as its shape changes with the drop in temperature. Moreover, the user is largely relieved of the burden of choosing an optimal weight. If the starting weight happens to be set much too high for the problem, only those few randomly generated weights that are unusually small will produce success, and the weight will be rapidly pulled down from its erroneous initial value. The converse will happen as well.

It is time to formalize the procedure. As in the pure stochastic method, let Δ be an n-dimensional random vector whose probability density function is given by Equation (2.5) on page 104. Let $g(t)$ be a density function whose mean is 1.0 and whose domain is the positive reals. Then the random variable wt, where w is a constant and t is a random variable with the density $g(t)$, obviously has mean w.

At some stage of the optimization process, we have a current center point, $\mathbf{x}$; the estimated value of the smoothed function there, $\psi(\mathbf{x}, T)$; the estimated negative gradient of the smoothed function, $\Phi(\mathbf{x}, T)$; and the current mean gradient weight, w. Generate a new random perturbation, Δ, according to the density $h(\Delta, T)$. Also generate a random gradient weight, t, according to the density $g(t)$. Evaluate the objective function at the point $\mathbf{x} + \Delta + wt\Phi(\mathbf{x}, T)$. If no improvement is made, abandon this point and generate a new random point. But if it improved, adjust the center point, the estimated smoothed function value, the gradient, and the mean gradient weight according to the new values of those quantities. The simple moving-average method described in conjunction with the pure stochastic method (page 110) is appropriate.

A code fragment is now shown that illustrates the details of this algorithm. This code is extracted from the MLFN2 program, so many declarations, memory allocations, and so forth, are omitted for clarity.

```
void LayerNet::ssg_core ()
{
  int ntemps, niters, setback ;
  int i, iter, itemp, n_good, n_bad, use_grad ;
  double tempmult, temp, fval, bestfval, starttemp, stoptemp, fquit ;
  double avg_func, new_fac, grad_weight, weight_used ;
  enum RandomDensity density ;

  use_grad = ...           // Use gradient for hinting?  (Yes, here)
  ntemps = ...             // Number of temperatures
  niters = ...             // Iterations per temperature
  setback = ...            // Set back after improvement
  starttemp = ...          // Starting temperature
  stoptemp = ...           // Stopping temperature
  density = ...            // Random density for perturbation
  fquit = ...              // Quit if error drops this low
```

Stochastic Smoothing with Gradient Hints

```
/*
   We will keep the current 'average' network weight set in avgnet.  This will be the moving
   center about which the perturbation is done.  Although not directly related to the
   algorithm itself, we keep track of the best network ever found in bestnet.  That is what
   the user will get at the end.
*/

   copy_weights ( bestnet , this ) ;   // Current weights are best so far
   copy_weights ( avgnet , this ) ;    // Center of perturbation
   bestfval = trial_error () ;

/*
   Initialize by cumulating a bunch of points
*/

   avg_func = 0.0 ;                    // Mean function around center
   if (use_grad) {
     for (i=0 ; i<n_grad ; i++)        // Zero the mean gradient
       avg_grad[i] = 0.0 ;
     }

   for (iter=0 ; iter<niters ; iter++) {  // Initializing iterations

     perturb ( avgnet , this , starttemp , density ) ; // Move randomly

     if (use_grad)                     // Also need gradient?
       fval = gradient ( grad ) ;      // Compute it along with function
     else                              // But if not
       fval = trial_error () ;         // Just find function

     avg_func += fval ;                // Cumulate mean function

     if (use_grad) {                   // Also need gradient?
       for (i=0 ; i<n_grad ; i++)      // Cumulate mean gradient
         avg_grad[i] += grad[i] ;
       }

     if (fval < bestfval) {            // If this iteration improved grand best
       bestfval = fval ;               // then update the best so far
       copy_weights ( bestnet , this ) ; // Keep the best network
```

```
      if (bestfval <= fquit)           // If we reached the user's
         goto FINISH ;                 // limit, we can quit
      }

   } // Loop: for all initial iters


   avg_func /= niters ;                // Mean of all points around avgnet
   new_fac = 1.0 / niters ;            // Weight of each point

   if (use_grad) {                     // Also need gradient?
      for (i=0 ; i<n_grad ; i++)       // Find gradient mean and length
         avg_grad[i] /= niters ;
      grad_weight = 0.5 ;              // Good for neural networks
      }


/*
   This is the temperature reduction loop and the iteration within
   temperature loop.
*/


   temp = starttemp ;
   tempmult = exp ( log ( stoptemp / starttemp ) / (ntemps-1) ) ;

   for (itemp=0 ; itemp<ntemps ; itemp++) {     // Temp reduction loop

      n_good = n_bad = 0 ;                       // Counts better and worse

      for (iter=0 ; iter<niters ; iter++) {     // Iters per temp loop

         if ((n_bad >= 10) && ((double) n_good / (double) (n_good+n_bad) < 0.15))
            break ;                             // Reduce temp if wasting time

         perturb ( avgnet , this , temp , density ) ;  // Randomly perturb about center

         if (use_grad)                          // Bias per gradient?
            weight_used = shift ( grad , this , grad_weight ) ;
```

Stochastic Smoothing with Gradient Hints

```
      if (use_grad)                            // Need gradient?
        fval = gradient ( grad ) ;
      else
        fval = trial_error () ;

      if (fval >= avg_func) {                  // If this would raise mean
        ++n_bad ;                              // Count this bad point for user
        continue ;                             // Skip it and try again
        }

      ++n_good ;                               // Count this improvement

      if (fval < bestfval) {                   // If this iteration improved record
        bestfval = fval ;                      // then update the best so far
        copy_weights ( bestnet , this ) ;      // Keep the network

        if (bestfval <= fquit)                 // If we reached the user's
          break ;                              // limit, we can quit

        iter -= setback ;                      // It often pays to keep going
        if (iter < 0)                          // at this temperature if we
          iter = 0 ;                           // are still improving
        }

      adjust ( avgnet , this , new_fac ) ;     // Move center slightly
      avg_func = new_fac * fval + (1.0 - new_fac) * avg_func ;

      if (use_grad) {
        grad_weight = new_fac * weight_used + (1.0 - new_fac) * grad_weight ;
        for (i=0 ; i<n_grad ; i++)             // Adjust mean gradient
          avg_grad[i] = new_fac * grad[i] + (1.0 - new_fac) * avg_grad[i] ;
        }
      }                                        // Loop: for all iters at a temp

/*
   Iters within temp loop now complete
*/
      if (bestfval <= fquit)                   // If we reached the user's
        break ;                                // limit, we can quit
      temp *= tempmult ;                       // Reduce temp for next pass
      }                                        // through this temperature loop
```

```
/*
   The trials left this weight set and neterr in random condition.
   Make them equal to the best, which will be the original
   if we never improved.
*/

FINISH:
   copy_weights ( this , bestnet ) ;   // Return best weights in this net
   neterr = bestfval ;                  // Trials destroyed weights, err
}
```

```
/*
--------------------------------------------------------------------------

   shift - Shift the weights toward the (negative) gradient

--------------------------------------------------------------------------
*/

double LayerNet::shift( double *grad , LayerNet *pert , double weight )
{
   int n ;
   double length, *outgrad, *hid1grad, *hid2grad, x1, x2 ;

/*
   Compute the random weight for the gradient vector.
   This is the weight parameter times a positive random variable with unit mean.
   We use 0.25 times a chi-square(4).
*/

   normal_pair ( &x1 , &x2 ) ;
   length = x1 * x1 + x2 * x2 ;
   normal_pair ( &x1 , &x2 ) ;
   length += x1 * x1 + x2 * x2 ;
   length *= 0.25 * weight ;        // This is the random weight

   if (nhid1 == 0) {                 // No hidden layer
      n = nout * (nin+1) ;
      outgrad = grad ;
```

```
      while (n--)
        pert->out_coefs[n] += outgrad[n] * length ;
      }

    else if (nhid2 == 0) {           // One hidden layer
      n = nhid1 * (nin+1) ;
      hid1grad = grad ;
      outgrad = grad + n ;
      while (n--)
        pert->hid1_coefs[n] += hid1grad[n] * length ;
      n = nout * (nhid1+1) ;
      while (n--)
        pert->out_coefs[n] += outgrad[n] * length ;
      }

    else {                            // Two hidden layers
      n = nhid1 * (nin+1) ;
      hid1grad = grad ;
      hid2grad = grad + n ;
      while (n--)
        pert->hid1_coefs[n] += hid1grad[n] * length ;
      n = nhid2 * (nhid1+1) ;
      outgrad = hid2grad + n ;
      while (n--)
        pert->hid2_coefs[n] += hid2grad[n] * length ;
      n = nout * (nhid2+1) ;
      while (n--)
        pert->out_coefs[n] += outgrad[n] * length ;
      }

  return length ;
}

/*
--------------------------------------------------------------------------

   adjust - slightly move the center

--------------------------------------------------------------------------
*/
```

```
void LayerNet::adjust ( LayerNet *cent , LayerNet *pert , double fac )
{
  int n ;
  double old ;

  old = 1.0 - fac ;

  if (nhid1 == 0) {                    // No hidden layer
    n = nout * (nin+1) ;
    while (n--)
      cent->out_coefs[n] = old*cent->out_coefs[n] + fac*pert->out_coefs[n] ;
    }

  else if (nhid2 == 0) {               // One hidden layer
    n = nhid1 * (nin+1) ;
    while (n--)
      cent->hid1_coefs[n]= old*cent->hid1_coefs[n] + fac*pert->hid1_coefs[n];
    n = nout * (nhid1+1) ;
    while (n--)
      cent->out_coefs[n] = old*cent->out_coefs[n] + fac*pert->out_coefs[n] ;
    }

  else {                               // Two hidden layers
    n = nhid1 * (nin+1) ;
    while (n--)
      cent->hid1_coefs[n] = old*cent->hid1_coefs[n] + fac*pert->hid1_coefs[n] ;
    n = nhid2 * (nhid1+1) ;
    while (n--)
      cent->hid2_coefs[n] = old*cent->hid2_coefs[n] + fac*pert->hid2_coefs[n] ;
    n = nout * (nhid2+1) ;
    while (n--)
      cent->out_coefs[n] = old*cent->out_coefs[n] + fac*pert->out_coefs[n] ;
    }
}
```

This code starts by setting the usual stochastic optimization parameters: the number of temperatures, iterations per temperature, setback amount, starting and stopping temperatures, random density, and user's quitting error. Also, the flag use_grad tells the algorithm to use gradient hints. Two network weight sets will be kept in scratch storage. One of them, avgnet, is the current mean point around which perturbation will be performed. At any time, this is the location of the most recent estimate of the minimum of the smoothed function. It is this point that will creep steadily toward better and better areas of the error surface. The other scratch weight set, bestnet, plays no direct role in the algorithm. Every time the error function is evaluated at a randomly selected point, the function value is compared to the record best. Whenever the record is broken, the lucky network that produced such good results is saved in bestnet. It is this network that will be returned to the user when the algorithm is complete.

The algorithm is initialized by performing niters random perturbations centered at the starting weight set. The averages of the function and the gradient are cumulated. The perturbations are done at the starting temperature. This provides a very smoothed function and gradient. The grand best network is also found for possible (though unlikely) return to the user. No setback is used. This is a very expensive operation, and there is no point in prolonging it any longer than necessary to get a rough estimate of the means.

After the initialization loop is complete, the function and gradient sums are divided by the number of samples that went into those sums, giving the means. Every time a good step is taken later, the new point will influence the current means by the new_fac amount. The most intuitive value for this factor is the contribution of each point to the ensemble of niters samples. Brave readers may wish to increase this quantity, understanding that the price paid will be reduced probability of locating the global minimum. Finally, grad_weight is initialized to 0.5, which is heuristically known to be generally good for neural network applications. This quantity specifies the mean value of the random number generator that supplies gradient weights. It will be adjusted later as needed.

The temperature reduction loop starts out at starttemp, and on each pass the temperature will be reduced by a factor of tempmult. At the beginning of each pass through this loop, the counters n_good and n_bad are zeroed so that they may be used to count the number of good (improved) and bad random points. These quantities play no part whatsoever in the actual algorithm. However, as previously discussed, it is good to print them for the user so that the performance of the algorithm, especially as regards convergence, can be ascertained.

The first action taken inside the internal iteration loop is to see if the fraction of trial points that are being accepted is small. If so, we are wasting time and the temperature should be reduced. Otherwise, randomly perturb the point around the current center, avgnet. If gradient hints are to be used, the perturbed point is shifted in the direction of the negative gradient. The shift routine returns the value of the random weight that was used for the shift. That allows the mean weight to be optimized later. Then the function value at that trial point is computed, perhaps along with the gradient.

If the function value at the trial point exceeds the average around the center, the trial point is abandoned. We obviously do not want to move in a direction that would increase the value of the smoothed function. If improvement was had, we take several actions. Check to see if this point is better than the grand best. If so, update the grand best and set back the iteration counter. Then slightly adjust everything. The center point, avgnet, and the mean function there are both adjusted. If gradient hinting is in use, the mean gradient weight and the gradient itself are adjusted.

At the bottom of the temperature loop, we must see if the user's quitting error was attained in the inner loop. If so, we are done. Otherwise, reduce the temperature and make another pass. When all passes are complete, retrieve the grand best network for the caller.

The shift subroutine generates a random weight using a distribution whose mean value is the weight calling parameter and whose domain excludes negative numbers. A reasonable choice may be based on a chi-square with four degrees of freedom. This distribution is never negative, and it has a moderately heavy right tail so that if the initial weight is grossly underestimated, rapid recovery is possible. This random variable is generated as the sum of the squares of four normal random deviates. The sum is multiplied by 0.25 to produce a unit mean, then multiplied by weight to provide the required mean. The network's weights are shifted by this random number times the gradient, and the random number is returned to provide for continuous optimization.

The adjust subroutine is called to adjust the current center, avgnet, in the direction of a successful trial point. Its actions are so trivial that it is almost a waste to print it here. But for the sake of completeness, this code is provided, so that no question on its operation may remain. The adjustment is exactly the same as that for the mean function, the gradient, and the gradient weight.

4

Probabilistic Neural Networks I: Introduction

- A strong intuitive foundation

- The mathematics of the original model

- Donald Specht's neural network architecture

- An effective training algorithm

- Complete source code for implementing the PNN

Sometimes the line between neural networks and traditional statistical techniques becomes a little thin. That is the case for members of the *probabilistic neural network* (PNN) family. The mathematical foundation on which they are built has been known for several decades, having been discovered long before neural networks were more than a twinkle in someone's eye. However, the unusually large computational requirements of the algorithm caused it to fade into obscurity. Even moderate-size problems required memory and CPU speed far beyond what was available at that time.

The mother of all PNNs was described by Meisel (1972), although it existed in other related forms even earlier. Despite its known theoretical power, it remained practically unused until Donald Specht (1990a) cast it in the form of a neural network by showing how this algorithm could be broken down into a great number of simple components that could largely operate in parallel. Because this neural network had its roots in probability theory, he called it a probabilistic neural network. Later in this chapter we will see how he organized the flow of operations into layers, and how he delegated separate responsibilities to the neurons in each layer. But to start out, we will present the method in a form closer to its statistical origin.

Foundations of the PNN

The PNN is fundamentally a classifier. Later, we will see that continuous mappings can be coaxed from it. But originally it was designed and formulated as an algorithm that is trained on members of two or more classes. Its ultimate use is to examine unknowns and to decide to which class they belong. Therefore, let us consider classification. For simplicity, we will work with two classes, each being described by two variables. Members of these classes can be plotted as a scatter plot. Each class member can be shown by a single symbol whose horizontal position is determined by the value of one variable, and whose vertical position is determined by the other.

Examine Figure 4.1. It is clear that the unknown, represented by a question mark, belongs to the lower-left class. This is despite the fact that it is actually closer to the centroid of the upper-right class. We see that good classifiers examine more than just central tendencies. They take into account the total pattern into which class members fall.

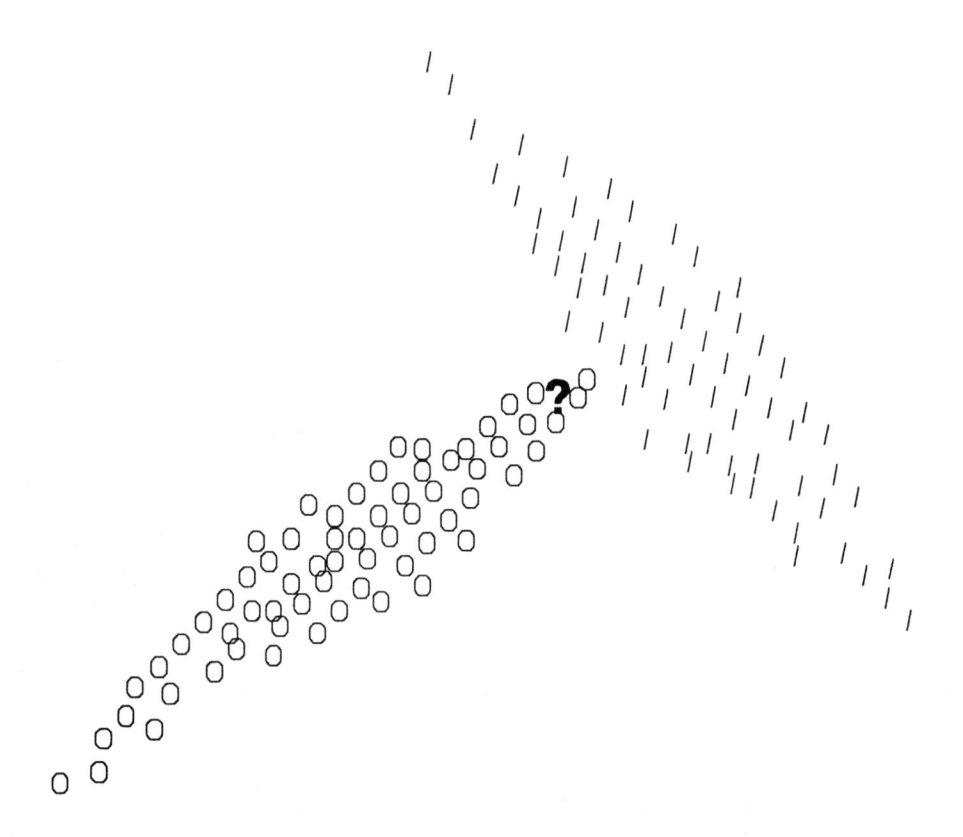

Figure 4.1 Classification must use overall shape.

Now examine Figure 4.2. There is quite excellent separation between the two classes, so we should be able to construct a successful classifier. Yet many (or most) traditional classification algorithms would fail when confronted with the bimodal distribution of one of these classes. Thus, a truly versatile classifier should be able to handle multiple modes.

Those two examples might lead the reader to devise a simple classification algorithm. This method computes the distance between the unknown and all members of the training set. It then assigns the unknown case to the class to which the closest training case belongs. This method will obviously work for both Figures 4.1 and 4.2. In fact, this is a commonly used method called the *nearest-neighbor* classifier. Unfortunately, Figure 4.3 shows us that it is not always foolproof.

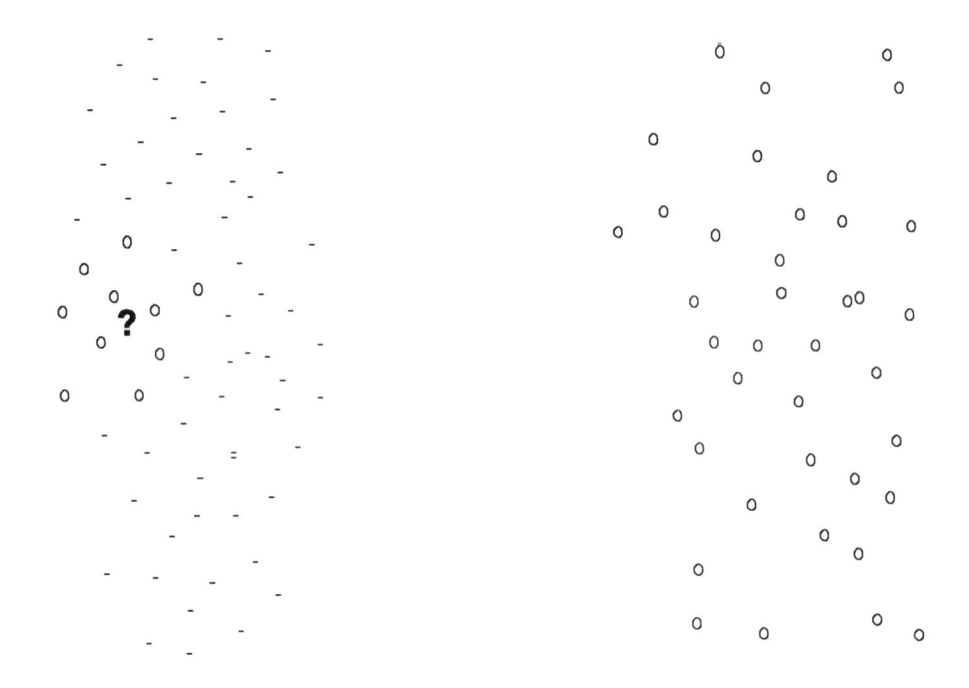

Figure 4.2 Classes may have multiple modes.

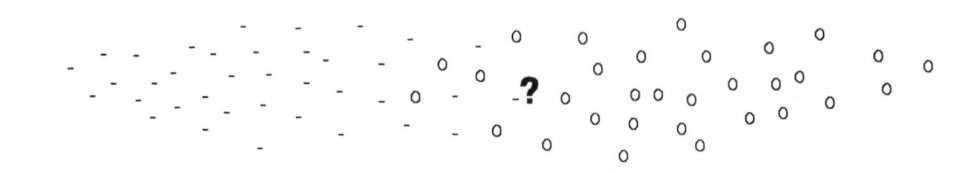

Figure 4.3 Nearest-neighbor methods can fail.

Figure 4.3 bears close examination. It should be apparent that the unknown probably belongs to the right class, and we must not be misled by the fact that it is closer to a member of the left class than to any member of the right class. Why do we believe that it is more likely a member of the right class? The reason is that the density of the left class is very thin where the unknown is located, while the density of the right class is much larger. There is only one member of the left class near the unknown, while members of the right class are all around. We are guided by more than mere proximity. We take into account the quantity of class representatives nearby. Since there are so many more members of the right class in the vicinity, we conclude that the unknown is more likely a member of that class than of the left class, which is so sparse there. This intuition is at the core of the PNN development that follows.

PNN versus MLFN versus Traditional Statistics

It is worthwhile to digress briefly so that we may see where PNNs fit into the overall classification picture. Nearly all standard statistical classification algorithms assume some knowledge of the distribution of the random variables used to classify. In particular, the multivariate normal distribution is frequently assumed, and the training set is used only to estimate the mean vectors and covariance matrix of the populations. While some deviation from normality is tolerated, large deviations usually cause problems. In particular, multimodal distributions cause even most nonparametric methods to fail. One of the beauties of neural networks is that they can typically handle even the most complex distributions. Multiple-layer feedforward networks (MLFNs) have been shown to be excellent classifiers. However, they have two problems: One is that little is known about how they operate and what behavior is theoretically expected of them. A more pragmatic criticism is that their training speed can be seriously slow. The PNN, on the other hand, has superb mathematical credentials, usually trains orders of magnitude faster than MLFNs, and classifies as well as or better than they do. Its principal disadvantages are that it is relatively slow to classify, and it requires large amounts of memory. (Some modifications of the basic PNN alleviate these difficulties at the expense of slower training.) Most important of all for many applications is that it can often provide mathematically sound confidence levels for its decisions. That fact alone has made the PNN a favorite for military applications.

Another situation in which the PNN is favored is if the data is likely to contain *outliers*, points that are very different from the majority. In most implementations of the model, outliers will have no real effect on decisions regarding the more frequent cases, yet they will be properly handled if they are valid data. Outliers are generally more of a threat to other neural network models, and they can totally devastate many traditional statistical techniques.

Bayes Classification

This section discusses what is probably the single most popular classification paradigm. The PNN is strongly based on Bayes' method of classification. So let us start by presenting an elementary but quite adequate description of Bayes' method.

We have a collection of random samples from K populations. The populations are indexed by k, $k = 1, ..., K$. Each of these samples is a vector $\mathbf{x} = [x_1, ..., x_m]$. In the most general case, we may want to allow for the possibility that the different populations may have different probabilities of delivering random samples to us. These *prior probabilities* are designated by h_k. When we misclassify a case that truly belongs to population k, the cost associated with this misclassification is c_k. In many or most applications, the prior probabilities, h_k, are treated as being equal. The same is true of the costs, c_k. We will often be able to ignore these quantities; however, in the spirit of generality, they will be included.

The complete collection of samples from known populations is called the *training set*. It contains n_1 samples from population 1, n_2 samples from population 2, and so forth, through n_K samples from population K. What we need to generate from this training set is an algorithm that will enable us to determine the population from which an unknown sample is taken. If we can find an algorithm whose expected misclassification cost does not exceed that of any other algorithm based on that training set, that algorithm is called *Bayes optimal*.

It can be proved that if we happen to know the true probability density functions $f_k(\mathbf{x})$ for all populations, then there is a Bayes optimal decision rule. What we do is classify an unknown sample $\mathbf{x}$ into population i if

$$h_i\, c_i\, f_i(\mathbf{x}) > h_j\, c_j\, f_j(\mathbf{x}) \tag{4.1}$$

for all populations j not equal to i.

The proof that the above decision rule does in fact minimize the expected cost of misclassification can be found in a vast number of statistics texts. The reader of this text will not be burdened with yet another presentation. That rule should satisfy the intuition, though. The density $f_k(\mathbf{x})$ corresponds to the concentration of class k cases around the unknown, as was discussed in conjunction with Figure 4.3

on page 160. The Bayes rule tells us to favor a class if it has high density in the vicinity of the unknown. The rule also tells us to favor a class if its prior probability is high, or if the cost of misclassifying it is high. These are all sensible criteria.

The problem with the above rule is that we generally do not know the probability density functions $f_k(\mathbf{x})$. All we have is a training set from which we must infer the density functions. If we are willing to go out on a limb by assuming that the densities have a particular form, such as the normal distribution, we may be able to estimate the parameters of each distribution with the training cases. That is risky, though. The fewer assumptions that we must endure, the better. This brings us to the next topic.

Parzen's Method of Density Estimation

Parzen (1962) presented an excellent method for estimating a univariate probability density function from a random sample. His estimator converges asymptotically to the true density as the sample size increases. Parzen's PDF estimator uses a weight function, $W(d)$ (called a *potential function* in Meisel (1972), and frequently called a *kernel*), which has its largest value at $d = 0$ and which decreases rapidly as the absolute value of d increases. One of these weight functions is centered at each training sample point, with the value of each sample's function at a given abscissa x being determined by the distance d between x and that sample point. His PDF estimator is a scaled sum of that function for all sample cases. This is illustrated in Figure 4.4.

In that figure we have eight sample points: 0.15, 0.20, 0.21, 0.25, 0.26, 0.35, 0.50, and 0.70. Each of these points is the center of a bell-shaped window function. The sum of these eight functions is also graphed. For this particular sample, and using this weight function, Parzen's density approximation would be that sum times a constant. It should be obvious that such an estimator is reasonable. In practice, it turns out that it is actually very good, and that as the sample size increases, it approaches the true density arbitrarily closely under quite loose conditions.

Let us state Parzen's method mathematically. We collect a sample of size n from a single population. The estimated density function for that population is shown in Equation (4.2).

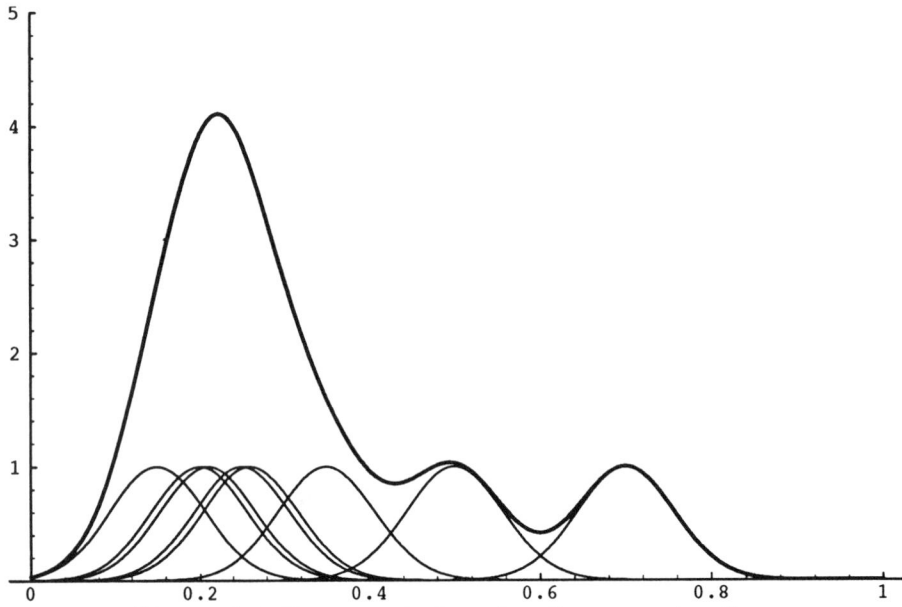

Figure 4.4 Parzen window density approximation.

$$g(x) = \frac{1}{n\sigma} \sum_{i=1}^{n} W\left(\frac{x-x_i}{\sigma}\right) \tag{4.2}$$

The scaling parameter sigma (σ) defines the width of the bell curve that surrounds each sample point. As will be seen in Equation (4.6), it should decrease as the sample size increases. As we will also see later, the choice of σ can have a profound influence on the performance of the PNN. Values that are too small cause individual training cases to exert too much influence, losing the benefit of aggregate information. Values of σ that are too large cause so much blurring that the details of the density are lost, often distorting the density estimate badly. See, for example, Figures 4.5 through 4.8. Those four figures are density estimates from the same data and bell-shaped window that were used in Figure 4.4. They show the effect of different choices for the window width, σ.

Foundations of the PNN

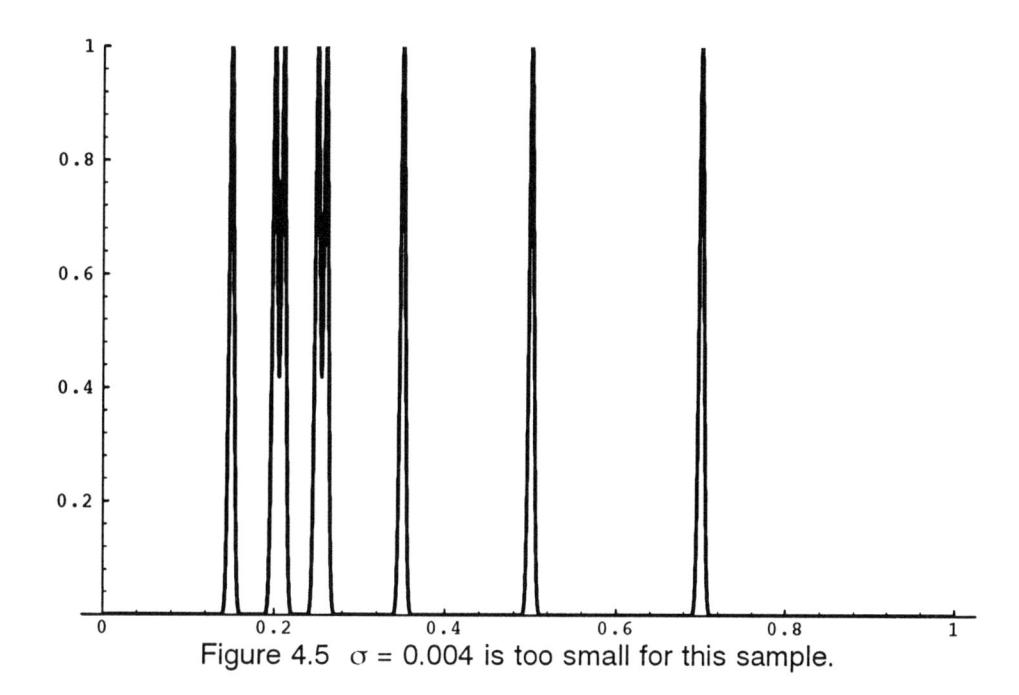

Figure 4.5 $\sigma = 0.004$ is too small for this sample.

Figure 4.6 $\sigma = 0.05$ is probably still too small.

Figure 4.7 σ = 0.1 is just about right.

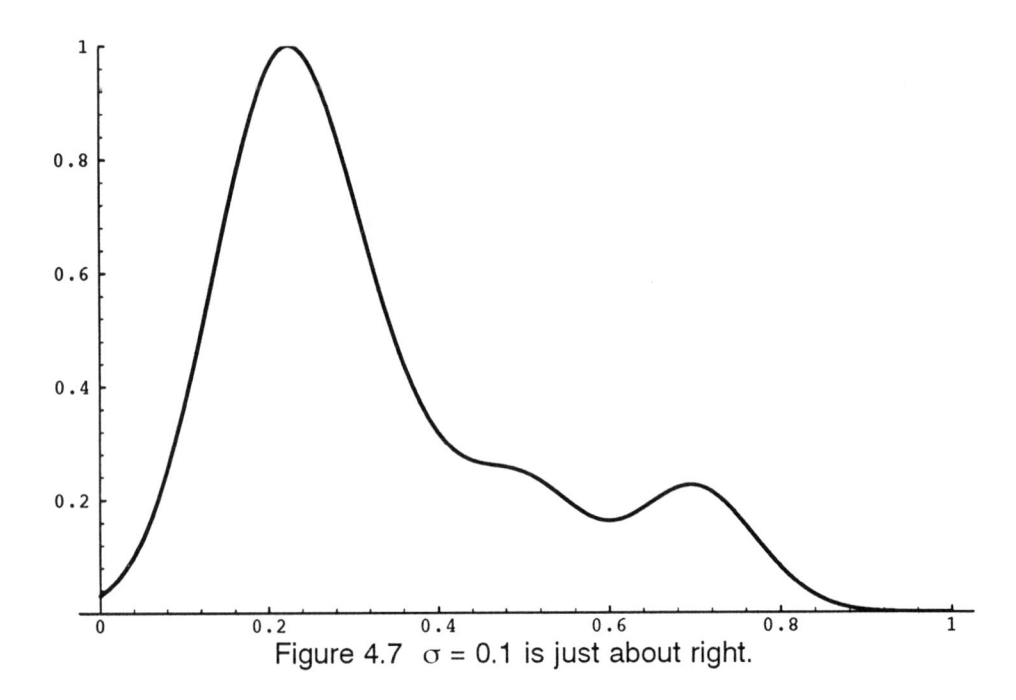

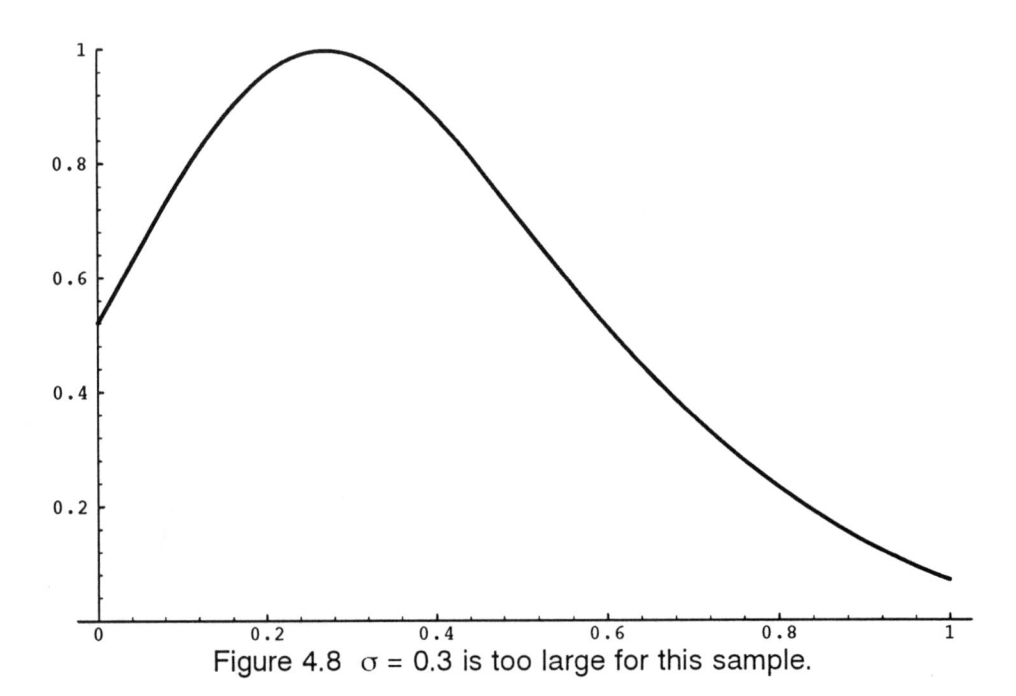

Figure 4.8 σ = 0.3 is too large for this sample.

Foundations of the PNN

We have considerable freedom in choosing the weight function. There are surprisingly few restrictions on its properties. Parzen (1962) and Specht (1990a) state them explicitly. Our presentation will be a bit less rigorous, being given only for the benefit of those few readers who might want to experiment with their own weight functions.

- The weight function must be bounded.

$$\sup_{d} |W(d)| < \infty \qquad (4.3)$$

- The weight function must rapidly go to zero as its argument increases in absolute value. This restriction, which is the most likely to be violated by careless experimenters, is expressed in two conditions.

$$\int_{-\infty}^{\infty} |W(x)| \, dx < \infty$$
$$\lim_{x \to \infty} |x W(x)| = 0 \qquad (4.4)$$

- The weight function must be properly normalized if the estimate is going to be a density function, rather than just a constant multiple of a density function.

$$\int_{-\infty}^{\infty} W(x) \, dx = 1 \qquad (4.5)$$

- In order to achieve correct asymptotic behavior, the window must become narrower as the sample size increases. If we express σ as a function of n, the sample size, two conditions must be true.

$$\lim_{n \to \infty} \sigma_n = 0$$
$$\lim_{n \to \infty} n \sigma_n = \infty \qquad (4.6)$$

The weighting function W most often employed is the Gaussian function. Note that this has nothing to do with normality assumptions. It is purely for the many conveniences supplied by the Gaussian function. That function is well behaved and easily computed. It satisfies the conditions required by Parzen's method. And last, but certainly not least, years of experience indicate that it is a reliable performer.

Despite the strong tradition inherent in the Gaussian function, it must be remembered that an infinite number of other choices is possible. For this reason, a few simple alternatives will be presented. One of these may be superior for the reader's application. On the other hand, I am of the firm opinion that the Gaussian is virtually always the best kernel function, so it will be prominently featured. The (normalized for unit area) Gaussian function is shown in Equation (4.7).

$$g(x) = \frac{1}{\sqrt{2\pi}\,\sigma} e^{\left(\frac{-x^2}{2\sigma^2}\right)} \tag{4.7}$$

The Gaussian kernel, shown in Figure 4.9(a), is so well behaved and widely accepted that there is little reason to look for alternatives. However, in case any readers want to experiment, a few alternatives will be mentioned.

There is one possible small problem with the Gaussian kernel. Since it involves an exponential, it can be slow to compute. In most practical cases, we will be working with multivariate samples (which will be discussed later). In such cases, the dominant eater-of-time is computing dot products, so the exponentiation is trivial. But if not, there are alternatives.

The most primitive fast alternative to the Gaussian kernel is a histogram bin. This is shown in Equation (4.8) and Figure 4.9(b).

$$W(x) = \begin{cases} \frac{1}{2\sigma} & |x| < \sigma \\ 0 & \text{otherwise} \end{cases} \tag{4.8}$$

It is easy to chop off the sharp corners of the bin approach. Equation (4.9) is probably a better kernel. See Figure 4.9(c).

Foundations of the PNN

a

b

c

d

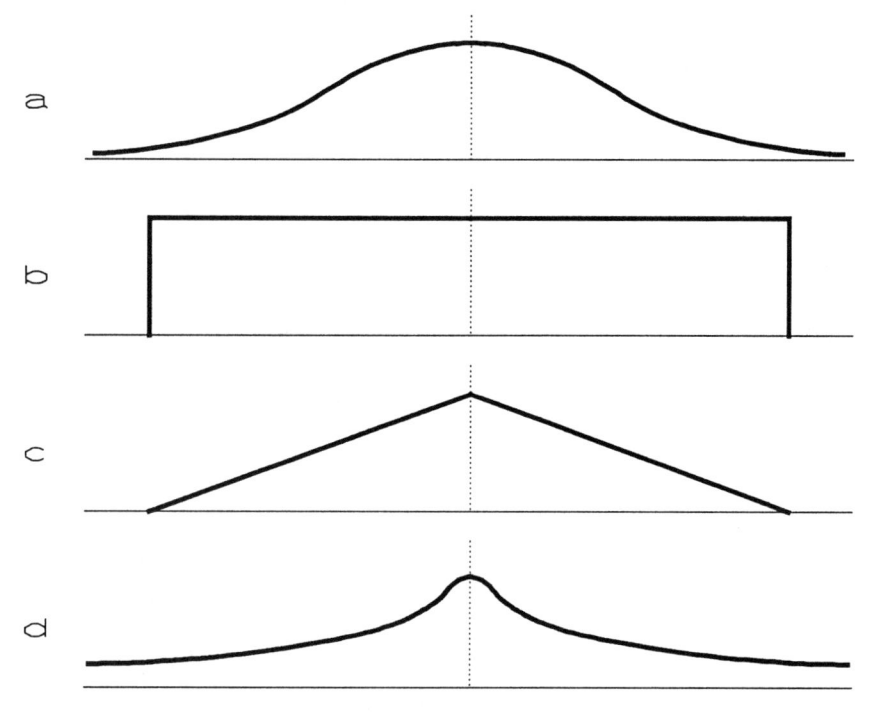

Figure 4.9 Four common Parzen kernels.

$$W(x) = \begin{cases} \dfrac{1}{\sigma}\left(1 - \left|\dfrac{x}{\sigma}\right|\right) & |x| < \sigma \\ 0 & \text{otherwise} \end{cases} \quad (4.9)$$

Both of those alternative kernels drop to zero at $x = \sigma$. That means that the estimated density can be zero in areas where the sample is sparse. It would usually be more realistic if the estimated density were some very small positive number. This can be attained with Equation (4.10). It is plotted in Figure 4.9(d).

$$W(x) = \dfrac{1}{\pi\sigma\left[1 + \left(\dfrac{x}{\sigma}\right)^2\right]} \quad (4.10)$$

Multivariate Extension of Parzen's Method

Cacoullos (1966) extended Parzen's method to the multivariate case. Things become much more complicated because the most general formulation allows each variable X_i to have its own scale factor σ_i, and the kernel function is multivariate. The fully general density estimator is shown in Equation (4.11).

$$g(x_1, ..., x_p) = \frac{1}{n\, \sigma_1\, \sigma_2 \cdots \sigma_p} \cdot \sum_{i=1}^{n} W\!\left(\frac{x_1 - x_{1,i}}{\sigma_1},\, ...,\, \frac{x_p - x_{p,i}}{\sigma_p}\right) \quad (4.11)$$

One or both of two common simplifications may be employed to reduce the complexity of that equation. First, we may assume that all sigmas are equal: $\sigma_0 = \sigma_1 = ... = \sigma$. This may be a reasonable assumption if all of the variables are normalized to approximately the same variation. However, as will be seen in the next chapter, the value of each σ can be optimized in such a way that each becomes almost a measure of that variable's importance. We cannot always afford the equality assumption. However, for the remainder of this chapter, we will live with it.

The other common simplification involves the nature of the multivariate kernel. We can achieve tremendous economy by letting it be the product of univariate kernels as shown in Equation (4.12).

$$W(x_1, ..., x_p) = \prod_{i=1}^{p} W_i(x_i) \quad (4.12)$$

That equation indexes the univariate kernels according to the variable on which they are used. In practice, we would nearly always use the same univariate kernel for every variable, with any differences being limited at most to different scalings.

By far the most common multivariate density estimator uses both of those simplifications along with the univariate Gaussian kernel of Equation (4.7). If we remember that $e^a\, e^b = e^{a+b}$, and that the squared length of a vector is the sum of the squares of its components, we can write that common density estimator as Equation (4.13). Bold roman typeface is used to remind the reader that **x** is a vector.

$$g(\mathbf{x}) = \frac{1}{(2\pi)^{p/2} \sigma^p n} \sum_{i=1}^{n} e^{-\frac{|\mathbf{x}-\mathbf{x}_i|^2}{2\sigma^2}} \qquad (4.13)$$

Just as was the case for a univariate density, the population density function estimated from the training set is the average of separate multivariate normal distributions. Each distribution is centered at a different case in the training set.

The density estimator shown in Equation (4.13) is essentially what we shall use for the remainder of this chapter (except for some trivial rescaling to reduce computational loads). That is the foundation of the original PNN as proposed by Donald Specht. It is also the estimator used in virtually every commercial neural network program available at the time of this writing. It has a long history of good-to-excellent performance, and its training speed is fast. In the next chapter we will explore more powerful alternatives, but this solid old workhorse must not be disparaged in any way.

The Original PNN

On page 162 we examined Bayes' method of classification and learned that it has the laudable property of minimizing the expected cost of misclassification. All that lacked was knowledge of the population density functions. Then, on page 163, we learned about an excellent method for estimating population densities from samples. Voilà! We have a classifier. And it's a good one, too. Provided that σ is not overly large, that classifier should be able to handle multiple modes such as depicted in Figure 4.2, a job that few other classifiers can touch. And it's even asymptotically Bayes optimal. One could hardly ask for more in regard to capabilities.

This amazing classifier, which was discovered decades ago, would have come into widespread use much earlier if sufficient computation power had been available. But the memory required to store every training sample for the Parzen density estimator, and the vast amount of computation needed for that estimator, far outreached the technology of the era. By the time sufficient power became widely available, the whole method somehow had been forgotten by all but a few people well-versed in statistics. Then Donald Specht discovered that the Bayes-Parzen classifier could be cast in the form of a neural network. In Specht (1990a) he showed how the algorithm could be split up into a large number of simple processes, each of which has its own dedicated procedure, and most of which can run in parallel. That is the essence of a neural network. The implication of this discovery is that extremely fast hardware implementations of the algorithm are possible. Specht's PNN architecture for a small network is shown in Figure 4.10.

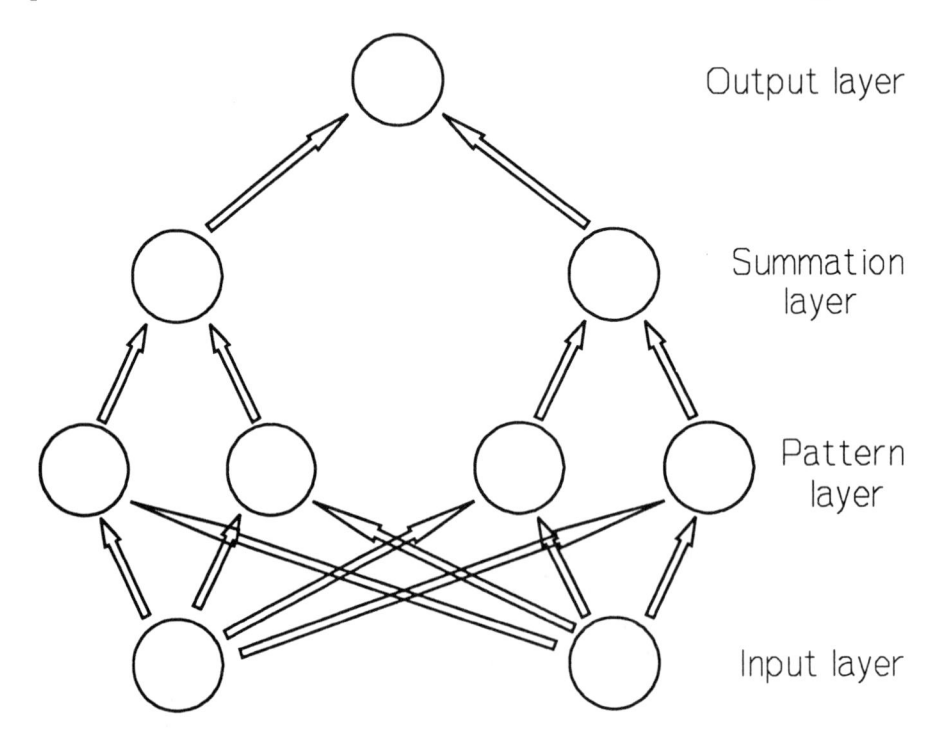

Figure 4.10 Specht's PNN architecture.

The network in Figure 4.10 is very small. It has two inputs, two classes, and two training cases in each class. The pattern layer contains one neuron for each training case. The summation layer has one neuron for each class. Execution starts by simultaneously presenting the input vector to all pattern layer neurons. Each pattern neuron computes a distance measure between the input and the training case represented by that neuron. It then subjects that distance measure to the neuron's activation function, which is essentially the Parzen window. The following layer contains summation units that have a modest task. Each summation neuron is dedicated to a single class. It simply sums the pattern layer neurons corresponding to members of that summation neuron's class. The attained activation of summation neuron k is the estimated density function value of population k. The output neuron is a trivial threshold discriminator. It decides which of its inputs from the summation units is the maximum. The PNN architecture is elegantly simple, yet capable of extremely highspeed operation if the pattern units can be operated in parallel.

Computation in the PNN

This section provides explicit instructions for all of the computations involved in the basic PNN. It also gives hints for improving efficiency in specialized cases, and lists C++ code for implementing an effective PNN.

Examine once again Equation (4.1) on page 162, which shows how to classify using Bayes' rule. Observe that an estimated density appears on both sides of the expression. If, rather than working with densities, we worked with constant multiples of densities, and if the constant were the same for all classes, the results obtained would be identical to those obtained by estimating true densities. In other words, for classification purposes, we can remove the restriction on $W(d)$ expressed in Equation (4.5). This lets us use a simpler weight function.

The elementary PNN that is the subject of this section uses identical scale factors σ for all classes. This throws σ into the role of being a constant factor in all densities. Thus, for classification purposes, it can be ignored along with the density normalizing factor. It also simplifies some of the mathematics if we absorb the constant 2 into σ, treating that quantity as a single scaling factor. A streamlined classification function (which is now just a *multiple* of a probability density) reduces to the general formulation shown in Equation (4.14).

$$g(\mathbf{x}) = \frac{1}{n} \sum_{i=1}^{n} W\left(\frac{\|\mathbf{x} - \mathbf{x}_i\|}{\sigma}\right) \qquad (4.14)$$

Use of the Euclidean distance in that equation is not mandatory. Other distance measures are possible, but are almost never used. Fukunaga (1972) provides a detailed listing of the requirements that the combination of the distance function with the weighting function must satisfy in order to achieve correct asymptotic results.

The most common weighting function is the unnormalized Gaussian, shown in Equation (4.15).

$$W(d) = e^{-d^2} \qquad (4.15)$$

The Gaussian kernel has many advantages. It has a fairly flat top, so the influence of a sample point carries over steadily across a modest range. Then it tapers off smoothly and becomes, for all practical purposes, zero after a certain distance. This prevents sample points from exerting distant influences. The Gaussian function has a long history of success and is generally recommended.

The only disadvantage of the Gaussian kernel is that computation of the exponentiation function may sometimes consume too much time. In that unusual case, a reasonable alternative is shown in Equation(4.16).

$$W(d) = \frac{1}{1+d^2} \qquad (4.16)$$

This alternative kernel is much faster to compute than the Gaussian. But it has a relatively peaked maximum, perhaps giving undue emphasis to individual sample points. Worse, its tails are very long. The influence of a sample point can extend for a considerable distance. Whether or not these tradeoffs are significant is problem dependent. It is likely that their severity will increase for smaller training sets. Figures 4.11 and 4.12 compare the effect of these two weight functions on four bivariate sample points.

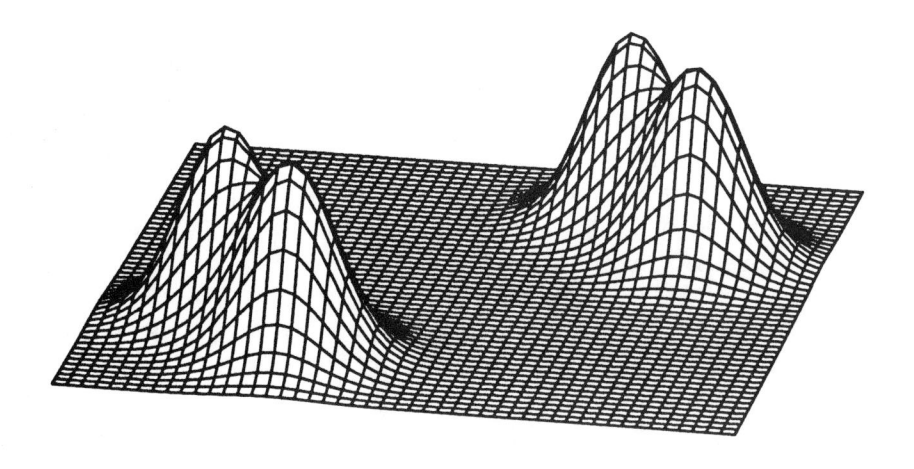

Figure 4.11 Gaussian kernel.

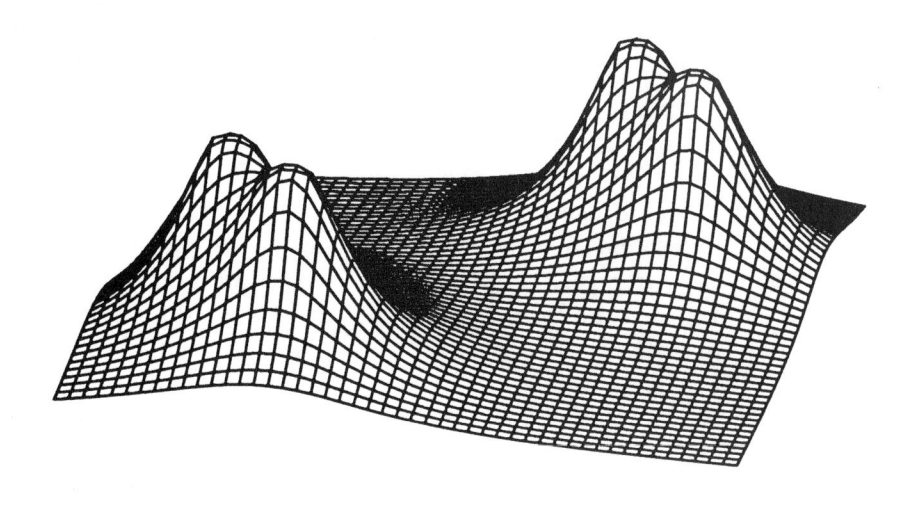

Figure 4.12 $1/(1+d^2)$ kernel.

A situation often arises in which a special property of the application's data can be used to effect a significant speedup of PNN computation. This happens when the problem is such that the X vectors that are sampled always lie on the surface of a sphere whose radius is constant. This property of constant length can sometimes be forced even when it may not appear to occur naturally. For example, suppose that the data is binary. The instinct may be to code all observations as 0 and 1. However, if they are coded as −1 and 1 instead, it can be seen that we have the property of constant length. How do we take advantage of this property? Look at the identity expressed in Equation (4.17).

$$d^2(X,Y) = (X-Y) \cdot (X-Y) = X \cdot X + Y \cdot Y - 2 X \cdot Y \quad (4.17)$$

Suppose the vector length of every case, whether unknown or in the training set, is constant. Then the $X \bullet X$ and $Y \bullet Y$ terms in the above equation will also be constant. Rather than subtracting two vectors and squaring the differences of each component, we only need to compute the dot product of the unknown with each training sample. And there is even another simplification if the data is binary. Computing the dot product of two binary vectors is equivalent to counting the number of variables in the two cases that have the same binary value. Careful coding can result in significant speed improvements.

Code for Computing PNN Classification

This section presents a short code fragment for implementing the basic PNN classifier already discussed. This is not a self-contained program. It is extracted from a C++ class function, so it refers to several private class variables. However, these variables are named in such a way that their meanings should be obvious. A complete listing of this subroutine in context can be found in the module BASIC.CPP on the accompanying code disk.

```
width = 1.0 / (sigma * sigma) ;          // Multiplies Euclidean distances

for (pop=0 ; pop<npop ; pop++)           // For each population
   out[pop] = 0.0 ;                      // will sum kernels here
```

The Original PNN

```
for (case=0 ; case<ncases ; case++) {        // Do all training cases

  dptr = ... ;                                // Point to this training case
  pop = ... ;                                 // Get its class (0 to npop-1)

  dsq = 0.0 ;                                 // Will sum distance here
  for (ivar=0 ; ivar<nin ; ivar++) {          // All variables in this case
    diff = input[ivar] - dptr[ivar] ;         // Unknown minus case
    dsq += diff * diff ;                      // Cumulate Euclidean distance
    }
  dsq *= width ;                              // Divide by sigma squared

  if (kernel == KERNEL_GAUSS)                 // If Gaussian kernel
    out[pop] += exp ( -dsq ) ;                // Sum that function
  else if (kernel == KERNEL_RECIP)            // Faster alternative
    out[pop] += 1.0 / ( 1.0 + dsq ) ;         // So sum it
  } // For all training cases

/*
  Return the class having highest output
*/

  best = -1.0 ;                               // Keep track of max across pops
  for (pop=0 ; pop<npop ; pop++) {            // For each population
    if (out[pop] > best) {                    // find the highest activation
      best = out[pop] ;
      ibest = pop ;
      }
    }
  return ibest ;
```

Optimizing Sigma

By now it should be clear that finding a good value of σ is crucial to competent performance, yet there is no universal, mathematically rigorous method for choosing the best value. Consider a bivariate sample of eight points from a single population. Suppose the population has two modes, and our sample contains four points from each. The density functions estimated with the Gaussian weighting function, for several different values of σ, are shown in Figures 4.13 through 4.16.

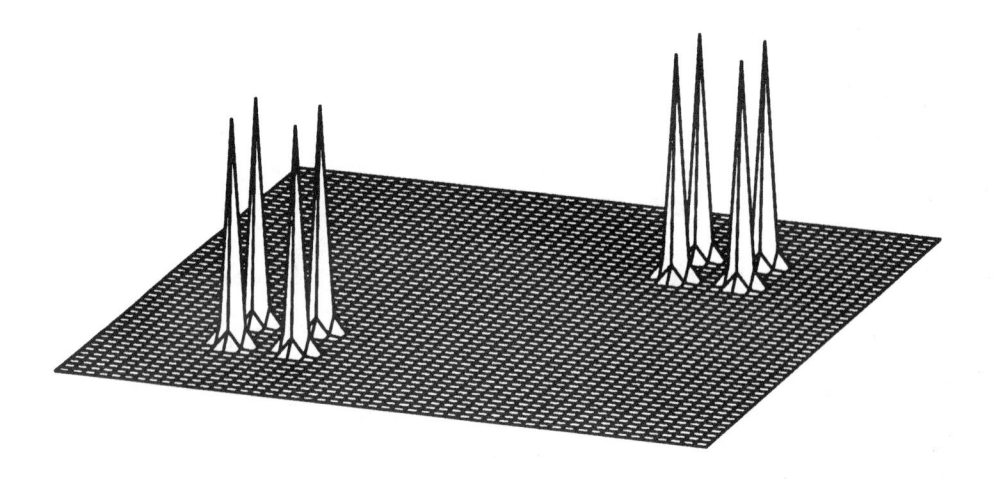

Figure 4.13 Sigma is too small.

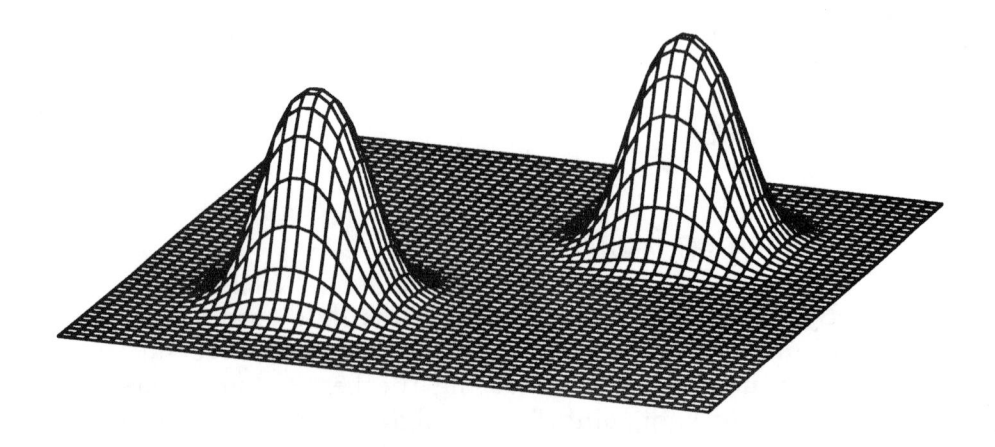

Figure 4.14 Sigma on the small side of good.

The Original PNN

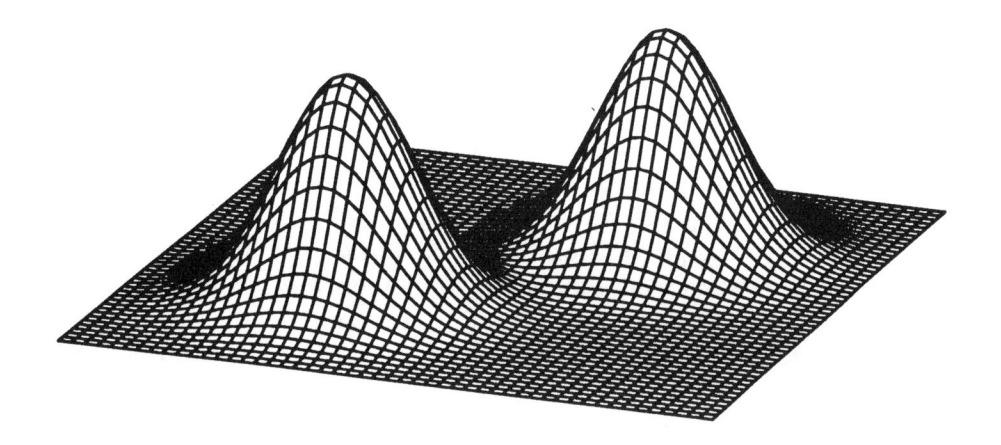

Figure 4.15 Sigma on the large side of good.

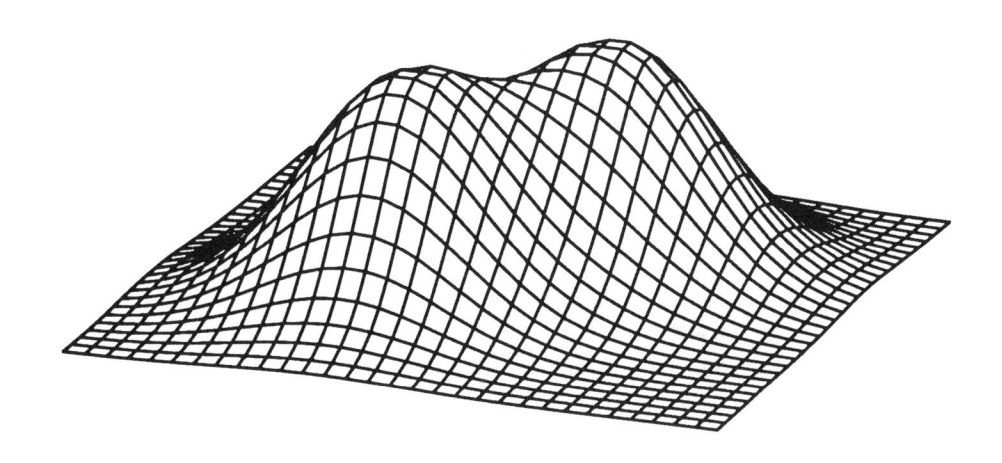

Figure 4.16 Sigma is too large.

Figure 4.13 shows the effect of the scaling parameter being too small. The combined influence of neighbors in a cluster is totally eliminated. We are left with essentially a nearest neighbor classifier. Figure 4.14 shows a good choice for σ, though perhaps a bit on the small side. Each of the two population modes is well defined, the samples work together to represent the mode, and the wilderness between the modes (where members of other populations may perhaps lie) remains isolated. Figure 4.15 is still a good σ, though it may be tending toward excessive size. The blurring between population centers may or may not be correct. Figure 4.16 shows the effect of σ being too large. The population density is blurred so badly that unless the other populations were extremely well separated from this, confusion would surely result. We can visually perceive when σ is much too large or small. But how can we automate that choice? And how can we trim it up for optimal behavior? That is the subject of this section.

Before becoming too deeply immersed in the subject of computing an optimal value of sigma, it would be good to ponder the question of whether we are undertaking a reasonable task. Let us consider a ridiculous, but revealing, situation. Suppose that our samples are bivariate. We measure the height and weight of experimental subjects in order to classify them in some way. What if we measure their height in millimeters and their weight in kilograms? The height variables would be vastly larger than the weight variables. That is not good. When the distance measure between an unknown case and a training case is computed, the height variable would dominate the distance. This is true regardless of the value of sigma. If such disparate measurements were absolutely necessary, a situation that I cannot envision, then the only recourse would be to use separate sigmas for the two variables. But that subject will not be covered until the next chapter. What do we do now, when we need to keep the PNN simple? There is only one choice. We must rescale the variables so that they are commensurate in variation. If we do not do so, there is no point in trying to optimize sigma, as the PNN itself will be crippled. Never forget that. It is crucial to good performance.

Now we can get back to the problem at hand. The optimal value of σ for every problem is different. It may be on the order of 100, or it may be on the order of 0.001. Larger sample sizes almost invariably benefit from smaller values of σ, but that rule is vague. We need to find a method for providing an effective value based on the training set. And be assured that this effort is not in vain. Figure 4.17 is based on an actual problem from my own case file. It shows the percent

Pct error

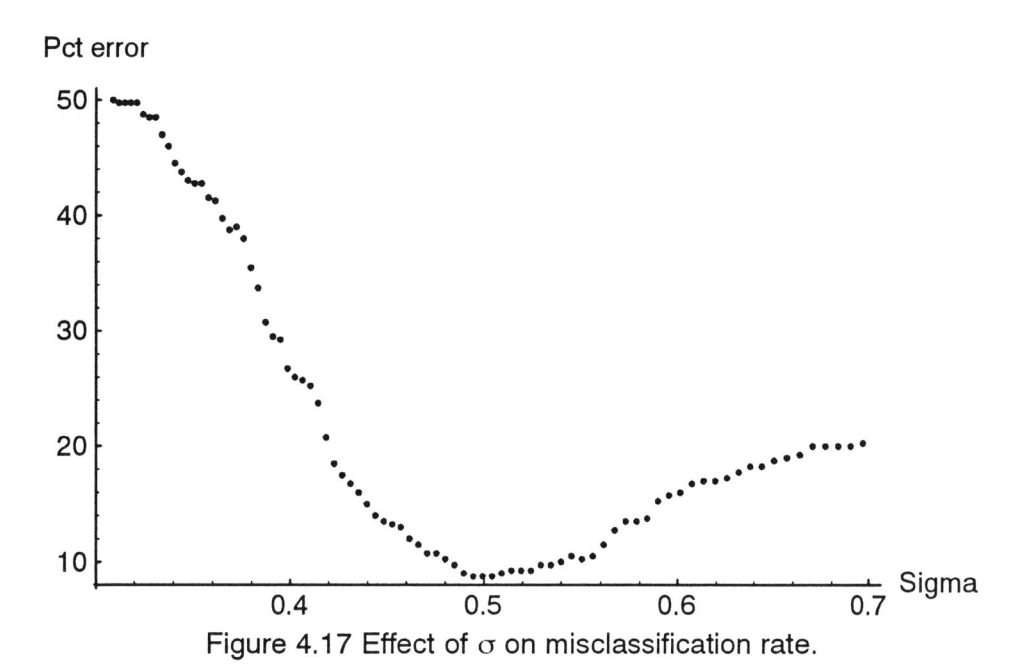

Figure 4.17 Effect of σ on misclassification rate.

misclassification of a large test set as a function of σ. Clearly, if finding an effective classification network for this data is important, casual selection of σ is not recommended.

There are two steps in the selection of an optimal σ: First we must define a criterion for judging the efficacy of a particular value of this parameter. Then we must choose an algorithm for optimizing this criterion. We will begin with the first step. What is a good criterion?

The obvious choice for a performance criterion is easily eliminated. Suppose that, for a particular trial value of σ, we define a set of Parzen density estimators based on the training set. Each of these estimators is defined by Equation (4.14) on page 173. Then we use this set of density estimators to classify every case in the training set according to the Bayes rule shown in Equation (4.1) on page 162. A good criterion would be the number of correctly classified cases. Or would it? Look closely at Equation (4.14). What happens when we reach the term in that summation for which the training case in the sum is the same as the training case being classified for the criterion computation? The distance measure will be zero, and the weight function will be large. That will produce a tremendously unfair bias toward correctly classifying each case. This criterion is obviously useless.

Fortunately, there is a simple solution. When a member of the training set is being classified, temporarily remove that member from the summation that determines the density estimate. That way no bias will be introduced by using a training case to influence its own classification decision. This criterion is actually very good. Experience indicates that as long as the training set is reasonably representative of the underlying populations, a σ chosen by maximizing the classification accuracy this way produces very good results when applied to the general population. In the next chapter, we will refine this criterion in a way that will let us resolve ties and use a more sophisticated optimization algorithm than the one presented later in this chapter. However, the improvement is rarely significant for the basic PNN discussed so far. A simple count of correct decisions is adequate for all but the most demanding tasks.

The following code fragment illustrates this technique for computing the misclassification error of a probabilistic neural network. This is extracted from a class library, so it frequently refers to private members of that class. However, the names have been chosen in such a way that the function of every variable should be obvious. A complete listing of this subroutine, in context, can be found in the module PNNET.CPP on the accompanying code disk.

The algorithm operates by permanently setting *last* to point to the last case in the training set. The contents of that slot will be the case being ignored. The number of cases, *ncases*, is decremented by one so that the PNN classifier *trial* does not use the last case in making the decision. After excluding the actual last case, successive cases (working toward the first) are swapped with the case in the last slot. In this way, each case spends one pass in the last slot, where it is excluded. This rearranges the training set order, but that is no problem.

```
exclude = ncases ;              // Will exclude this case
--ncases ;                      // Use one less case to classify
last = data + size * ncases ;   // Point to last slot

tot_err = 0.0 ;                 // Total error will be cumulated here
first = 1 ;                     // For first trial no swapping needed

while (exclude--) {             // Exclude each training case

  if (! first) {                // If not first trial, swap excluded to end
    exclude_ptr = data + size * exclude ;
```

```
   for (i=0 ; i<size ; i++) {        // Each variable in this case
      temp = exclude_ptr[i] ;         // Gets swapped to end slot for ignoring
      exclude_ptr[i] = last[i] ;
      last[i] = temp ;
      }
   }

   first = 0 ;                        // Flag that we swap from now on
   oclass = trial ( last ) ;          // Evaluate network for excluded case
   tclass = ... ;                     // True class in training set
   if (tclass != oclass)              // Same as PNN classified class?
      tot_err += 1.0 ;                // If not, inc error

   } // for all excluded

   ++ncases ;                         // Undo shrinking
   neterr = tot_err / ncases ;        // Mean per presentation
```

Now that we have a means of evaluating the efficacy of any given value of σ, we need a means for computing the optimal value. The minimization algorithm must satisfy several requirements. First, we must pay attention to speed. The time needed to evaluate one σ via this technique is proportional to the square of the number of training cases, which can be large. Therefore, we want to do as few evaluations as possible. But that is in conflict with two other properties of this problem. One is that multiple minima are possible. We dare not lock into the first local minimum we find. Some degree of global search is necessary, despite its pain. The other conflict with economy is that the error function may not be smooth. It often has large high-order derivatives. The implication is that we are unable to make effective use of quadratic (or higher-order!) interpolation or extrapolation to the minimum. Sophisticated algorithms like Brent's method are out of the question. They would lead us astray with wild projections so many times that the expense of their mistakes would surpass their general economy. By the time we get close enough to the minimum for the derivatives to have settled down enough to justify projection, we would likely be satisfied with the σ obtained and be ready to quit.

The minimization I would recommend is performed in two steps: The first step is a global search over a reasonable range, with insurance against a poorly specified range. This provides three points (values of σ) such that the center point has lesser error than its neighbors. The second step refines that trio. Code for the first step was given on page 11 when the glob_min subroutine was listed.

How many points are needed for the global search? The minimum is three, as we need to verify a local minimum at the center. This might be appropriate if the network has been trained once, with just minor modification in the training set. The σ from the previous training set could be made the center point, with endpoints slightly below and above it. But in general, as many points as training time allows should be used to ensure securing the global minimum.

After a rough minimum has been found with the primitive glob_min algorithm, we need to refine the estimate. I use the *golden-section* method, as it is nearly as optimal as we can get without unstable fitting of polynomials. The Fibonacci algorithm is slightly faster if the number of refinement iterations is known in advance, but for this application, that is impossible. The golden-section algorithm will now be described for those unfamiliar with it.

As in most minimization schemes, we always keep three points, as closely spaced as possible, such that the function value of the center point is less than that of either of its neighbors. For each iteration, we evaluate the function at a fourth point that lies within the interval spanned by the three current points. This allows us to shrink the current interval by discarding one of the endpoints. We iterate in this manner until either the width of the interval becomes small enough, or until the difference in function values between the points becomes small enough. The two possible outcomes of a function evaluation at a fourth point are shown in Figure 4.18.

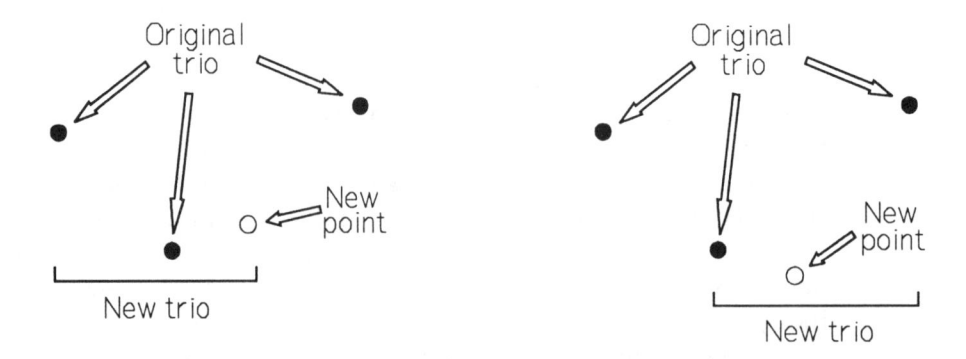

Figure 4.18 Outcomes in a golden-section iteration.

The question begging to be answered is, "Where do we place the new point?" It should be apparent that if the widths of the intervals to the left and right of the center point are different, we should split the wider of them. This is the area where the least is known about the function, so by checking on it here, we gain the most additional knowledge about its behavior. A first guess might be to split the interval exactly in half by placing the new point precisely between the center point and most distant endpoint. In fact, this is not a terribly bad strategy. But we can do a little better.

Our intuition might tell us that we should place the new point closer to the center point than exactly halfway. This way, if we end up discarding the more distant endpoint, we have narrowed the spanned interval by more than if we placed the new point exactly halfway between the center and the distant endpoint. On the other hand, we may not want to take that idea too far. It leaves us with a more narrow interval to be possibly discarded on the next iteration. What we gained on this iteration may be lost on the next iteration. Some rigor is needed.

It is possible to explicitly compute performance figures for any given placement rule. The derivation of the optimum will not be shown here, as it strays too far from the subject of this text, and it can be found in most textbooks on numerical optimization. Suffice it to say that the intuition developed above is correct. If the interval is scaled so that the left and right endpoints lie at 0 and 1, then the two interior points should lie at about 0.382 and 0.618. (The actual value of the latter figure is $2 / (1 + \sqrt{5})$, and the former figure is 1 minus the latter.) These values are the golden-section numbers that have a long history in mathematics. It can be shown that if we are ever able to attain such placement, and continue to split the larger interval according to the golden ratio, this placement will be maintained forever. Furthermore, this placement rule, for any fixed number of function evaluations, will give us the minimum-width final interval of any other uniformly specified placement rule. Only Fibonacci placement can do better, and its superiority is only slight. And since the Fibonacci algorithm does not use a uniform placement rule, it requires that we know the number of function evaluations in advance, a stringent requirement.

There are (at least) two common methods for achieving golden-section spacing when the initial trio of points does not have that spacing. The more common method computes the position of the new point by sectioning the total interval defined by the outermost pair of points. The location of the center point is ignored except for using it to determine which is the wider interval in which the new point will be placed. This method fairly rapidly converges to the overall golden section, at the price of possibly poor spacing for the first few iterations. The other method, presented here, applies the golden-section rule to the wider of the two intervals, ignoring the other endpoint. This method does not actually "converge" to ultimate golden-section spacing. Rather, the first time that function improvement is had at the new point, it jumps directly to that magic spacing. I prefer this method for problems that will probably require relatively few function evaluations to provide satisfactory convergence. This is usually the case for optimizing σ in PNNs. The more traditional method is usually preferred for problems in which a great many function evaluations will be performed in order to provide highly accurate location of the minimum. But both methods are excellent, there being little real difference between them in terms of performance.

We now present a subroutine for golden-section minimization. The parameters are similar to those for the global minimization routine, glob_min, already shown. The three pairs of points in the parameter list act as both input and output. The parameters log_space and critlim serve the same function as before. Only tol is new. It provides an alternate means of terminating iteration. If the relative difference between the best and worst function values among the three current points drops to this level, it decides that further work is not worthwhile, and so it quits. If the user wants to achieve the last bit of accuracy possible, tol should be set to 0. This forces iteration to continue until the limit of machine precision is attained. (That supposed limit is reflected in the constant 3.e-8 in the code below, which is appropriate for double precision on most hardware. It should, in general, be slightly less than the square root of the minimum computable difference between two numbers.)

```
int gold_min (
    int log_space ,                 // Space by log?
    double critlim ,                // Quit if crit drops this low
    double tol ,                    // Quit if relative improvement this low
    double (*criter) (double) ,     // Criterion function
    double *x1,                     // Input and output
    double *y1 ,                    // Lower X value and function there
    double *x2,
    double *y2 ,                    // Middle (best)
```

The Original PNN

```
      double *x3,
      double *y3                    // And upper
      )

{
   double left_width, right_width, x, y, numer, denom ;
   double gold = 2.0 / (1.0 + sqrt(5.0)) ; // About 0.618

   for (;;) {

      if (*y2 < critlim)            // Do we satisfy user yet?
         break ;

      if ((*x3 - *x1) < (3.e-8 * *x2))   // Avoid refining beyond
         break ;                     // double precision

      numer = (*y1 > *y3) ? *y1 - *y2 : *y3 - *y2 ;
      denom = (fabs(*y2) > tol) ? fabs(*y2) : tol ;

      if (numer / denom < tol)      // Relative error check
         break ;

      if (user_pressed_escape())    // Was the ESCape key pressed?
         return 1 ;

      if (log_space) {
         left_width = *x2 / *x1 ;
         right_width = *x3 / *x2 ;
         }
      else {
         left_width = *x2 - *x1 ;
         right_width = *x3 - *x2 ;
         }

      if (left_width > right_width) {    // Left interval larger so split it

         if (log_space)
            x = exp ( log(*x1) + gold * log(*x2 / *x1) ) ;
         else
            x = *x1 + gold * (*x2 - *x1) ;
```

```
      y = criter ( x ) ;

      // If we improved, or tied with left side favored, discard right pt
      if ((y < *y2)  ||  ((y == *y2)  &&  (*y1 < *y3))) {
         *x3 = *x2 ;
         *y3 = *y2 ;
         *x2 = x ;
         *y2 = y ;
         }
      else {  // Didn't improve so discard left point
         *x1 = x ;
         *y1 = y ;
         }
      } // Left interval larger

   else {                           // Right interval larger so split it

      if (log_space)
         x = exp ( log(*x3) + gold * log(*x2 / *x3) ) ;
      else
         x = *x3 + gold * (*x2 - *x3) ;

      y = criter ( x ) ;

      // If we improved, or tied with right side favored, discard left pt
      if ((y < *y2)  ||  ((y == *y2)  &&  (*y1 > *y3))) {
         *x1 = *x2 ;
         *y1 = *y2 ;
         *x2 = x ;
         *y2 = y ;
         }
      else {                        // Didn't improve so discard right point
         *x3 = x ;
         *y3 = y ;
         }
      } // Right interval larger
   }

   return 0 ;
}
```

Operation of the above routine is straightforward. It begins each iteration by seeing if the central (best) point is good enough for the user. It then checks to see if the location of the optimal point is as accurate as can be attained with the available precision. As previously mentioned, the constant used for this check should be somewhat less than the square root of the precision to which floating-point numbers can be represented on the hardware. Then it does one last convergence check by seeing if we are working in a flat area where further refinement in x is not justified by improvement in y. Note that this is not a foolproof test. It may be that vast improvement lurks somewhere in the current interval. It is more of a heuristic test that has been found useful in practice. Finally, it checks to see if an impatient user has pressed the escape key.

The widths of the intervals on either side of the center point are computed according to the spacing method requested by the user. The wider interval is selected for splitting, and the new golden-section point is found. The endpoint to discard is selected based on the function value (see Figure 4.18), and appropriate housekeeping is done.

This may be a good time to discuss the thorny issue of integrating general-purpose subroutines, such as the minimization routines just given, with class member functions. If we simply make the subroutine a member of the class with which it is associated, everything seems straightforward. The criterion function (criter in these routines) is also made a member, and everybody has full access to whatever is needed. But it is exceedingly poor style to restrict the use of a widely usable routine by imprisoning it in whatever class happens to need it.

There is a better way, although it appears a little messy. The problem is that we need to call the general subroutine from a certain class member function; and the general subroutine, in turn, needs to call another subroutine that needs access to class variables but that cannot be a member of the class. In fact, this secondary function may need access to class variables from more than one class, and we certainly don't want to become involved with multiple inheritance (at least, I don't). Our solution is to make the secondary function static and define static variables as needed to pass information to it. Look at the following code fragment, extracted from the complete listing in the module BASIC.CPP on the accompanying code disk.

```
static double basic_crit ( double sig ) ;        // Local criterion to optimize
static TrainingSet *local_tptr ;                 // These two statics pass class data
static PNNbasic *local_netptr ;                  // to the local criterion routine
```

```
void PNNbasic::learn ( TrainingSet *tptr , struct LearnParams *lptr )
{
  .
  .
  .
  local_netptr = this ;
  local_tptr = tptr ;

  k = glob_min ( lptr->siglo , lptr->sighi , lptr->nsigs , 1 , lptr->quit_err ,
            &basic_crit , &x1 , &y1 , &x2 , &y2 , &x3 , &y3 ) ;
  .
  .
  .
}


static double basic_crit ( double sig )
{
  local_netptr->sigma = sig ;
  return local_netptr->trial_error ( local_tptr ) ;
}
```

The PNNbasic learning routine first sets the static variables to contain whatever the static criterion routine will need, then calls the general optimization routine. That routine, when it needs to evaluate the criterion for a trial sigma, calls the static criterion routine. This roundabout method is the technique I prefer. Other methods, more in the spirit of hard-core C++, are possible. But I find them even more complex and intimidating than the above and so I prefer this solution.

Accelerating the Basic PNN

This section will suggest several ways in which the basic PNN can be made to run faster. No computational details will be given, as they are either trivially simple, or beyond the scope of this text. These are seeds for thought.

The most important consideration is that the distance computation must be optimized for the nature of the data. All of the PNN programs in this text use the fully general case of floating-point data. If the data is integers, by all means use integer arithmetic (but watch out for overflow in computing dot products!). We may even get away with rescaling floating-point data as integers to allow total integer operation. This is especially true on native 32-bit machines. The time savings can be substantial.

If the data resides on the surface of a sphere, use Equation (4.17) to avoid many subtractions. This property is attainable in a surprising number of problems.

If the data is binary, the dot product can be avoided entirely by simple counting. If runs of identical bits can be expected, use run-length compression to store the training set and perhaps even the input data. Count intelligently, using the run lengths. Long bit runs are common in many pattern-matching and shape classification problems, so this method should always be considered.

If the training set is large and the data is discrete, consider the possibility that many duplicate training cases may be present. Keep one of each and weight its contribution by the number of duplicates in the original set. But beware of this approach if there is not massive duplication. The weighting operation is fairly expensive.

Elimination of duplicates can be generalized into clustering. Use any of the widely available clustering algorithms to reduce the number of cases in the training set. Train with the cluster centroids, weighted by the size of each cluster. In many cases, execution time can be cut in half, or even better, with almost no loss of accuracy.

If the dimensionality of the data vectors is large, classification time can be significantly reduced by prescreening based on principal components. Before training begins, compute the first few principal components of the training set taken as a whole (all classes together). Then compute and store the scores of each training case on each of the first few principal components. When classifying an unknown, first compute its principal component scores. Then, when passing through the training set with the unknown, cumulating density estimates, compare the score of the unknown on the first principal component with that of the current training case. If they are too different, skip this case. If they are close, try the next component. The point of diminishing returns is reached quickly, and the choice of a cutoff for *too different* is subjective. But in important problems where speed is of the essence, this method can be a lifesaver. A few scalar comparisons are worthwhile if there is a high probability that they can let us avoid an expensive dot product.

Bayesian Confidence Measures

One property of the PNN that makes it the neural network of choice for some situations is that it often has the ability to provide mathematically sound confidence estimates for its decisions. This may *not* always be so. In many (most?) practical classification problems, there is a possibility that unknown samples may not be drawn from any of the trained classes. A text-reading program may employ a neural network that was trained on all of the letters, numbers, and common symbols. But if the program's input is from a human, garbage characters may be encountered. When such unexpected input is possible, one cannot compute Bayesian confidence estimates based on Parzen density estimates. For some appropriate alternative methods of computing confidences, see Masters (1993).

But sometimes we may get lucky in our application. When the classes are mutually exclusive and exhaustive (meaning roughly that no case can possibly fall into more than one population, and that the training set encompasses all populations fairly), then Bayes' theorem can be applied. This theorem lets us compute the probability that an observation X was the product of population A.

$$P[A|X] = \frac{g_A(X)}{\sum_k g_k(X)} \qquad (4.18)$$

Each of the density estimates $g_k(X)$ in the numerator and denominator of the above formula could, of course, be multiplied by prior probabilities and/or cost constants if such biasing is desired.

We shall not dwell on this subject. Masters (1993) presents a thorough discussion of computing confidences in neural network decisions, both PNN and otherwise. Also, Bayes classification is widely discussed in standard statistical references. It should be sufficient to remind the reader that the ability to compute Bayes confidence figures is a major advantage of probabilistic neural networks relative to most other models.

5

Probabilistic Neural Networks II: Advanced Techniques

- Models employing separate sigma weights

- A continuous error criterion

- Gradient computation

- Multivariate optimization

- Complete source code

The previous chapter provided a solid introduction to the probabilistic neural network. It described in detail the PNN algorithms that are currently in widespread use. However, many improvements are possible. The learning algorithms can be made faster and more accurate. The models can be generalized into more powerful versions. And the very foundation on which PNNs are built, Bayesian classification, can be replaced with a general function mapping model. Let us begin.

Different Variables Rate Different Sigmas

Aside from possible time and memory constraints, the greatest current impediment to effective use of probabilistic neural networks is the fact that the popular model presented in the previous chapter uses a single value of the σ parameter to scale all of the variables. This one-sigma-fits-all approach is a terrible handicap. The poor user is burdened with the task of providing the network with variables whose variations are all commensurate. If that is not done, good performance is unlikely. Worse still is the fact that even when care is taken to properly scale the data, performance may still suffer. This is because the user probably does not know in advance which variables are important and which are not. The presence of variables whose variation is meaningless has a dilutive effect on the useful variables. Ideally, we would want the variation of unimportant variables to be small so that they exert minimal influence on the distance measure computed between an unknown point and each training case. This distance measure should be dominated by the important variables. Examination of Figure 5.1 will make this more clear.

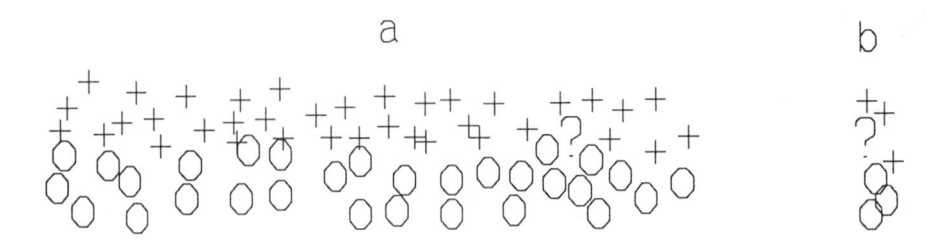

Figure 5.1 Unequal scaling hinders performance.

Different Variables Rate Different Sigmas

The left part of that figure, labeled *a*, depicts a training set consisting of two classes. Two variables are measured. The cases are plotted in such a way that the value of the first variable, which we shall call *x*, determines the horizontal position of the symbol used to identify each case. The second variable, *y*, determines the vertical position. Several things should be clear. The two classes are fairly well separated, so classification of unknowns should not be too difficult. The *x* variable is obviously worthless for determining the class membership of an observed case. Only the *y* variable discriminates between the classes.

An unknown case, represented by a question mark, is in the midst of that training set jumble. Most observers would agree that the unknown probably belongs to the + class. Now let's think about how the traditional PNN would make a decision.

The usual algorithm starts by estimating (a multiple of) the density function of the + class at the ? point. To do this, a + case is selected and the Euclidean distance separating that case from the ? case is computed. The distance is divided by σ and the kernel function is evaluated for that weighted distance. This is repeated for every + case, and the mean of all of those kernel functions is found. Then the same process is repeated for the other class. The class having the greatest mean weight function is the winner.

How does the value of σ affect this process? Suppose that σ is very small. Distances will be magnified as a result of the division by σ, so the weight function will be minuscule for all but the closest training cases. Most of the training set will be ignored; only those few cases that are in the immediate neighborhood of the unknown will enter into the decision. The danger of that approach is apparent in Figure 5.1. When one considers the value of the vital *y* variable, the unknown case is clearly in the + camp. Yet the chance cluster of a few cases in the other class near the unknown spells disaster if only the nearest neighbors are used. We must somehow bring the more distant neighbors into play. Only by examining the training set in its totality can we ascertain the importance of the *y* variable.

So now let's try a larger σ, one that will keep the argument to the kernel function small enough that more distant cases will enter into the density estimate. This will definitely improve the situation. But it is still not all that we could hope for. The (squared) Euclidean distance separating the unknown case from a training case is the sum of two components. One is the squared difference between the *x* variables, and the other is the squared difference between the *y* variables. Unfortunately, in the example being studied here, we end up with precisely the opposite of what we want. For most training cases, the distance will be dominated by the relatively large difference in x variables. The distance component due to the y variable will be practically ignored. But that is the variable that we want to emphasize! It's too bad that its contribution to the distance measure will be diluted by the contribution of the x variable that is essentially random noise. Pity the poor optimization algorithm that is faced with the difficult task of choosing a σ that somehow compromises between diluting the important variable and ignoring a large part of the training set.

The user can help. Look at the right side of Figure 5.1, labeled b. That shows the effect of a careful user manually scaling the variables in such a way that the less important variable has less variation. We now see that the distance measure will be dominated by the important variable. This is exactly what we want. The optimum σ and all classification decisions will be based primarily on the distribution of the y variable.

That approach is not usually feasible, though. It is unreasonable to expect a user to decide in advance which variables are important and which are not. In a trivial case like the one shown here, that may be possible. But when there are many variables, many classes, and multiple modes, such decisions are nearly impossible.

The solution to this problem is to use a separate σ weight for each variable. If we can devise a training algorithm that varies each σ separately, we can let that algorithm automatically convert the distribution shown in Figure 5.1(a) into that shown in Figure 5.1(b).

In the basic PNN model, we computed the density estimate using Equation (4.14) on page 173. That equation will no longer do the job, as it computes the Euclidean distance first, then divides by the common σ. We now need the more general distance function shown in Equation (5.1). That distance function uses a different σ for each of the p variables. It expresses the weighted Euclidean distance separating an observed case $\mathbf{x}$ from a training case $\mathbf{x}_i$. The subscript j indexes the individual variable within the vector case.

$$D(\mathbf{x}, \mathbf{x}_i) = \sum_{j=1}^{p} \left(\frac{x_j - x_{ij}}{\sigma_j} \right)^2 \tag{5.1}$$

With that general distance measure in hand, we are in a position to define a (multiple of a) density estimator. This is done in Equation

(5.2). Note that the Gaussian kernel function is explicitly included in this equation, as that function will be assumed throughout the remainder of this chapter.

$$g(\mathbf{x}) = \frac{1}{n} \sum_{i=1}^{n} \exp(-D(\mathbf{x}, \mathbf{x}_i)) \qquad (5.2)$$

We now have everything that we need to devise a much more powerful form of the probabilistic neural network. Given a training set, and given a set of σ weights for the variables, we can compute density estimates for each class at any given point. That is all we need in order to classify. But there is a catch. How do we determine the optimal σ weights? We can still employ the *leave-one-out* misclassification count that was presented in the previous chapter. Just vary the σ weights until the misclassification is minimized. However, as anyone who has taken Numerical Methods 101 knows, that is a mighty tall order when the criterion function can take on only integer values. In order to be able to use efficient optimization algorithms, we need a better error criterion.

A Continuous Error Criterion

In this section we will generalize the discrete counting criterion into one that is a continuous function of the σ weights. This will allow us to break the ties that frequently occur for several close values of σ. Even more importantly, it allows us to compute derivatives of the error function with respect to the sigma weights. The value of derivatives in optimization problems is immense.

Much of the mathematics that is essential to the topic of this section was (apparently) developed independently by two unrelated research efforts. One of these was headed by Donald Specht. His formulation of *generalized regression* will appear later as a topic studied on its own. The other is the team of Henrik Schioler and Uwe Hartmann. Their work will be most often quoted in this section. It should be emphasized that the two presentations are essentially identical from a mathematical point of view. I have chosen to honor the excellent work of both by citing Schioler and Hartmann first in the development of the continuous error criterion, then later devoting an entire chapter to the broader work of Donald Specht.

We will start by briefly reviewing the *general linear models* approach to classification. Suppose we have K classes. Define a delta function that indicates whether or not a given case in the training set belongs to a particular class.

$$\delta_k(i) = \begin{cases} 1 & \text{if training case } i \text{ is a member of class } k \\ 0 & \text{otherwise} \end{cases} \quad (5.3)$$

We can represent the fact that a given case belongs to class k by means of a K-vector that is entirely 0 except for a single 1 in the k position. In other words, a case that belongs to the second of four classes would have that fact signified by the vector (0, 1, 0, 0). Using the notation of Equation (5.3), the class vector for training case i is $(\delta_1(i), ..., \delta_K(i))$. A neural network that maps $\Re^p$ to $\Re^K$ could then be made to act as a classifier. Simply train the network to map an independent variable $\mathbf{X}$ to a class vector $\mathbf{Y} = (Y_1, ..., Y_K)$. An unknown case would then be classified by assigning it to the class corresponding to the largest element in its computed class vector. If we know the true class of that case, we can compute an error measure as the squared Euclidean distance between the computed class vector and the correct class vector.

But how can we make a PNN serve as a general mapping function? An answer is found in Schioler and Hartmann (1992). This section will briefly summarize their method. Readers interested in full details should consult that reference. Also, a parallel mathematical development can be found in Chapter 6 when Donald Specht's generalized regression is discussed. Finally, it should be pointed out that the reader is about to encounter some moderately advanced mathematics. Feel free to skim for a while. Understanding the development of this continuous error criterion at a deep mathematical level is not a prerequisite to understanding or using the criterion itself.

If we are in the happy position of knowing the joint PDF of $\mathbf{X}$ and $\mathbf{Y}$, then it is very easy to estimate $\mathbf{Y}$ given $\mathbf{X}$. As is well known in statistical circles, the expected squared error is minimized when we choose the conditional expectation of $\mathbf{Y}$. This conditional expectation, which is the optimal prediction of $\mathbf{Y}$ for a given $\mathbf{X}$, is defined in Equation (5.4). Following Schioler and Hartmann, we use a single integral, understanding that it is applied to each element of $\mathbf{Y}$.

A Continuous Error Criterion

$$E_{Y|X}(x) = \frac{\int_{-\infty}^{\infty} y \cdot f_{XY}(x, y) \, dy}{\int_{-\infty}^{\infty} f_{XY}(x, y) \, dy} \qquad (5.4)$$

We do not know the joint distribution of X and Y, but we certainly have the tool for estimating it. If we concatenate the p-vector X and the K-vector Y into a single vector of $p+K$ elements, we can use the multivariate Parzen method of Equation (5.2) to estimate $f_{XY}(x, y)$. Substituting that estimator into Equation (5.4), we see that our estimate of Y conditional on X is given by Equation (5.5).

$$\hat{\phi}(x) = \frac{\int_{-\infty}^{\infty} y \cdot g_{XY}(x, y) \, dy}{\int_{-\infty}^{\infty} g_{XY}(x, y) \, dy} \qquad (5.5)$$

That equation could probably be evaluated by numerical means. However, such an approach would be hopelessly slow in any practical situation. Luckily, Schioler and Hartmann make an important observation. They show that when the Gaussian kernel is used for the Parzen window, the integrals in Equation (5.5) simplify tremendously. They are ultimately able to express the conditional predictor as the ratio shown in Equation (5.6), where the numerator and denominator are given by Equations (5.7) and (5.8), respectively.

$$\hat{\phi}(x) = \frac{A(x)}{S(x)} \qquad (5.6)$$

$$A(x) = \sum_{i=1}^{n} y_i \cdot \exp(-D(x, x_i)) \qquad (5.7)$$

$$S(x) = \sum_{i=1}^{n} \exp(-D(x, x_i)) \qquad (5.8)$$

There are a few aspects of those equations that should be noted. The distance function, D, was defined in Equation (5.1). The numerator term, $\mathbf{A}(\mathbf{x})$, is a vector because $\mathbf{y}$ is a vector. The denominator is a scalar. As was done with the PNN, the version given here uses a separate distance weight for each variable and absorbs the constant 2 into the weight for computational efficiency.

Look closely at the prediction vector defined by the above equations when the $\mathbf{y}$ vectors in the training set are the canonical class membership vectors described at the beginning of this section. Recall that every element of each of these vectors is 0 except for the position corresponding to the case's class, which is a 1. Thus, the ith element of the numerator vector is the sum of the exponential terms corresponding to class i. In other words, it is simply a scaled density estimator, similar to that defined in Equation (5.2), but not normalized per the number of cases in each class. The denominator is the sum of the elements of the numerator vector. Thus, the elements of the predicted $\mathbf{Y}$ vector are Bayesian confidences, with priors proportional to the number of cases in each training class! (In many practical applications, this bias is what we want, so the development will follow in this line. Later we will see how to avoid such bias and/or include prior probabilities and costs.) Thus, when we minimize the squared error of the predicted $\mathbf{Y}$, we are actually minimizing the sum of squared errors in the Bayesian classification probabilities. How's that for everything coming together in the end?

We close this section by formally defining the error function whose minimum we will seek by varying the σ weights. The usual procedure for evaluating the performance of a set of weights is to use the leave-one-out method already described. We will develop the notation in a more general way so as to make it clear that a separate set of known cases may be used instead. If, as is most likely, the user wishes to simply cross validate the training set by leaving each case out once, then it is understood that the training set referred to here will be modified by the removal of each current test case.

Suppose we are evaluating the PNN for some observation $\mathbf{x}$ whose class membership is known. Let us define K activation functions, one for each class. These functions, shown in Equation (5.9), are identical to those of Equation (5.2) except that normalization per the class size is not done. They are also the components of the numerator vector in Schioler and Hartmann's class mapping, Equation (5.7).

$$h_k(\mathbf{x}) = \sum_{i=1}^{n} \delta_k(i) \exp(-D(\mathbf{x}, \mathbf{x}_i)) \qquad (5.9)$$

Derivatives of the Error Function

We can then define the Bayesian confidences as shown in Equation (5.10). Note that these are also the components of Schioler and Hartmann's final predictions, Equation (5.6). In particular, note that the denominator terms, $s(\mathbf{x})$ here and $S(\mathbf{x})$ there, are exactly the same quantity.

$$b_k(\mathbf{x}) = \frac{h_k(\mathbf{x})}{s(\mathbf{x})}$$

$$s(\mathbf{x}) = \sum_{k=1}^{K} h_k(\mathbf{x}) \tag{5.10}$$

Assume that $\mathbf{x}$ is known to belong to class k. We thus hope that $b_k(\mathbf{x}) = 1$ and that $b_j(\mathbf{x}) = 0$ for $j \neq k$. The error attributed to this observation is shown in Equation (5.11).

$$e_k(\mathbf{x}) = [1 - b_k(\mathbf{x})]^2 + \sum_{j \neq k} [b_j(\mathbf{x})]^2 \tag{5.11}$$

Specht (1992) suggests the use of the first term of that sum as a continuous error criterion. That certainly has appeal. However, the error measure used here is probably superior due to its inclusion of squared values of the other errors. The effect of including these terms is that the error is increased by *close seconds*. If only the probability for the correct class were used, the distribution of probabilities for the incorrect classes would be ignored. By also summing the squares of the other probabilities, we inflict a greater penalty if the error is concentrated in a single class than if the error is equally distributed among all other classes. This agrees with intuition, which warns us that a single major threat is more likely to cause misclassification than many small threats.

Derivatives of the Error Function

In this section we obtain the first and second derivatives of the error defined in Equation (5.11) with respect to each of the sigma weights. Knowledge of these derivatives enables us to optimize the error using efficient second-order gradient algorithms instead of terribly slow gradient-free methods.

Straightforward differentiation gives us the gradient, shown in Equation (5.12). Differentiating once more gives us the second derivatives, shown in Equation (5.13).

$$\frac{\partial e_k(\mathbf{x})}{\partial \sigma_j} = 2[b_k(\mathbf{x}) - 1]\left[\frac{\partial b_k(\mathbf{x})}{\partial \sigma_j}\right]$$
$$+ 2 \sum_{i \neq k} \left[b_i(\mathbf{x}) \frac{\partial b_i(\mathbf{x})}{\partial \sigma_j}\right] \quad (5.12)$$

$$\frac{\partial^2 e_k(\mathbf{x})}{\partial \sigma_j^2} = 2[b_k(\mathbf{x}) - 1]\left[\frac{\partial^2 b_k(\mathbf{x})}{\partial \sigma_j^2}\right] + 2\left[\frac{\partial b_k(\mathbf{x})}{\partial \sigma_j}\right]^2$$
$$+ 2 \sum_{i \neq k} \left[b_i(\mathbf{x}) \frac{\partial^2 b_i(\mathbf{x})}{\partial \sigma_j^2}\right] + 2 \sum_{i \neq k} \left[\frac{\partial b_i(\mathbf{x})}{\partial \sigma_j}\right]^2 \quad (5.13)$$

All that we lack is the first and second partial derivatives of the Bayesian probabilities, $b_k(\mathbf{x})$, with respect to the sigma weights. In the development that follows, notation will be simplified if we do a bit of abbreviation. We will have frequent need for the derivatives with respect to σ_j of the quantities in the numerator and denominator of Equation (5.10). Since the denominator of that equation is the sum of the numerator terms across all classes, the derivative of the denominator is the sum of the derivatives of the numerators. These abbreviations and their definitions are shown in Equations (5.14) through (5.17).

$$\frac{\partial h_k(\mathbf{x})}{\partial \sigma_j} \equiv v_{kj}(\mathbf{x}) = 2 \sum_{i=1}^{n} \delta_k(i) \exp[-D(\mathbf{x}, \mathbf{x}_i)] \frac{(x_j - x_{ij})^2}{\sigma_j^3} \quad (5.14)$$

$$\frac{\partial s(\mathbf{x})}{\partial \sigma_j} \equiv V_j(\mathbf{x}) = \sum_{k=1}^{K} v_{kj}(\mathbf{x}) \tag{5.15}$$

$$\frac{\partial^2 h_k(\mathbf{x})}{\partial \sigma_j^2} \equiv w_{kj}(\mathbf{x}) = 2 \sum_{i=1}^{n} \delta_k(i) \exp[-D(\mathbf{x}, \mathbf{x}_i)] \cdot$$
$$\left[2 \frac{(x_j - x_{ij})^4}{\sigma_j^6} - 3 \frac{(x_j - x_{ij})^2}{\sigma_j^4} \right] \tag{5.16}$$

$$\frac{\partial^2 s(\mathbf{x})}{\partial \sigma_j^2} \equiv W_j(\mathbf{x}) = \sum_{k=1}^{K} w_{kj}(\mathbf{x}) \tag{5.17}$$

We are now in a position to find the partial derivatives of the Bayesian probabilities with respect to the σ weights. Tedious but straightforward application of the rule for differentiating quotients gives us Equations (5.18) and (5.19).

$$\frac{\partial b_k(\mathbf{x})}{\partial \sigma_j} = \frac{v_{kj}(\mathbf{x}) - V_j(\mathbf{x}) b_k(\mathbf{x})}{s(\mathbf{x})} \tag{5.18}$$

$$\frac{\partial^2 b_k(\mathbf{x})}{\partial \sigma_j^2} = \frac{w_{kj}(\mathbf{x}) - W_j(\mathbf{x}) b_k(\mathbf{x})}{s(\mathbf{x})}$$
$$+ \frac{2 V_j^2(\mathbf{x}) b_k(\mathbf{x}) - 2 v_{kj}(\mathbf{x}) V_j(\mathbf{x})}{s^2(\mathbf{x})} \tag{5.19}$$

We have just discussed how to compute the derivatives of the error of a single observation. We compute the derivative of the sum of the errors for a collection of cases by summing the derivatives for each case. If we are evaluating the error by cross validating the training set, the set of cases summed in Equations (5.14) and (5.16) will be slightly different for each test case because that case is temporarily removed.

It should be noted that mixed partial derivatives can also be computed. However, that is rarely, if ever, justified. The amount of additional computation required to find the pure partials along with the error is small. The added computation for also computing mixed partials is much greater. Since the partial derivatives do not generally stabilize until the optimization is nearly complete, the tremendous extra work per iteration is almost never worth the small reduction in total number of iterations.

Incorporating Prior Probabilities

The preceding discussion has focused on a straightforward implementation of an error function. The use of unweighted sums implies Bayesian prior probabilities proportional to the number of training cases in each class. We may want to impose a different set of prior probabilities and/or cost functions. Or we may simply want to specify equal priors by removing the effect of different class counts. This is trivially accomplished.

Let $\{c_k, k = 1, ..., K\}$ be the set of Bayesian weights that we wish to impose on the classifier. If our goal is simply to remove the effect of unequal class representation in the training set, we can use $c_k = 1 / n_k$. We will not ask that these weights satisfy any normalization requirements, such as summing to one; their effect is relative only.

In accordance with Bayes' theorem, we must modify Equation (5.10) as shown in Equation (5.20). The definition of the error function, Equation (5.11), remains the same. The partial derivatives of the error, Equations (5.12) and (5.13), are unchanged. The derivatives of the activation functions, Equations (5.14) and (5.16), are also unaffected by the inclusion of prior probabilities. In fact, the only change needed to include Bayesian weighting in the derivatives is that the values of v_{kj} and w_{kj} computed in Equations (5.14) and (5.16) must be multiplied by c_k before being used in any other equations. (Those equations are (5.15), (5.17), (5.18), and (5.19).) It is left as an almost trivial exercise for the reader to verify that fact.

$$b_k(\mathbf{x}) = \frac{c_k h_k(\mathbf{x})}{s(\mathbf{x})}$$

$$s(\mathbf{x}) = \sum_{k=1}^{K} c_k h_k(\mathbf{x})$$

(5.20)

Here is another little exercise for interested readers. It is not difficult and can be enlightening. *Intuitively* verify the correctness of the modifications to incorporate priors that were just described. Start with the original formulation in which priors were implicitly defined by the number of cases in each class. Assume equal priors by virtue of having an equal number of cases in each class. Now duplicate every case in one class, thus increasing its prior probability. What happens in the computations of that method? How is that effected in the modifications just described?

Efficient Computation

Since evaluating the error and its derivatives can be an extremely expensive operation, it is vital that every effort be made to keep the computation as efficient as possible. This section will present an algorithm that computes these quantities using a minimum of effort. At the end of this section, we will also discuss potential numerical pitfalls and how to avoid those pitfalls. The first presentation of the algorithm will be as pseudocode, for that more clearly portrays the relatively complex procedure. After the numerical discussion, some code fragments in C will be shown to illustrate the fine details. Complete source code can be found in the module SEPVAR.CPP on the accompanying code disk.

The computation for each test case involves two separate steps. In the first step, we traverse the training set, cumulating the output activations and the v and w terms for each class and variable. This is the slow step, and hence it is the step in which efficiency is most vital. In the second step, we compute the error and its derivatives. This step is very fast, being independent of the number of training cases. Our aim in presenting the second step will be more for clarity of expression than for efficiency.

A cardinal rule of computation is to use the associative law to pull common factors out of loops to avoid redundant operations. Close examination of Equations (5.14) and (5.16) reveals that a little trick will enable us to extract a factor of σ_j from the former and a factor of σ_j^2 from the latter. That avoids a significant amount of expensive division in this long loop. To see how to do this, remember how the distance function D is computed for each case. For each variable, the term $((x_j - x_{ij}) / \sigma_j)^2$ enters into the generalized distance sum. This is an expensive term to compute. It pays to preserve the p-vector of terms that go into the sum, because those same terms appear in Equations (5.14) and (5.16). If we rewrite those equations to reflect the use of those terms and to reflect removal of the common σ_j factor, we get Equations (5.21) and (5.22), respectively.

$$v_{kj}(\mathbf{x}) = \frac{2}{\sigma_j} \sum_{i=1}^{n} \delta_k(i) \exp[-D(\mathbf{x}, \mathbf{x}_i)] \left(\frac{x_j - x_{ij}}{\sigma_j}\right)^2 \quad (5.21)$$

$$w_{kj}(\mathbf{x}) = \frac{2}{\sigma_j^2} \sum_{i=1}^{n} \delta_k(i) \exp[-D(\mathbf{x}, \mathbf{x}_i)] \cdot \left[2\left(\frac{x_j - x_{ij}}{\sigma_j}\right)^4 - 3\left(\frac{x_j - x_{ij}}{\sigma_j}\right)^2\right] \quad (5.22)$$

In the first step, we will use i to index the training set case, with i running from 1 through n, the number of cases. The input variable will be indexed by j, which runs from 1 through p. The value of the jth variable in training case i is x_{ij}. The test case is $\mathbf{x}$, and it belongs to class t. There are K classes. Early in the main loop, we will save the work vector *dsqr* for use later in the loop to avoid expensive recomputation. This is the vector discussed in the previous paragraph. The pseudocode for this loop demonstrates the mathematics by exactly following the equations that have been presented. However, it ignores several vital aspects related to numerical stability in pathological situations. Readers should also study the code fragments that appear later.

Derivatives of the Error Function

```
for k from 1 to K
    h_k ← 0
    for j from 1 to p
        v_kj ← 0
        w_kj ← 0

for i from 1 to n
    k ← class of training case i
    dist ← 0
    for j from 1 to p
        diff ← (x_j - x_ij) / σ_j
        dsqr_j ← diff * diff
        dist ← dist + dsqr_j
    edist ← exp(-dist)
    h_k ← h_k + edist
    for j from 1 to p
        temp ← edist * dsqr_j
        v_kj ← v_kj + temp
        w_kj ← w_kj + temp * (2.0 * dsqr_j - 3.0)
```

The vast majority of the computation time is spent in the two loops over j. The first loop cumulates the squared weighted distance (Equation (5.1)) between the test case and the current training case. This quantity is saved in $dsqr$ because it will be needed in the second loop. Since we are using a Gaussian window, we cumulate exp(-$dist$) into the appropriate sum (Equation (5.9)).

The second inner loop cumulates the essence of v and w using Equations (5.21) and (5.22), respectively. The difference between those equations and the code shown above is that the common factors of $2 / \sigma_j$ for v and $2 / \sigma_j^2$ for w are omitted in the code. Since those factors are constant for all training cases, there is no point in including them in this expensive loop. They are included later, outside the training set loop.

The critical part is now done. The remainder of the effort does not involve the training set, so its speed is unimportant in nearly all practical situations. Pseudocode for computing the Bayesian probabilities (Equation (5.20)), including priors, is now shown. A floor is placed under s to prevent division by zero. A slightly more sophisticated approach to ensuring numerical stability will be shown when actual C code is given later.

```
s ← 0
for k from 1 to K
    h_k ← h_k * c_k
    s ← s + h_k
if s < 1.e-40
    s ← 1.e-40
for k from 1 to K
    b_k ← h_k / s
```

The Bayesian probabilities of class membership have been computed. Now find the error associated with this result using Equation (5.11). Recall that this case belongs to class t.

```
err ← 0
for k from 1 to K
    if k == t
        err ← err + (1.0 - b_k) * (1.0 - b_k)
    else
        err ← err + b_k * b_k
```

We are ready for the final step, computation of the derivatives. This is done separately for each variable in two loops. The first loop multiplies v and w by the Bayesian priors, multiplies by the common factors $2/\sigma_j$ and $2/\sigma_j^2$, divides by $s(\mathbf{x})$ to simplify Equations (5.18) and (5.19), and cumulates the sums shown in Equations (5.15) and (5.17). The second loop computes the partial derivatives of b_k with respect to σ_j using Equations (5.18) and (5.19). (Note how the division by $s(\mathbf{x})$ is avoided because it was done in the first loop.) Then it uses Equations (5.12) and (5.13) to compute the derivatives of the error, *grad* and *dergrad*. This pseudocode is shown below.

```
for j from 1 to p
    vtot ← 0
    wtot ← 0
    for k from 1 to K
        v_kj ← v_kj * 2.0 * c_j / (s * σ_j)
        w_kj ← w_kj * 2.0 * c_j / (s * σ_j * σ_j)
        vtot ← vtot + v_kj
        wtot ← wtot + w_kj
    grad_j ← 0
    dergrad_j ← 0
```

```
for k from 1 to K
    der1 ← v_kj - b_k * vtot
    der2 ← w_kj + 2.0 * b_k * vtot * vtot
           - 2.0 * v_kj * vtot - b_k * wtot
    if k == t
        temp ← -2.0 * (1.0 - b_k)
    else
        temp ← 2.0 * b_k
    grad_j ← grad_j + temp * der1
    dergrad_j ← dergrad_j + temp * der2
               + 2.0 * der1 * der1
```

There is one obvious numerical pitfall to be avoided and another that is not so obvious. It is clear that we must never let any of the σ weights become zero, or we will divide by zero in the distance scaling, as well as in a few other places. However, we must also be wary when any σ becomes even fairly small, or when any test case is dramatically different from all training cases. When that happens, the weighted distances separating the test case from the training cases become large. The exponential in the Gaussian window function can then underflow easily, causing it to falsely return a value of zero. As long as this does not occur for *every* training case, things are fine. But if it happens for all of the cases, $s(\mathbf{x})$ will be zero, causing problems when b, v and w are divided by $s(\mathbf{x})$. An effective solution is to set a floor under $s(\mathbf{x})$, preventing it from being any smaller than some tiny limit. This also has a sometimes agreeable side-effect. When a test case is really wild, all of the Bayesian probabilities will be zero. They will no longer sum to one, but that is an excellent tradeoff for the valuable information that the case fits into none of the classes.

This is not an absolutely perfect solution, though. An artificial floor can occasionally cause errors in the derivative computation. This is almost never a serious problem in practical applications. Nevertheless, it is disagreeable to perfectionists. Also, significant problems *can* occur in pathological situations. A better solution is to impose the floor earlier than it was done above, as each training case is processed. Also, use the floor only for computing the output activations (and hence s). Use the possibly underflowed value to compute the derivatives. In the interest of clarity, and with only trivial loss of robustness, this was not shown in the pseudocode given above. However, it is done in the C code fragment that now appears.

```
for (pop=0 ; pop<nout ; pop++) { // For each population (class)
   out[pop] = 0.0 ;                // Will sum kernels here
   for (ivar=0 ; ivar<nin ; ivar++) { // For each input variable
      v[pop*nin+ivar] = 0.0 ;      // Will store v terms here
      w[pop*nin+ivar] = 0.0 ;      // And w terms here
      }
   }


for (tset=0 ; tset<ntrain ; tset++) { // Do all training cases

   dptr = ... ;                     // Point to this case

   dist = 0.0 ;                     // Will sum distance here
   for (ivar=0 ; ivar<nin ; ivar++) { // All variables in this case
      diff = input[ivar] - dptr[ivar] ; // Test input minus training case
      diff /= sigma[ivar] ;         // Scale per sigma
      dsqr[ivar] = diff * diff ;    // Squared weighted distance
      dist += dsqr[ivar] ;          // Cumulate for all vars
      }

   dist = exp ( -dist ) ;           // Apply kernel function
   truedist = dist ;                // Need this for derivatives
   if (dist < 1.e-40)               // If this case is far from all
      dist = 1.e-40 ;               // prevent zero density via floor

   pop = ... ;                      // Class of this training case
   out[pop] += dist ;               // Cumulate this class's density
   vptr = v + pop * nin ;           // Point to this row in v
   wptr = w + pop * nin ;           // And w

   for (ivar=0 ; ivar<nin ; ivar++) { // All variables in this case
      temp = truedist * dsqr[ivar] ; // Except for common factors,
      vptr[ivar] += temp ;          // This is Equation (5.21)
      wptr[ivar] += temp * (2.0 * dsqr[ivar] - 3.0) ; // and Equation (5.22)
      }
   } // For all training cases

/*
   Deal with priors.  Divide by the class count to remove the effect of unequal counts.
*/
```

```
    psum = 0.0 ;
    for (pop=0 ; pop<nout ; pop++) {           // For each class
      out[pop] *= priors[pop] / n[pop] ;       // Numerator of Eqn (5.20)
      psum += out[pop] ;                       // Cumulate denominator
      }

    if (psum < 1.e-40)                         // Even though we kept dist away from 0 above
      psum = 1.e-40 ;                          // Pathological priors can still cause problems

    for (pop=0 ; pop<nout ; pop++)             // For each class
      out[pop] /= psum ;                       // Compute b_k per Eqn (5.20)

/*
   Compute the derivatives.
*/

    for (ivar=0 ; ivar<nin ; ivar++) {                         // For each var's sigma
      vtot = wtot = 0.0 ;                                      // Will be summing these

      for (outvar=0 ; outvar<nout ; outvar++) {                // For all classes
        v[outvar*nin+ivar] *= priors[outvar] / n[outvar] ;     // Must also deal with
        w[outvar*nin+ivar] *= priors[outvar] / n[outvar] ;     // Priors and class counts
        v[outvar*nin+ivar] *= 2.0 / (psum * sigma[ivar]) ;     // Common factors in Eqn
        w[outvar*nin+ivar] *= 2.0 / (psum * sigma[ivar] * sigma[ivar]) ; // (5.21), (5.22)
        vtot += v[outvar*nin+ivar] ;                           // Equation (5.15)
        wtot += w[outvar*nin+ivar] ;                           // Equation (5.17)
        }

      for (outvar=0 ; outvar<nout ; outvar++) {                // For each class
        der1 = v[outvar*nin+ivar] - out[outvar] * vtot ;       // Equation (5.18)
        der2 = w[outvar*nin+ivar] + 2.0 * out[outvar] * vtot * vtot -
             2.0 * v[outvar*nin+ivar] * vtot - out[outvar] * wtot ; // Equation (5.19)
        if (outvar == tclass)
          temp = 2.0 * (out[outvar] - 1.0) ;
        else
          temp = 2.0 * out[outvar] ;
        deriv[ivar] += temp * der1 ;                           // Equation (5.12)
        deriv2[ivar] += temp * der2 + 2.0 * der1 * der1 ;      // Equation (5.13)
        }
      } // For each variable's sigma
```

Classes May Deserve Their Own Sigmas, Too

In the previous section, we generalized the traditional probabilistic neural network to allow each variable to have its own σ weight. In most applications that is an excellent compromise between extreme generality and practical parsimony. But for the sake of completeness, we will now take this model to the next logical generalization by not only allowing different weights for each variable, but also by having a separate weight vector for each class. There is often a high price to pay for this extra freedom. With more free parameters, overfitting can easily happen, so thorough validation is crucial. Also, training time becomes more of a problem. This is due not only to the increased number of parameters over which optimization must occur, but also to the fact that the interaction inherent in these parameters makes the optimization process unstable. This model should be employed only when there is strong reason to believe that the classes must have significantly different weights due to variation in natural scaling or importance. For example, it may be that three classes must be distinguished. Some variable is crucial to the decision regarding class one versus class two; but that same variable is worthless in regard to class three. Such is the case for the variable represented by the vertical axis in Figure 5.2. When this situation arises, it may be beneficial to permit the scale for that variable to be greater for class three than it is for the other classes, so that its importance to that membership decision is diminished relative to the other, more important variables.

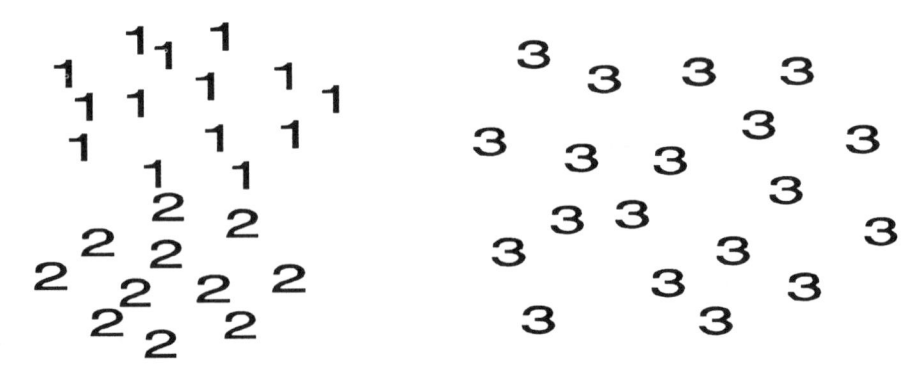

Figure 5.2: Classes may need their own sigmas.

Using separate weight vectors for each class introduces an annoying complication into the computations. Look back at Equation (4.11) on page 170. That is the general multivariate Parzen density approximator that is evaluated for each class. When the σ vector is the same for all classes, their product in the denominator of the normalizing factor in front of that equation can be ignored. The product cancels in the Bayesian classification formula. But when each class has its own weight vector, these factors no longer cancel. They must be explicitly included in the density estimator. Keeping with our tradition of assuming a Gaussian window, the activation function that we must now use is shown in Equation (5.23). Note that each class has its own distance function, shown in Equation (5.24). We use σ_{kj} to designate the weight in class k of variable j.

$$h_k(\mathbf{x}) = \frac{1}{\sigma_{k1} \sigma_{k2} \cdots \sigma_{kp}} \sum_{i=1}^{n} \delta_k(i) \exp(-D_k(\mathbf{x}, \mathbf{x}_i)) \quad (5.23)$$

$$D_k(\mathbf{x}, \mathbf{x}_i) = \sum_{j=1}^{p} \left(\frac{x_j - x_{ij}}{\sigma_{kj}} \right)^2 \quad (5.24)$$

Many of the equations for this model will be nearly identical to those of the model described in the previous sections. We just saw that the distance function for this model is the same as that of the previous model except that each class has its own personal weight vector. The activation function for this model is that of the previous model except that we divide each class' activation by the product of the σ weights for that class. The formula for converting activations into Bayesian probabilities, Equation (5.10) on page 201, is exactly the same for both models. The error measure, Equation (5.11), is also identical. The formulas for the first and second partial derivatives of the error, Equations (5.12) and (5.13) respectively, are nearly identical. The only difference is that the weights in the previous model now need to have a second index to indicate the class. If we just mentally substitute a σ_{ij} for each σ_j in those two monstrous equations, we can avoid rewriting them.

Now things begin to get a little awkward. We need to think about the partial derivatives of the activation of class k with respect to σ_{ij}. How many of these partial derivatives are there? It seems as though there are K^2p of them (K activations times Kp sigmas). Expanding on the notation of the previous section, we will let v_{kij} stand for the partial derivative of the activation of class k, h_k, with respect to σ_{ij}. But wait. Things may not be so bad after all. Remember that the activation of a class is not impacted by the weight vectors of other classes. So most of those partial derivatives are zero! In particular, $v_{kij} = 0$ whenever $k \neq i$. This lets us revert to a simpler notation using just two indices. We let $v_{kj} \equiv v_{kkj}$ stand for the nonzero partial derivatives. The second partials, symbolized by w instead of v, are handled the same way. Throughout the remainder of this section, we will use the two-index and three-index abbreviations interchangeably, according to whichever is more convenient at the time.

We now write the precise definitions of these quantities. To ease the pain, this is done in two steps: We start by computing a pair of intermediate quantities, p_{kj} and q_{kj}, in Equations (5.25) and (5.26), respectively. These are the partial derivatives of the activation functions *without* division by the product of the weights. As such, it is not surprising that they are practically identical to Equations (5.14) and (5.16) for the previous model.

$$p_{kj}(\mathbf{x}) = 2 \sum_{i=1}^{n} \delta_k(i) \exp[-D_k(\mathbf{x}, \mathbf{x}_i)] \frac{(x_j - x_{ij})^2}{\sigma_{kj}^3} \qquad (5.25)$$

$$q_{kj}(\mathbf{x}) = 2 \sum_{i=1}^{n} \delta_k(i) \exp[-D_k(\mathbf{x}, \mathbf{x}_i)] \cdot \left[2 \frac{(x_j - x_{ij})^4}{\sigma_{kj}^6} - 3 \frac{(x_j - x_{ij})^2}{\sigma_{kj}^4} \right] \qquad (5.26)$$

On to step two. To find the partial derivatives of the activation function that we are using for this model, which includes division by the σ weights, we use the rule for differentiating quotients. Remember that all of the weights except for the one in the differentiation are constants, which means that they simply appear as a linear factor. It will simplify notation if we let $\tau_k = \sigma_{k1}...\sigma_{kp}$ be the product of the weights for class k.

With these facts in mind, we see that the partial derivatives can be computed as shown in Equations (5.27) and (5.28), respectively.

$$\frac{\partial h_k(\mathbf{x})}{\partial \sigma_{kj}} \equiv v_{kj}(\mathbf{x}) = \frac{p_{kj}(\mathbf{x})}{\tau_k} - \frac{h_k(\mathbf{x})}{\sigma_{kj}} \quad (5.27)$$

$$\frac{\partial^2 h_k(\mathbf{x})}{\partial \sigma_{kj}^2} \equiv w_{kj}(\mathbf{x}) = \frac{q_{kj}}{\tau_k} + 2\frac{h_{kj}}{\sigma_{kj}^2} - 2\frac{p_{kj}}{\tau_k \sigma_{kj}} \quad (5.28)$$

This gives us the partial derivatives of the numerators of the Bayesian probabilities. Next we need the derivatives of the sum, $s(\mathbf{x})$, that is the denominator. We saw back in Equations (5.15) and (5.17) on page 203 that for the previous model, this quantity could be found by simply summing the partial derivatives of the numerators. But things are actually easier for this current model. Reverting back to our three-index abbreviations, look at Equation (5.29). All but one of the terms in the sum are zero. The same holds true for w.

$$\frac{\partial s(\mathbf{x})}{\partial \sigma_{ij}} = \sum_{k=1}^{K} v_{kij}(\mathbf{x}) = v_{ij} \quad (5.29)$$

Since we know the partial derivatives of the numerator and denominator of Equation (5.10), we are finally in a position to find the partial derivatives of the Bayesian probabilities with respect to the σ weights. As before, straightforward application of the rule for differentiating quotients gives us Equations (5.30) and (5.31).

$$\frac{\partial b_k(\mathbf{x})}{\partial \sigma_{ij}} = \frac{v_{kij}(\mathbf{x}) - v_{ij}(\mathbf{x})b_k(\mathbf{x})}{s(\mathbf{x})} \quad (5.30)$$

Note that these two equations freely mix the two-index and three-index versions of v and w. When implementing these equations, please remember that v_{kij} and w_{kij} are zero whenever $k \neq i$. This leads to significant simplification. In the C code that follows, the condition

$$\frac{\partial^2 b_k(\mathbf{x})}{\partial \sigma_{ij}^2} = \frac{w_{kij}(\mathbf{x}) - w_{ij}(\mathbf{x}) b_k(\mathbf{x})}{s(\mathbf{x})}$$
$$+ \frac{2 v_{ij}^2(\mathbf{x}) b_k(\mathbf{x}) - 2 v_{kij}(\mathbf{x}) v_{ij}(\mathbf{x})}{s^2(\mathbf{x})} \tag{5.31}$$

of equality (or lack thereof) leads to the use of two different, separately optimized, computations.

We now present a code fragment that implements the model described in this section. It computes the Bayesian probabilities and the partial derivatives of the error with respect to all weights. The complete routine can be found in the module SEPCLASS.CPP on the accompanying disk. This code is very similar to the code given in the previous section, so the description that follows the code will focus on only those aspects that are unique to this model.

```
for (pop=0 ; pop<nout ; pop++) { // For each population
   out[pop] = 0.0 ;                // Will sum kernels here
   for (ivar=0 ; ivar<nin ; ivar++) {
      v[pop*nin+ivar] = 0.0 ;      // Scratch for derivative stuff
      w[pop*nin+ivar] = 0.0 ;      // Ditto
      }
   }

for (tset=0 ; tset<ntrain ; tset++) { // Do all training cases

   dptr = ... ;                     // Point to this case
   pop = ... ;                      // Its class

   dist = 0.0 ;                     // Will sum distance here
   for (ivar=0 ; ivar<nin ; ivar++) { // All variables in this case
      diff = input[ivar] - dptr[ivar] ; // Unknown input minus case
      diff /= sigma[pop*nin+ivar] ; // Scale per sigma
      dsqr[ivar] = diff * diff ;    // Squared weighted distance
      dist += dsqr[ivar] ;          // Cumulate for all vars
      }

   dist = exp ( -dist ) ;           // Use Gaussian kernel
```

Classes May Deserve Their Own Sigmas, Too

```
    truedist = dist ;              // Need this for derivatives
    if (dist < 1.e-180)            // If this case is far from all
        dist = 1.e-180 ;           // prevent zero density

    out[pop] += dist ;             // Cumulate this class' density
    vptr = v + pop * nin ;         // Point to this row in v
    wptr = w + pop * nin ;         // And w
    for (ivar=0 ; ivar<nin ; ivar++) { // All variables in this case
        temp = truedist * dsqr[ivar] ;  // Use Equations (5.25) and (5.26)
        vptr[ivar] += temp ;       // (except for common factors)
        wptr[ivar] += temp * (2.0 * dsqr[ivar] - 3.0) ; // to find $p_{kj}$ and $q_{kj}$
        }

    } // For all training cases


/*
    Scale the outputs per the sigmas.
    Make the v's and w's be the actual derivatives of the activations.
*/


    for (outvar=0 ; outvar<nout ; outvar++) {   // k in $sigma_{kj}$, $v_{kj}$
        temp = 1.0 ;                            // Will cumulate $t_k$, the
        for (ivar=0 ; ivar<nin ; ivar++)        // product of all sigmas
            temp *= sigma[outvar*nin+ivar] ;    // for the outvar class
        out[outvar] /= temp ;                   // Scale outputs per sigmas
        for (ivar=0 ; ivar<nin ; ivar++) {      // j in $sigma_{kj}$, $v_{kj}$
            v[outvar*nin+ivar] *= 2.0 / sigma[outvar*nin+ivar] ; // Common factors
            w[outvar*nin+ivar] *=                                // as in Eqns (5.21) and (5.22)
               2.0 / (sigma[outvar*nin+ivar] * sigma[outvar*nin+ivar]) ;

            // At this point, v and w are derivatives of activation before scaling
            v[outvar*nin+ivar] /= temp ;        // Also scale first and
            w[outvar*nin+ivar] /= temp ;        // second derivatives
            // Apply Equations (5.27) and (5.28) to compute revised derivatives
            w[outvar*nin+ivar] += 2.0 / sigma[outvar*nin+ivar] *
               (out[outvar] / sigma[outvar*nin+ivar] - v[outvar*nin+ivar] ) ;
            v[outvar*nin+ivar] -= out[outvar] / sigma[outvar*nin+ivar] ;
            }
        }
```

```
/*
   Deal with class count normalization and prior probabilities.
*/

   psum = 0.0 ;
   for (pop=0 ; pop<nout ; pop++) {
     out[pop] *= priors[pop] / n[pop] ;
     psum += out[pop] ;
     }

   if (psum < 1.e-190)              // Even though we kept dist away from 0 above
     psum = 1.e-190 ;               // Pathological priors can still cause problems

   for (pop=0 ; pop<nout ; pop++)
     out[pop] /= psum ;


/*
   Compute the derivatives.  We must also worry about priors.
*/

   for (ivar=0 ; ivar<nin ; ivar++) {                    // j in sigma_{kj}, v_{kj}

     for (outvar=0 ; outvar<nout ; outvar++) {           // Apply priors to derivs
       v[outvar*nin+ivar] *= priors[outvar] / n[outvar] ;
       w[outvar*nin+ivar] *= priors[outvar] / n[outvar] ;
       v[outvar*nin+ivar] /= psum ;                      // Doing this now
       w[outvar*nin+ivar] /= psum ;                      // Saves a little time later
       }

     for (outvar=0 ; outvar<nout ; outvar++) {           // This is the K summed terms
       if (outvar == tclass)                             // in Equations (5.12) and (5.13)
         temp = 2.0 * (out[outvar] - 1.0) ;              // First (correct class) term
       else                                              // And other (wrong class) terms
         temp = 2.0 * out[outvar] ;                      // in the sum

       for (i=0 ; i<nout ; i++) {                        // k in sigma_{kj}, v_{kj}
         vij = v[i*nin+ivar] ;                           // Simplified sum from
         wij = w[i*nin+ivar] ;                           // Equation (5.29)
```

```
      if (i == outvar) {                       // Split Equations (5.30) and (5.31)
         der1 = vij * (1.0 - out[outvar]) ;    // into two cases according to
         der2 = wij * (1.0 - out[outvar]) +    // whether k==i for v_kij and w_kij
            2.0 * vij * vij * (out[outvar] - 1.0) ; // Which lets us simplify
         }
      else {                                   // Case of k not equal to i
         der1 = -out[outvar] * vij ;           // So many terms are zero
         der2 = out[outvar] * (2.0 * vij * vij - wij) ;
         }                                     // Der1 and 2 are derivs of b_k
      deriv[i*nin+ivar] += temp * der1 ;       // Equations (5.12)
      deriv2[i*nin+ivar] += temp * der2 + 2.0 * der1 * der1 ; // and (5.13)
      } // For i to nout (sigma[ij])
   } // For outvar in Eqn (5.12) and (5.13) sums
} // For ivar (j in sigma[ij])
```

The first step in the above code is to zero the vector where the scaled density for each class will be cumulated. The matrix that will hold the nonzero partial derivatives is also zeroed. The next step is to pass through the entire training set, cumulating the densities and partial derivatives of the classes *as if the densities were not divided by the products of the weights for each class*. This code is exactly the same as the code for the model of the previous section.

The next loop accomplishes several tasks. The weights for this class are multiplied together, as their product will be a scaling factor used for the activations (per Equation (5.23)) as well as the derivatives. Also, recall that for the sake of efficiency, the common factor of $2 / \sigma$ was omitted from the expensive loop over the training set. That common factor must be included, as shown in Equations (5.21) and (5.22). Once that is done, the v and w arrays contain the p and q terms defined in Equations (5.25) and (5.26), respectively. These are the partial derivatives of the activations before division of those activations by the product of the weights. The last few lines in this loop use Equations (5.27) and (5.28) to compute the partial derivatives of the activations *after* division by the weight product, which is the activations that this model actually uses. After this loop is complete, v and w contain the true partial derivatives. At this same point in the code for the model of the previous section, they were not quite the true derivatives, as the common factors had not yet been included.

The next step is the straightforward incorporation of prior probabilities to compute the Bayesian probabilities from the activations. This is identical to the code for the previous model.

The last step is computation of the partial derivatives of the error. This operation is considerably more complicated for this model than for the previous model, as three loops are needed. There are K (classes) times p (variables) partial derivatives, and each of these is found by summing over all of the classes in Equations (5.12) and (5.13).

The outermost loop covers the input variables. For each, the first action is to incorporate the prior probabilities into the derivatives, exactly as was done in the previous model. Also, the derivatives are divided by psum to save a little effort later. Then we use outvar to loop over the summation in Equations (5.12) and (5.13). Each of these summations consists of two parts. The first part is a term for the correct class, and the second part is a summation over all incorrect classes. The only difference between these two parts is a single factor, so that factor is placed in temp, and the remainder of the computation is independent of the class.

For each term in that sum, we compute the partials with respect to the weights for variable ivar in each class. For a given class and variable, we retrieve the partial derivatives of the activation of that class with respect to that weight. This is also the quantity shown in Equation (5.29) and the equivalent for w. Now we use Equations (5.30) and (5.31) to compute the derivatives of the Bayesian probabilities. As suggested on page 215, we split this computation into two cases. One case is when we are summing a term in Equation (5.12) (or (5.13)) in which the class is the same as the class of the weight on which we are working. The other case occurs for all other classes. In that latter case, the v_{kij} and w_{kij} quantities are zero, so considerable simplification is possible.

Once the derivatives of the Bayesian probabilities are found, we act exactly as we did for the previous model. We cumulate the gradient and second partials using Equations (5.12) and (5.13), respectively.

Optimizing Multiple-Sigma Models

In Chapter 4 the probabilistic neural network was based on a single σ weight. Choosing an optimal value for that weight was not a difficult process. It was just a matter of trying a handful of values across the likely domain of possibilities to find a rough global minimum, then applying a crude algorithm to zoom in on the nearest local minimum. One-dimensional searches like this are quite manageable.

The two models presented in this chapter impose a more formidable challenge, though. In order to efficiently optimize a function of several variables, we need a sophisticated algorithm. We have a lot going for us. The continuous error criterion presented earlier in this chapter is much easier to optimize than the elementary counting criterion previously employed. And we can compute not only the gradient, but even the second partial derivatives of this continuous criterion. All that remains is to find a way to make efficient use of this information.

This section will present the learning algorithm that I use. It is based on sound mathematics, and experience indicates that it performs well. Beyond that, no claims of optimality are made. This is probably fertile ground for more thorough investigation. In particular, it is likely that more effective use of the second derivatives could be made. Readers in search of a thesis topic, please take note.

In any optimization problem in which computation of derivatives is feasible, the first choice to be made is among three possibilities. The simplest method, which also has the lowest overhead, is to focus on the gradient and use a member of the conjugate gradient family. This is my choice. The second derivatives are not needed as a normal part of that algorithm, but some use of them is possible. There are two other choices. One can use quasi-Newton methods in which the entire Hessian matrix (or its inverse) is approximated and stored. These methods are generally only marginally superior to conjugate gradient methods, if they are superior at all. And they require storage and manipulation of a square matrix whose number of rows and columns is equal to the number of parameters being optimized. In neural network applications, that can be a very large number. For this reason, I avoid quasi-Newton methods.

The third choice is to use Newton's method directly. We have the theoretical capability of computing all mixed partials. The equations for doing this are not presented in this text, but they can be easily derived. However, this method requires the same mass storage as quasi-Newton methods. Worse, there can be an awful lot of mixed partials to compute, and most of that computation must take place in the expensive loop that passes through the entire training set. In all but the smallest problems, the horrendous overhead of finding all mixed partials would almost surely swamp out any gains due to the excellence of Newton's method.

One decision has been made. We will use a conjugate gradient algorithm. It has excellent convergence properties, yet it avoids storage of the potentially gigantic Hessian matrix. Two more questions must be answered. How do we best perform a global search to find a starting point for the descent to a local minimum? Can we find enough of a use for the second derivatives (which are not needed by the basic conjugate gradient algorithm) to justify the time spent computing them? These questions will be answered one at a time.

In order to locate a good starting point, one hopefully near the global minimum, it is tempting to use the same approach that was used earlier in this book for training multiple-layer feedforward networks. However, simulated annealing is usually a poor choice for this particular problem. In the case of an MLFN, local minima abound, and even the approximate location of the one that is the best is difficult or impossible to predict in advance. We have no choice but to cast about with wild abandon. Such is not usually the case for probabilistic neural networks. Unless the user has been extraordinarily careless, the basin of attraction of the global minimum will be broad, and all weights will have similar orders of magnitude. Thus, there is a simple approach that has always worked well for me: Start by treating the PNN as a basic single-sigma model. Perform a rough line minimization of that single weight. Use that nearly optimal value as the starting point for all sigmas in the general model. This method is fast, easy, and it seems to be reliable.

The second question is more difficult to answer. Just what do we do with those second derivatives? Their computation does not add a lot to the expense of computing the error and the gradient, but it adds something. How can we justify that expense? Should we even try to justify it, or should we just abandon second derivatives? If we were using a quasi-Newton method, we could probably set the diagonal of the Hessian to those values, and scale the mixed partials accordingly. But we aren't using that method. The conjugate gradient algorithm, at least as I have seen it, has no place for second derivatives. In fact, its whole point is to avoid them. Nonetheless, there is a valuable role for the vector of pure second derivatives that we can so easily compute along with the gradient. We use it to estimate an efficient scaling factor for the line search that is at the core of the conjugate gradient algorithm. If the reader has not yet studied Chapter 1, now is the time. The global line search that is used for the initial univariate sigma optimization is discussed on page 8. That same algorithm is also used by the conjugate gradient algorithm, which is itself discussed on page 31. Finally, the use to which the vector of second derivatives is put is described on page 26.

6

Generalized Regression

- Review of ordinary regression

- Multiple and polynomial regression

- Mathematical derivation of generalized regression

- An intuitive look at generalized regression

- Donald Specht's GRNN architecture

- Gradient computation

- Complete source code

When Donald Specht recast a decades-old statistical classification algorithm as a neural network, he reintroduced to the world one of the best general-purpose classifiers ever devised. Unfortunately, that original algorithm is deeply and fundamentally limited to the single task of classification. That statement is not meant to cast aspersions on the utility of the algorithm. Classification is an extremely important and widely used technique. But the more general function-mapping capabilities of other neural networks like the ubiquitous multiple-layer feedforward net meant that Specht's powerful new probabilistic neural network could not compete in a very large arena. Thus, when he modified the algorithm to include function mapping, he added a formidable new tool to the neural network toolbox. This chapter will discuss his *general regression neural network (GRNN)*, often referred to as *generalized regression*. Both his original design and recent modifications that allow separate sigmas will be presented. But first, let us review ordinary regression as it is traditionally implemented.

Review of Ordinary Regression

The tremendous versatility of generalized regression will be appreciated all the more when it is seen in comparison to traditional regression. For this reason, as well as for the sake of those who need a refresher course in regression, this section reviews the salient features of the technique.

The basic idea behind regression is that we use a set of one or more measured values, called *independent variables*, to predict the value of a single *dependent variable*. We will follow the tradition of limiting the discussion to the prediction of just one variable. The general case of predicting several variables simultaneously is handled by treating each dependent variable as a separate regression problem.

There are many reasons why we might want to be able to predict some variable given some other variables. The variable might be unmeasurable but valuable, as for example, next week's price of some favorite stock or bond. Or the variable may be important to the stable control of an industrial process. We will not be concerned with the reason or nature of the prediction. All we know is that there is hope of being able to predict the dependent variable with useful accuracy. Two simple examples of attempts to predict one variable from another are shown in Figures 6.1 and 6.2, respectively.

Review of Ordinary Regression

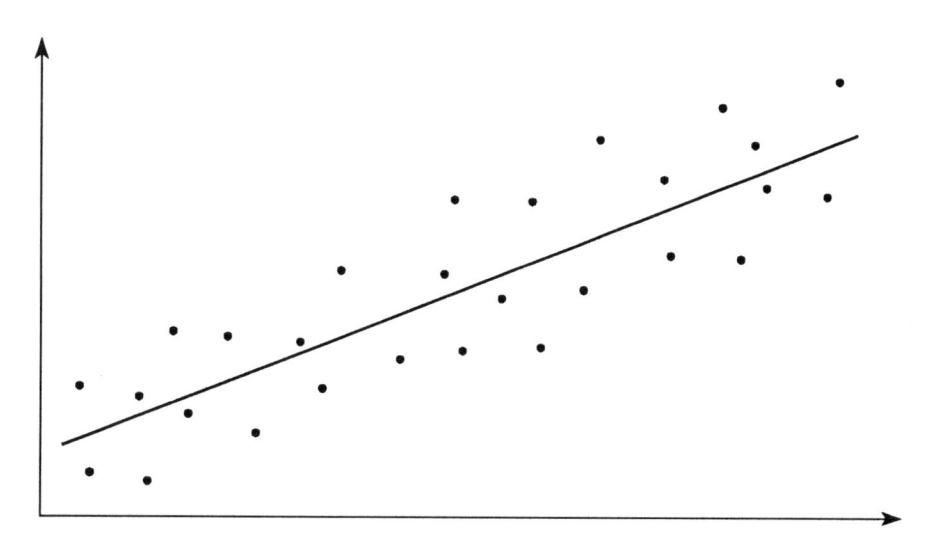

Figure 6.1 Appropriate linear regression.

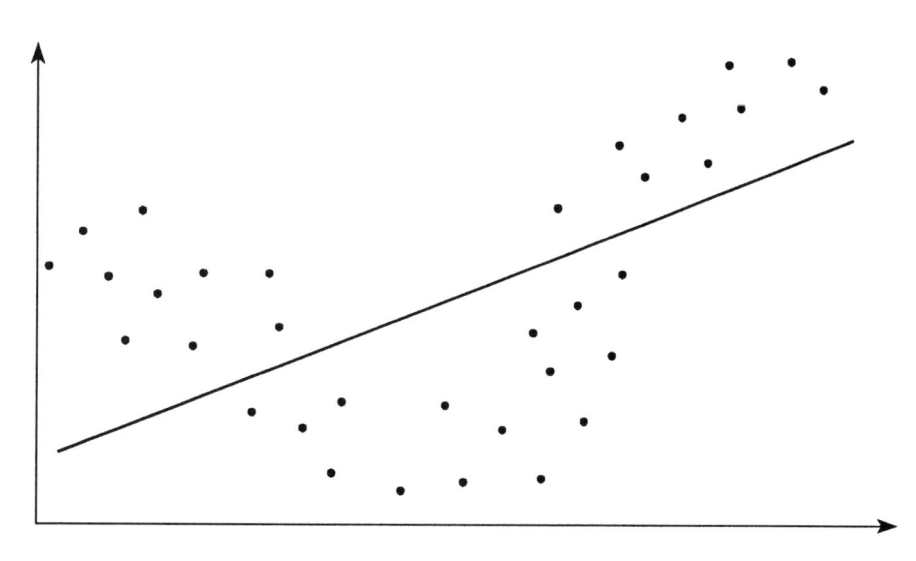

Figure 6.2 Inappropriate linear regression.

Simple Linear Regression

The easiest case is simple linear regression with one independent variable. By *linear* we mean that the function that will be used to model the data is a straight line. We thus implicitly assume that the data does indeed lie on a straight line (except for random noise). In particular, we assume that the situation is more like that shown in Figure 6.1, rather than that of Figure 6.2. It is amazing how often this seemingly obvious assumption is ignored. Univariate linear regression is expressed as the simple relationship shown in Equation (6.1).

$$y = ax + b \tag{6.1}$$

Given a training set, computation of the slope, a, and the intercept, b, is done in three steps. Start by finding the mean of each variable, as defined in Equation (6.2). Then cumulate the sum of squares and cross-products as shown in Equation (6.3). Finally, compute the slope and intercept using Equation (6.4). The resulting linear equation will minimize the mean squared error of the predicted y values in the training set.

$$\bar{x} = \frac{1}{n}\sum_{i=1}^{n} x_i$$
$$\bar{y} = \frac{1}{n}\sum_{i=1}^{n} y_i \tag{6.2}$$

$$SS_x = \sum_{i=1}^{n}(x_i - \bar{x})^2$$
$$SS_{xy} = \sum_{i=1}^{n}(x_i - \bar{x})(y_i - \bar{y}) \tag{6.3}$$

$$a = \frac{SS_{xy}}{SS_x}$$

$$b = \bar{y} - a * \bar{x}$$
(6.4)

Multiple Regression

When there are several independent variables, the situation is a little more complicated. A typical example in which there are three independent variables is shown in Equation (6.5). Note that we always need one more coefficient than there are variables so as to allow for a constant offset.

$$y = \beta_1 x_1 + \beta_2 x_2 + \beta_3 x_3 + \beta_4$$
(6.5)

It is easiest to express this problem using matrix notation. Even more simplification is attained by augmenting the independent vector **x** by placing the constant 1.0 at the end. In the example of Equation (6.5) in which there are three independent variables, each observed **x** vector would contain four components, $\{x_1, x_2, x_3, 1\}$. If we let this be a row vector and let the coefficients form a column vector, Equation (6.5) can be compactly expressed as in Equation (6.6).

$$\mathbf{x}\beta = y$$
(6.6)

How do we compute the β vector of coefficients so as to minimize the mean squared error of the predictions within the training set? This question is answered in nearly every intermediate-level statistics book ever written, so we will mercifully dispense with the details here. In summary form, the procedure is as follows: Augment each observed vector by placing 1.0 at its end, exactly as was done above. Stack these row vectors into a matrix that we will call **A**. This matrix contains as many rows as there are observations, and as many columns as there are independent variables, plus one more column that is entirely 1's. Place the measured values of the dependent variable corresponding to each independent variable vector in a column vector that we will call **Y**. We then hope that Equation (6.7), which expresses perfect prediction for each member of the training set, will be true.

$$\mathbf{A}\beta = \mathbf{Y} \tag{6.7}$$

This equation has an exact solution if, and only if, **Y** lies in the subspace spanned by the columns of **A**. Unfortunately, this solution is not guaranteed to be unique. This fact can cause serious difficulties that must be dealt with. Furthermore, random sampling errors do in practice guarantee that **Y** will virtually never lie in the subspace spanned by the columns of **A**. So we must find a solution, ß, that approximately solves Equation (6.7). Nearly any statistics text will show that the β vector given in Equation (6.8) minimizes the mean squared error in the predicted values of **Y**.

$$\beta = (\mathbf{A'A})^{-1} \mathbf{A'Y} \tag{6.8}$$

Alas, that traditional old workhorse of an equation does us little good in practice. In most realistic applications, the matrix that must be inverted will often be either totally singular, and hence not invertible, or so ill-conditioned that it might as well be singular. It is unfortunate that the majority of textbooks that discuss multiple regression emphasize Equation (6.8). Computing β by direct application of that equation, which includes inverting the matrix as indicated, is the *worst possible method*. It is numerically unstable, it invites division by zero (a cardinal sin), and it is just plain ugly and disgusting to programmers with any class at all. Last but not least, in those rare cases when it does give a reasonably correct answer, finding that answer requires far more computation than many methods that are numerically superior. Don't even think about doing it this way.

So how do we find β quickly and correctly? There are several choices, but they all start out the same way. Without proof, which can be found in many common sources, we state that the least squares solution satisfies what are generally known as the *normal equations* of the problem. This set of simultaneous linear equations is expressed in matrix form in Equation (6.9). Note that our old quasi-friend, Equation (6.8), gives (in simple situations) a solution to the normal equations.

$$\mathbf{A'A}\beta = \mathbf{A'Y} \tag{6.9}$$

As any student of numerical methods knows, there is a vast array of tools for solving for β in Equation (6.9). Many of us have demonstrated to a professor our understanding of *Gauss-Jordan elimination* by laboriously solving a small system of equations, armed with nothing more than pencil, paper, and perhaps a calculator. Provided we are confident that the system is not singular, that method is fast and respectable. Its close relative, *LU decomposition*, is a little faster and has similar numerical characteristics. Those who desire a somewhat more sophisticated approach, one that is slower but has superior numerical properties, may want to use *QR decomposition*. However, staunch numerical conservatives like myself will almost always want the comfort and security obtained by using the best that there is, *singular value decomposition*. The mathematics of that algorithm is beyond the scope of this text. Press *et al.* (1992) gives a good summary along with excellent C code. Forsythe *et al.* (1977) is even more detailed. A good intuitive discussion of the technique, including both the basic mathematics and the motivation for that mathematics, is in Masters (1993). But all that the reader needs to know right now is that the singular value decomposition approach to multiple regression, though relatively slow, handles every significant problem that may arise. Data sets that are ill conditioned, or even totally singular, are dealt with in an effective manner.

It should be pointed out that computing several β vectors, each one for predicting a different dependent variable from the same set of independent variables, is only slightly more time consuming than finding just one β vector. This entire chapter focuses on the common situation of having a single *y* variable. But if more than one is to be predicted based on the same set of independent variables, take care to do it efficiently. For all of the solution methods just discussed, including singular value decomposition, the vast majority of the computational load is involved with the matrix of independent variables, **A**. Once the required decomposition has been found, applying that decomposition to a column vector **Y** to compute a β vector is fast and easy. Be sure to code your implementation in such a way as to isolate the tedious decomposition, which need only be performed once, from the simple final step. The best reference for readers who want to implement multiple regression this way is Press *et al.* (1992).

Polynomial Regression

Look back at Figure 6.2 on page 225. Obviously, ordinary linear regression is not an effective method for modeling a function that looks like that one. So how can we handle such a situation? As will be seen a little later, generalized regression usually does an excellent job. But first let us examine the traditional approach.

When one wants to model a complicated curved function, it is often reasonable to assume that the function is the weighted sum of several simpler curved functions. And there is usually no better choice for simple basis functions than the polynomials. There is a famous theorem, the Weierstrass approximation theorem, which, in essence, states that a continuous function defined on a compact interval can be approximated to any degree of accuracy by a polynomial. This means that, in principle at least, we can find a polynomial that does what we want. We can model the training data to any desired accuracy by finding a high-degree polynomial that passes through a large number of the points in the training set, and hope that the polynomial so determined will do a good job on data that is not in the training set. There is a problem with this brute-force approach, though. It doesn't work. In fact, 99 times out of 100, we find that the more we try to accurately fit a high-degree polynomial to a training set, the worse the fit becomes in areas that are not included in the training set. If one makes a plot of a polynomial found this way, one almost invariably finds that the plot goes wildly off scale, shooting out the top of the plot between one pair of training points, then plunging into the ground between the next pair. Of course, the polynomial dutifully passes through each and every point that went into its definition. But so what? It is worthless everywhere else.

Instead of trying to use a high-order polynomial to exactly fit a small set of representative training points, what we need to do is use a low-order polynomial to provide a least-squares fit to a large collection of training points. Only by the wildest coincidence will any one point be fit exactly. But they will all be fit approximately. And most importantly, the use of a relatively low-order polynomial will ensure smooth interpolation across the domain.

Superficially, it seems easy to accomplish this task. Compute a set of polynomials from the independent variable for each training point. Arrange these polynomials as a vector of *independent variables* and then use the multiple regression technique of the previous section to compute the coefficient of each polynomial. In fact, that is exactly what we will do. But the catch comes when we decide just what polynomials to use. The obvious choice is $f_1(x) = x$, $f_2(x) = x^2$, $f_3(x) = x^3$, and so on. This a terrible choice. Why? Because these functions are not very different in terms of the information that they extract from the raw data. The even powers are different from the odd powers, but that's about it. Large positive values of x produce large positive values of all of the functions, with the relationship being monotonic. If x is negative, all of the odd powers behave in the same way, as do all of the even powers. The bottom line is that we end up with a set of independent variables that are highly correlated. The **A'A** matrix would be nearly singular, and as a result, the computed β would be very unstable and dangerously at the whim of random noise.

Instead of this simplistic choice, we need polynomials that are relatively independent of one other, that is, polynomials that behave very differently within some reasonable domain. No matter what the value of x is within that domain, we hope that when x changes some of the polynomials go up and some go down. Furthermore, we want this pattern to change throughout the domain. The resulting variety of extracted features is just what we need to induce stability in the multiple-regression model.

We now introduce an extremely popular family of polynomials for use in multiple regression: the Chebyshev polynomials. They actually have a wealth of uses, especially in numerical approximation. They can be found in nearly any book on numerical methods; those uses will not be covered here. We are strictly interested in using them for least-squares fitting of curved functions via polynomial regression.

For this family, and indeed for any family of polynomials, there is one small problem to be dealt with right up front: All polynomials blow up as the absolute value of x increases. This is an inescapable fact of life. For very large absolute values of x, every even-order polynomial behaves similarly to every other even-order polynomial. And the same is true of odd-order polynomials. Therefore, if our valuable independence properties are to be preserved, we must limit the domain over which x is allowed to travel, regardless of what family is used. The Chebyshev polynomials are allowed to range from −1 to 1. If the raw data does not readily fit in this interval, it must be transformed so that it does. For the remainder of this discussion, it will be assumed that all raw input values lie within this domain. For best results, the actual raw inputs should cover as wide an expanse of this domain as possible. This rescaling should always be possible.

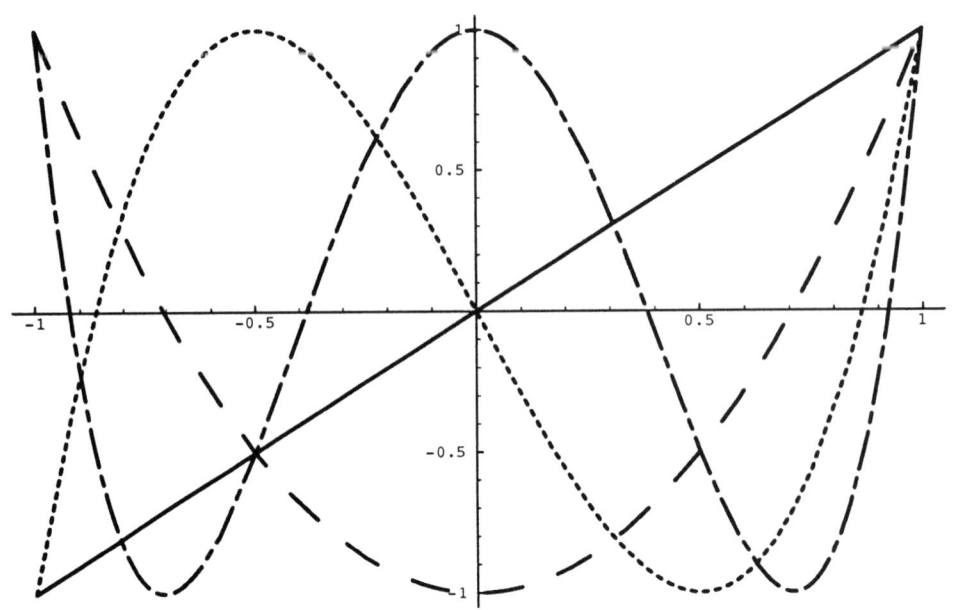

Figure 6.3 The first four Chebyshev polynomials.

$$T_1(x) = x$$
$$T_2(x) = 2x^2 - 1$$
$$T_3(x) = 4x^3 - 3x \quad (6.10)$$
$$T_4(x) = 8x^4 - 8x^2 + 1$$

The Chebyshev polynomials are usually written T_k, where k is the degree of the highest power in the polynomial. The letter T is in deference to an older spelling, Tchebycheff. The first four Chebyshev polynomials are plotted in Figure 6.3. T_1 is a solid line, T_2 is long dashes, T_3 is short dashes, and T_4 is alternating dashes. Their definitions are shown in Equation (6.10).

Notice that once these polynomials reach the end of their (−1, 1) range, they head off to infinity with no turning back. In order to make proper use of their ability to extract valuable information from the input data, the data absolutely must be scaled to lie within that range as closely as possible.

Review of Ordinary Regression

It is rare that higher degrees are ever needed. If they are needed, they can be computed from the recursive formula shown in Equation (6.11).

$$T_k(x) = 2xT_{k-1}(x) - T_{k-2}(x) \qquad (6.11)$$

Here is a short subroutine for computing Chebyshev polynomial function values from a raw input. It uses the recursion in Equation (6.11).

```
void cheby (
   int n ,                    // Highest degree to compute
   double x ,                 // Input of raw value in [-1,1]
   double *t                  // Output: t[k] = T{k+1}(x), 0<=k<n
   )
{
   int i ;

   t[0] = x ;
   t[1] = 2.0 * x * x - 1.0 ;

   for (i=2 ; i<n ; i++)
      t[i] = 2.0 * x * t[i-1]  -  t[i-2] ;
}
```

Many readers will by now be asking why so much space has been devoted to a traditional statistical technique when this is supposedly a book about neural network algorithms. There are two reasons. The first is to help readers appreciate even more the generalized regression neural network that is about to take center stage. Look at all the work that we had to do to have even a chance of modeling an arbitrary nonlinear function using traditional techniques. We had to transform the domain of the input variable to a predefined interval. We had to make an arbitrary decision as to how high a degree of polynomial we wanted to include. And then we had to hope that the degree is high enough to follow the curves. None of this is necessary for generalized regression. We throw in the data, and the network follows the curves. It is beautiful.

The other reason for expounding on Chebyshev polynomials is that they have a lot of applicability for preprocessing data that will be presented to traditional neural networks. Notice that these polynomials map from the domain [−1, 1] to the range [−1, 1]. That range makes them particularly suitable for neural network inputs. I have seen many problems that benefited greatly from adding a few extra inputs to the neural network. These extra inputs are low-order Chebyshev polynomials based on one or more measured variables. The information extracted by this preprocessing often is immediately useful to the network, making its job easier than if the network itself had to learn to extract information about nonlinearities in the data. Do not take this lightly. Sometimes the improvement is surprising.

The General Regression Neural Network

We'll jump right in with the mathematics of this model, then back off and develop an intuitive feel for it. Readers who are intimidated by this fierce introduction may safely skip to the intuitive discussion on page 237. Note that this section relies heavily on notation and concepts introduced in Chapters 4 and 5. Readers should be familiar with that material before proceeding.

As is our custom, we will assume that the independent variable **x** is a vector, and that the dependent variable y is a scalar. It is well known that the best predicted value for y (in the sense of minimum expected squared error) is its conditional expectation given **x**. That expectation is shown in Equation (6.12).

$$E_{Y|\mathbf{X}}(\mathbf{x}) = \frac{\int_{-\infty}^{\infty} y \cdot f_{XY}(\mathbf{x}, y)\, dy}{\int_{-\infty}^{\infty} f_{XY}(\mathbf{x}, y)\, dy} \qquad (6.12)$$

In practice, we never know the joint density $f_{XY}(\mathbf{x}, y)$. However, we can append the y variable to the end of the **x** vector and use the good old multivariate Parzen estimator to approximate that joint density. Define distance functions for **x** and y as shown in Equations (6.13) and (6.14), respectively. Parzen's density approximation is then shown in Equation (6.15).

The General Regression Neural Network

$$D_X(\mathbf{x}, \mathbf{x}_i) = \sum_{j=1}^{p} \left(\frac{x_j - x_{ij}}{\sigma_j} \right)^2 \tag{6.13}$$

$$D_Y(y, y_i) = \left(\frac{y - y_i}{\sigma_y} \right)^2 \tag{6.14}$$

$$g(\mathbf{x}, y) = \frac{1}{n \, c_X \, c_Y} \sum_{i=1}^{n} \exp(-D_X(\mathbf{x}, \mathbf{x}_i) - D_Y(y, y_i))$$

$$= \frac{1}{n \, c_X \, c_Y} \sum_{i=1}^{n} \exp(-D_X(\mathbf{x}, \mathbf{x}_i)) \exp(-D_Y(y, y_i)) \tag{6.15}$$

The two normalizing constants are functions of the σ weights, and their purpose is to ensure that the density approximator integrates to unity. In particular, c_Y is defined as shown in Equation (6.16), and c_x is defined in the corresponding way, understanding that the integral is taken over the entire multivariate domain.

$$c_Y = \int_{-\infty}^{\infty} \exp(-D_y(y, 0)) \, dy \tag{6.16}$$

If we replace the exact density used in Equation (6.12) with the approximation given in Equation (6.15), we can express the predicted value of y as shown in Equation (6.17). The numerator and denominator are defined in Equations (6.18) and (6.19), respectively.

$$\hat{y}(\mathbf{x}) = \frac{N(\mathbf{x})}{D(\mathbf{x})} \tag{6.17}$$

$$N(\mathbf{x}) = \int_{-\infty}^{\infty} \frac{y}{nc_X c_Y} \sum_{i=1}^{n} \exp(-D_X(\mathbf{x}, \mathbf{x}_i)) \exp(-D_Y(y, y_i)) \, dy$$
$$= \frac{1}{nc_X c_Y} \sum_{i=1}^{n} \exp(-D_X(\mathbf{x}, \mathbf{x}_i)) \int_{-\infty}^{\infty} y \cdot \exp(-D_y(y, y_i)) \, dy \qquad (6.18)$$
$$= \frac{1}{nc_X} \sum_{i=1}^{n} y_i \cdot \exp(-D_X(\mathbf{x}, \mathbf{x}_i))$$

$$D(\mathbf{x}) = \int_{-\infty}^{\infty} \frac{1}{nc_X c_Y} \sum_{i=1}^{n} \exp(-D_X(\mathbf{x}, \mathbf{x}_i)) \exp(-D_Y(y, y_i)) \, dy$$
$$= \frac{1}{nc_X c_Y} \sum_{i=1}^{n} \exp(-D_X(\mathbf{x}, \mathbf{x}_i)) \int_{-\infty}^{\infty} \exp(-D_y(y, y_i)) \, dy \quad (6.19)$$
$$= \frac{1}{nc_X} \sum_{i=1}^{n} \exp(-D_X(\mathbf{x}, \mathbf{x}_i))$$

Those last two equations deserve close examination, for they are at the heart of the GRNN. Let us start with the denominator, Equation (6.19), as it is a little easier to handle. The first line is just a straightforward substitution of the estimator of Equation (6.15) into the denominator of Equation (6.12). Two separate steps are necessary to get to the second line. First we interchange the order of integration and summation. The integral of a sum is equal to the sum of the integrals. Then we factor the term involving $\mathbf{x}$ out of the integral. It is constant throughout the integration, so it can be brought out to the front. Finally, look back at Equation (6.16) to see the value of the integral. The c_Y constants cancel, and we are left with the last line of that equation.

The numerator, Equation (6.18), is only a little trickier. The first line is a direct substitution, as was the case with the denominator. Also, we arrive at the second line by the exact same interchange of operations and removal of the common factor. The magic happens in the transition to the last line. We leave it as a small exercise for the reader to verify that the value of that integral is y_i times c_Y. Here is a hint: What is the integral (from minus infinity to infinity) of

The General Regression Neural Network

$f(x) = x \cdot \exp(-x^2)$? (Think about symmetry.) Now write the integral at the end of Equation (6.18) using the full definition of D_Y as given in Equation (6.14). Expand it and see what happens.

To wrap this up, insert the quantities shown in Equations (6.18) and (6.19) into Equation (6.17). The constants cancel. It is also interesting to observe that the scaling factor for y, σ_Y, vanished. We are left with Equation (6.20). That is the fundamental equation of the general regression neural network.

$$\hat{y}(\mathbf{x}) = \frac{\sum_{i=1}^{n} y_i \exp(-D(\mathbf{x}, \mathbf{x}_i))}{\sum_{i=1}^{n} \exp(-D(\mathbf{x}, \mathbf{x}_i))} \qquad (6.20)$$

An Intuitive Approach

We can devise a solution to the general regression problem by looking at it from an entirely different viewpoint. Think about finding the weighted mean of a collection of data values. Suppose, for example, that we regularly collect three sequential samples of a variable generated by some process. We need the mean of those three values, but we want to weight the last sample twice as heavily as the first two samples. All that we do is double the last sample, add in the first two samples, and divide by four (1+1+2). The mean of 3, 5, and 4 computed this way would be (3+5+2•4) / 4 = 4. In other words, we multiply each observed value by the weight that we give it, then divide by the sum of the weights.

Now suppose that the weights are not fixed constants. Instead, the weight that is assigned to each sample value is dynamically determined by the value of some other variable that is measured at the same time. And even the rule by which that associated variable determines the weight is itself changeable. It's time for a picture. Look at Figure 6.4.

This figure shows a scatterplot of a collection of sampled points. The horizontal axis is used for what we shall call x, and the vertical axis is used for y. The center of each circle represents a single observation. For the moment, ignore the fact that the circles are filled differently.

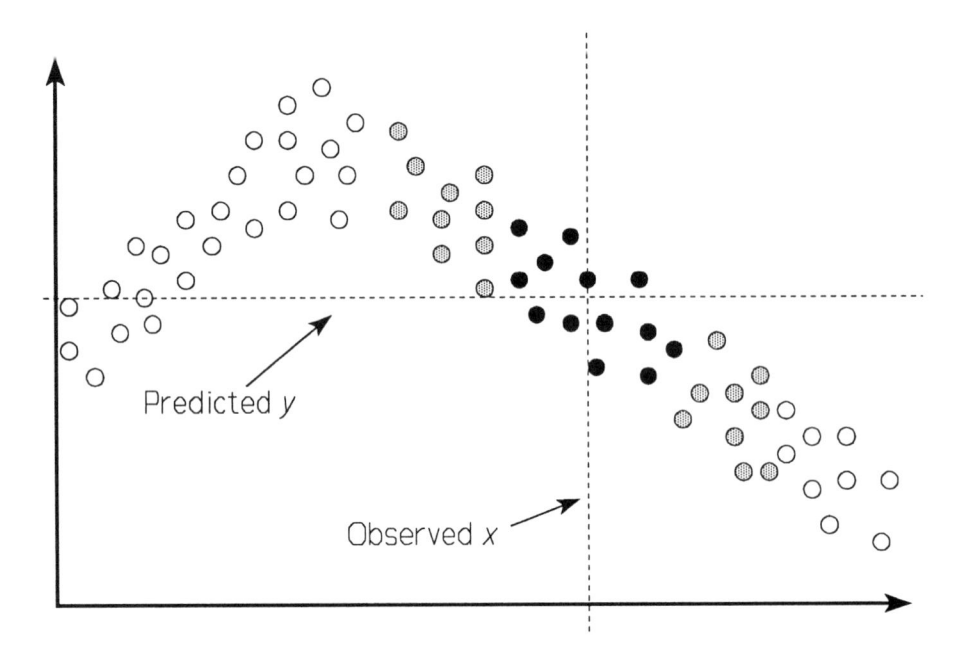

Figure 6.4 Generalized regression.

At some later time we are given a value for the *x* variable, and we are asked to estimate what the corresponding value of *y* would be. The vertical dotted line is placed at the observed *x* value. We can easily make a pretty good eyeball estimate of a probable *y* value. But can we come up with a more rigorous approach?

Intuition first tells us that our *y* estimate should primarily be based on the *y* values of the sample points that are near the newly observed *x*. Points whose *x* value is distant from the newly observed *x* should be essentially ignored. In fact, a good method would be to compute some measure of the distance separating the newly observed point from each old sample point, and then find the weighted mean of the *y* values of those old sample points. The weight for each point would be determined by the distance separating the observed point from the sample point, with greater distances yielding lower weights. To compute this weighted mean, we would multiply the *y* value of each sample by its weight (as determined by its *x* relative to the new *x*), sum those quantities across the entire collection, then divide by the sum of the weights. Now look back at Equation (6.20). That's exactly what the GRNN is doing. In Figure 6.4 the circles representing sample points have been colored according to their x distance from the newly observed point. Empty circles are so far away that for all practical purposes they do not enter into the estimate. Lightly filled circles have moderate weights, and fully filled circles contribute heavily to the weighted mean of y values. This weighted mean, which is our predicted y, is plotted as a horizontal dotted line.

Donald Specht's GRNN Architecture

Since this is a book about neural networks, it is incumbent on the author to show how the above algorithm really *is* a neural network. Actually, there is an even more important reason for portraying it in neural network form. One of the key selling points of neural networks is that they can be implemented as a large number of simple processes that are able to execute mostly in parallel. This property lets neural networks be both cheap to construct and fast to execute. The best way to present the structure of the GRNN is to go straight to the source. Figure 6.5 is adapted from an illustration in Specht (1991).

Operation of the GRNN neural network is very similar to operation of the ordinary PNN described in Chapter 4. The pattern layer contains one unit per training case. In this illustration there are four training cases. The independent variable input vector, which here contains three variables, is simultaneously presented to all pattern units. These units each compute a distance measure separating the training case represented by that unit from the input case. This distance is acted on by the activation function, which is, in effect, the Parzen window.

Up until this point, the GRNN and the PNN are identical in operation. The difference occurs in the connection to the summation units. In the PNN, there is a separate summation unit for each class. Each pattern unit connects only to the summation unit corresponding to the class of the training case embodied in that pattern unit. In the GRNN, every pattern unit connects to both summation units. For the denominator summation unit, the weight vector is unity, so a simple sum is performed. For the numerator summation unit, the weight connecting each pattern unit is equal to the value of the dependent variable for the training case of that pattern unit.

The only (arguably) nonneural operation in this architecture is that of the output unit. It must divide the output of the numerator summation by the output of the denominator summation. In at least

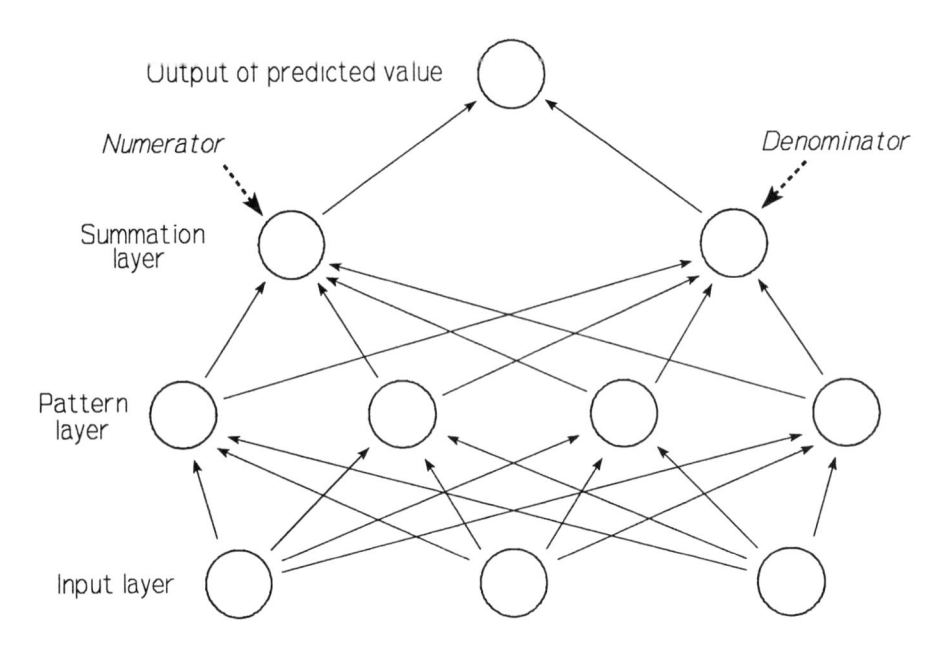

Figure 6.5 Donald Specht's GRNN.

one hardware implementation of the GRNN known to the author, division is not supported on the chip. This operation must be offloaded to another processor. And there is general (though not universal) agreement that biological neurons are incapable of division. But that is a small point of criticism of this extremely powerful model.

It should be obvious that this architecture can easily be expanded to perform multivariate prediction. All that is needed is to include a numerator summation unit for each dependent variable. The remainder of the structure remains the same.

Computing the Gradient

We shall now demonstrate how the gradient of the error of the GRNN can be computed. The method is very similar to that for the PNN. Therefore, the reader who wishes to understand this section must be familiar with the corresponding material in Chapter 5. Since there are so many similarities, this presentation will be made rather quickly and with little in the way of explanation. We use exactly the same distance function as was used previously. For the reader's convenience, this distance function is reproduced in Equation (6.21).

$$D(\mathbf{x}, \mathbf{x}_i) = \sum_{j=1}^{p} \left(\frac{x_j - x_{ij}}{\sigma_j} \right)^2 \qquad (6.21)$$

So that the reader can more easily follow the parallel flow of the ensuing derivation, symbols that are similar to those used in Chapter 5 will be employed. The output of the GRNN that corresponds to a particular input is shown in Equation (6.22). The numerator and denominator of that equation are shown in Equations (6.23) and (6.24), respectively. Note that these correspond to Equations (6.17) through (6.19) given earlier on page 235.

$$b(\mathbf{x}) = \frac{h(\mathbf{x})}{s(\mathbf{x})} \qquad (6.22)$$

$$h(\mathbf{x}) = \sum_{i=1}^{n} y_i \exp(-D(\mathbf{x}, \mathbf{x}_i)) \qquad (6.23)$$

$$s(\mathbf{x}) = \sum_{i=1}^{n} \exp(-D(\mathbf{x}, \mathbf{x}_i)) \qquad (6.24)$$

Since the GRNN does not need to deal with multiple classes, its error measure is considerably simpler than that of the PNN. The usual squared error attributed to an observation is shown in Equation (6.25).

$$e(\mathbf{x}; y) = [b(\mathbf{x}) - y]^2 \qquad (6.25)$$

We now obtain the first and second derivatives of the error defined in Equation (6.25) with respect to each of the sigma weights. Straightforward differentiation gives us the gradient, shown in Equation (6.26). Differentiating once more gives us the second derivatives, shown in Equation (6.27).

$$\frac{\partial e(\mathbf{x};y)}{\partial \sigma_j} = 2[b(\mathbf{x})-y]\left[\frac{\partial b(\mathbf{x})}{\partial \sigma_j}\right] \quad (6.26)$$

$$\frac{\partial^2 e(\mathbf{x};y)}{\partial \sigma_j^2} = 2[b(\mathbf{x})-y]\left[\frac{\partial^2 b(\mathbf{x})}{\partial \sigma_j^2}\right] + 2\left[\frac{\partial b(\mathbf{x})}{\partial \sigma_j}\right]^2 \quad (6.27)$$

We continue this development in parallel with that of the PNN in Chapter 5. Once again, the derivatives with respect to σ_j of the quantities in the numerator and denominator of Equation (6.22) are shown in Equations (6.28) through (6.31).

$$\frac{\partial h(\mathbf{x})}{\partial \sigma_j} \equiv v_j(\mathbf{x}) = 2\sum_{i=1}^{n} y_i \exp[-D(\mathbf{x},\mathbf{x}_i)]\frac{(x_j-x_{ij})^2}{\sigma_j^3} \quad (6.28)$$

$$\frac{\partial s(\mathbf{x})}{\partial \sigma_j} \equiv V_j(\mathbf{x}) = 2\sum_{i=1}^{n} \exp[-D(\mathbf{x},\mathbf{x}_i)]\frac{(x_j-x_{ij})^2}{\sigma_j^3} \quad (6.29)$$

$$\frac{\partial^2 h(\mathbf{x})}{\partial \sigma_j^2} \equiv w_j(\mathbf{x}) = 2\sum_{i=1}^{n} y_i \exp[-D(\mathbf{x},\mathbf{x}_i)] \cdot \left[2\frac{(x_j-x_{ij})^4}{\sigma_j^6} - 3\frac{(x_j-x_{ij})^2}{\sigma_j^4}\right] \quad (6.30)$$

$$\frac{\partial^2 s(\mathbf{x})}{\partial \sigma_j^2} \equiv W_j(\mathbf{x}) = 2 \sum_{i=1}^{n} \exp[-D(\mathbf{x}, \mathbf{x}_i)] \cdot$$
$$\left[2 \frac{(x_j - x_{ij})^4}{\sigma_j^6} - 3 \frac{(x_j - x_{ij})^2}{\sigma_j^4} \right]$$
(6.31)

We can finally find the partial derivatives of the GRNN output with respect to the σ weights. Tedious but straightforward application of the rule for differentiating quotients gives us Equations (6.32) and (6.33).

$$\frac{\partial b(\mathbf{x})}{\partial \sigma_j} = \frac{v_j(\mathbf{x}) - V_j(\mathbf{x}) b(\mathbf{x})}{s(\mathbf{x})}$$
(6.32)

$$\frac{\partial^2 b(\mathbf{x})}{\partial \sigma_j^2} = \frac{w_j(\mathbf{x}) - W_j(\mathbf{x}) b(\mathbf{x})}{s(\mathbf{x})}$$
$$+ \frac{2 V_j^2(\mathbf{x}) b(\mathbf{x}) - 2 v_j(\mathbf{x}) V_j(\mathbf{x})}{s^2(\mathbf{x})}$$
(6.33)

This section will be completed by providing a code fragment for computing these partial derivatives. No real explanations are needed, as the code and equations are straightforward modifications of the PNN code already studied in depth. The only significant exception is that this code handles the general case of predicting one or more dependent variables. There are nout outputs. The complete text of this subroutine can be found in the module SEPVAR.CPP on the accompanying program disk.

```
for (pop=0 ; pop<nout ; pop++) {  // For each population
   out[pop] = 0.0 ;                // Will sum kernels here
   for (ivar=0 ; ivar<nin ; ivar++) {
      v[pop*nin+ivar] = 0.0 ;      // Scratch for derivative stuff
      w[pop*nin+ivar] = 0.0 ;      // Ditto
      }
   }

psum = 0.0 ;                       // Denominator sum

vsptr = ... ;                      // Will cumulate vsum here
wsptr = ... ;                      // and wsum here
for (ivar=0 ; ivar<nin ; ivar++) { // One for each sigma
   vsptr[ivar] = 0.0 ;
   wsptr[ivar] = 0.0 ;
   }

for (tset=0 ; tset<ntrain ; tset++) { // Do all training cases

   dptr = ... ;                    // Point to this case

   dist = 0.0 ;                    // Will sum distance here
   for (ivar=0 ; ivar<nin ; ivar++) { // All variables in this case
      diff = input[ivar] - dptr[ivar] ; // Input minus case
      diff /= sigma[ivar] ;        // Scale per sigma
      dsqr[ivar] = diff * diff ;   // Squared weighted distance
      dist += dsqr[ivar] ;         // Cumulate for all vars
      }

   dist = exp ( -dist ) ;

   truedist = dist ;               // Need this for derivatives
   if (dist < 1.e-40)              // If this case is far from all
      dist = 1.e-40 ;              // prevent zero density

   dptr = ... ;                    // Point to start of y vector
   for (ivar=0 ; ivar<nout ; ivar++)// Cumulate numerator for each $y_i$
      out[ivar] += dist * dptr[ivar] ;
   vptr = v ;                      // Cumulate v and w now
   wptr = w ;
```

```
   for (outvar=0 ; outvar<nout ; outvar++) {        // For each y
     for (ivar=0 ; ivar<nin ; ivar++) {             // And each x
       temp = truedist * dsqr[ivar] * dptr[outvar] ;
       *vptr++ += temp ;                            // Equation (6.28)
       *wptr++ += temp * (2.0 * dsqr[ivar] - 3.0) ; // And (6.30)
       }
     }
   for (ivar=0 ; ivar<nin ; ivar++) {               // Cumulate vsum and wsum
     temp = truedist * dsqr[ivar] ;
     vsptr[ivar] += temp ;                          // Equation (6.29)
     wsptr[ivar] += temp * (2.0 * dsqr[ivar] - 3.0) ; // And (6.31)
     }
   psum += dist ;                                   // Cumulate denominator
   } // For all training cases

 for (pop=0 ; pop<nout ; pop++)                     // Compute each output y
   out[pop] /= psum ;                               // Using Equation (6.22)

/*
   Compute the derivatives.
*/

 for (ivar=0 ; ivar<nin ; ivar++) {                 // For each variable (i.e., sigma)

   vtot = vsptr[ivar] * 2.0 / (psum * sigma[ivar]) ;    // Common factors
   wtot = wsptr[ivar] * 2.0 / (psum * sigma[ivar] * sigma[ivar]) ;
   for (outvar=0 ; outvar<nout ; outvar++) {        // For each output y
     v[outvar*nin+ivar] *= 2.0 / (psum * sigma[ivar]) ;// Common factors
     w[outvar*nin+ivar] *= 2.0 / (psum * sigma[ivar] * sigma[ivar]) ;
     }

   for (outvar=0 ; outvar<nout ; outvar++) { // Derivatives computed here
     der1 = v[outvar*nin+ivar] - out[outvar] * vtot ;       // Eqn (6.32)
     der2 = w[outvar*nin+ivar] + 2.0 * out[outvar] * vtot * vtot -  // Eqn (6.33)
         2.0 * v[outvar*nin+ivar] * vtot - out[outvar] * wtot ;
     temp = 2.0 * (out[outvar] - target[outvar]) ;
     deriv[ivar] += temp * der1 ;                   // Equation (6.26)
     deriv2[ivar] += temp * der2  +  2.0 * der1 * der1 ;  // Equation (6.27)
     }
   }
```

The GRNN in Action

It is instructive to see how a GRNN works at solving a problem. Let us use a simple cubic polynomial as a model of the true underlying structure of a collection of sample data. This polynomial is graphed in Figure 6.6. In order to generate a training set, this polynomial is sampled at a wide variety of points, and random noise is added. Furthermore, one wild point is included. This training set is shown in Figure 6.7. Notice the single outlier about one-quarter of the way in from the left.

We now examine the effect produced by a variety of values of σ, the smoothing parameter. In Figure 6.8 we see what happens when a very small value is used. The GRNN follows the training data closely, almost moving from point to point. If the data is known to be clean, the GRNN makes an excellent interpolating algorithm. But since in most cases we know that the data is contaminated by noise, straightforward interpolation is not what we want.

Figure 6.9 is obtained by using a moderately small smoothing parameter. Observe that the wild point succeeds in pulling the function a bit out of line. If we are confident that any supposed wild points are actually valid data, then this is just what we want. But usually this degree of data following is not appropriate. A somewhat larger smoothing parameter gives us the function shown in Figure 6.10. Most people would consider this to be essentially ideal.

Finally, we must be wary of taking a good thing too far. Figure 6.11 illustrates the effect of a smoothing parameter that is too large. The global shape of the training set has swamped out all of the details. Granted, we usually want the fine details, which are due to noise, to be eliminated. On the other hand, this is ridiculous.

What is the moral of this story? Actually, there are two morals: First, it should be obvious that there most definitely *is* an optimal value of the smoothing parameter. In a multivariate problem, there would be an optimal vector of values. The leave-one-out approach that has been espoused for all members of the PNN family seems to work well for finding that optimal value. The second moral is that whenever possible, we should visually examine the function implemented by the GRNN. It is risky to just blindly accept whatever it provides.

The GRNN in Action

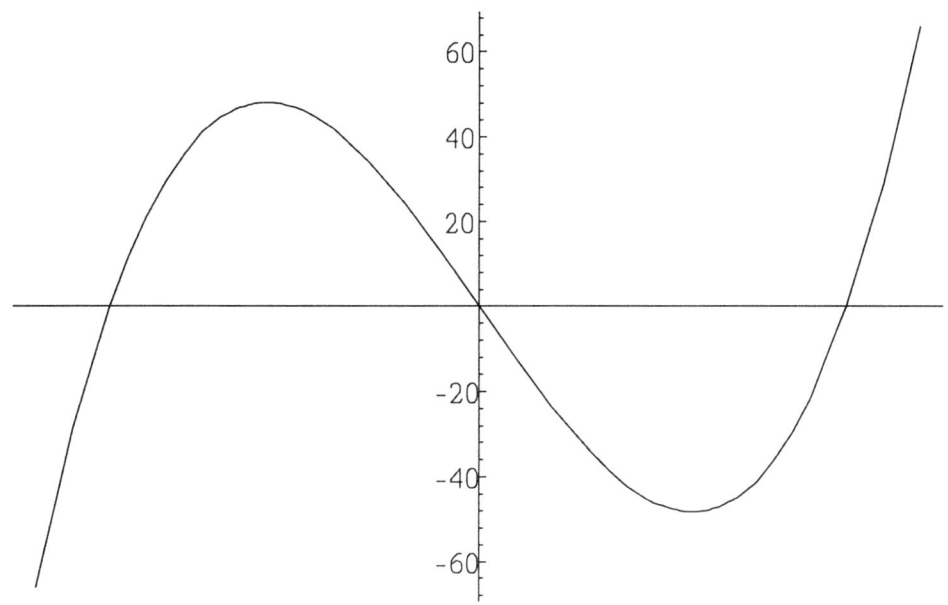

Figure 6.6 A cubic polynomial.

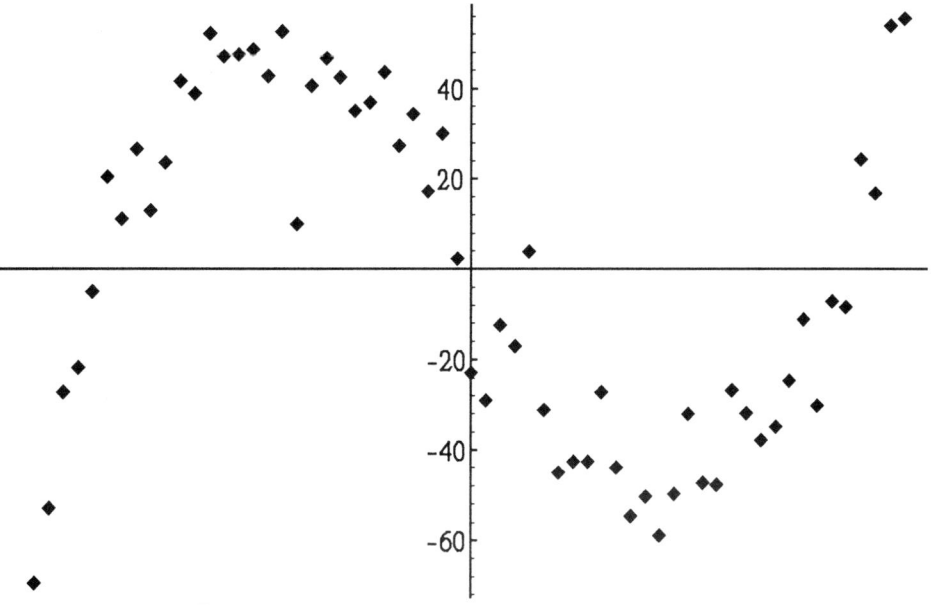

Figure 6.7 A cubic polynomial plus noise.

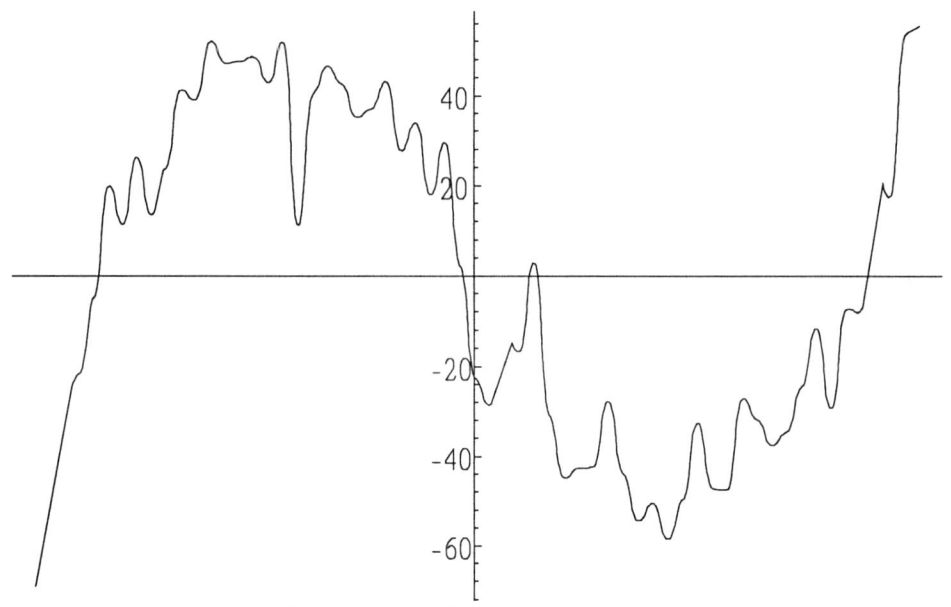

Figure 6.8 Sigma is too small.

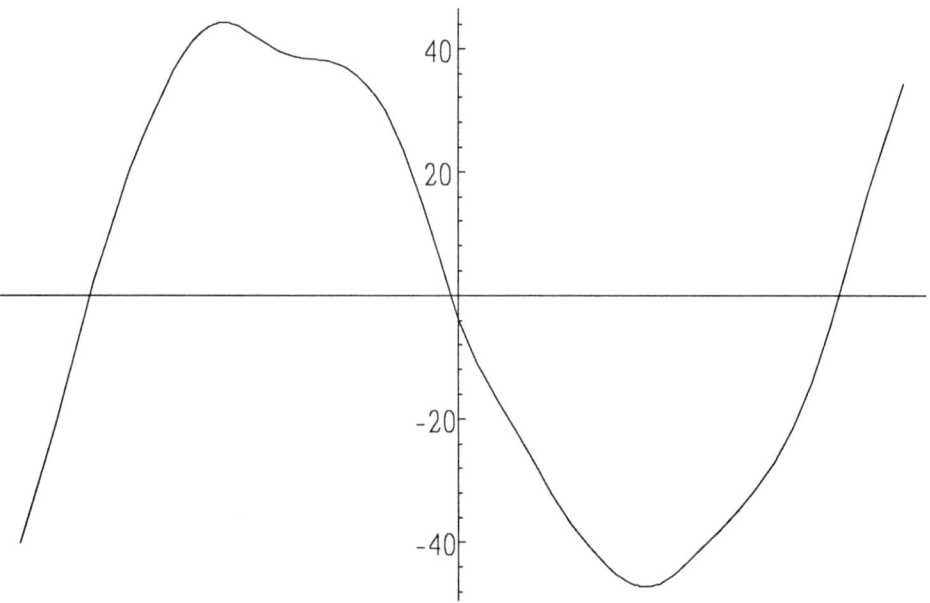

Figure 6.9 Sigma is perhaps a bit small.

The GRNN in Action

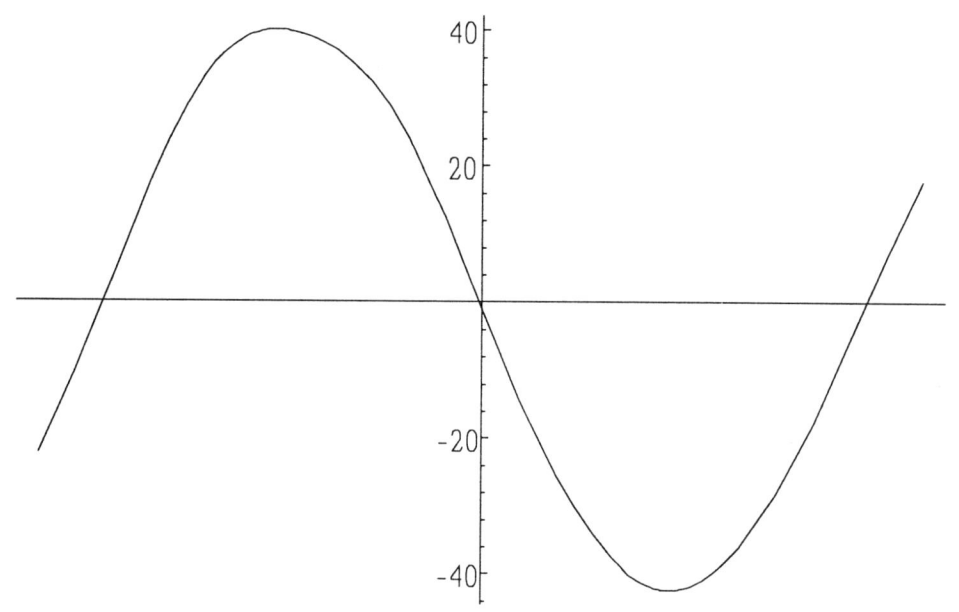

Figure 6.10 Sigma is perfect.

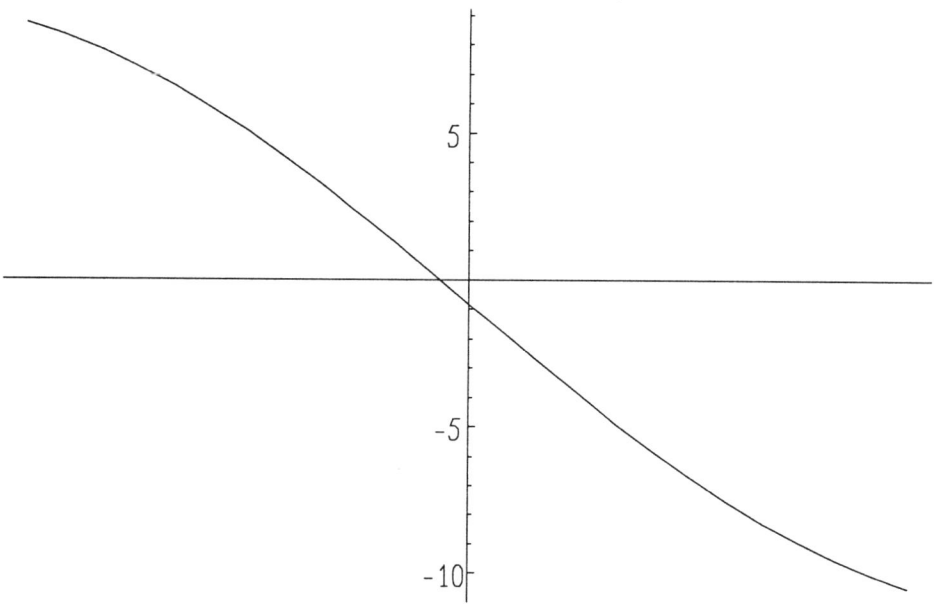

Figure 6.11 Sigma is far too large.

7

The Gram-Charlier Neural Network

- An intuitive description of this model

- Moon Kim's neural network implementation

- The prerequisite mathematical foundation

- The mathematics of the original model

- Edgeworth's modification

- Complete source code for all algorithms

- Comparative performance evaluations

The Gram-Charlier neural network (GCNN) is a close relative of the probabilistic neural network in that its foundation is statistical. As was the case with the PNN, the training set guides the neurons in the network to collectively approximate the density functions of the parent distributions. Classification is then based on Bayesian likelihood tests. However, the similarity ends there. The PNN and the GCNN approach the approximation problem very differently, and hence they have very different properties. The PNN is more robust, being able to handle distributions of virtually any shape. One must be careful with the GCNN, as it can fail badly in some circumstances. On the other hand, when the GCNN works, it has some truly wonderful advantages over other models. Training is extremely fast — far faster than even single-sigma optimization for a PNN and light-years beyond MLFN training. At the same time, execution speed is also extremely rapid, commensurate with the MLFN. And memory requirements are minuscule. When it can be used, this model has all of the advantages of the MLFN and the PNN with none of their disadvantages. It is definitely worth pursuing.

This chapter will first focus on the original Gram-Charlier neural network as proposed in Kim and Arozullah 1992a. Their pioneering results will be reviewed. Then it will be shown how the range of applicability of this model can be extended by means of a statistical technique developed by F. Y. Edgeworth in 1905. Finally, a pair of theoretical and practical demonstrations will be done. These will compare the performance of the PNN and the GCNN so as to help the reader choose an appropriate model for solving a particular problem.

An exceptional amount of quite advanced mathematics will appear in this chapter. This is because the GCNN, and especially Edgeworth's modification, are deeply rooted in theoretical statistics. Readers must not be intimidated by this. Complete source code for all algorithms is given, as well as intuitive explanations of that code. Understanding of the mathematics is not a prerequisite to use of the GCNN. This unusual level of detail is provided mainly for one reason: It is not widely available elsewhere. I am aware of only three published papers on the actual GCNN. And explicit details of the underlying statistical techniques are buried deeply inside relatively few advanced statistics texts. Now that this immensely useful neural network is entering the arena of mainstream applications, it is time for its mathematics to see the light of day. Disinterested readers may safely skim over the details.

Structure and Overview of Functionality

On a superficial level, the GCNN and the PNN are quite similar. They are fundamentally classifiers. They both use the training set to estimate the probability density function of each class's parent population. Then they both use the Bayesian likelihood method to classify unknown samples. However, their implementations of these two steps are very different. The PNN uses the neurons to collectively approximate the density by means of Parzen windows. That algorithm intrinsically demands that most or all of the training data be stored and processed each time classification is performed. In return, a generally excellent approximation to each density is obtained. The GCNN uses its neurons to collectively approximate the Gram-Charlier series expansion of the density. Compared with the PNN, the adequacy of this density approximation is much less certain. In fact, it is so unreliable that Bayesian confidences should not be computed unless exceptionally rigorous validation is done first. On the other hand, the Gram-Charlier estimator requires negligible storage, and classification can be performed extremely quickly. Training is almost instantaneous, with all weights able to be computed with simple, explicit formulas. For data on which it works, this is truly a best-of-all-worlds model. It trains fast, runs fast, and has minimal hardware requirements. Not many neural networks can make that boast. In this section we will provide an overview of the model. The physical structure of the network, with an eye toward parallel implementations, will be emphasized. Mathematical details will follow in later sections.

Let us start by briefly reviewing the Bayesian method of classification. This was already discussed in Chapter 4, so we will be terse here. Also, since the majority of the GCNN development will focus on univariate (scalar) samples, the Bayes classifier will be presented the same way. Later in this text, some methods for extending the GCNN to multivariate samples will be discussed.

Each random sample is a random variable X. The K populations from which our samples are drawn will be indexed by k, $k = 1, ..., K$. The prior probability of an unknown sample being drawn from population k is h_k. The cost associated with misclassifying a sample from population k is c_k. The training set consists of n_1 samples known to be from population 1, and n_2 samples known to be from population 2, and so forth, through n_K samples from population K. The probability density function of X when it is drawn from class i is $f_i(X)$. In practice, we will estimate $f_i(X)$ based on the n_i training cases from that class. The *Bayes optimal* decision rule is to classify an unknown sample X into population i if

$$h_i\, c_i\, f_i(X) > h_j\, c_j\, f_j(X) \tag{7.1}$$

for all populations j not equal to i.

How do the neurons in the GCNN approximate a density function? The exact mathematics will have to wait for a while. For now, let it be known that the unknown observation is standardized and then fed to a small set of simple functions. These functions are labeled $\alpha(x)$ and $H_i(x)$ for i from 3 through a small integer. They are identical for all neurons in all implementations of the model. Thus, it is easy to construct GCNNs using specialized hardware. The training process involves computation of a set of weights and a pair of constants for standardizing the observations. The outputs of the functions just mentioned are combined in a special way using the trained weights. The result is an approximation to the value of the probability density corresponding to the observation.

The above procedure can be made more clear by means of a pair of diagrams. These diagrams also illustrate how the GCNN can be implemented in parallel hardware if one wishes to increase its already prodigious speed. First, examine Figure 7.1.

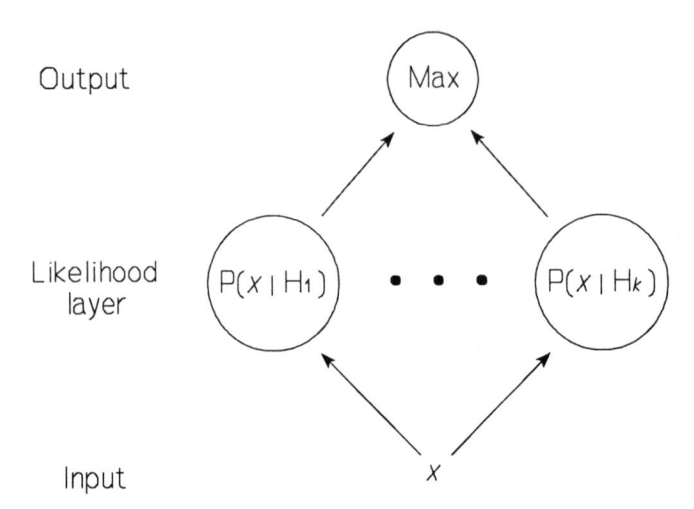

Figure 7.1 Global structure of the GCNN.

That figure depicts the global structure of the network. It is essentially identical to that of the PNN. The input sample is sent to every processor in the likelihood layer. These processors, which can run in parallel, compute the likelihood of x under each of the k hypotheses. The classification decision is made by determining which likelihood is the maximum. This is a simple and straightforward operation. The real complexity happens inside the likelihood processors. (The term *processor* is used instead of *neuron* because each of them is composed of a set of even more primitive operations.)

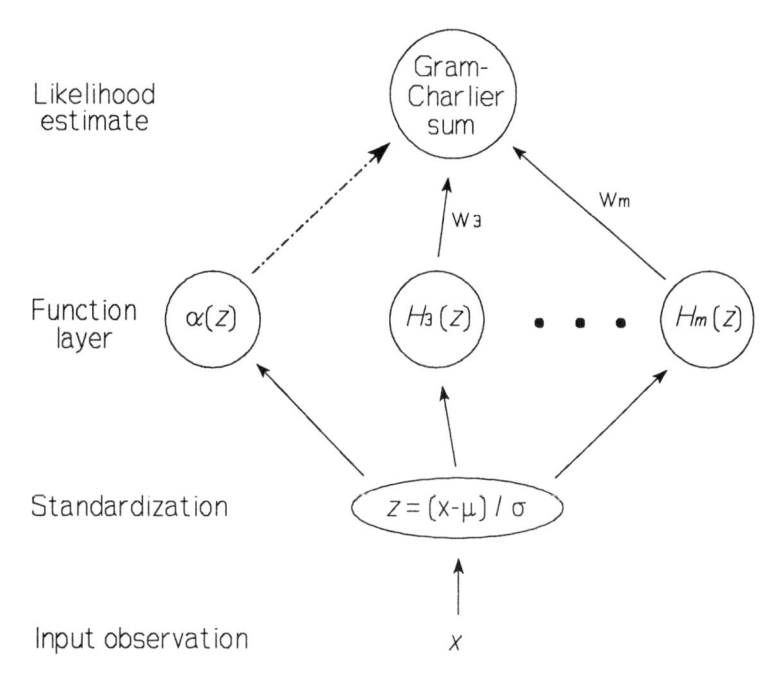

Figure 7.2 Likelihood processor in the GCNN.

Figure 7.2 illustrates a single likelihood processor. There is one such unit for each class. They are all identical in operation. The only difference is that the standardization constants, μ and σ, and the weights, w_3 through w_m, are learned from the training samples. The input sample is first sent to a standardization neuron that does nothing more than subtract a constant and divide by another constant. The standardized value, z, is then passed on to every neuron in a specialized function layer. Each neuron in this layer computes a different function. These functions are intrinsic to the GCNN paradigm and are independent of the training set and the particular implementation. The only difference among various implementations is the actual number of functions used, specified by m. The function outputs corresponding to $H_k(z)$ for k from 3 through m are weighted by their respective weights w_k. These weights are learned from the training samples. The weighted function outputs are then combined with the remaining function, $\alpha(z)$, in a special GCNN neuron. The output of this final neuron is the estimated likelihood of the input x under the hypothesis corresponding to this likelihood processor. Note that $\alpha(z)$ and all of the $H_k(z)$ functions can be computed in parallel by dedicated processors.

The architecture just described is a quite universal depiction of the GCNN in all of its forms. Most variation is obtained by changing the number of $H_k(z)$ functions. The enhancements described later in this chapter involve only the computation of the w_k weights. The inventor of the GCNN, Moon Kim, has proposed a much more complicated version using Parzen windows. However, I have not had a lot of success with that variation, so it will not be described here. Details can be found in Kim and Arozullah (1992a).

Parallel implementation of the GCNN has been discussed. However, the computation performed by each neuron is very fast. In practice, only the most time-critical applications would need a parallel architecture.

Motivation

The next few sections will be devoted to an exploration of the problem of estimating a probability density function based on a sample. We already saw that Parzen's windowing technique has superb mathematical credentials, and that it is highly effective in most practical problems. Unfortunately, that method is sometimes impossible to use. It may be that the necessary training set is too large to fit in the memory that is available. More commonly, the execution time of the PNN algorithm may exceed constraints imposed by the application. In such cases we would welcome a more parsimonious algorithm.

The motivation for the GCNN is that many applications are almost but not quite adequately served by traditional statistical methods. The distributions of the variables (perhaps after suitable transformation) are vaguely similar to a normal distribution. Good old maximum-likelihood classification based on a normal distribution would do a marginally passable job, but skewness or other irregularities prevent excellent performance. If training samples, memory, and time are all abundant, the PNN is an excellent choice. If training time is not a problem, the MLFN is also a possibility. However, we long for the simplicity that is almost but not quite ours. We want to use some explicit formulas to quickly estimate a small set of parameters (weights, in neural network parlance). Then we want to plug observations equally quickly into some simple formulas to perform a classification. Enter the GCNN.

It must be emphasized that this model is limited in its capabilities. The key factor was mentioned in the paragraph above. *The distributions of the variables must be reasonably close to normal.* One tremendous advantage of the PNN is that it can handle distributions that have modes (clusters of cases) that lie scattered all around the input space. Wild outliers are swallowed alive. No problem. The GCNN does not share this rigor. Ideally, the distributions should be unimodal. If not, then at least the modes should be close and be connected by continuous high density. Skewness and kurtosis (heavy tails) are the very reasons for using the GCNN rather than linear discriminant analysis. Nonetheless, the skewness and kurtosis cannot be extreme. It is difficult to quantify just what is meant by extreme. Suffice it to say that thorough validation is mandatory. These issues will be explored in more detail later, but the user should be aware of them right up front.

One more anomaly of the GCNN must be emphasized. Its strength lies in tough classification calls in densely populated regions. Its performance relative to other models is best when there is significant overlap among the classes, making classification difficult. When the classes are well separated, meaning that the most important decisions must be made out in the tails of the distributions, the GCNN is at a competitive disadvantage. Other methods should be tried. In summary, the GCNN is appropriate under the following conditions:

- The problem is difficult in that the classes are fairly similar.

- The distributions of the variables are moderately non-normal, so that traditional classification is compromised.

- Training and execution must be fast.

- Memory is limited.

Series Expansions of Densities and Distributions

Here is the problem that must be solved. A collection of samples of a random variable has been taken from a population. We need to estimate the probability density function of that variable so that we may later use that function to perform Bayesian classification. It is known that the distribution of the variable is vaguely reminiscent of a normal distribution, but that it is sufficiently nonnormal as to preclude assuming normality in the Bayesian classification. How do we do it?

A strongly intuitive answer to this question is that we start with a normal density function and perturb it based on the samples. In particular, let $f(x)$ denote the (unknown) population density function, and let $\alpha(x)$ be the normal density as defined in Equation (7.2).

$$\alpha(x) = \frac{1}{\sqrt{2\pi}} e^{-x^2/2} \tag{7.2}$$

As long as we are basing our estimated density on the normal density, we might as well do the perturbation using derivatives of the normal density. It turns out that this choice provides a useful orthogonality relationship that we will take advantage of later. For now, understand that there is no compelling mathematical reason for this choice. It simply seems like a nice, sensible thing to do. Therefore, let us boldly proclaim that the parent density can be approximated by a series of the form shown in Equation (7.3). The tenuous nature of that assumption will be taken up later.

$$f(x) \approx c_0 \alpha(x) + c_1 \alpha'(x) + c_2 \alpha''(x) + \ldots \tag{7.3}$$

The use of the normal density and its derivatives to provide a series expansion of an arbitrary density function gives rise to several questions, among which are the following:

- What are the derivatives of the normal density function, and how do we compute them?

- Given a theoretical density to match, or a collection of random samples, how can we find suitable coefficients c_j so as to satisfactorily approximate the density function?

Series Expansions of Densities and Distributions

- If we have a method for finding those coefficients, how can we be sure that the series does in fact converge to $f(x)$?

- Since we obviously must truncate the series to compute the approximation in our lifetime, how good is the truncated series?

Not surprisingly, it is the last question that is the killer. The naive approach that we will study first turns out to give an exceedingly poor answer to that last question. Fortunately, there is an alternative. Let us attack those questions one at a time.

Hermite Polynomials and Normal Density Derivatives

Notation for the remainder of this chapter will be vastly simplified by defining a differentiation operator. This operator, D, maps one function to another function. To be specific, the function on which D operates is mapped to its derivative. This definition is shown in Equation (7.4).

$$D \equiv \frac{d}{dx} \tag{7.4}$$

Readers who are versed in calculus might want to compute the first few derivatives of the normal density shown in Equation (7.2). Three of them are shown in Equation (7.5), which also illustrates the D operator.

$$\begin{aligned} D\,\alpha(x) &= -x\,\alpha(x) \\ D^2\,\alpha(x) &= (x^2-1)\,\alpha(x) \\ D^3\,\alpha(x) &= -(x^3-3x)\,\alpha(x) \end{aligned} \tag{7.5}$$

By considering the rule by which products are differentiated, it should be obvious that the rth derivative of the normal density will be a polynomial of degree r times the normal density. This enables us to express the derivatives of the normal density in the compact form shown in Equation (7.6). Note how the sign change for odd derivatives is accommodated so that the coefficient of the highest power is always unity.

$$D^r \alpha(x) = (-1)^r H_r(x) \alpha(x) \qquad (7.6)$$

The polynomials referred to in Equation (7.6) have a name. They are called the *Hermite* polynomials. (An older name for them is the *Tchebycheff-Hermite* polynomials.) In practice, when many of them must be computed, it is usually most efficient to use the recurrence relationship shown in Equation (7.7).

$$H_r(x) = x H_{r-1} - (r-1) H_{r-2} \qquad (7.7)$$

By convention, it is agreed that $H_0(x) = 1$. The first three Hermite polynomials can be seen in Equation (7.5). Three more of them are shown in Equation (7.8).

$$\begin{aligned} H_4(x) &= x^4 - 6x^2 + 3 \\ H_5(x) &= x^5 - 10x^3 + 15x \\ H_6(x) &= x^6 - 15x^4 + 45x^2 - 15 \end{aligned} \qquad (7.8)$$

Kendall and Stuart (1969) derive an explicit formula for Hermite polynomials of arbitrary order using a fascinating method of matching coefficients in a Taylor expansion. This formula is shown in Equation (7.9). Note that it has little or no apparent practical utility. The Hermite polynomials are almost always best evaluated using the recursion relationship given earlier.

$$H_r(x) = x^r - \frac{r^{[2]}}{2 \cdot 1!} x^{r-2} + \frac{r^{[4]}}{2^2 \cdot 2!} x^{r-4} - \frac{r^{[6]}}{2^3 \cdot 3!} x^{r-6} + \dots \qquad (7.9)$$

In that equation, the notation $r^{[n]}$ stands for the product of n factors. The first is r, the second is $(r-1)$, and so forth. For example, $r^{[4]} = r \cdot (r-1) \cdot (r-2) \cdot (r-3)$.

It is interesting to see what the Hermite polynomials look like. Some of them are plotted (with scaling) in Figure 7.3. If those functions are multiplied by the normal density, the result is derivatives of the normal density. They are shown in Figure 7.4. The key for identifying the functions plotted in those illustrations is given at the bottom of the figure. The justification for the choice of scaling constants will become clear later.

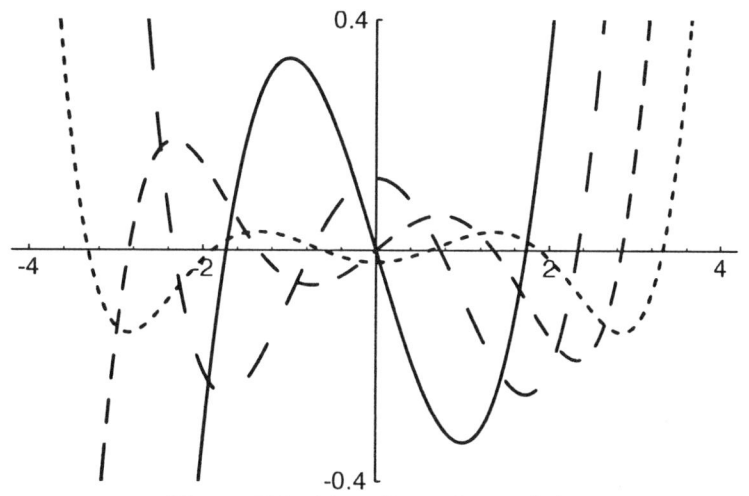

Series Expansions of Densities and Distributions

Figure 7.3 Hermite polynomials.

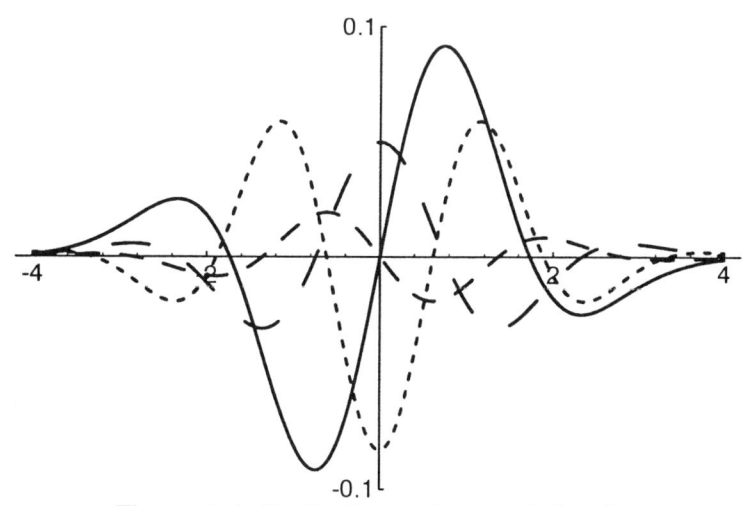

Figure 7.4 Derivatives of normal density.

$H_3 / 3!$	————————————	$D_3 \alpha / 3!$
$H_4 / 4!$	—— —— ——	$D_4 \alpha / 4!$
$H_5 / 5!$	— — — — — — —	$D_5 \alpha / 5!$
$H_6 / 6!$	··············	$10\, D_6 \alpha / 6!$

The Hermite polynomials are orthogonal when weighted by the normal density, as shown in Equation (7.10). This property will be used in the next section when we compute the coefficients in the series expansion given in Equation (7.3). This result, whose full derivation can be found in Kendall and Stuart (1969), is achieved by repeated integration by parts.

$$\frac{1}{n!} \int_{-\infty}^{\infty} H_m(x) H_n(x) \alpha(x) \, dx = \begin{cases} 0 & m \neq n \\ 1 & m = n \end{cases} \quad (7.10)$$

Before leaving this section, it should be noted that there is another definition of the Hermite polynomial floating around. That definition, more common in Europe than in the US, is a linear rescaling of the domain and range of the function given here. This alternative will not be shown, lest the reader become confused. The version given in this text is by far the more common version. Readers who perhaps stumble on a different definition should not be surprised.

An Alternative Representation of the Density

This section started out with the straightforward expansion of the density shown in Equation (7.3). We will continue to use that expansion in principle, but we will rewrite it in a form that is more fitting now that we know what the derivatives of the normal density look like. Look back at their definition in Equation (7.6). Notice that every derivative contains the normal density, $\alpha(x)$, as a factor. If we pull that common factor out of the original expansion, absorb the sign changes into the coefficients, and express the derivatives in terms of the Hermite polynomials, we get the expansion shown in Equation (7.11).

$$f(x) \approx \alpha(x) \left[c_0 + c_1 H_1(x) + c_2 H_2(x) + c_3 H_3(x) + \dots \right] \quad (7.11)$$

Remember that this expression of the density approximation is exactly the same as that given at the beginning of this section in Equation (7.3) *except* that the sign changes that relate the derivatives of the normal density to the Hermite polynomials have been absorbed into the coefficients. Thus, the even-subscripted coefficients here are the same as those in the original equation, while the odd-subscripted coefficients have the opposite sign. We will find this latter representation more convenient than the former. For the remainder of this chapter, whenever we speak of the c_i coefficients, we will be referring to those in the expression above.

This representation may also be more pleasing to the intuition than the original. Very soon we will see that in all cases of practical interest, $c_0 = 1$. This tells us that our density approximator is equal to a normal density times one plus a polynomial. That multiplier determines the distortion that must be imposed on the normal density in order to fit the density being approximated.

Computing Hermite Polynomials

We will frequently need to compute the values of the first few Hermite polynomials. In case only a few are needed, it is probably best to embed the coefficients in the program code and use the standard nesting algorithm for polynomial evaluation (taking advantage of the fact that all powers are even or odd, of course). But in many cases, we need to evaluate several of the polynomials at the same abscissa. The fastest and most accurate way to do that is to use the recurrence relationship shown in Equation (7.7). A code fragment for performing that computation for a fixed number of polynomials is shown below. It should be obvious how to extend this algorithm for more polynomials.

```
h2 = x * x - 1.0 ;
h3 = x * (h2 - 2.0) ;
h4 = x * h3 - 3.0 * h2 ;
h5 = x * h4 - 4.0 * h3 ;
h6 = x * h5 - 5.0 * h4 ;
h7 = x * h6 - 6.0 * h5 ;
h8 = x * h7 - 7.0 * h6 ;
h9 = x * h8 - 8.0 * h7 ;
```

Computing the Coefficients

There is a simple and straightforward method for computing the c_j coefficients in the expansion of Equation (7.11). If we multiply both sides of that equation by $H_r(x)$ and then integrate from minus infinity to infinity, the result is as shown in Equation (7.12).

$$\int_{-\infty}^{\infty} f(x) H_r(x) \, dx = \sum_{j=0}^{\infty} c_j \int_{-\infty}^{\infty} H_j(x) H_r(x) \alpha(x) \, dx \qquad (7.12)$$

Now look back at the orthogonality relationship shown in Equation (7.10). The integral in the right side of Equation (7.12) will be equal to zero for all values of j except $j = r$. We immediately see that if the density $f(x)$ that we are trying to approximate is known, the coefficients can be computed using Equation (7.13).

$$c_r = \frac{1}{r!} \int_{-\infty}^{\infty} f(x) H_r(x) \, dx \qquad (7.13)$$

That is actually a very pretty little result. It says in essence that to find the coefficients for approximating $f(x)$ in terms of the Hermite polynomials times a normal density, we simply project f onto the Hermite polynomials and scale. This is not quite the same thing as if we were operating with a true orthogonal basis, as the presence of $\alpha(x)$ in the series expansion complicates things. But it is close enough for intuitive appeal. Readers who are versed in the use of Fourier and Gabor techniques will surely be comfortable with this approach.

There is an alternative way of expressing the constants that is in common use. Recall how the *moments* of a distribution are defined. The zeroth moment is defined to be equal to one. (Examination of the next few equations should convince the reader that this is reasonable.) The first moment, otherwise known as the *mean* of the distribution, is shown in Equation (7.14). Other moments are traditionally defined in terms of differences from the mean. These *central moments* are shown in Equation (7.15).

$$\mu_1 = \int_{-\infty}^{\infty} x f(x) \, dx \qquad (7.14)$$

$$\mu_r = \int_{-\infty}^{\infty} (x - \mu_1)^r f(x) \, dx \qquad (7.15)$$

Series Expansions of Densities and Distributions

To keep things simple, let us assume without loss of generality that the mean of $f(x)$ is zero. This can be obtained by shifting any distribution by an amount equal to its mean. The moments defined in Equation (7.15) are more compact when $\mu_1 = 0$. Expand the expression for c_r given in Equation (7.13) into all of the terms of the polynomial. Replace each term by the corresponding moment as defined in Equation (7.15). It should now be clear that the coefficients for approximating the centered density can be expressed in terms of the central moments in a method analogous to the Hermite polynomials. For example, see Equation (7.16). Recall that by the definition of the zeroth moment, we have $c_0 = 1$, and that by centering, we have $c_1 = 0$.

$$\begin{aligned} c_2 &= \frac{1}{2!}(\mu_2 - 1) \\ c_3 &= \frac{1}{3!}\mu_3 \\ c_4 &= \frac{1}{4!}(\mu_4 - 6\mu_2 + 3) \\ c_5 &= \frac{1}{5!}(\mu_5 - 10\mu_3) \end{aligned} \qquad (7.16)$$

In practice, we will nearly always make the further assumption that the density is standardized to unit standard deviation. This will stabilize the approximation. Since now $\mu_2 = 1$, the coefficients can be simplified even further. It is immediately seen that $c_2 = 0$ and that standardization does not affect the odd coefficients (other than indirectly through scaling of the domain variable). Two of the even coefficients for approximating this standardized density are shown in Equation (7.17).

$$\begin{aligned} c_4 &= \frac{1}{4!}(\mu_4 - 3) \\ c_6 &= \frac{1}{6!}(\mu_6 - 15\mu_4 + 30) \end{aligned} \qquad (7.17)$$

Finding the Coefficients from a Sample

So far we have only dealt with the problem of computing the coefficients to approximate a density whose functional form is explicitly known. In real problems we will almost never have a need for that capability. If we already know the density, why bother approximating it? Just compute it directly. Instead, our customary task will be to use a collection of random samples to approximate an unknown density. It is not difficult.

The traditional method of computing the coefficients from a training set relies on the final technique discussed in the previous section. The mean and standard deviation of the sample are computed. These quantities are saved, as they will be needed when the density approximator is evaluated for unknown points at a later date. The mean is subtracted from each sample point, and that difference is divided by the standard deviation. The moments of this standardized sample are computed. The values of c_3 and c_5 are found from Equation (7.16). The values of c_4 and c_6 can be found from Equation (7.17). In the extremely unlikely event that more coefficients are desired, the method described in the next paragraph is the best choice.

The method of computing moments first, then computing coefficients, seems to be the traditional approach. This is despite the fact that the mathematical derivation of the coefficients took place in exactly the reverse order. I prefer to compute the coefficients by directly implementing the discrete version of Equation (7.13). This method, shown in Equation (7.18), may involve somewhat more computational effort than the former method. When time is critical, this direct method should probably be avoided. On the other hand, I have an (unproven) gut feeling that the direct projection method enjoys better numerical stability under finite floating-point operations.

$$c_r = \frac{1}{n\,r!} \sum_{i=1}^{n} H_r(x_i) \qquad (7.18)$$

We now present code for a Gram-Charlier neural network class. The constructor uses the direct projection method for computing the coefficients. Some users may prefer to use the moment method. Later in this chapter, when Edgeworth's enhancements are discussed, code for computing moments will appear. Users can easily substitute that code for the projection code given here, then apply Equations (7.16) and

Series Expansions of Densities and Distributions

(7.17) to compute the coefficients. The subroutine hermite that is called here is implemented with the code fragment shown on page 263.

```
class GCnet {

public:
   GCnet ( const int ndata , const double * const data ) ;
   double density ( const double x , const int n_moments ) ;

private:
   double mean, std ;
   double c3, c4, c5, c6, c7, c8 ;
} ;


GCnet::GCnet (
   const int n ,
   const double * const data
   )
{
   int i ;
   double diff ;

/*
   Compute the mean and standard deviation for standardizing the data
*/

   mean = std = 0.0 ;

   i = n ;
   while (i--)
      mean += data[i] ;
   mean /= n ;

   i = n ;
   while (i--) {
      diff = data[i] - mean ;
      std += diff * diff ;
      }
   std = sqrt ( std / n ) ;
```

```
/*
    Compute the GC coefficients via direct projection on the Hermite polynomials
*/

    c3 = c4 = c5 = c6 = c7 = c8 = 0.0 ;
    i = n ;
    while (i--) {
        diff = (data[i] - mean) / std ;     // Standardize to mean 0 and unit variance
        hermite ( diff ) ;                  // Compute h3 through h8 (see page 263)
        c3 += h3 ;
        c4 += h4 ;
        c5 += h5 ;
        c6 += h6 ;
        c7 += h7 ;
        c8 += h8 ;
        }

    c3 /= (n * 6.0) ;                       // Divide by sample size and r!
    c4 /= (n * 24.0) ;
    c5 /= (n * 120.0) ;
    c6 /= (n * 720.0) ;
    c7 /= (n * 5040.0) ;
    c8 /= (n * 40320.0) ;
    }
```

The member function density computes the density approximation for a specified point. The caller of this function must also specify the number of moments beyond the implicit first and second (which just define a standard normal density) that are to be used in the approximation. As will be shown later, most practical applications are best served by specifying n_moments = 1, which causes only the third moment to be used. The upper limit for the code given here is n_moments = 6, invoking moments up to the eighth order. Using this many moments is nearly always counterproductive. The rare user who actually wants to go higher should be able to modify this code easily. Note that this function ignores the constant involving the square root of two pi shown in Equation (7.2). Readers who want a true density must divide the returned value by that constant. This is generally a waste of time, for whenever the GCNN is used for classification, the constant cancels out across all classes.

Series Expansions of Densities and Distributions

```
double GCnet::density ( const double x , const int n_moments )
{
  double z, a, b ;

  z = (x - mean) / std ;              // Standardize
  a = exp ( -0.5 * z * z ) ;          // Normal density (times sqrt(2 pi))
  h2 = z * z - 1.0 ;                  // Second-degree Hermite polynomial
  h3 = z * (h2 - 2.0) ;               // And third
  b = 1.0  +  c3 * h3 ;               // First extra moment term (3rd moment)
  switch (n_moments) {
    case 2: h4 = z * h3 - 3.0 * h2 ;              // Compute Hermite by recursion
         b += c4 * h4 ;
         break ;
    case 3: h4 = z * h3 - 3.0 * h2 ;
         h5 = z * h4 - 4.0 * h3 ;
         b += c4 * h4 + c5 * h5 ;
         break ;
    case 4: h4 = z * h3 - 3.0 * h2 ;
         h5 = z * h4 - 4.0 * h3 ;
         h6 = z * h5 - 5.0 * h4 ;
         b += c4 * h4 + c5 * h5 + c6 * h6 ;
         break ;
    case 5: h4 = z * h3 - 3.0 * h2 ;
         h5 = z * h4 - 4.0 * h3 ;
         h6 = z * h5 - 5.0 * h4 ;
         h7 = z * h6 - 6.0 * h5 ;
         b += c4 * h4 + c5 * h5 + c6 * h6 + c7 * h7 ;
         break ;
    case 6: h4 = z * h3 - 3.0 * h2 ;
         h5 = z * h4 - 4.0 * h3 ;
         h6 = z * h5 - 5.0 * h4 ;
         h7 = z * h6 - 6.0 * h5 ;
         h8 = z * h7 - 7.0 * h6 ;
         b += c4 * h4 + c5 * h5 + c6 * h6 + c7 * h7 + c8 * h8 ;
         break ;
   }

  return a * b ;
}
```

What's Wrong with This Picture?

There is a serious difficulty with the algorithms discussed so far. To put it bluntly, in a large number of practical situations, they simply don't work. In many cases, the infinite series shown in Equation (7.3) (and, equivalently except for signs, in Equation (7.11)) does not converge to the density that was used to compute the coefficients. And in those cases in which it does converge, all too often it is useless anyway. When we truncate an infinite series, as we certainly must do if it is to be computed in a finite time, we hope that the magnitude of the sum of the terms that are truncated is less than the magnitude of the last term that is kept. Unfortunately, that is not the case in a disturbingly large number of applications. Summing $k+1$ terms may actually provide a worse approximation than summing k terms. That is not good. A little later in this chapter (Figure 7.6 and following), we will see a graphic illustration of this phenomenon.

This is not just a vague theoretical difficulty. It has immense practical implications. The Hermite polynomials, especially those of high order, oscillate and blow up to great magnitudes as they move away from zero. Multiplication by the normal density serves to tame them to harmless levels when they are very far from zero, but not before some pretty wild fluctuations have taken place. The end result is that although the quality of the approximation is usually quite good near the center of the distribution, it can be extremely poor out in the tails. In fact, negative density estimates are not unusual! Unfortunately, many or most common statistical procedures are primarily concerned with the tails of the distribution. This is especially true when decision confidences are important. So the GCNN may be at its weakest just when we need it the most.

What to do? First of all, we validate thoroughly. This is vital in any work, but it is particularly vital when the GCNN is employed. Second, we make use of the significant improvements to the basic GCNN that are discussed in the next section. Third, we keep in mind the heuristics that will be presented later. Finally, we may be able to glean a little information from some theoretical results that will now be shown. In general, these results are so weak that they are useless in practice. But sometimes they can be a comfort. At the very least, they provide some insight for those who understand them. They will be shown here without proof, with references given as needed. Readers who are not mathematically inclined may safely skip the remainder of this section.

Let's start out simple. If one had to designate a single property of a distribution that determined most reliably whether a truncated Gram-Charlier series could adequately represent it, that property would be the skewness. In the case of standardized variables, which we have here, the skewness is just the third moment. It should be near zero. In other words, a truncated GCNN series does a poor job on distributions that are highly skewed. In many applications, we will want to restrict ourselves to at most the third or fourth moment, as stability suffers when higher-order moments are used. However, when moments higher than the fourth are discarded, Barton and Dennis (1952) compute disturbingly small explicit limits on the skewness in order for the Gram-Charlier approximation function to be unimodal and non-negative.

Cramer (1926) provides some of the most rigorous results concerning sufficient conditions for the Gram-Charlier series to converge properly. For example, assume that the function $f(x)$ has a continuous derivative, and that $f(x)$ tends to zero as x tends to plus or minus infinity. (Note that this result is not contingent on $f(x)$ being a density.) Then if the integral shown in Equation (7.19) exists, the Gram-Charlier series is absolutely and uniformly convergent for all x.

$$\int_{-\infty}^{\infty} \left(\frac{df}{dx}\right)^2 e^{\frac{1}{2}x^2} dx \qquad (7.19)$$

In that same reference, it is shown that if $f(x)$ is of bounded variation, and if the integral shown in Equation (7.20) exists, then the Gram-Charlier series converges at all continuity points of the density.

$$\int_{-\infty}^{\infty} |f(x)| e^{\frac{1}{4}x^2} dx \qquad (7.20)$$

Unfortunately, these two sufficient conditions do not give us much. The exponentials in the integrals blow up so quickly that the other term must go to zero at an almost unreasonable speed. A great many distributions that one encounters in practice fail to satisfy either of these conditions. Granted, failure to satisfy these conditions does not automatically mean that the series will fail to converge. They are sufficient conditions, not necessary. On the other hand, experience indicates that they are not too far from being necessary. It is not difficult to find examples of distributions that only marginally fail to satisfy these conditions and that do not have convergent Gram-Charlier series expansions.

Other Problems

Even when the theoretical conditions are right for a Gram-Charlier series to converge to the density that determined its coefficients, we are still not home free. The method used to compute those coefficients may not be as good as could be hoped for. In the next section, we will see how to improve the situation, but a short discussion of the problem is in order.

We need to introduce the concept of statistical *efficiency*. When we use mathematical formulas to compute one or more individual numbers from a sample of data that was collected, we are implicitly discarding a lot of information from that sample. If we sample ten random numbers and distill them down into two, it is only under the most unusual of circumstances that those two numbers capture all of the information contained in the original sample of ten numbers. When we, in turn, use those few distilled numbers to perform a task for us, we should be legitimately concerned about how much useful information was discarded in the process of distilling the sample down into those special numbers. The smaller the quantity of useful information that is discarded, the more efficient those numbers are at performing our task. If, in fact, those few distilled numbers tell us everything that we can possibly glean from the sample *that is useful for performing the task*, then those calculated numbers are 100 percent efficient for the task.

That is exactly what we are doing with the Gram-Charlier series expansion of a density. Our task is to estimate an unknown density function based on a random sample from that population. For our set of distilled numbers, we compute the mean, the standard deviation, and some central moments of the sample. Those few numbers determine the coefficients of the Gram-Charlier series expansion. All other information contained in the sample is ignored. And therein lies the problem. We have thrown away some potentially useful information. Our use of the sample moments to compute the coefficients as derived earlier in this chapter had some pretty mathematics associated with it, but we could have done better. In statistical parlance, we say that the sample moments are not maximally efficient for computing the coefficients.

One of the worst practical implications of all this is the effect of random error on the computed coefficients. High-order moments can have immense variation in response to sample error. Suppose, for example, that we use moments up to the sixth order. A single outlier in the sample, when raised to the sixth power, becomes gigantic. That one sample point swamps out the contributions of all of the other points and causes the coefficient of H_6 to be unreasonably large. As a result, the approximation function may oscillate wildly, especially in the tails. This is especially true for small samples. If the sample is very large, the effect of random outliers is reduced by the masses of other points.

This leads to a heuristic rule for deciding how many moments to use. Recall that since we have standardized the samples, the first and second moments are ignored. (The first moment is zero and the second is one.) In a surprising number of cases, we are best off stopping at the third moment! That single extra moment is able to inflict a large amount of distortion on the normal density, often sufficient to do a good modeling job. Higher moments can provide additional distortion for more complex fits, but they come at a steep price in stability. Thus, we should let the expected random error in the sample, and the size of the sample, determine the number of moments that are used. Nobody ever seems to use moments beyond the sixth.

I am not aware of any known method for fully efficient computation of the Gram-Charlier coefficients. However, we can do significantly better than the method discussed so far. This is the subject of the next section.

Edgeworth's Expansion

We will now explore an alternative method for expanding a density function as an infinite series involving the normal density and its derivatives. The mathematics of this expansion is extremely complicated, so a large number of intermediate steps and details will be omitted from this treatment. The reader will be referred to other sources frequently. Most readers will not want to chase down these sources, as a very advanced mathematical background is required to understand the material. The comprehensive outline presented here should be sufficient for all practical purposes.

There is a curious aspect of the infinite series that we will now use. *It is exactly the same series as the Gram-Charlier expansion*, yet in practice it often gives superior results. Why? Because the terms in the series are reordered. In the Gram-Charlier expansion, the H_3 term appears in its entirety first. This is followed by the H_4 term, and so on. In Edgeworth's expansion, the various Hermite polynomial terms are scattered throughout the series. A given Hermite polynomial term may appear early in the series with a coefficient different from that in the Gram-Charlier expansion; then that same term may appear later in the series with a coefficient that, when combined with the earlier coefficient, produces a net result equal to the Gram-Charlier coefficient. When the two competing series are considered in their infinite entirety, they are exactly equal. But the key fact is that when the series are truncated, as must always be done, they are not by any means equal. And it turns out that in many or most cases, the approximation defined by the truncated Edgeworth series is superior to that of the truncated Gram-Charlier series.

Before plunging into the mathematics of the Edgeworth expansion, let us please the reader with an intuitive explanation of why the particular reordering that we are about to pursue improves the quality of the truncated series approximation. This explanation is not by any means the complete story, but it is a substantial part of the story. The difference between the two methods involves the way that the sample moments enter into the coefficients of the Hermite polynomials that comprise the expansion. We already know that higher-order moments have greater instability in the presence of random noise. We also know from the definition of the Gram-Charlier expansion that each Hermite polynomial in the Gram-Charlier expansion is based on the moment whose order equals the degree of the polynomial (and usually moments of lesser order). For example, the coefficient of H_6 depends on moments up to the sixth order. To obtain a good theoretical fit, polynomials that high are often needed. Unfortunately, moments that high are notoriously unstable. This is a serious conflict.

Edgeworth's expansion solves this conflict nicely. Cramer (1946) provides a very advanced demonstration showing that, under quite reasonable conditions, this matching of polynomial powers with moment orders makes little mathematical sense. In reality, moments of much lower order are all that are required to determine the coefficients of the Hermite polynomials in the early terms of the reordered series expansion. The higher-order moments become involved only in the coefficients of these same Hermite polynomials that appear further out in the

Edgeworth's Expansion

series, past the point at which the series is truncated. Thus, the Edgeworth expansion provides the best of both worlds. We get the fitting power of high-degree polynomials, along with the relative stability of low-order moments.

It must be emphasized that even more is involved than stability in the presence of sampling error. Even when theoretical distributions having no sampling error are matched, this reordering of terms is usually superior to the simplistic Gram-Charlier order. However, the mathematics needed to support that statement is best left to the reference cited earlier and to others.

Mathematics of the Edgeworth Expansion

Anyone who has seen much calculus has seen power series expansions of functions. One of the most famous of these is the series expansion of the exponentiation function. This is shown in Equation (7.21).

$$e^x = 1 + x + \frac{x^2}{2!} + \frac{x^3}{3!} + \frac{x^4}{4!} + \ldots \qquad (7.21)$$

We will now introduce a twist on this power series expansion. For those who have never seen it before, it may seem bizarre. But it is a powerful tool, and we will need it. What we are going to do is replace the variable x with an operator. In particular, recall the D operator that was defined in Equation (7.4) on page 259. This operator maps a function to its derivative. Thus, $Df(x) = f'(x)$.

Strange as it may seem, we can actually raise e to the power of the D operator. What we get is another operator. That operator can be represented by a power series not unlike the series shown in Equation (7.21). So that we can conveniently save some tedious manipulation later, let us work with e raised to the power of a constant times the D operator. The power series expansion of that operator is shown in Equation (7.22). The result of applying that operator to a function is an infinite sum whose terms are that function and all of its derivatives.

$$\{e^{KD}\}f(x) = \left\{1 + KD + \frac{(KD)^2}{2!} + \frac{(KD)^3}{3!} + \ldots\right\}f(x) \quad (7.22)$$

Moments are one set of constants that describe a distribution. We now need to present an alternative set of descriptive constants called *cumulants*. We shall deliberately avoid an explicit definition of these beasts, as the definition is extremely complicated and involves concepts from advanced statistics. For those who are desperately curious, the cumulants are the coefficients of the terms in the power series expansion of the log of the characteristic function of the distribution. Satisfied? If not, Kendall and Stuart (1969) is the definitive reference.

For our purposes, all we need to know is that the cumulants, usually represented by the Greek letter kappa (κ), can easily be expressed in terms of the moments. For the standardized densities that we are using, the moments and cumulants are equivalent up to the third: $\kappa_1 = 0$, $\kappa_2 = 1$, and $\kappa_3 = \mu_3$. The next few are shown in Equation (7.23).

$$\begin{aligned}
\kappa_4 &= \mu_4 - 3 \\
\kappa_5 &= \mu_5 - 10\mu_3 \\
\kappa_6 &= \mu_6 - 15\mu_4 - 10\mu_3^2 + 30
\end{aligned} \quad (7.23)$$

We are now in a position to write the formal definition of Edgeworth's expansion of a density function; it is shown in Equation (7.24). The theoretical justification for that equation is beyond the scope of this text. A thorough derivation can be found in Kendall and Stuart (1969).

$$f(x) = \exp\left\{-\kappa_3 \frac{D^3}{3!} + \kappa_4 \frac{D^4}{4!} - \kappa_5 \frac{D^5}{5!} + \ldots\right\}\alpha(x) \quad (7.24)$$

That expression is actually a lot more complicated than might appear at first glance. It involves the *product* of an infinite number of infinite power series. Recall that $e^{a+b} = e^a e^b$. The exponent in Equation (7.24) is the sum of an infinitude of terms, so the operator in front of the normal density $\alpha(x)$ is the product of an infinite number of operators. But each one of those operators is itself of the form shown

Edgeworth's Expansion

on the left side of Equation (7.22) and hence is defined by a power series of D operators. It's not a pretty sight.

It should be apparent that except for very low powers, terms in that product involving any given order derivative D^j accumulate from products of multiple sets of terms in the sets of series. How do we order them, and which ones do we keep when we truncate? These issues are covered in Cramer (1946). We will content ourselves with a summary. Designate the jth derivative of the normal density as $\alpha^{(j)}$. Edgeworth's series is shown in Equation (7.25).

$$f(x) = \alpha(x) + \sum_{j=1}^{\infty} (-1)^j \left[b_{j,j+2\cdot 1} \alpha^{(j+2\cdot 1)} + b_{j,j+2\cdot 2} \alpha^{(j+2\cdot 2)} + \ldots + b_{j,3j} \alpha^{(3j)} \right]$$
(7.25)

This series is truncated by stopping at some value of j. For each j, all of the terms enclosed in square brackets are included. The derivatives corresponding to a particular value of j are of the degree $j + 2h$, where h runs from 1 through whatever value gives a total of $3j$. Each of the $b_{j,j+2h}$ factors is a polynomial in the cumulants κ_3 through κ_{j-h+3}.

Let us examine the few special cases that will be of practical use. The first term in the infinite series arises from $j = 1$. There will be only one term in the bracketed summation, corresponding to $h = 1$, because $j + 2 = 3j$. The $b_{1,3}$ factor will be a polynomial involving κ_3 only. This first term in the infinite series, which we shall call e_3, is shown in Equation (7.26). We leave it as a simple (yet valuable) exercise for the reader to verify that the Edgeworth expansion that is truncated here at $j = 1$ is identical to the Gram-Charlier series truncated at the same third-degree term.

$$e_3 = \frac{-\kappa_3}{3!} \alpha^{(3)}(x)$$
(7.26)

The term corresponding to $j = 2$ will have two terms in the bracketed summation. These will involve $\alpha^{(4)}$ and $\alpha^{(6)}$. The multiplier for the former will be a polynomial through κ_4. (In this particular case, κ_3 vanishes.) The multiplier for the latter will be a polynomial in κ_3 only. This term is shown in Equation (7.27).

There are several notable details in that equation. The first is the key to the performance of the Edgeworth expansion. Observe that

$$e_4 = \frac{\kappa_4}{4!} \alpha^{(4)}(x) + \frac{10\kappa_3^2}{6!} \alpha^{(6)}(x) \tag{7.27}$$

we have gotten all the way up to the sixth derivative of the normal density, so we will have the fitting power of a sixth-degree Hermite polynomial. Yet we have needed to invoke moments only up to the fourth order, resulting in relative stability under noisy conditions. Second, readers may wonder where the coefficients came from, especially the factor of ten in the numerator of the second term. Alas, there is no simple formula; it involves brutal algebraic manipulation. Truly interested and ambitious readers can work it out for themselves. Here is a sketch of the process: We are using terms up to that of κ_4 in the definition of the Edgeworth expansion, Equation (7.24). So we will (mercifully) be working with the product of only two infinite power series. Write each of these using the definition shown in Equation (7.22). Now observe that when they are multiplied, a term involving D^6 will arise only once. That coefficient will have in its denominator a factor of 3! twice, arising from squaring the 3! in the first term of Equation (7.24). There will also be a factor of 2! from the definition in Equation (7.22). Thus, we see that the final coefficient is 1/72, which is the same as 10/6!. Any reader who sits down and works through that outline in full detail will gain an appreciation for the complexity of the situation.

We now show without derivation the next term in the Edgeworth expansion, given by $j = 3$. In practical situations, this is as far as we will ever want to go. It is given in Equation (7.28).

$$e_5 = -\frac{\kappa_5}{5!} \alpha^{(5)}(x) - \frac{35\kappa_3\kappa_4}{7!} \alpha^{(7)}(x) - \frac{280\kappa_3^3}{9!} \alpha^{(9)}(x) \tag{7.28}$$

Now we have gotten up to a ninth-degree polynomial but have used only moments up to the fifth order. Extremely ambitious readers can compute the coefficients in exactly the same way as was done earlier. But this time there are three infinite power series to multiply! Have fun.

This mathematical derivation will be concluded by showing in Equation (7.29) the final form of the Edgeworth expansion that will be used. Note that it is given on three separate lines. These lines are the truncation points. If one uses the first line only, one has nothing more

Edgeworth's Expansion

than the ordinary Gram-Charlier series expansion truncated at the same point. In many practical situations, that is all we want. If sampling noise is low, we can include the second line. In those rare situations that sampling noise is extremely low, we may also want to include the third line. The coefficients are shown in Equation (7.30).

$$f(x) \approx \alpha(x)(1 + c_3 H_3(x) \\ + c_4 H_4(x) + c_6 H_6(x) \\ + c_5 H_5(x) + c_7 H_7(x) + c_9 H_9(x)) \tag{7.29}$$

$$\begin{aligned} c_3 &= \mu_3 / 3! \\ c_4 &= (\mu_4 - 3) / 4! \\ c_5 &= (\mu_5 - 10\mu_3) / 5! \\ c_6 &= 10\mu_3^2 / 6! \\ c_7 &= 35\mu_3(\mu_4 - 3) / 7! \\ c_9 &= 280\mu_3^3 / 9! \end{aligned} \tag{7.30}$$

Code for a GCNN with Edgeworth's Modification

We now present a class that is similar to the GCnet that was shown earlier. The EWnet class constructor is called with a training set. It computes the moments, then uses Equation (7.30) to compute and save the coefficients. Here is the class definition and the constructor.

```
class EWnet {

public:
   EWnet ( const int ndata , const double * const data ) ;
   double density ( const double x , const int n_moments ) ;

private:
   double mean, std ;
   double c3, c4, c5, c6, c7, c9 ;
} ;
```

```
EWnet::EWnet (
   const int n ,
   const double *const data
   )
{
  int i ;
  double diff, prod, m3, m4, m5 ;

/*
   Compute the mean and standard deviation for standardizing the data
*/

   mean = std = 0.0 ;

   i = n ;
   while (i--)
      mean += data[i] ;
   mean /= n ;

   i = n ;
   while (i--) {
      diff = data[i] - mean ;
      std += diff * diff ;
      }
   std = sqrt ( std / n ) ;

/*
   Compute the moments
*/

   m3 = m4 = m5 = 0.0 ;
   i = n ;
   while (i--) {
      diff = (data[i] - mean) / std ;
      prod = diff * diff * diff ;
      m3 += prod ;
      prod *= diff ;
      m4 += prod ;
      prod *= diff ;
      m5 += prod ;
      }
```

Edgeworth's Expansion

```
   m3 /= n ;
   m4 /= n ;
   m5 /= n ;

/*
   Compute the Edgeworth coefficients
*/

   c3 = m3 / 6.0 ;
   c4 = (m4 - 3.0) / 24.0 ;
   c5 = (m5 - 10.0 * m3) / 120.0 ;
   c6 = m3 * m3 / 72.0 ;
   c7 = (m4 - 3.0) * m3 * 35.0 / 5040.0 ;
   c9 = m3 * m3 * m3 * 280.0 / 362880.0 ;
}
```

The density member function of this class is not unlike that of the GCnet class. It is called with a single data point and an indicator of the number of additional moments (beyond the implicit first and second) to be used. Remember that using just one more is equivalent to a GCnet with n_moments = 1. We allow only values of one, two, and three, as three already gets us up to ninth-order polynomials. Nothing higher is ever used in practice.

```
double EWnet::density ( const double x , const int n_moments )
{
   double z, a, b ;

   z = (x - mean) / std ;           // Standardize
   a = exp ( -0.5 * z * z ) ;       // Normal density (times a constant)
   h2 = z * z - 1.0 ;               // Second-degree Hermite polynomial
   h3 = z * (h2 - 2.0) ;            // And third
   b = 1.0  +  c3 * h3 ;            // First extra moment term (3rd moment)

   switch (n_moments) {
      case 2: h4 = z * h3 - 3.0 * h2 ;
              h5 = z * h4 - 4.0 * h3 ;
              h6 = z * h5 - 5.0 * h4 ;
              b += c4 * h4 + c6 * h6 ;
              break ;
```

```
    case 3: h4 = z * h3 - 3.0 * h2 ;
            h5 = z * h4 - 4.0 * h3 ;
            h6 = z * h5 - 5.0 * h4 ;
            h7 = z * h6 - 6.0 * h5 ;
            h8 = z * h7 - 7.0 * h6 ;
            h9 = z * h8 - 8.0 * h7 ;
            b += c4 * h4 + c5 * h5 + c6 * h6 + c7 * h7 + c9 * h9 ;
            break ;
    }

    return a * b ;
}
```

Comparing the Models

In this section we will briefly compare the pure Gram-Charlier neural network with that obtained from Edgeworth's modification. When appropriate, their performance will also be judged against the probabilistic neural network and a simple maximum-likelihood classifier based on an assumption of normality.

These comparisons are deliberately performed using extremely difficult problems in order to best illustrate the strengths and weaknesses of the models. We know that these neural networks work by starting with a normal distribution, then warping it to fit the desired density. It has already been pointed out that one of the best ways to make sure that the infinite series fails to converge is to try to fit a highly skewed distribution. So to thoroughly illustrate what can happen when we inadvertently do that in a real problem, we will start this demonstration with a decidedly skewed distribution, a chi-square with two degrees of freedom. In the figures that follow, note that the distribution has been shifted and scaled to have zero mean and unit variance.

Start by examining Figure 7.6. The solid line depicts a (shifted and scaled) chi-square density with two degrees of freedom. This is obviously nothing that we would want to try to fit with the methods of this chapter, but it sure provides a tough test of these methods. The dotted line in that figure is the approximation to this density obtained with just one term of the series. Recall that when only the first term is used, the Gram-Charlier series and the Edgeworth series are the same. The coefficient c_3 is computed by numerically evaluating Equation (7.13) on page 264. Note that despite the fact that we are asking for an extremely unreasonable approximation feat, the fit is surprisingly good. This is typical of real-life situations. It is not at all unusual for this single-term model to be the best performer of the family.

Figure 7.7 shows what happens when we add one more term of the series. Things deteriorate badly. And it just keeps getting worse and worse. Figure 7.8 results from including another term, and Figure 7.9 from one more still. That brings us up to a sixth-order polynomial, and what a polynomial it is. The density approximation is strongly negative in the vicinity of the mean!

Now let's see what happens when we rearrange the terms according to Edgeworth's modification. Recall that when one term is used, the Gram-Charlier and Edgeworth approximations are the same. So Figure 7.6 can be considered the first use of the Edgeworth expansion as well as the first of the Gram-Charlier. If we add one more term, we get the results shown in Figure 7.10. Note how much better this is than its Gram-Charlier compatriot in Figure 7.7. And adding still another term gives us Figure 7.11. Is the Edgeworth approximation improving as we append terms? Probably not; look closely at Figures 7.6, 7.10, and 7.11. In a manner reminiscent of a Taylor series expansion about a point, the fit is definitely improving around the mean of zero. But at the same time, the tails are having problems. The level of oscillatory error is definitely increasing. And in most cases of practical interest, the tails are the most important part of the density. The boundaries in classification decisions will usually lie somewhere in the overlapping tails. This is precisely where we would like the *best* approximation to occur.

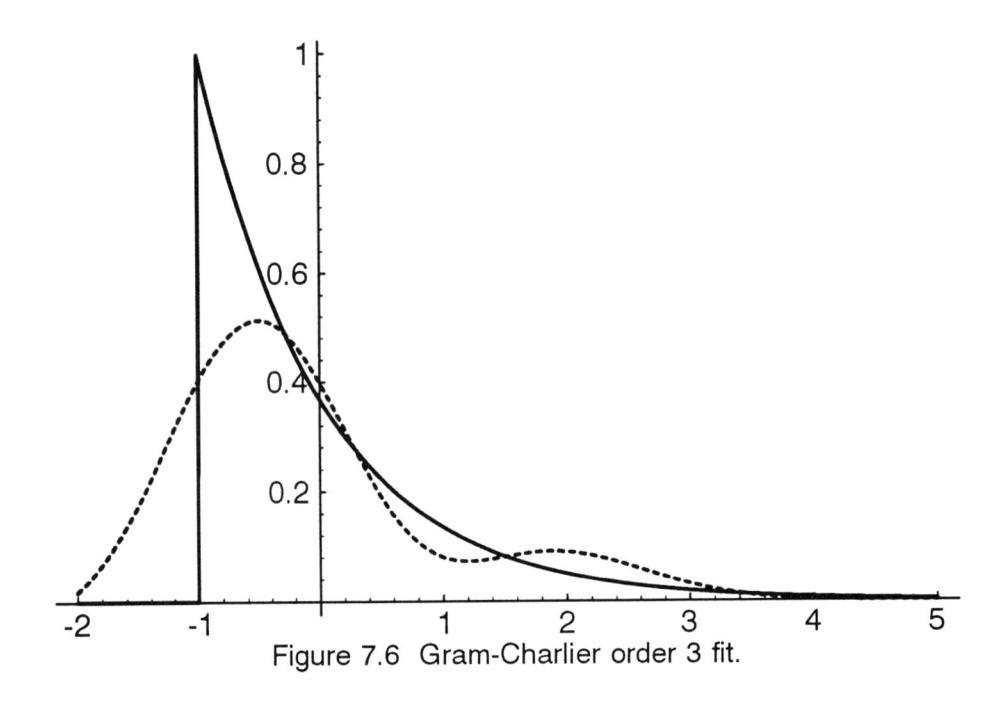

284   *The Gram-Charlier Neural Network*

Figure 7.6 Gram-Charlier order 3 fit.

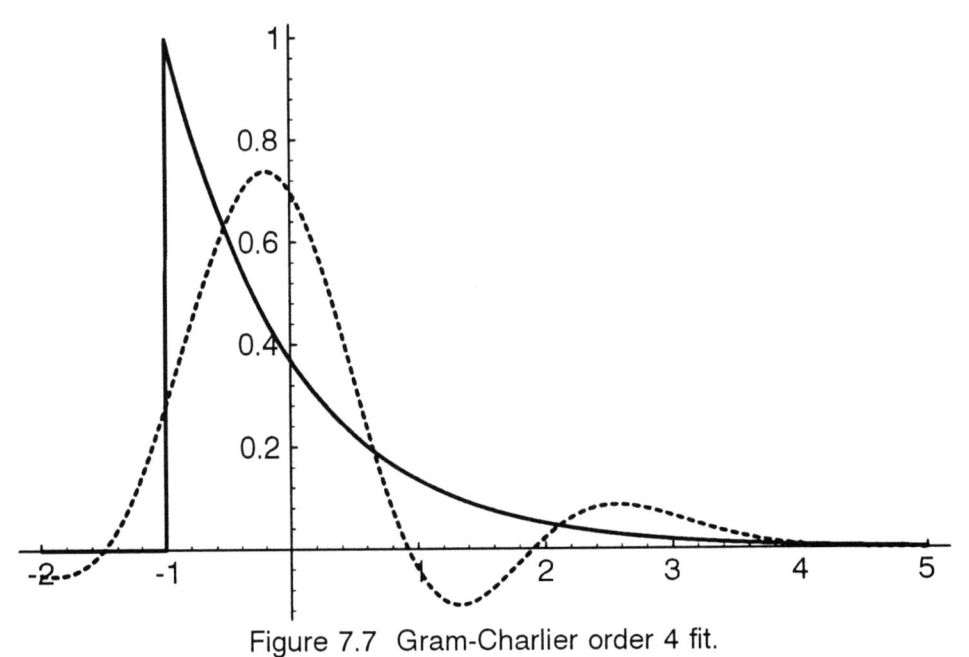

Figure 7.7 Gram-Charlier order 4 fit.

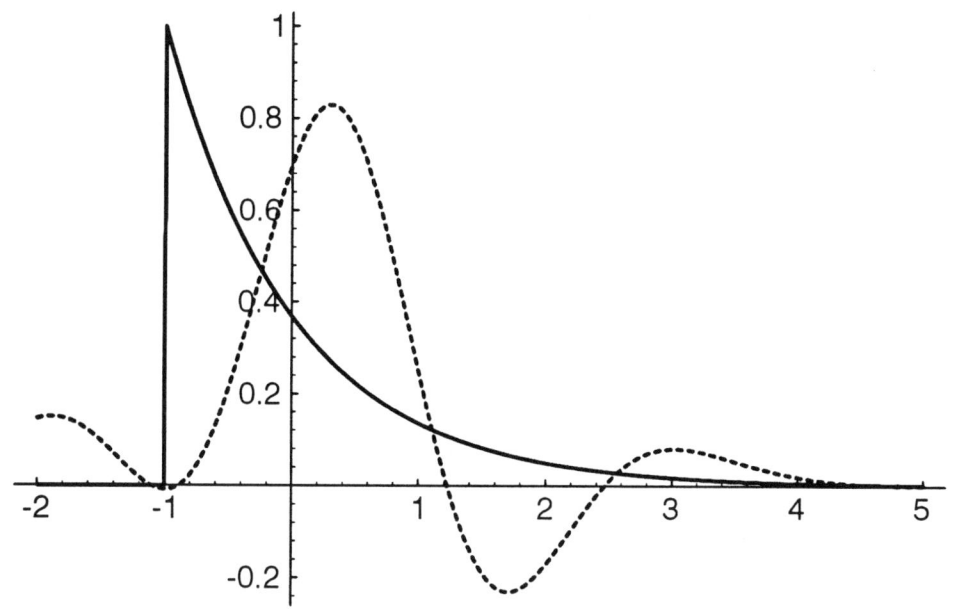

Figure 7.8 Gram-Charlier order 5 fit.

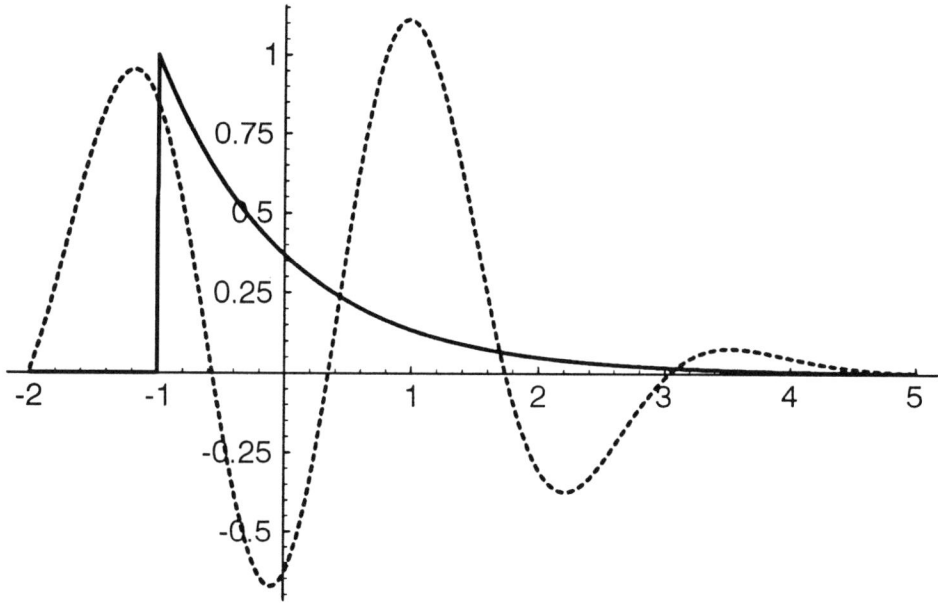

Figure 7.9 Gram-Charlier order 6 fit.

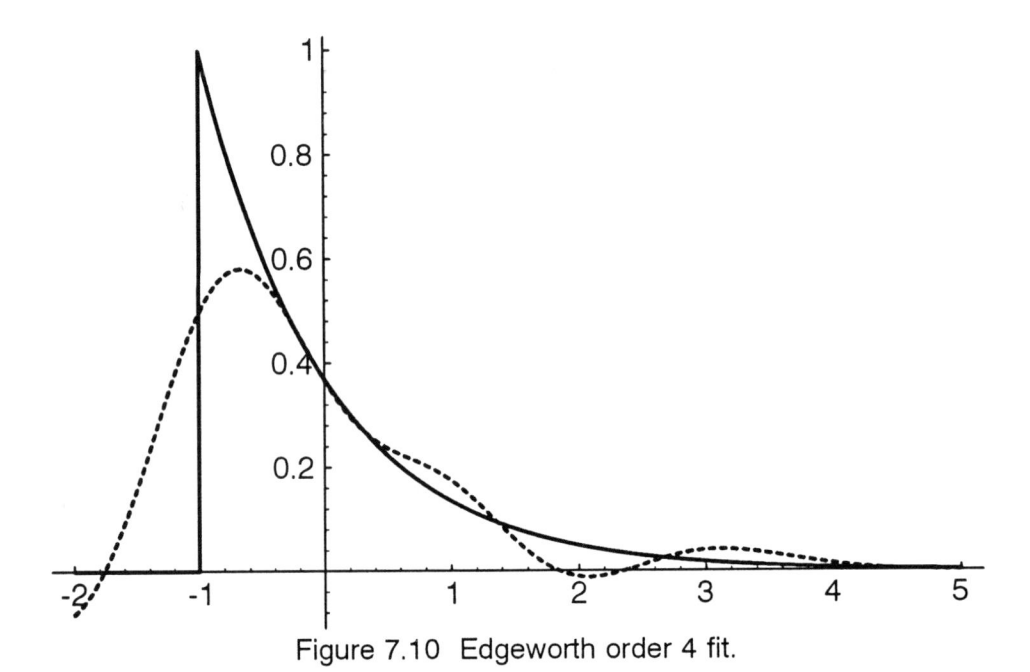

Figure 7.10 Edgeworth order 4 fit.

Figure 7.11 Edgeworth order 5 fit.

Enough of theory. Let's look at some real data. Suppose we are dealing with an application that generates samples whose random error follows a log-normal distribution. Suppose also that we do not know the exact nature of the distribution, but we do observe that it has a heavy tail in the positive direction. Therefore, we apply a square-root transformation. The resulting distribution will be less skewed, but will still be decidedly nonnormal. We will compare here the results of a signal-detection application that would be obtained by a variety of models for each of four degrees of signal strength relative to noise. These four degrees of difficulty might arise from different amounts of random error in any application.

In addition to testing the Gram-Charlier and Edgeworth models, we will also compare them with two other methods. One method is the standard probabilistic neural network. The other method is a straight-forward maximum-likelihood test based on the assumption that the error distribution is normal. This is the test that a traditional statistician (who carelessly neglected to examine a histogram of the data) would probably use. Several thousand replications of a Monte-Carlo test of the performances were run, and the results are shown in the following table. The four columns correspond to four degrees of noise level (from difficult to easy). The numbers in the table are percent misclassification. One hundred sample points were used for each trial.

```
Model           High <-------- Noise Level --------> Low

Normal ML       37.7         25.4         14.9         7.3
PNN             36.4         22.3         12.8         7.2
GC3 & EW3       35.8         22.2         13.3         7.9
GC4             37.5         24.4         14.0         8.7
GC5             40.3         27.4         17.0        10.8
GC6             41.8         31.5         21.6        13.7
EW4             35.2         22.0         13.5         7.5
EW5             36.4         23.6         14.3         9.1
```

It should not be surprising that the best neural network models outperform the normal maximum-likelihood test. Since the distributions are not normal, this is to be expected. The departure from normality is not extreme, so the relative performance is not extreme. But it is there.

It might be a little surprising that the best GCNN models actually beat the PNN at high noise levels. The GCNN starts failing only at low noise levels, where decisions are being made out in the tails.

That is known to be the weak point of GCNNs. But remember that *the goal is not to beat the PNN in accuracy*. If we do, that's just gravy. All we really need to do is remain in the ballpark. The reason is that we are inclined to favor the GCNN over the PNN only when speed is necessary. The GCNN is hundreds or thousands of times faster than the PNN. That alone is a powerful argument in its favor. We see from the above table that the GCNN and the PNN are quite competitive in performance.

We have already discussed the dangers of using high moments in computing the series expansion coefficients. The theoretical fit to a chi-square distribution presented earlier in this section illustrated that clearly. This chart also supports that contention. For all four Gram-Charlier models (3–6), the lowest-order model is the best at all noise levels. Adding more terms to the series causes performance to deteriorate significantly. This is the rule, not the exception.

We fare a little better when the Edgeworth modification is employed. For three of the four noise levels, adding one more term improves performance. The single small exception is probably a statistical fluke. On the other hand, adding still another Edgeworth term causes a notable decline in accuracy. Be warned.

The reader may legitimately wonder how well these models fare when the noise distribution is truly normal. In that case, the quick and easy normal maximum-likelihood test is theoretically optimal. Do we expose ourselves to danger when we use one of these neural networks unnecessarily? Not really. The next table compares the same models when the error is normal.

```
Model           High <-------- Noise Level -------> Low

Normal ML       31.1        16.4        7.0         2.4
PNN             31.8        16.8        7.1         2.4
GC3 & EW3       31.4        16.3        7.0         2.3
GC4             31.1        16.0        6.9         2.4
GC5             30.9        16.1        7.0         2.4
GC6             31.5        16.2        7.1         2.5
EW4             31.2        16.3        7.0         2.5
EW5             31.0        15.8        6.7         2.3
```

That table should make it clear that there is nothing to lose by using any of these network models when it is not needed. The theoretically optimal normal maximum-likelihood method does not enjoy any practical superiority even when the error really *is* normal.

Multivariate Versions of the GCNN

Thus far, we have considered only univariate versions of the GCNN. This is obviously a serious weakness of the model. As will be seen, it is not an easy weakness to overcome. However, there are at least two ways of handling the situation. The simpler and more practical one will be discussed here.

Let us first dismiss the method that perhaps has good initial appeal but that appears to be impractical. Chambers (1967) shows how the Edgeworth expansion can be generalized to the multivariate case. Unfortunately, the generalization is very complicated and does not seem to work well in practice. I am not aware of any practical applications of the direct method. Interested readers may wish to consult that reference and experiment.

There is a much more straightforward approach to using the GCNN in a multivariate situation. Statisticians are aware that as long as a collection of random variables are mutually independent, the joint likelihood of any multivariate case is the product of the individual univariate likelihoods. The condition of independence is crucial, though. Look at Figure 7.12, which shows a bivariate population along with a single peculiar case.

The filled black circles represent cases in a randomly sampled collection from a bivariate population. The marginal (univariate) probability density function of each of the two variables is shown at the bottom and right sides of the scatterplot. A single case is shown as a hollow circle. It is obvious that this case does not belong to the population. Its joint likelihood would be just about zero. But look at the marginal likelihoods associated with this case. Each is fairly large. If we try to compute the joint likelihood by multiplying the marginals, we would get a number that is most definitely not near zero. What is the cause of this serious error? It is because the two variables are not independent. The scatterplot shows that when one variable is high, the other variable tends to be high also. It should be clear that if we are to use multiple univariate GCNNs to compute a multivariate likelihood by multiplication, we *must* be sure that the variables are reasonably independent.

How do we make sure that the variables are independent? That can be difficult. We may be lucky and just get them that way. And the Sun may rise in the West, too. In practice, we have to work for independence and then say our prayers and hope. It is some consola-

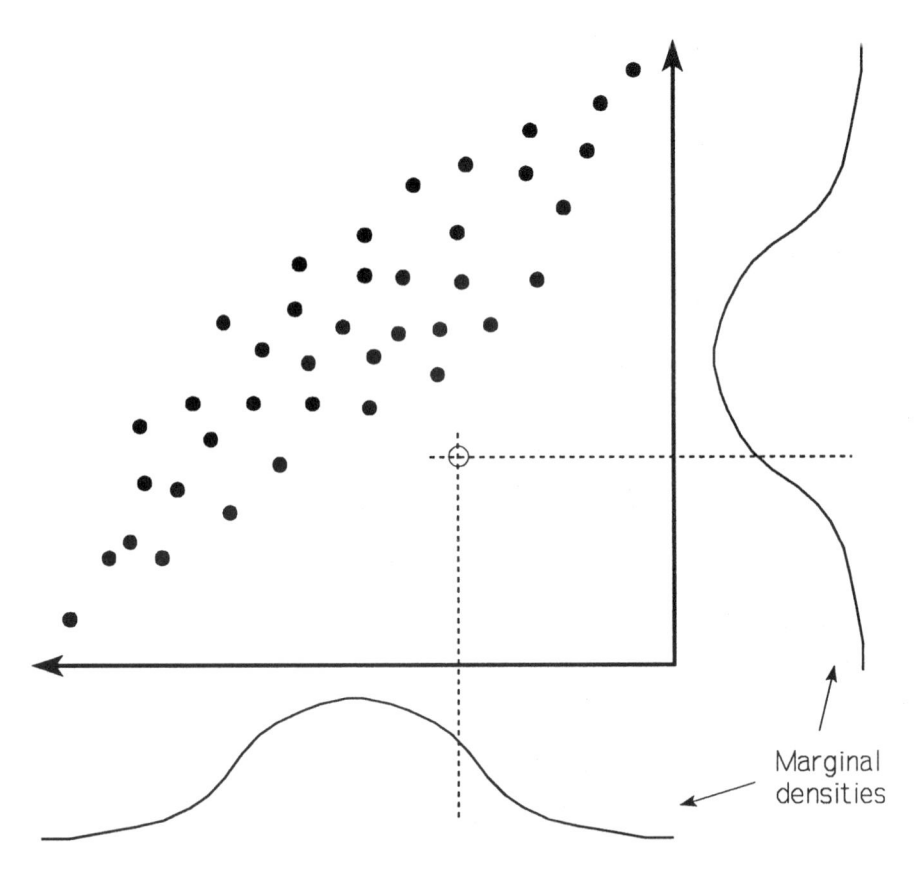

Figure 7.12 Independence is crucial.

tion that absolutely strict independence is not needed. Errors introduced by slight amounts of correlation will generally be slight. Thorough validation will often convince us that we are standing on sufficiently solid ground. But some work will almost always be needed.

Never neglect intelligent design of the measured variables as a means of achieving independence. It is too easy to get hung up on fancy mathematical methods and ignore what should be obvious. For example, suppose we measure the temperature and pressure within a reaction vessel. We hope to use that information to help us classify the state of the process into one of several categories. We know from the physics of the reaction that the temperature and pressure are quite highly correlated, though not perfectly correlated (or one would be redundant). This knowledge may lead us to try using the temperature and the log of the ratio of the pressure to temperature as our two variables. A quick statistical test would possibly show that those two variables are nearly independent.

If we cannot take advantage of our knowledge in that way, we are stuck with statistical methods. Several possibilities are discussed in Chapter 8.

In summary, here is the best way to use the GCNN in a multivariate situation. First and foremost, try to start out with variables that are as independent as possible. Use differences or (log) ratios of variables that are highly correlated. Then test for independence by examining scatterplots and correlation matrices. Clusters of correlated variables that are independent of other variables can each be treated separately. Transform them by using linear discriminant functions or some relative. Then test for independence once more. To use the network, train a separate univariate GCNN based on each variable. To compute the likelihood for a case, send each variable for the case to that variable's GCNN. Multiply the outputs from the GCNNs. Just be sure to validate performance carefully. That is the ultimate test. Even if the GCNN is given a set of variables that exhibits some moderate dependencies, correct validation will reveal what can be expected in practice. If we are satisfied with what we see, then we needn't worry about the variables being correlated.

8

Dimension Reduction and Orthogonalization

- Principal components of data arrays

- Principal components based on class centroids

- Linear discriminant functions

The curse of many or most neural network applications is that the number of potentially important variables can be overwhelming. When we want to predict the future behavior of a particular stock or bond, which variables are important? Yesterday's price? The day before? How about last week, or the price a year ago? And that is just looking at price variables. What about a stock's PE ratio, or its dividend? Then there are debt/equity ratios, order backlogs, ad infinitum. Or perhaps we are looking at a potential target in an infrared image. We have computed Gabor quadrature-pair filter values for eight orientations and ten frequencies. That gives us 160 variables, a quantity that pushes the limits of any neural network.

There are two major problems with having to process a very large number of variables. One problem is speed. The sheer size of the computational burden can slow even the fastest computers to the point of uselessness. The other major problem is overfitting. When there is a large number of variables compared with the number of training cases, neural networks can commit the error of focusing on meaningless idiosyncrasies of individual training cases instead of seeing the broad picture that is vital to generalization beyond the training set.

There is a third potential problem associated with having a large number of variables: There can be substantial correlation between variables. Granted, this is not strictly a problem caused by having many variables. It is possible to have total correlation with only two variables, and it is possible to have total independence with hundreds of variables. But it is an indisputable fact that the more variables that are present, the higher the probability of significant interdependencies. Whether or not correlation is a legitimate concern depends on the network model. Multiple-layer feedforward networks generally handle even massive amounts of correlation with no complaints. Probabilistic neural networks can be hindered to some degree, as groups of redundant variables exert undue influence on the decision process. And the Gram-Charlier neural network is totally undone by redundancy.

In this chapter we will discuss methods for extracting the bulk of the useful information present in a large set of variables, leaving the redundant information behind. The result will be far fewer variables, each of which will be relatively independent of the others. As will be pointed out, none of the methods discussed here is absolutely guaranteed to extract the information that is most important to the task at hand. There is always the possibility that some vitally important piece of information will be inadvertently left behind, buried under a pile of redundancies. However, in practice, the probability of this happening is very small. Decades of experience with these techniques in many disciplines indicate that, in the vast majority of cases, they do a superb job of extracting the important information while leaving the noise behind.

Principal Components

We start this discussion with the most common method of data reduction. *Principal components* are extracted from a collection of multivariate cases as a way of accounting for as much of the variation in that collection as possible by means of as few new variables as possible. It may be that the collection is composed of samples from several different classes. If it is, we don't care (often to our peril). The data is treated as one single group. Any categorization inherent in the collection is ignored when principal components are computed.

Each principal component is a scalar variable computed as the dot product of a case and a predefined weight vector. The mathematics of this chapter will follow the common tradition of treating all vectors as columns. So, for example, we may have a weight vector $\mathbf{v} = (v_1, v_2, ...)'$ where the prime (') indicates the transpose operation. A single observation would be $\mathbf{x} = (x_1, x_2, ...)'$. Assume that the weight vector $\mathbf{v}$ has been computed in such a way that it is appropriate for generating a principal component of the data set. (The method for finding such vectors will be discussed shortly.) Then the principal component defined by $\mathbf{v}$ is computed for a case $\mathbf{x}$ as shown in Equation (8.1).

$$y = \mathbf{v}'\mathbf{x} = v_1 x_1 + v_2 x_2 + ... \qquad (8.1)$$

That equation concerns a single principal component, a scalar variable. In practice we will almost always work with several principal components. There will, in general, be far fewer of them than there are original x variables, as data reduction is the primary purpose of this whole operation. In particular, let us say that we measure m variables, and for each case we wish to extract p principal components. In nearly all cases of practical interest, $1 \leq p \ll m$. We can now modify Equation (8.1) by computing a p-vector of principal components defined by an m by p weight matrix, each of whose p columns is a weight vector defining a different principal component. This is shown in Equation (8.2).

$$\mathbf{y} = \mathbf{V}'\mathbf{x} \tag{8.2}$$

We've come a long way without even defining what we mean by the term *principal component*. There are many questions to be considered. What properties would we like this new variable to possess? Once some properties are expressed, how can we define **V** to provide those properties? These questions will now be answered.

Let's start out simple. Suppose that we want to extract just one single principal component from the data. In other words, for each case **x** in our collection of samples, we want to compute a scalar y by dotting **x** with some vector **v**. What would be a desirable property for the collection of y values that will be obtained from the data collection? Most people would agree that y should represent the variation among the cases to the greatest degree possible. In other words, y would do us little good if it had about the same value for every case in the collection. Instead, we want y to take on as great a variety of values as possible throughout the collection. In mathematical terms, we want to define **v** in such a way that the variance of $\mathbf{v}'\mathbf{x}$ is maximized relative to the universe of possible vectors. Astute readers will immediately see that posing the problem with that single condition is of no use, since all we need to do is increase the length of **v** to increase the variance of $\mathbf{v}'\mathbf{x}$. We need the small additional condition that the length of **v** is fixed at some constant, typically 1.

There is an interesting geometric interpretation of the condition of maximum variance. Suppose that we create a scatterplot of the cases. If the cases are bivariate, this can be easily done on paper. Now draw a line through the centroid of the scatterplot. Project each case onto that line. The projections of the cases on the line represent the values of the dot product $\mathbf{v}'\mathbf{x}$. Rotate the line until the projections are spread out as much as possible. If the data falls into an ellipsoid shape, this line will correspond to the major axis of the ellipse. This line represents the vector **v** that provides us with the first principal component. A typical bivariate scatterplot showing two principal components is given in Figure 8.1.

We have just defined a property that we would like for a single principal component. But what if we now want a second? What would be a desirable property for this new variable? For convenience, let us refer to the defining vector for the first principal component as $\mathbf{v}_1$. That lets us use $\mathbf{v}_2$ to refer to the vector for the second principal component that we seek. The property of capturing maximum variation from the

Principal Components

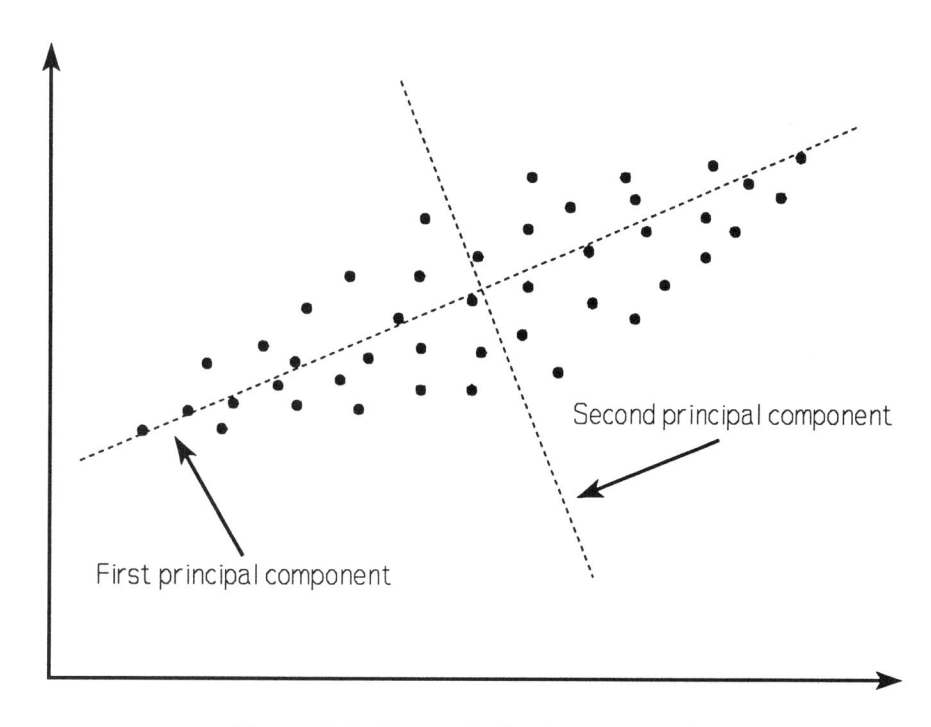

Figure 8.1 Two principal components.

collection is important. But we can't use precisely that property again, or we would just end up with the same vector as we did before. Remember that another of our goals is to eliminate redundancy from the measured variables. This tells us that we want our second principal component to be independent of the first. We can now state the property that we want for this quantity. The second principal component should have maximum variance across the data collection, subject to the restriction that it be uncorrelated with the first principal component. In geometric terms, this implies that $\mathbf{v}_2$ must be orthogonal to $\mathbf{v}_1$.

This scheme can be repeated as needed. Each successive principal component is computed in such a way that it has the maximum possible variance, subject to the condition that it is uncorrelated with all previous principal components. A set of variables computed this way will capture the maximum obtainable variance from the collection of sample cases relative to all possible collections of that many variables. And their independence is a very nice side effect.

Now that the properties we want for the principal components have been clearly stated, we need to know how to compute the **V** matrix whose p columns are the vectors to be dotted with the raw data. Full derivation of the mathematics is not difficult, but it is beyond the scope of this text. Interested readers have a large variety of sources that may be consulted. My favorite is the eminently readable, yet thoroughly detailed Cooley and Lohnes (1971). Readers in search of extremely detailed mathematics should procure the classic Anderson (1958). For our purposes, we will simply state the algorithm used to compute **V**.

As with most statistical procedures, the first step is to compute the mean so that the data can be centered. Let x_{ij} stand for the measured value of variable j in case i of the collection of n cases that comprises the training set. Then the mean of variable j is computed by summing across the training set and dividing by the number of cases that went into the sum. This elementary fact is shown in Equation (8.3).

$$\mu_j = \frac{1}{n} \sum_{i=1}^{n} x_{ij} \qquad (8.3)$$

The covariance matrix for the training set is an m by m symmetric matrix whose diagonal contains the variances of each of the m measured variables and whose off-diagonal area contains their covariances. We will call this matrix **W**. Each of its elements is computed using Equation (8.4). Note that some authorities divide by $n-1$ rather than n so as to compute population estimates. For our purposes this is irrelevant.

$$w_{ij} = w_{ji} = \frac{1}{n} \sum_{k=1}^{n} (x_{ki} - \mu_i)(x_{kj} - \mu_j) \qquad (8.4)$$

Many readers will not be surprised to learn that the vectors that define the principal components are the eigenvectors of the covariance matrix, and that the eigenvalues are the variances of the principal components. So our task is simple: Compute the eigenstructure of **W**. Let the eigenvector corresponding to the largest eigenvalue be the first column of **V**. The eigenvector corresponding to the second-largest eigenvalue will be the second column of **V**, and so on. We stop adding columns to **V** when the eigenvalues become small enough that we no longer consider them an important contribution to the variation in the training set.

How do we know how to choose p, the number of principal components (the number of columns in **V**)? This question does not have a firm answer. There are some statistical tests that can be performed, but I strongly encourage avoidance of such tests, as they can be dangerously misleading in many practical situations. The best approach is a mixture of heuristics and common sense. The sum of the eigenvalues of **W** is equal to the sum of the variances of the original variables (the diagonal of **W**). It is perfectly reasonable to consider the fraction of this total variance that has been captured by a set of principal components. An excellent heuristic method for choosing p is to plot the fraction (0 to 1) of the total variance as a function of p. As principal components are appended, the sum of their eigenvalues will steadily increase until all of the variance is accounted for. In most applications, the first eigenvalue alone will account for a very sizeable fraction of the total variance. Adding the second will produce a significant boost. It will almost always be seen that after including only a few eigenvalues, nearly all of the variance in the training set will be accounted for. Visual inspection of such a plot usually enables one to choose p easily. Figure 8.2 is typical of what might be seen in real applications.

If there is a reason for keeping a human out of the loop, and strictly automatic choice of p is demanded instead, the arbitrary nature of the decision can be somewhat reduced. Simply choose in advance a fraction of the variance that will be considered satisfactory. One might, for example, agree that it is sufficient to extract 90 percent of the variance. One then keeps including principal components until the sum of their eigenvalues reaches or exceeds 90 percent of the total. This is a common practice, but a visual inspection is to be preferred if at all possible.

Use of principal components is not foolproof. Throughout this entire discussion, we have made a vital assumption that has been glibly ignored thus far. Our main concern has been with accounting for the majority of the variation in the training set. But what guarantee do we have that by doing so, we have extracted the information that is important to our task? Strictly speaking, we have no guarantee at all. It may be that the bulk of the variation is due to irrelevant processes, or perhaps even due to random noise. We are in big trouble if the information that we need is hidden away in some components that correspond to small eigenvalues that are discarded. The truth of the

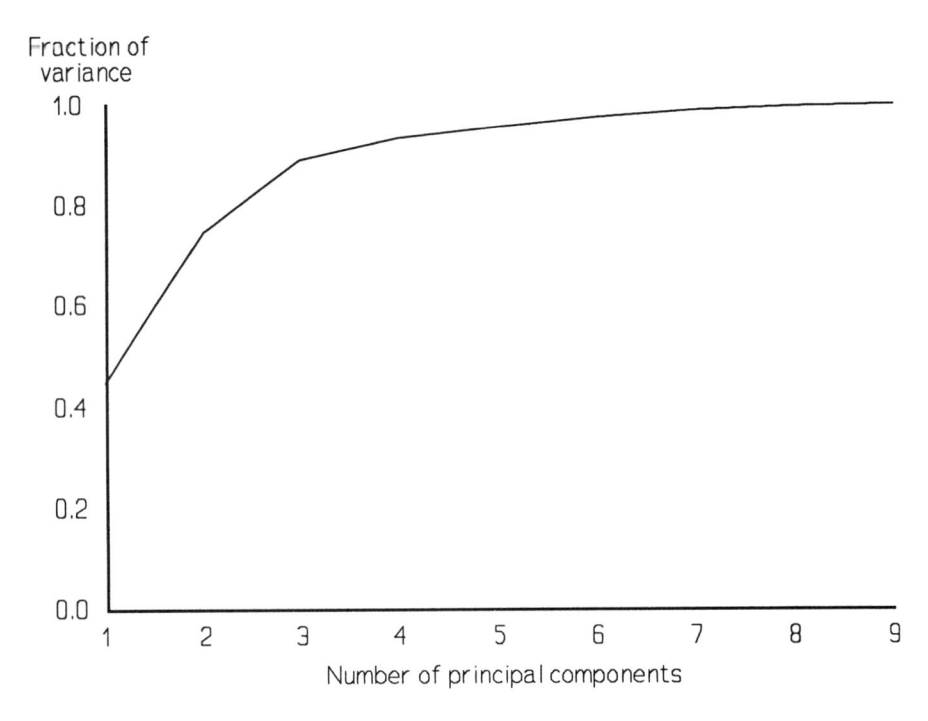

Figure 8.2 Successively accounting for variance.

matter is that such events can happen. On the other hand, many years of experience with this technique in a tremendous variety of applications indicate that our implicit assumption is almost always valid. In the vast majority of situations I and many other researchers have seen, there is an extremely strong tendency for the important information in a data set to be concentrated in the first few principal components. The remaining components are almost always the home of the system noise. But be warned: This may not always be the case.

Scaling and Computation Issues

We have seen that the basic method for computing principal components is to compute the covariance matrix of a training set using Equation (8.4), find its eigenstructure, keep (in the columns of $\mathbf{V}$) a few of the eigenvectors corresponding to the largest eigenvalues, then freely compute the principal components for observed cases using Equation

(8.2). There are several small modifications to this simple technique that we will usually want to employ.

The first issue involves centering of the principal components. Direct use of Equation (8.2) gives us variables whose mean is generally different from zero. Especially when we use these variables as neural network inputs, we would like them to be centered. This is easily done. Simply subtract the mean of each measured variable before multiplying by **V'**. In other words, let the mean vector be designated as $\boldsymbol{\mu} = (\mu_1, \mu_2, ...)'$. Then compute the principal components using Equation (8.5).

$$\mathbf{y} = \mathbf{V}'(\mathbf{x} - \boldsymbol{\mu}) \tag{8.5}$$

The next issue involves scaling of the principal components. The first will have the maximum variance, and each succeeding principal component will have less variance. In neural network applications, that will tend to emphasize the importance of the first components, something that may not be justifiable. Also, it will often require that the network learn weights that are quite disparate. This can slow learning and increase the likelihood of landing in a local minimum. In most (though perhaps not all) situations, we would like the computed principal components to have equal variance. Scaling them to unit variance is a good choice. This is easily done. Recall that the eigenvalue corresponding to each column of **V** is the variance of that principal component. So all we need to do is to divide each computed principal component by the square root of its corresponding eigenvalue. In mathematical terms, let **L** be a p by p diagonal matrix. Its diagonal elements are the eigenvalues corresponding to the columns of **V**, and all of its other elements are zero. Then we can use Equation (8.6) to compute principal components having unit variance as well as zero mean.

$$\mathbf{y} = \mathbf{L}^{-\frac{1}{2}} \mathbf{V}'(\mathbf{x} - \boldsymbol{\mu}) \tag{8.6}$$

There is one last scaling issue that is sometimes important and sometimes not. Should we let the variances of the raw variables influence the definitions of the principal components? If all of the original measured variables have about the same variance, this question is not important. But suppose that the variances of those variables differ by large amounts. In particular, suppose that we measure two variables. The first is a person's height in millimeters.

The second variable is that person's weight in kilograms. Typical values for the first variable might range from 1500 to 2500, while the second would likely fall in the range of 50 to 90. The variance of the first variable might be about 1000 times that of the second. Now think about a scatterplot of a set of experimental subjects. If we plot the huge height variable on the horizontal axis, the principal axis of the rough ellipsoid of plotted cases will be nearly horizontal. The larger eigenvalue will be many times greater than the smaller, and the eigenvector corresponding to the larger eigenvalue will be nearly equal to the trivial vector $(1, 0)'$. The implication is that an automated scheme for choosing p will conclude that only one principal component is needed, as that single component accounts for nearly 100 percent of the variance. Furthermore, when we compute that first principal component, its value will be based almost entirely on the subject's height, with the weight practically ignored. Is that what we really want? Probably not. It is more likely that we want to normalize the raw variables before computing the principal components. In the example just cited, that would probably give us a first principal component roughly equal to height plus weight, a measure of overall size. The second principal component would probably be height minus weight, a measure of obesity.

The obvious method for accomplishing this normalization is to compute the variance of each raw variable and divide each centered value by the square root of the variance before computing **W**. When we actually do the computation, there is a slightly easier method. Compute **W** using the unscaled raw variables. Then normalize each element of **W** according to Equation (8.7). The net result is exactly the same as if the variables were standardized first. Observe that the resulting matrix, called a *correlation matrix* by statisticians, has the value 1.0 along its diagonal. This normalization is not mandatory. In some situations it may be appropriate that variables having larger variance should exert more influence. But that situation is not frequent.

$$w'_{ij} = \frac{w_{ij}}{\sqrt{w_{ii} w_{jj}}} \tag{8.7}$$

Code for Principal Components

We now present code for a class that enables easy computation of principal components. The class constructor is called with a training set. The user also specifies either the number of principal components to compute, or the fraction of the total variance that is required. The constructor returns in its parameter list the number of components actually found. It also saves the information that will be needed to compute principal components from cases. The class header and constructor now appear.

```
class PrincoData {

public:
   PrincoData ( int ncases , int nvars , double *data , int stdize ,
            int maxfacs , double frac , int *nfacs ) ;
   ~PrincoData () ;
   void factors ( int ncases , double *data ) ;

private:
   int nvars, nfacs ;
   double *means, *evals, *evect, *work1 ;
} ;


PrincoData::PrincoData (
      int ncases ,              // Number of cases (rows in data array)
      int nv ,                  // Number of variables (columns in data array)
      double *data ,            // Input (ncases by nv) matrix
      int stdize ,              // Standardize inputs to equal variance?
      int maxfacs ,             // Maximum number of output factors
      double frac ,             // Fraction (0-1) of variance to retain
      int *nfactors             // Output: Number of factors retained
      )

{
   int n, icase, var, var2, fac ;
   double *dptr, *std, diff1, diff2, sum, temp, *work2, *covar ;
```

```
/*
   Copy parameters to private area and allocate memory.
   Also realize that the number of factors cannot exceed one less than
   the number of cases.  This becomes important when we are using group
   means rather than raw data to define the factors.
*/

if (maxfacs > ncases-1)
   maxfacs = ncases-1 ;

nvars = nv ;

if (stdize) {
   std = (double *) malloc ( nvars * sizeof(double) ) ;
   if (std == NULL) {
      *nfactors = nfacs = -1 ; // Error flag
      return ;
      }
   }
else
   std = NULL ;

means = (double *) malloc ( nvars * sizeof(double) ) ;
evals = (double *) malloc ( nvars * sizeof(double) ) ;
evect = (double *) malloc ( nvars * nvars * sizeof(double) ) ;
covar = (double *) malloc ( nvars * nvars * sizeof(double) ) ;
work1 = (double *) malloc ( nvars * sizeof(double) ) ;
work2 = (double *) malloc ( nvars * sizeof(double) ) ;

if ((means == NULL) || (evals == NULL) || (evect == NULL) ||
    (covar == NULL) || (work1 == NULL) || (work2 == NULL)) {
   if (means != NULL)
      free ( means ) ;
   if (evals != NULL)
      free ( evals ) ;
   if (evect != NULL)
      free ( evect ) ;
   if (std != NULL)
      free ( std ) ;
   if (covar != NULL)
      free ( covar ) ;
```

Principal Components

```
      if (work1 != NULL)
        free ( work1 ) ;
      if (work2 != NULL)
        free ( work2 ) ;
      *nfactors = nfacs = -1 ;  // Error flag
      return ;
      }
```

```
/*
   Compute means and covariances
*/
```

```
   for (var=0 ; var<nvars ; var++)     // Zero the mean vector
     means[var] = 0.0 ;

   n = nvars * nvars ;                 // Zero the covariance matrix
   while (n--)
     covar[n] = 0.0 ;

   for (icase=0 ; icase<ncases ; icase++) { // Cumulate means
     dptr = data + icase * nvars ;     // Point to this case
     for (var=0 ; var<nvars ; var++)   // All variables in this case
       means[var] += dptr[var] ;
     }

   for (var=0 ; var<nvars ; var++)     // Mean is sum divided by n
     means[var] /= ncases ;            // Equation (8.3)

   for (icase=0 ; icase<ncases ; icase++) { // Cumulate covariances
     dptr = data + icase * nvars ;     // Point to this case
     for (var=0 ; var<nvars ; var++) {
       diff1 = dptr[var] - means[var] ;
       for (var2=var ; var2<nvars ; var2++) {
         diff2 = dptr[var2] - means[var2] ;
         covar[var*nvars+var2] += diff1 * diff2 ;
         }
       }
     }
```

```
   for (var=0 ; var<nvars ; var++) {              // Divide sums by n
      for (var2=var ; var2<nvars ; var2++) {      // To get covariance matrix
         covar[var*nvars+var2] /= ncases ;        // Equation (8.4)
         if (var != var2)                         // Symmetrically duplicate
            covar[var2*nvars+var] = covar[var*nvars+var2] ;
         }
      }

/*
   If we are to standardize, save the standard deviations and adjust
   the covariance matrix.
*/

   if (std != NULL) {
      for (var=0 ; var<nvars ; var++) {           // Each variable's variance
         std[var] = sqrt ( covar[var*nvars+var] ) ; // is in the diagonal
         covar[var*nvars+var] = 1.0 ;             // which then becomes unity
         }
      for (var=0 ; var<nvars-1 ; var++) {         // Adjust covariances
         for (var2=var+1 ; var2<nvars ; var2++) { // for standardization
            covar[var*nvars+var2] /= (std[var] * std[var2]) ; // Equation (8.7)
            covar[var2*nvars+var] = covar[var*nvars+var2] ;
            }
         }
      }


/*
   Compute eigenstructure and number of factors to retain
*/


   jacobi ( nvars , covar , evals , evect , work1 , work2 ) ;

   sum = 0.0 ;
   for (var=0 ; var<nvars ; var++)
      sum += evals[var] ;                         // Sum the eigenvalues

   frac *= sum ;                                  // User wants this much of sum retained
```

Principal Components

```
      sum = 0.0 ;
      for (nfacs=0 ; nfacs<maxfacs ; nfacs++) {
         sum += evals[nfacs] ;        // We have retained this much so far
         if (sum >= frac) {            // Compare it to user's request
            ++nfacs ;                  // If there, break out with number of factors
            break ;
            }
         }
```

/*
   We now do one or two things to avoid expensive operations in the 'factors' routine.
   Equation (8.6) says we must divide each factor by the square root of the corresponding eigenvalue in order to produce unit standard deviations for the factors. If the user wants standardization of the input variables, divide the factor weights by the standard deviations now so we don't have to do it for each case later.
*/

```
   for (fac=0 ; fac<nfacs ; fac++) {
      if (evals[fac] > 0.0)
         temp = 1.0 / sqrt ( evals[fac] ) ;
      else
         temp = 0.0 ;
      for (var=0 ; var<nvars ; var++)
         evect[var*nvars+fac] *= temp ;
      }

   if (std != NULL) {
      for (var=0 ; var<nvars ; var++) {
         for (fac=0 ; fac<nfacs ; fac++)
            evect[var*nvars+fac] /= std[var] ;
         }
      }

   if (std != NULL)
      free ( std ) ;
   free ( covar ) ;
   free ( work2 ) ;  // We keep work1 for use by 'factors'

   *nfactors = nfacs ;
}
```

The constructor listed above is provided with a training set when it is invoked. The training set is in the form of a matrix strung out into a vector. The nv variables of the first case appear first. Those of the second case follow, and so on, for all ncases cases. The input flag stdize indicates (by being nonzero) that the user wishes to standardize all raw input variables so that they have an equal effect on the principal components. This was discussed on page 301 and involves Equation (8.7).

There are two methods for the user to specify the number of principal components that are extracted. The input parameter maxfacs places an upper limit on the number. The input parameter frac tells the constructor to be satisfied when that fraction (0–1) of the total variance is accounted for. Principal components will be successively extracted until at least that fraction of the variance is obtained, except that no more than maxfacs will be extracted. In order to specify an exact number via maxfacs, set frac equal to 1.0 or more. In order to specify a fraction of the variance via frac, set maxfacs equal to nv or more. The number of principal components actually extracted is returned to the user in nfactors.

The first action taken by the constructor is to limit maxfacs to one less than the number of cases. For the applications discussed up until now, this will never be an issue. In the next section, we will see that it can be important. Also, memory for both permanent (during the life of the class object) and scratch use is allocated. Note that the vector of standard deviations is allocated only if the user requested standardization.

Computation of the mean vector and covariance matrix is a simple and straightforward application of Equations (8.3) and (8.4), respectively. Note that we take advantage of symmetry and compute only half of the covariance matrix. If the user wants the input variances standardized, we save the standard deviations for use later, then adjust the covariance matrix according to Equation (8.7).

We use the subroutine jacobi to compute the eigenstructure of the covariance matrix. This routine will be discussed at the end of this section. The total variance is found, and the number of principal components is computed according to the user's specification.

The last step is adjusting the **V** matrix (in evect) in one or two ways. First, we divide each column (eigenvector) by the square root of the corresponding eigenvalue, as shown in Equation (8.6). This causes the principal components to have unit variance. Then, if the user wants to standardize the input variables, we divide each row of **V** by the standard deviation of the corresponding variable. This saves having to perform that expensive operation for each and every case that may be processed later. Finally, we free the work areas that are no longer needed and return the number of principal components to the user.

The destructor is trivial. It uses the private variable nfacs to see if the constructor failed. If not, it simply frees all allocated memory. The destructor is now listed.

```
PrincoData::~PrincoData ()
{
  if (nfacs < 0)
    return ;
  free ( means ) ;
  free ( evals ) ;
  free ( evect ) ;
  free ( work1 ) ;
}
```

After the constructor has been called with a training set on which the computed **V** matrix is based, we may compute principal components for individual cases. This is done with the member function factors. The cases are arranged in the data array exactly as they were for the constructor. We do not need to specify the number of variables, as it is the same as when the constructor was called (or at least it had better be). This function is a trivial implementation of Equation (8.5). The only unusual thing to notice is that the column dimension of the input/output array data generally changes. On input, it has as many columns as there are input variables (nv in the constructor call). On output, it has only nfacs columns. This dimension change facilitates subsequent use of the array by other routines.

```
void PrincoData::factors (
  int ncases ,              // Number of cases (rows in data array)
  double *data              // In (ncases by nvars) and out (ncases by nfacs)
  )

{
  int icase, var, fac ;
  double *dptr, sum, diff ;
```

```
for (icase=0 ; icase<ncases ; icase++) {        // For each case
   dptr = data + icase * nvars ;                // Point to this case
   for (fac=0 ; fac<nfacs ; fac++) {            // For each factor to be found
      sum = 0.0 ;                               // Will dot evect with case
      for (var=0 ; var<nvars ; var++) {         // All variables in this case
         diff = dptr[var] - means[var] ;        // Must be centered
         sum += evect[var*nvars+fac] * diff ;   // Cumulate dot product
      }
      work1[fac] = sum ;                        // This case's factor 'fac'
   }
   dptr = data + icase * nfacs ;                // nfacs <= nvars, so may compress
   for (fac=0 ; fac<nfacs ; fac++)              // Replace original variables
      dptr[fac] = work1[fac] ;                  // With principal factors
   }
}
```

The last tidying up to do is to deal with computation of the eigenstructure of the covariance matrix. In the constructor, we called the subroutine jacobi. This routine is one of the most elementary methods for computing the eigenstructure of a real symmetric matrix. There are faster, more advanced algorithms available, and the user may want to seek them out. On the other hand, this algorithm is nothing to be ashamed of. It is reasonably fast, extremely reliable, and much shorter than its competitors. Despite its simplicity, we will avoid a full discussion of its operation here. Interested readers may consult any good numerical methods text for a full discussion. The version given here is loosely based on the program in Press *et al.* (1992), although I have made a few minor optimization changes that seem to improve its performance in statistical applications.

A rough sketch of the operation of jacobi is the following. When one performs an orthogonal rotation on a matrix, its eigenvalues remain constant and its eigenvectors are rotated by the same angle. If a matrix is strictly diagonal, its eigenvalues are arrayed along the diagonal. So we find a rotation that will zero some off-diagonal element, and we perform that rotation. We simultaneously rotate an identity matrix to keep track of the rotations. The act of zeroing a particular element will, unfortunately, undo the zeroing of other elements. But the key is that the undoing will be relatively slight. So we just keep going around the off-diagonal area of the matrix, zeroing everything in sight, until we are left with a diagonal matrix. The original form of this algorithm, which was intended for hand calculation on small matrices, zeroed the largest

Principal Components

remaining element each time. However, with the advent of fast computers that make operation on large matrices possible, the time required to search for the largest element becomes significant. So the method used here is popular. Just pass through the entire off-diagonal area, zeroing all of the elements in order, regardless of their size. This blunt-instrument approach leaves the door open for optimization. On early sweeps, we may want to skip elements that are small. On later sweeps, we may want to cheat a little and arbitrarily zero elements that are already extremely tiny. These refinements are of no great significance to overall operation and involve fairly arbitrary tradeoffs in performance. Note that this subroutine destroys the input matrix.

```
inline void rotate ( double *mat , int i , int j , int k , int l , double sine , double tau , int n )
{
   double t1, t2 ;

   t1 = mat[i*n+j] ;
   t2 = mat[k*n+l] ;
   mat[i*n+j] = t1 - sine * (t2 + t1 * tau) ;
   mat[k*n+l] = t2 + sine * (t1 - t2 * tau) ;
}

void jacobi (
   int n ,                       // Size of matrix
   double *mat ,                 // Square symmetric real matrix
   double *evals ,               // Output of n eigenvalues
   double *evect ,               // Output of n by n eigenvectors (each is a column)
   double *work1 ,               // Work vector n long
   double *work2                 // Work vector n long
   )
{
   int i, j, k, ibig, sweep ;
   double err, *dptr, threshold, test, diff, theta ;
   double corr, sine, cosine, tangent, tau, big, mat_ij ;

/*
The rotations will be cumulated in the evect matrix, each of whose columns will be a
normalized eigenvector.  Initialize this to the identity.  The output vector evals will always
contain the current diagonal of mat, so initialize it now.  The corrections to the diagonal
as a result of rotation will be maintained in work1 and work2, so also initialize them.
*/
```

```
   for (i=0 ; i<n ; i++) {
     dptr = evect + i * n ;            // Point to row i
     for (j=0 ; j<n ; j++)             // Set entire row to 0
       dptr[j] = 0.0 ;
     dptr[i] = 1.0 ;                   // But set diagonal to 1
     evals[i] = work1[i] = mat[i*n+i] ; // Matrix diagonal
     work2[i] = 0.0 ;
   }
```

/*
   This is the main loop which does a single sweep through the matrix. It is rare that
   more than a dozen sweeps will be needed do zero the above-diagonal region.
   However, just for safety, we impose a limit here.
*/

```
   for (sweep=0 ; sweep<200 ; sweep++) {
```

/*
   Start by checking for convergence. We simply sum the magnitude of the
   elements above the diagonal. When they become tiny we are done.
*/

```
     err = 0.0 ;
     for (i=0 ; i<n-1 ; i++) {
       dptr = mat + i * n ;            // Point to row i
       for (j=i+1 ; j<n ; j++)         // Above-diagonal area
         err += fabs ( dptr[j] ) ;     // Will be all zero when done
       }
     if (err < 1.e-60)                 // Safer for portability than using zero
       break ;                         // Although numerically slightly inferior
```

/*
   We can save a lot of time in the early sweeps by skipping a zeroing rotation for matrix
   elements that are already small. Set the threshold slightly smaller than recommended in
   Press et al to be more conservative. After four sweeps (1 more than Press uses), use a
   threshold of zero so that we do the rotation no matter how small.
*/

```
     if (sweep > 4)
       threshold = 0.0 ;
     else
       threshold = 0.15 * err / (n * n) ;
```

Principal Components

```
/*
   This is the so-called "cyclic Jacobi" method.  We pass through the entire above-
   diagonal region in this nested loop.  For small matrices it is more efficient to zero
   the largest element each time.  But for large matrices the search for the largest
   becomes too expensive.
*/

   for (i=0 ; i<n-1 ; i++) {          // Row i
      for (j=i+1 ; j<n ; j++) {       // And column j
         mat_ij = mat[i*n+j] ;        // This is the element to be zeroed
```

```
/*
   Compute a test value as a moderate multiple of the off-diagonal element currently
   being zeroed.  Many decisions will be based on the significance of this value, which
   is determined by adding it to the appropriate quantity and seeing if the result is the
   same to machine precision.
*/
         test = 128.0 * fabs ( mat_ij ) ;
```

```
/*
   Here we cheat a little, though not until a sweep later than Press does.  If the off-
   diagonal being zeroed is already tiny compared to both of its corresponding
   diagonals, we cross our fingers and surreptitiously set this element to zero without
   actually doing the work.  Shameful, but it saves time with no real cost in accuracy.
*/

         if ((sweep > 5)  &&
            (fabs(evals[i]) == (fabs(evals[i])+test))  &&
            (fabs(evals[j]) == (fabs(evals[j])+test))) {
            mat[i*n+j] = 0.0 ;
            continue ;
            }
```

```
/*
   This is another time saver.  It is not cheating at all.  On the first few iterations there
   is no point in bothering with zeroing small elements.  Stick with the big ones.  Only
   after we have a few sweeps under our belt do we get picky.  The threshold was
   computed earlier.
*/
         if (fabs ( mat_ij ) < threshold)
            continue ;
```

/*
   This is it. We can no longer avoid it. We must do the rotations to zero the (i,j) above-diagonal element. Start by computing the rotation angle, theta, then find our ultimate goal, its tangent. If the denominator of the strict formula would be tiny, use an approximation that is essentially perfect in that instance.
*/

```
            diff = evals[j] - evals[i] ;
            if (fabs(diff) == (fabs(diff) + test)) {
              if (diff != 0.0)
                tangent = mat_ij / diff ;
              else
                tangent = 0.0 ;
            }
            else {
              theta = 0.5 * diff / mat_ij ;
              tangent = 1.0 / (fabs ( theta ) + sqrt ( theta * theta + 1.0 )) ;
              if (theta < 0.0)
                tangent = -tangent ;
            }
```

/*
   Do the rotations. We break it up into three steps, as this is an efficient way to handle the requirement that we only do the elements above the diagonal.
*/

```
            cosine = 1.0 / sqrt ( tangent * tangent + 1.0 ) ;
            sine = cosine * tangent ;
            tau = sine / (cosine + 1.0) ;

            for (k=0 ; k<i ; k++)      // Rows above (less than) i
              rotate ( mat , k , i , k , j , sine , tau , n ) ;
            for (k=i+1 ; k<j ; k++)   // Rows between i and j
              rotate ( mat , i , k , k , j , sine , tau , n ) ;
            for (k=j+1 ; k<n ; k++)   // Rows beyond j
              rotate ( mat , i , k , j , k , sine , tau , n ) ;
```

/*
   Now apply this same rotation to the eigenvector matrix
*/

Principal Components

```
            for (k=0 ; k<n ; k++)
                rotate ( evect , k , i , k , j , sine , tau , n ) ;
```

/*
   The last step in this (i,j) zeroing is to cumulate (across the sweep)
   the terms that will be needed to update the diagonal (eigenvalues)
   at the end of the sweep. Also, we do not actually compute the value
   of the zeroed term, as it is zero (or should be). Just set it.
*/

```
            corr = tangent * mat_ij ;
            evals[i] -= corr ;
            work2[i] -= corr ;
            evals[j] += corr ;
            work2[j] += corr ;

            mat[i*n+j] = 0.0 ;
            } // j
        }// i
```

/*
   A sweep is completed. Update the eigenvalues (diagonal) and work vectors.
*/

```
      for (k=0 ; k<n ; k++) {
         work1[k] += work2[k] ;
         evals[k] = work1[k] ;
         work2[k] = 0.0 ;
         }

      } // sweep
```

/*
   We are essentially done. The final step is to sort the eigenvalues
   in descending order and simultaneously swap the vectors.
*/

```
   for (i=0 ; i<n ; i++) {              // End of each pass gets next biggest
      big = evals[i] ;                  // Keep track of biggest eval here
      ibig = i ;                        // And its location in array
      for (j=i+1 ; j<n ; j++) {         // Check for any bigger below
```

```
         if (evals[j] > big) {         // If we find a bigger eval
            big = evals[j] ;            // Update our record
            ibig = j ;                  // And its location
            }
         }
      if (ibig == i)                    // If nothing bigger was found below
         continue ;                     // Then no swap necessary
      evals[ibig] = evals[i] ;          // Swap this small one into big's place
      evals[i] = big ;                  // And put big one up here
      for (j=0 ; j<n ; j++) {           // Also must swap corresponding vectors
         test = evect[j*n+i] ;          // All rows of this pair of columns
         evect[j*n+i] = evect[j*n+ibig] ;
         evect[j*n+ibig] = test ;
         }
      }
   }
```

Principal Components of Group Centroids

We have discussed a method for extracting the majority of the variation in a data set, expressing that variation in relatively few independent variables. This is a useful technique when the problem is one of general function mapping. When the entire training set represents a universe of possibilities, and the principal components will serve as the inputs to a neural network that predicts one or more output variables, the technique just described is often appropriate. But what if the problem is one of classification? What if the training set consists of cases from more than one class, and the ultimate goal is to build a classifier network? The previously discussed method may not be ideal. Let's consider why.

In a classification problem, there are two general sources of case-to-case variation. One source of variation is the noise or other contamination that is not related to differences between the classes. This is called the *within-class* variance. It has nothing to do with differences between the classes. It is simply the variation that naturally occurs within each class. The other source of variation among the cases in the training set is due to the fact that the classes are different. (At least we hope that is true!) Some of the cases belong to one class, so their variables tend to cluster around some area or areas.

Other cases belong to another class, so their variables cluster around some other area. This source of training set variation is called the *among-class* variance, or sometimes the *between-class* variance. A little thought tells us that the among-class variance is our friend. That is what allows us to discriminate cases from different classes based on their measured variables. The within-class variance is our nemesis. It casts a cloud of confusion about us, masking the differences among the classes with noise or extraneous effects.

So how does this relate to principal components? When we compute new variables that account for variance in the training set, we would obviously like to focus our energy on the good variance, the among-class part. But if we just clump the whole training set together and define principal components based on the conglomerate of all classes, we have mixed the within-class and the between-class variance parts. Our new variables will be extracting the useless noise along with the good information. How can we remedy the situation?

I do not know of any excellent, generally applicable method for solving this problem. However, there is a method that is extremely simple and is often effective. A slightly more sophisticated variation on this method will be shown in the next section. For now, let's keep things on a primitive level. A crucial assumption of the method to be discussed is that each class is at least roughly unimodal. In other words, the cases that belong to a given class will tend to cluster in one area and not be split up into two or more subgroups. When that assumption is valid, we can approximate the among-class variation by simply looking at the class centroids. For each class, find the mean vector of all training cases in that class. Treat that mean vector as a single representative of that class. Then base the principal components on the collection of class means. That way, the variation within each class is ignored, and only the variation among classes remains. Figure 8.3 illustrates this with three classes. The two dotted lines represent the two principal components defined using the group centroids.

There are several important weaknesses of this technique that must be noted. Here's a quick quiz: How many principal components can we compute? Even if we measure a huge number of variables, there is a strict and usually small limit on the number of new variables we can compute. The answer is that we are limited to one less than the number of classes. It all comes down to elementary geometry. Two points determine a line. So if we have two classes, we can have only one principal component based on their centroids. Three points determine a plane, and so forth. In an ideal situation, this would be no

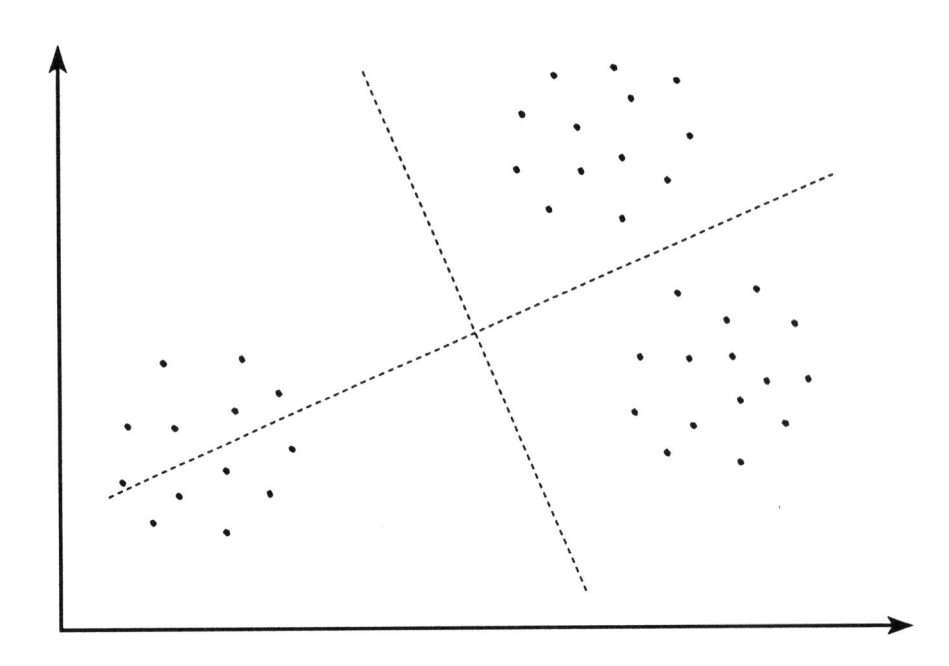

Figure 8.3 Principal components from group centroids.

problem. The information contained in that limited number of principal components would be sufficient to perform nearly optimal classification. (And the method discussed in the next section would be optimal under fairly reasonable conditions.) But if we had an ideal situation, we probably would not be using neural networks. Traditional statistical methods would be adequate. The unfortunate fact of the matter is that the actual distributions of the data within each class will often be such that limiting ourselves to this small number of new variables would be discarding useful information. The moral of the story is that this method should be used with extreme caution. Look at scatterplots. Try alternatives. Perhaps use these principal components, but also include a few other promising variables. Be wary and flexible.

An even more dangerous potential problem lies with the assumption that each class is unimodal. Violations of this assumption can be deadly. The centroid of a class that is split into several parts may be wildly unrepresentative of that class. The centroid can easily lie in an area of the problem space that is far from any members of that class. It does us no good whatsoever to base principal components on such false information. One way of solving this problem is to use clustering to isolate the subgroups, then find principal components of the cluster centroids. This is also a good way of artificially increasing the number of principal components that can be computed. But it is a lot of work. The decision is problem dependent.

Discriminant Functions

In the previous section, we presented a method for defining principal components based on group centroids. That let us focus on the valuable among-class variance, while avoiding inclusion of the within-class variance in the definition of the principal components. If we are not willing to assume anything about the distributions within each class other than that they are unimodal, that method is about the best we can do. But if we are willing to assume that the covariance matrix within each class is about the same for each class, we can do somewhat better. In many applications, this is not as severe an assumption as one might think at first. Certainly there are situations in which the different physical processes that give rise to the cases in different classes will also give rise to different noise distributions. On the other hand, it is often the case that the source of noise is the same for all classes, and the only difference among classes is a different central tendency. When this is so, the more sophisticated algorithm given in this section is appropriate. There are statistical tests to help one determine whether the covariance matrices are the same. It has been my experience that these tests are misleading more often than they are useful, so they will not be discussed here. I prefer simply to look at the numbers and make a common-sense decision. Readers who are determined to find more rigor are timidly referred to any of the excellent multivariate statistics texts available.

It is tempting to think that when one wants to compute a new variable that will optimally discriminate between classes, only the difference between classes is important, and the error distribution within the classes may be ignored. That is wrong; examination of Figure 8.4 will show why.

That figure shows two different situations involving discrimination between a pair of classes. In both cases, the group centroids differ only in regard to the variable plotted on the horizontal axis. If one were to base the discriminant function on only that one variable, it can be seen that a significant amount of overlap between the classes would

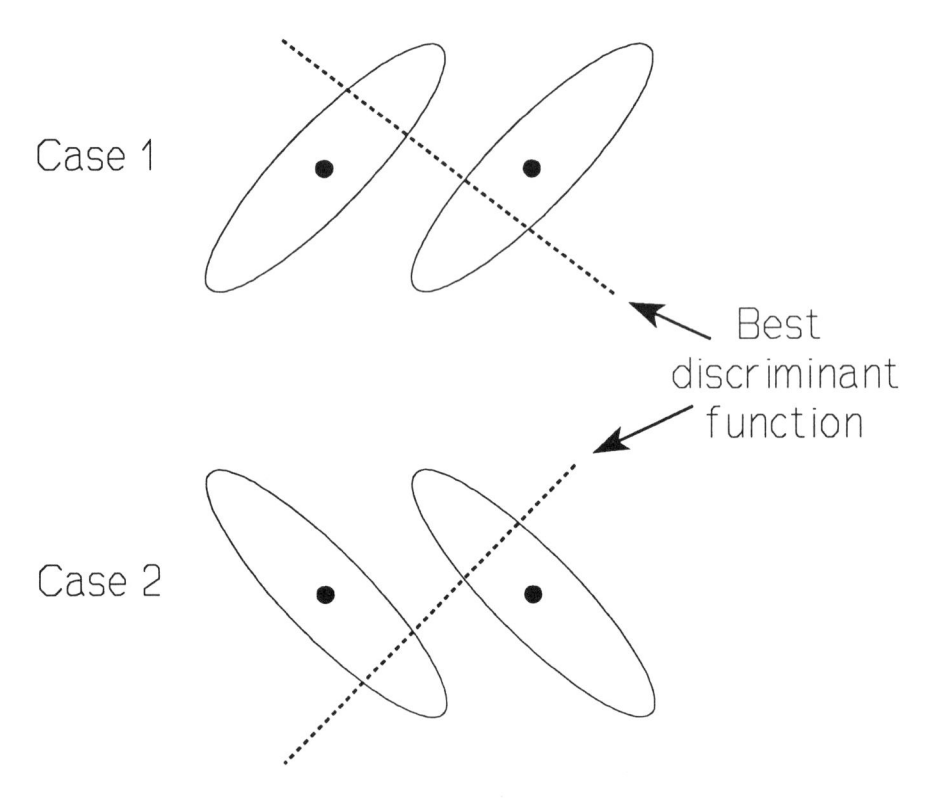

Figure 8.4 Discriminant functions depend on error distributions.

occur. Performance would be poor. We can take advantage of the shape of the within-class error distribution to compute a new variable that is very effective at discriminating between the classes. Observe how important that shape is to the definition of the optimal discriminant function. Figure 8.4 illustrates two cases in which the group centroids are identically placed, yet the within-class variances produce optimal discriminant functions that are perpendicular to each other! The function that is best for one case is worthless for the other case.

In this section we will explore how to compute this optimal discriminant function, which is analogous to the principal components discussed earlier in this chapter. It must be stressed, however, that the method described here has a vital assumption. It assumes that the within-class variance is the same for all classes. If it is not, this method will not work well. Look back at Figure 8.4 and think about what would happen if one of those ellipses were rotated significantly.

It becomes an entirely different problem, and one that is not easily solved.

Also, the same warning applies here as in the previous section in which the principal components were based on the group centroids. The number of discriminant functions that can be computed is, at most, one less than the number of classes. In many practical problems, this will force us to discard potentially useful information. This method should be used only with the greatest caution. An excellent, safe use is to compute these variables as *supplements* to other variables. In most situations, they will contribute a great deal of important information. Remember the goal of the techniques presented in this chapter. We have measured a large and unwieldy number of variables. They contain a lot of redundancy. We want to use this battery of variables to compute a much smaller set of variables that have little or no redundancy but that hopefully capture the essence of the original set. The catch is the word *hopefully*. We have no guarantee that the discarded information is worthless. Keep covered.

Purists should be informed that unlike the case of principal components, the new variables about to be computed are not strictly independent. Within each class there may be some correlation. The vectors that make up the columns of the **V** matrix here are not exactly orthogonal. However, the redundancy is usually small and unavoidable. It may be safely ignored.

Let us start by briefly reviewing the material we have seen so far in this chapter, within the context of a training set consisting of samples from each of several different classes. That training set exhibits case-to-case variation. The total variation across the training set is due to two ingredients: One is the variation within each class. The other is the variation due to the differences among classes. If we base the principal components on the entire training set, as described in the first section of this chapter, the **V** matrix will be the (perhaps scaled) eigenvectors of the total variance. Both the among-classes variance, **A**, and the within-classes variance, **W**, will contribute to the definition in a cumulative manner. It is probably not good to pollute the valuable **A** information this way. If we base the principal components on the among-classes variance alone, as described in the second section of this chapter, the **V** matrix will be the (perhaps scaled) eigenvectors of the **A** matrix. That is generally a better approach. However, if we are willing to assume that every class has about the same within-class variance, **W**, then the method of this section is best. We compute the **V** matrix as the (perhaps scaled) eigenvectors of the matrix product $\mathbf{W}^{-1}\mathbf{A}$. The precise reason for doing this involves mathematics that is beyond the scope of this text. Interested readers are referred to any standard multivariate statistics book.

There are some similarities and some differences relative to what we have done so far. Although the $\mathbf{W}^{-1}\mathbf{A}$ matrix is the product of two symmetric matrices, it itself is not symmetric. That means that its eigenvectors will not be orthogonal. On the other hand, its eigenvalues will still be real, and the value of each, relative to the sum of all eigenvalues, is still a reflection of the contribution of the corresponding eigenvector relative to the total discriminating power of all eigenvectors. Therefore, it is still reasonable to determine the number of discriminant functions to keep by looking at the sum of their eigenvalues relative to the sum of all eigenvalues. On the other hand, remember that the number we can keep is limited to one less than the number of classes. Unless there is a large number of classes, we will usually want to keep all of them.

One notable difference between this method and ordinary principal components is the issue of standardization of the raw variables. On page 301 we pointed out that it is often desirable to equalize the variance of the measured variables so as to equalize their contributions to the definitions of the principal components. In the method of this section, that is not an issue. The use of $\mathbf{W}^{-1}$ takes care of this standardization, and nothing else needs to be done.

As before, we will usually want to generate new variables whose variance is unity. This is a little more difficult here. The eigenvalues are no longer the variances of the discriminant functions, so Equation (8.6) no longer applies. We must explicitly compute the variance of each discriminant function, then divide the columns of $\mathbf{V}$ by the square root of that quantity. Statisticians will know that the variance of a linear function is given by the quadratic form over the covariance matrix of the raw variables. For a particular column of $\mathbf{V}$, the variance of that discriminant function within each class is given by Equation (8.8). Note that some authorities use the total variance instead of the within-class variance. This is a purely personal decision and has no real import.

$$\theta = \mathbf{v}'\mathbf{W}\mathbf{v} \tag{8.8}$$

That's about all of the mathematics of this method that is within the scope of this text. We now present code for a class that allows us to compute discriminant function values for any number of cases, with

Discriminant Functions

the definitions of the functions based on a training set. Use of this class is essentially identical to the PrincoData class presented earlier. The constructor is called with the training set and a few user parameters. It returns the number of functions retained and encapsulates the information that will be needed to compute discriminant functions from cases later. The class header and constructor now appear.

```
class Discrim {

public:
   Discrim ( int ncases , int nvars , int nclasses , double *data ,
      int *classes , int maxfacs , double frac , int *nfacs ) ;
   ~Discrim () ;
   void factors ( int ncases , double *data ) ;

private:
   int nvars, nclasses, nfacs ;
   double *means, *evals, *evect, *work1 ;
} ;

Discrim::Discrim (
   int ncases ,              // Number of cases (rows in data array)
   int nv ,                  // Number of variables (columns in data array)
   int nc ,                  // Number of classes
   double *data ,            // Input (ncases by nv) matrix
   int *classes ,            // Class ID of each case (0 to nc-1)
   int maxfacs ,             // Maximum number of output factors
   double frac ,             // Fraction (0-1) of variance to retain
   int *nfactors             // Output: Number of factors retained
   )
{
   int n, icase, iclass, var, var2, fac, *counts ;
   double *dptr, diff1, diff2, sum, temp, *work2 ;
   double *within, *among, *gpmeans, *gmptr, *scratch ;

/*
   Copy parameters to private area and allocate memory.
   Also realize that the number of factors cannot exceed one less than
   the number of classes.
*/
```

```c
   if (maxfacs > nc-1)
      maxfacs = nc-1 ;

   nvars = nv ;
   nclasses = nc ;

   means = (double *) malloc ( nvars * sizeof(double) ) ;
   evals = (double *) malloc ( nvars * sizeof(double) ) ;
   evect = (double *) malloc ( nvars * nvars * sizeof(double) ) ;
   within = (double *) malloc ( nvars * nvars * sizeof(double) ) ;
   among = (double *) malloc ( nvars * nvars * sizeof(double) ) ;
   work1 = (double *) malloc ( nvars * sizeof(double) ) ;
   work2 = (double *) malloc ( nvars * sizeof(double) ) ;
   gpmeans = (double *) malloc ( nvars * nclasses * sizeof(double) ) ;
   counts = (int *) malloc ( nclasses * sizeof(int) ) ;
   scratch = (double *) malloc ( nvars * nvars * sizeof(double) ) ;

   if ((means == NULL) || (evals == NULL) || (evect == NULL) ||
       (within == NULL) || (among == NULL) || (work1 == NULL) ||
       (work2 == NULL) || (gpmeans == NULL) || (counts == NULL) ||
       (scratch == NULL)) {
      if (means != NULL)
         free ( means ) ;
      if (evals != NULL)
         free ( evals ) ;
      if (evect != NULL)
         free ( evect ) ;
      if (within != NULL)
         free ( within ) ;
      if (among != NULL)
         free ( among ) ;
      if (work1 != NULL)
         free ( work1 ) ;
      if (work2 != NULL)
         free ( work2 ) ;
      if (gpmeans != NULL)
         free ( gpmeans ) ;
      if (counts != NULL)
         free ( counts ) ;
      if (scratch != NULL)
         free ( scratch ) ;
```

Discriminant Functions

```
      *nfactors = nfacs = -1 ;  // Error flag
      return ;
      }


/*
   Compute group means and covariances within classes
*/


   memset ( counts , 0 , nclasses * sizeof(int) ) ;  // Cases in each class

   n = nvars * nclasses ;                            // Zero the group mean vectors
   while (n--)
      gpmeans[n] = 0.0 ;

   n = nvars * nvars ;                               // Zero the covariance matrix
   while (n--)
      within[n] = 0.0 ;

   for (icase=0 ; icase<ncases ; icase++) {          // Cumulate means
      dptr = data + icase * nvars ;                  // Point to this case
      iclass = classes[icase] ;                      // Class of this case
      ++counts[iclass] ;                             // Count cases in each class
      gmptr = gpmeans + iclass * nvars ;             // Its mean vector
      for (var=0 ; var<nvars ; var++)                // All variables in this case
         gmptr[var] += dptr[var] ;                   // Cumulate mean
      }

   for (iclass=0 ; iclass<nclasses ; iclass++) {     // For each class
      if (! counts[iclass])                          // If user is careful, impossible
         counts[iclass] = 1 ;                        // But take out cheap insurance
      gmptr = gpmeans + iclass * nvars ;             // Its mean vector
      for (var=0 ; var<nvars ; var++)                // For all variables
         gmptr[var] /= counts[iclass] ;              // Mean is sum divided by n
      }

   for (icase=0 ; icase<ncases ; icase++) {          // Cumulate covariances
      dptr = data + icase * nvars ;                  // Point to this case
      iclass = classes[icase] ;                      // Class of this case
      gmptr = gpmeans + iclass * nvars ;             // Its mean vector
```

```
    for (var=0 ; var<nvars ; var++) {
      diff1 = dptr[var] - gmptr[var] ;
      for (var2=var ; var2<nvars ; var2++) {
        diff2 = dptr[var2] - gmptr[var2] ;
        within[var*nvars+var2] += diff1 * diff2 ;
        }
      }
    }

    for (var=0 ; var<nvars ; var++) {          // Divide sums by n
      for (var2=var ; var2<nvars ; var2++) {   // To get covariance matrix
        within[var*nvars+var2] /= ncases ;     // This many went into sum
        if (var != var2)                       // Symmetrically duplicate
          within[var2*nvars+var] = within[var*nvars+var2] ;
        }
      }
```

/*
   Compute the grand mean and the among-classes covariance matrix
*/

```
    n = nvars ;                                // Zero the grand mean vector
    while (n--)
      means[n] = 0.0 ;

    n = nvars * nvars ;                        // Zero the covariance matrix
    while (n--)
      among[n] = 0.0 ;

    for (iclass=0 ; iclass<nclasses ; iclass++) {   // For all classes
      gmptr = gpmeans + iclass * nvars ;            // Each group mean vector
      for (var=0 ; var<nvars ; var++)               // gets summed into
        means[var] += gmptr[var] ;                  // the grand mean
      }

    for (var=0 ; var<nvars ; var++)            // To get the grand mean
      means[var] /= nclasses ;                 // Must divide by n

    for (iclass=0 ; iclass<nclasses ; iclass++) {   // For all classes
      gmptr = gpmeans + iclass * nvars ;            // Each group mean vector
```

Discriminant Functions

```
      for (var=0 ; var<nvars ; var++) {
        diff1 = gmptr[var] - means[var] ;
        for (var2=var ; var2<nvars ; var2++) {
          diff2 = gmptr[var2] - means[var2] ;
          among[var*nvars+var2] += diff1 * diff2 ;
          }
        }
      }

    for (var=0 ; var<nvars ; var++) {          // Divide sums by n
      for (var2=var ; var2<nvars ; var2++) {   // To get covariance matrix
        among[var*nvars+var2] /= nclasses ;
        if (var != var2)                       // Symmetrically duplicate
          among[var2*nvars+var] = among[var*nvars+var2] ;
        }
      }
```

```
/*
   Compute eigenstructure and number of factors to retain.
   We must copy the within covariance matrix to a scratch area,
   as eigen_bia is destructive, and we need this later.
*/
```

```
    for (var=0 ; var<nvars ; var++) {
      for (var2=0 ; var2<nvars ; var2++)
        scratch[var*nvars+var2] = within[var*nvars+var2] ;
      }

    eigen_bia ( nvars , among , scratch , evals , evect , work1 , work2 ) ;

    sum = 0.0 ;
    for (var=0 ; var<nvars ; var++)
      sum += evals[var] ;          // Sum the eigenvalues

    frac *= sum ;                  // User wants this much of sum retained

    sum = 0.0 ;
    for (nfacs=0 ; nfacs<maxfacs ; nfacs++) {
      sum += evals[nfacs] ;        // We have retained this much so far
```

```
      if (sum >= frac) {                    // Compare it to user's request
         ++nfacs ;                          // If there, break out with number of factors
         break ;
         }
      }

/*
   Compute the variance of each discriminant function within classes,
   then use this to scale the coefficients to produce unit variance.
   Note that some authorities normalize the total (among+within) variance.
   This is a matter of personal preference and has no practical implications.
*/

   for (fac=0 ; fac<nfacs ; fac++) {        // Find variance of each factor
      sum = 0.0 ;                           // Cumulate it here
      for (var=0 ; var<nvars ; var++) {     // It comes from interaction of
         for (var2=0 ; var2<nvars ; var2++) // all pairs of variables
            sum += evect[var*nvars+fac] * evect[var2*nvars+fac] *
                   within[var*nvars+var2] ; // Standard quadratic form
         }                                  // Equation (8.8)
      work1[fac] = sum ;                    // This factor's variance within classes
      }

   for (fac=0 ; fac<nfacs ; fac++) {        // Normalize each factor
      if (work1[fac] > 0.0)                 // This is the usual case
         temp = 1.0 / sqrt ( work1[fac] ) ; // Need standard deviation
      else                                  // Pathological case
         temp = 0.0 ;                       // Needs cheap insurance
      for (var=0 ; var<nvars ; var++)       // For all vars in this factor
         evect[var*nvars+fac] *= temp ;     // Apply factor's scaling factor
      }

   free ( within ) ;
   free ( among ) ;
   free ( gpmeans ) ;
   free ( counts ) ;
   free ( scratch ) ;
   free ( work2 ) ;   // We keep work1 for use by 'factors'
   *nfactors = nfacs ;
}
```

Discriminant Functions

Operation of the preceding constructor is very similar to PrincoData, so a detailed explanation will be avoided. The parameter list specifies the number of cases, variables, and classes. The input variables are arranged in data just as they were for PrincoData. All variables for case one come first, then case two, and so forth. The class membership of each case is indicated in the vector classes, each of whose ncases elements is an integer from 0 through nc-1. The number of factors (or, perhaps more properly, discriminant functions) is determined and returned via the last three parameters just like in PrincoData. At most, maxfacs factors will be retained. Subject to that restriction, at least frac (0–1) fraction of the total classification power will be retained. I find that in most applications, I will set frac equal to 1.0 and set maxfacs equal to the number of variables. That way, the geometric limit of one less than the number of classes will be retained. The actual number retained is returned in nfactors.

The first action (after memory allocation and other busywork) is to compute the mean vector for each class. Then the within-class covariance matrix, **W**, is cumulated. Note that each case is centered by subtracting the mean for its class. That removes the effect of differences among classes. We also count the number of cases in each class and insure against disaster caused by a careless user forgetting to include any cases in some class.

The next step is to compute the grand mean vector, the mean of the class means. Then we can compute the covariance matrix among the classes, **A**. It should be mentioned that when we divide the sums of cross-products to get **A** and **W**, we do not divide by the degrees of freedom as is usually done for statistical purposes. We take the more straightforward route of just dividing by the number of items that were summed. For our purposes there is no difference at all. This was only pointed out to appease statisticians who may have been outraged by this act. All others should ignore this comment.

The eigenstructure of the $W^{-1}A$ matrix is computed with the eigen_bia subroutine, which will be discussed later. Then the number of discriminant functions is determined in exactly the same way as for PrincoData. The only slightly unusual action here is that the **W** matrix is copied to a scratch area from which it is passed to the eigen_bia routine. The reason is that this routine destroys its input matrices, and we will need **W** later when the discriminant functions are normalized.

That, in fact, is precisely what is done next. The quadratic form expressed in Equation (8.8) is computed for each column of **V**. This provides the variance of each discriminant function as defined by the columns of **V**. Each of those columns is then divided by the square root of that computed variance so that the net result will be discriminant functions with unit variance.

The destructor and the function that computes the discriminant functions (perhaps inappropriately called factor for consistency with the PrincoData class) are both trivial. The destructor simply frees all memory that was not freed at the end of the constructor. The factor function is practically identical to that routine in the PrincoData class. Their listings now appear with no further explanation.

```
Discrim::~Discrim ()
{
  if (nfacs < 0)
    return ;
  free ( means ) ;
  free ( evals ) ;
  free ( evect ) ;
  free ( work1 ) ;
}


/*
   factors - Convert raw data to discriminant factors
*/

void Discrim::factors (
  int ncases ,                  // Number of cases (rows in data array)
  double *data                  // In (ncases by nvars) and out (ncases by nfacs)
  )
{
  int icase, var, fac ;
  double *dptr, sum, diff ;

  for (icase=0 ; icase<ncases ; icase++) {      // For each case
    dptr = data + icase * nvars ;               // Point to this case
    for (fac=0 ; fac<nfacs ; fac++) {           // For each factor to be found
      sum = 0.0 ;                               // Will dot evect with case
      for (var=0 ; var<nvars ; var++) {         // All variables in this case
        diff = dptr[var] - means[var] ;         // Must be centered
        sum += evect[var*nvars+fac] * diff ;    // Cumulate dot product
        }
```

```
        work1[fac] = sum ;                    // This case's factor 'fac'
      }
    dptr = data + icase * nfacs ;             // nfacs <= nvars, so may compress
    for (fac=0 ; fac<nfacs ; fac++)           // Replace original variables
       dptr[fac] = work1[fac] ;               // With principal factors
    }
  }
```

The final bit of business involves computation of the eigenstructure of the $\mathbf{W}^{-1}\mathbf{A}$ matrix. The jacobi routine already presented only works for symmetric matrices. There are some excellent algorithms available for computing the eigenstructure of real general matrices. However, they are all long and complicated. Also, in order to use them, one must invert the $\mathbf{W}$ matrix. That is no great burden, but it is avoidable. Cooley and Lohnes (1971) provide a slick little algorithm for avoiding the inversion and computing this eigenstructure directly by calling jacobi twice and doing a small amount of other matrix manipulation. We will briefly summarize the mathematics, then provide source code. For the sake of those readers who wish to compare this short presentation with the much more thorough derivation found in the text just cited, we will adopt their notation and temporarily use $\mathbf{B}$ instead of $\mathbf{W}$. In other words, for this brief section we will be seeking the eigenstructure of $\mathbf{B}^{-1}\mathbf{A}$.

The whole basis of this technique is the fact that the matrix $\mathbf{B}^{-1/2\prime}\mathbf{A}\mathbf{B}^{-1/2}$ has the same eigenvalues as $\mathbf{B}^{-1}\mathbf{A}$, but that former matrix is symmetric and hence can be handled by jacobi. Moreover, the eigenvectors of $\mathbf{B}^{-1}\mathbf{A}$ are equal to $\mathbf{B}^{-1/2}$ times the eigenvectors of $\mathbf{B}^{-1/2\prime}\mathbf{A}\mathbf{B}^{-1/2}$. The derivation of those facts is really not terribly difficult. Some readers might be interested in trying it as an exercise.

So the first step is to compute $\mathbf{B}^{-1/2}$, a beastie that is essentially the square root of the inverse of $\mathbf{B}$. It's not difficult. Let $\mathbf{U}$ be the eigenvectors of $\mathbf{B}$, and let $\mathbf{K}$ be the corresponding diagonal matrix of eigenvalues. We state without proof the definition shown in Equation (8.9).

$$B^{-1/2} = U K^{-1/2} \qquad (8.9)$$

Once that matrix is computed (by a call to jacobi and some simple matrix operations), we must premultiply and postmultiply $\mathbf{A}$ by that matrix (with a transpose up front). The result is a symmetric matrix whose eigenstructure we compute by means of a second call to jacobi. That gives us the eigenvalues that we need. The final step is to multiply those eigenvectors by $\mathbf{B}^{-1/2}$ in order to arrive at the eigenvectors that we seek. Code for this algorithm is now shown.

```
void eigen_bia (
   int n ,                 // Size of matrix
   double *a ,             // Square symmetric real matrix (destroyed)
   double *b ,             // Ditto (destroyed)
   double *evals ,         // Output of n eigenvalues of (B inverse) * A
   double *evect ,         // Output of n by n eigenvectors (each is a column)
   double *work1 ,         // Work vector n long
   double *work2           // Work vector n long
   )

{
   int i, j, k ;
   double *dptr, temp ;

/*
   Replace B with itself raised to the -1/2 power
*/

   jacobi ( n , b , evals , evect , work1 , work2 ) ;

   for (i=0 ; i<n ; i++) {
      if (evals[i] > 1.e-6)            // This is the usual condition
         temp = 1.0 / sqrt ( evals[i] ) ; // But avoid division by 0
      else                              // This generally signals a very
         temp = 0.0 ;                   // bad singularity condition!
      for (j=0 ; j<n ; j++)
         b[j*n+i] = evect[j*n+i] * temp ;
      }

/*
   Premultiply A by the transpose of this matrix, and postmultiply by it
*/

   for (i=0 ; i<n ; i++) {
      for (j=0 ; j<n ; j++) {          // Compute (B^-1/2)' * A
         temp = 0.0 ;
```

Discriminant Functions

```
        for (k=0 ; k<n ; k++)
          temp += b[k*n+i] * a[k*n+j] ;
        evect[i*n+j] = temp ;      // Temporarily save product here
        }
      }

    for (i=0 ; i<n ; i++) {        // Postmultiply
      for (j=0 ; j<n ; j++) {
        temp = 0.0 ;
        for (k=0 ; k<n ; k++)
          temp += evect[i*n+k] * b[k*n+j] ;
        a[i*n+j] = temp ;
        }
      }
```

/*
  Find the eigenstructure of the matrix just computed, then compute the
  final eigenvectors by premultiplying by the matrix in B.
*/

```
    jacobi ( n , a , evals , evect , work1 , work2 ) ;

    for (i=0 ; i<n ; i++) {        // Premultiply eigenvectors by B
      for (j=0 ; j<n ; j++) {
        temp = 0.0 ;
        for (k=0 ; k<n ; k++)
          temp += b[i*n+k] * evect[k*n+j] ;
        a[i*n+j] = temp ;          // Temporarily save eigenvectors here
        }
      }
```

/*
  Normalize the column eigenvectors to unit length
*/

```
    for (i=0 ; i<n ; i++) {        // Column i is an eigenvector
      temp = 0.0 ;                 // Will cumulate squared length here
      for (j=0 ; j<n ; j++)        // Run down the rows of this column
        temp += a[j*n+i] * a[j*n+i] ;  // Cumulating squared length
```

```
      if (temp > 0.0)                  // Should always be true
        temp = 1.0 / sqrt ( temp ) ;   // But take no chances
      for (j=0 ; j<n ; j++)            // Run down the rows of this column
        evect[j*n+i] = a[j*n+i] * temp ; // Normalizing to unit length
      }
   }
```

There is only one sticky point about the above routine. The first step, computing $\mathbf{B}^{-1/2}$, involves dividing the eigenvectors of $\mathbf{B}$ by the square roots of the eigenvalues. As long as $\mathbf{B}$ is of full rank, this is no problem. But if $\mathbf{B}$ happens to be singular, which may occur when there is a very large amount of redundancy in the original measured variables, then tiny eigenvalues will appear. That signals trouble. The method used for handling this situation here is primitive, but it appears to work reasonably well. Understand that this is not a weakness of this particular algorithm. It is a deep, fundamental problem. Singularity will equally plague users who try to invert $\mathbf{B}$ so that the eigenstructure of $\mathbf{B}^{-1}\mathbf{A}$ can be directly computed with more general algorithms. Readers who find this to be a severe problem would do well to investigate the use of a pseudoinverse routine to invert $\mathbf{B}$, followed by multiplication by $\mathbf{A}$ and use of a general eigenstructure algorithm. Such techniques are beyond the scope of this text.

9

Assessing Generalization Ability

- Bias and random error in parameter estimates

- Special formulas for the population mean

- The jackknife and the bootstrap

- Cross validation

- Bootstrap error estimation

- Efron's E0 and E632 statistics

It's easy to boast about how well one's neural network learned its training set. "I trained my model on a year's worth of XYZ daily closing price, and it got the prediction error down to a quarter of a point!" The truth is, it doesn't much matter how low the training set error is. Granted, if the training set error is high, we know we are in trouble. But a low training set error means nothing. What matters is the error on the *validation set*. You do have one, don't you? A validation set is a collection of known data, just like the training set. The key is that none of the data in this set may be used during training in any way whatsoever. If both the training set and the validation set are representative of the underlying population, the performance of the neural network on the validation set is the real indicator of the ability of the neural network to perform its task.

This might be a good time to make a comment about a disturbingly common error. A researcher dutifully splits the known data into a training set and a validation set. The neural network is trained for a while on the training set, then the network's performance is evaluated by testing it on the validation set. The results are recorded, and then training is continued. This sequence of training with the training set and then testing with the validation set repeats. What nearly always happens is that the validation set error decreases at first, then turns upward as the network starts focusing on idiosyncratic details of the training set to the exclusion of important general features. The final network selected is the one that produced the lowest error on the validation set. *That action invalidates the validation set!* What one supposed to be a validation set has really become part of the training set. There is some disputation about whether or not the procedure just described is a good training method. I feel that it would often be better just to merge the two sets from the start and base the training on the total set. But what is absolutely not disputable is that one *must* collect a completely independent new test set. To do otherwise is to bury one's head in the sand. Real validation sets don't take part in training.

A good subtitle for this chapter is "Waste not, want not." We may have an unlimited supply of known data. I think I heard of that happening once. The sad truth is that known data is almost always a scarce and expensive resource. It seems a pity to have to dedicate a large fraction of the data to testing, ignoring it in the training process. A major focus of this chapter will be on ways to maximize use of the precious known data while still achieving good estimates of performance.

Bias and Variance in Statistical Estimators

We start by laying a theoretical and practical foundation for the subject of generalization ability. Of necessity, much of the mathematics contained in this chapter will be somewhat specialized, though not at an unreasonably high level. Readers who are intimidated are encouraged to move slowly and try to absorb everything along the way if at all possible. In most other chapters of this text, skipping the mathematics is allowed. The code and verbal explanations are sufficient for effective use of the material. But this chapter is different. A little knowledge is a dangerous thing when it comes to statistics. The algorithms of this chapter cannot be used blindly, and they can be easily abused by the unwary. Readers who use these techniques must have at least a basic knowledge of what they are doing and why they are doing it.

The field of statistics deals heavily with the following problem: Some population, such as red-headed American men, is under study. This population is characterized by one or more parameters that are of particular interest. For example, we may be interested in the average weight of members of this population, so the mean population weight would be the parameter of interest. If only we could get every member of this population on a scale, we could determine the parameter that we want. Unfortunately, in real life the population is, for all practical purposes, infinite in size. We must make do with a (usually small) finite sample. We collar a random set of red-headed American men, weigh them, and base our estimate of the population mean on their weights. But just how good is this estimate? In particular, we need to answer at least two questions. Is there a tendency for our estimate to consistently over or underestimate the true population mean weight? If so, we say that our estimate has a *bias*. The other question concerns uncontrollable random variation in our estimate. If we were to repeat the collection procedure, chances are that the resulting estimate of the parameter would be different from the first. How much variability due to sampling can be expected in our estimate? If we rounded up only three redheads and weighed them, we should not be too confident in our ability to draw a conclusion about the entire population. But if we fairly sampled 1,000 of them, we could be quite confident of finding a close estimate of the true mean weight of the entire population. We need to quantify these concepts. As is usual throughout the sciences, a consistent system of notation will make life easier.

Notation

This short section looks painful, and many readers will be tempted to skip it. *Don't do it!* The notation developed here is fairly universal in the literature, and we will be making heavy use of it throughout the remainder of this chapter. Bite the bullet and dig in. Be comforted that absolute statistical rigor is avoided. This will be kept as simple as possible, despite objections by a few purists. Readers will be asked only to absorb what is necessary.

There exists some population of interest, often infinite in size or nearly so. This population gives rise to a random variable that can be sampled. In most of the examples throughout this chapter, the random variable will be a real scalar, although there is no reason it cannot be a vector or any arbitrary construct with suitable modifications as needed. This random variable has a probability distribution that we shall call G. In the example given earlier, G may be the distribution of weights of red-headed American men.

We have the ability to sample values of the random variable. When we speak of a random sample in an abstract sense, we will use the symbol X, perhaps with a subscript. Thus, we may speak of a hypothetical set of n independent cases, $(X_1, X_2, ..., X_n)$, from the distribution G. When we actually collect a sample, so that the values are honest-to-goodness observed quantities, we use the symbol x, again perhaps with a subscript.

We are interested in some parameter depending on G, which we shall call α. In order to emphasize the fact that this parameter concerns G, we will often refer to it as $\alpha(G)$. In the example above, $\alpha(G)$ is the mean of the distribution of weights in this population. In practice, α might represent the median or the variance of G, or some other arbitrary percentile or expectation. Later, we will see an example in which α is a ratio: the ninetieth percentile divided by the median.

We collect n cases from the population: $(x_1, x_2, ..., x_n)$. This sample defines a discrete distribution function having mass $1/n$ at each of the n sample points. Call this new distribution function $\hat{G}$. It is hoped that the $\hat{G}$ defined by observation is a reasonable approximation to the G that is unknown. With that hope as motivation, we compute the *statistic* $\hat{\alpha} = \alpha(\hat{G})$ as an estimator of $\alpha(G)$. (For our purposes, a statistic is just a random variable that is defined as a function of other random variables.) How good is this estimator? We will soon explore this question. But a few more definitions are still needed.

Bias and Variance in Statistical Estimators

Statisticians love to deal with something called the *expectation* of a random variable. When a random variable X is distributed according to G, the expected value of X under that distribution is often written as $E_G[X]$. When G is a discrete distribution, the expectation is defined by the top line of Equation (9.1). When G is a continuous distribution, the bottom line defines the expectation. Note that $g(x)$ is the probability density function associated with G.

$$E_G[X] = \sum_x x g(x)$$
$$E_G[X] = \int_{-\infty}^{\infty} x g(x)\, dx \qquad (9.1)$$

For readers who are uncomfortable with these definitions, know that the expectation of a random variable is the average value of the random variable that we would expect to see over a very large number of repetitions. In other words, it is just the mean. It's that simple.

We are at last in a position to define the bias of our statistical estimator $\tilde{\alpha} = \alpha(\hat{G})$. Recall that we would like to know the value of some parameter $\alpha = \alpha(G)$. Unfortunately, since G is the unknown distribution of the entire population, we cannot directly compute $\alpha(G)$. The best we can do is collect a sample that defines $\hat{G}$, a discrete approximation to G, then compute the parameter based on that sample. Since we have randomly collected the sample, $\tilde{\alpha}$ is subject to statistical variation and other anomalies. It may consistently overestimate the true value of α. In other words, its expected value, $E_G[\alpha(\hat{G})]$, may exceed $\alpha(G)$. Or it may underestimate the true value. The difference between the expected value of our statistic derived from a random sample and the true value of the parameter in the entire parent population is the bias. This is defined in Equation (9.2).

$$\text{Bias} = E_G[\alpha(\hat{G})] - \alpha(G) \qquad (9.2)$$

Bias is not the only problem faced when estimating a population parameter based on a random sample. In fact, a problem that is usually even more serious is statistical variability. If the sample size is gigantic, we can probably be fairly sure that $\hat{G}$ represents G well enough that our computed $\tilde{\alpha}$ is close to the true value of α. But what if the sample is small? We may have accidentally collected an uncharacteristic sample that causes $\tilde{\alpha}$ to be unusually small. Or a bad sample may result in $\tilde{\alpha}$ being much larger than it should be. Note that this problem is different from bias. Bias is a *consistent tendency* toward overestimation or underestimation. Here we are concerned with random variation around the average value of $\tilde{\alpha}$, sometimes high and sometimes low. It is possible for $\tilde{\alpha}$ to have one of these problems and not the other. It may exhibit no consistent error, giving the correct value on average, but nevertheless exhibit wide variation from sample to sample. Or $\tilde{\alpha}$ may be very stable, giving almost exactly the same value from sample to sample, but be consistently too large or too small. Bias and statistical variation are different problems and should not be confused with one another.

How do we characterize the statistical variation of $\tilde{\alpha}$? The most straightforward approach is to use its variance. Recall that the variance of a random variable is the expected value of its squared deviation from its mean. This is expressed in Equation (9.3).

$$Var = E_G\left[(\hat{\alpha} - E_G[\hat{\alpha}])^2\right] \qquad (9.3)$$

One small but important final point should be made. The estimator $\tilde{\alpha} = \alpha(\hat{G})$ is computed from $\hat{G}$, which, in turn, is defined by the sample $(x_1, x_2, ..., x_n)$. Thus, we could just as well write $\tilde{\alpha} = \tilde{\alpha}(x_1, x_2, ..., x_n)$. Note that this function is invariant to permutation in its arguments. That fact will be crucial later. We will use $\tilde{\alpha} = \alpha(\hat{G})$ and $\tilde{\alpha} = \tilde{\alpha}(x_1, x_2, ..., x_n)$ interchangeably, according to whichever is more convenient at the time.

What Good Are They?

Suppose that we are able to estimate the bias and the variance of our estimator, $\tilde{\alpha}$. What good are they for us? Quite a lot, actually. There is an obvious heuristic benefit. Any conscientious researcher who uses some statistic to draw important conclusions will welcome any and all information regarding the quality of that statistic. Just looking at the numbers is useful. Sometimes they will be surprising.

We may wish to make explicit use of the estimated bias to correct the statistical estimate of the parameter. In other words, suppose we collect a sample and use that sample to compute both the parameter estimate, $\tilde{\alpha}$, and its estimated bias, β. We know that on the

Bias and Variance in Statistical Estimators

average, $\tilde{\alpha}$ will overestimate α by an amount equal to the true bias, whatever that may be. So if we could subtract the true bias from $\tilde{\alpha}$, we would have an unbiased statistic. Alas, we do not know the true bias. All we have is an estimate, β, derived from the sample. We hope that the new statistic $\alpha' = \tilde{\alpha} - \beta$ will be an improvement over plain old $\tilde{\alpha}$. In fact, it usually will be better. The bias of the corrected estimate will almost always be significantly less than the bias of the raw estimate. There is one potential problem, though. The bias estimate is itself a statistic derived from the sample. It has random variation that cannot be quantified in any way I know of. In some (but probably few) situations, the error variance added by inclusion of β may actually exceed the reduction in error variance due to removal of the squared bias. In other words, the variance of β may cause the variance of $\alpha' = \tilde{\alpha} - \beta$ to exceed the variance of just plain $\tilde{\alpha}$ to such a degree that the reduction of bias is not worthwhile. The price is too high. This does not appear to be a serious general problem, but the reader should be aware of the possibility. In particular, if the estimated bias is much less than the estimated standard deviation (square root of the variance), it is probably not worth doing a bias correction unless it is definitely known that a net improvement will result. The potential loss will not be worth the comparatively small gain.

An estimate of the variance of $\tilde{\alpha}$ is generally more useful than an estimate of the bias. It gives us a concrete idea of the reliability of $\tilde{\alpha}$ as an estimator of α. The standard deviation of $\tilde{\alpha}$ immediately tells us the rough range of variability due to nothing more than unavoidable randomness in sample selection from the population. Let us use the symbol $\sigma_{\tilde{\alpha}}$ to designate the estimated standard deviation of $\tilde{\alpha}$. Even though we may know nothing about the distribution of $\tilde{\alpha}$, we can immediately say that if we collect more samples of the same size, the values of $\tilde{\alpha}$ computed from those samples could easily vary by several times $\sigma_{\tilde{\alpha}}$, due to the randomness of the sampling procedure. Knowledge of that fact, coupled with knowledge of $\sigma_{\tilde{\alpha}}$, has been known to cause grown men and women to weep. Take it seriously.

Bias and Variance of the Sample Mean

The most common parameter that we wish to estimate is the mean of a distribution. For example, we may be using a neural network to predict the future value of a time series. We test the trained network with an independent validation set and record the error of each prediction. There are lots of things we may want to know about the error distribution. Its RMS value, its median, and its ninetieth percentile are all possibly of interest. But in practice, one of the most useful measures is the mean absolute value of the error. This quantity tells us precisely what error we can expect on average. So we take our randomly sampled collection of validation cases and treat the absolute errors as random variables sampled from an unknown distribution G. (For this example we assume that exactly one variable is predicted, so the errors are each a scalar quantity.) The statistic that we use to estimate the mean of G is the mean of $\hat{G}$, which is expressed in Equation (9.4) with x_i being the absolute error of the ith case.

$$\hat{\alpha} = \frac{1}{n} \sum_{i=1}^{n} x_i \qquad (9.4)$$

What do we know about the bias and variance of this estimator? The bias is easy. There is none. By definition, the expected value of each x_i is equal to α, the mean of G. So the expected value of their mean is also α (a simple result of addition being a linear operation). We will not attempt a proof here, but it can be shown that an excellent estimator of the standard deviation of $\hat{\alpha}$ is expressed in Equation (9.5).

$$\sigma_{\hat{\alpha}} = \sqrt{\frac{1}{n(n-1)} \sum_{i=1}^{n} (x_i - \hat{\alpha})^2} \qquad (9.5)$$

This equation is a powerful and immensely useful result. It is true regardless of the parent distribution G (assuming, of course, that the variance exists!). What this means is that whenever we are using the sample mean to estimate the mean of a distribution, Equation (9.5) provides (an approximation to) the standard deviation of that estimate. Ignore it at your peril.

Sometimes we may be willing to assume that $\hat{\alpha}$ follows an approximately normal distribution. This is especially true if n is large and the x_i values are independent and identically distributed, for then the central limit theorem charges to the rescue. When we are willing to assume normality of $\hat{\alpha}$, we may make probability statements about the true value of α and compute confidence intervals. For example, we may state that the interval defined by $\tilde{\alpha}$ plus and minus 1.96 $\sigma_{\tilde{\alpha}}$ has a 95 percent chance of enclosing the true value of α. Fanatics may even wish to employ Student's t. This discussion is going in a dangerous direction, and nothing more will be said lest the reader be encouraged to build a house on a foundation of quicksand. Zealous readers should consult any standard statistics text and pray liberally.

The Jackknife and the Bootstrap

We just saw that when we wish to estimate the mean of a distribution, the sample mean provides an unbiased estimate whose standard deviation also is easily estimated. That's wonderful, but what about other parameters? For example, we may be predicting a time series and be especially interested in the occurrence of unusually large errors. Are there methods like Equations (9.4) and (9.5) that let us directly compute unbiased estimates of arbitrary parameters, along with their standard deviations? Sadly, no; in a few special cases, such equations can be found, but this is rare. In general, we must resort to heuristic methods that usually *seem* to do a pretty good job. If that statement sounds discouraging, good. The two algorithms described in this section are not magic. They come with no performance guarantees. Verification of their correct operation is tricky at best, and often impossible. But the fact of the matter is that they are based on fairly sound mathematical foundations, and they have a long history of working much more often than they fail. For lack of anything better, the jackknife and the bootstrap will now be presented.

Readers should be reassured that the mathematics of these methods is not particularly difficult, and the algorithms themselves are surprisingly simple. Code to implement them is short and straightforward. However, to facilitate understanding of the procedures, it is strongly recommended that the reader be familiar with the notation developed starting on page 338. It will be used heavily.

The Jackknife

A fundamental assumption of the jackknife method of bias estimation is that in a great many situations, the bias of $\tilde{\alpha}$ is inversely related to the sample size in an approximately linear manner. Double the sample

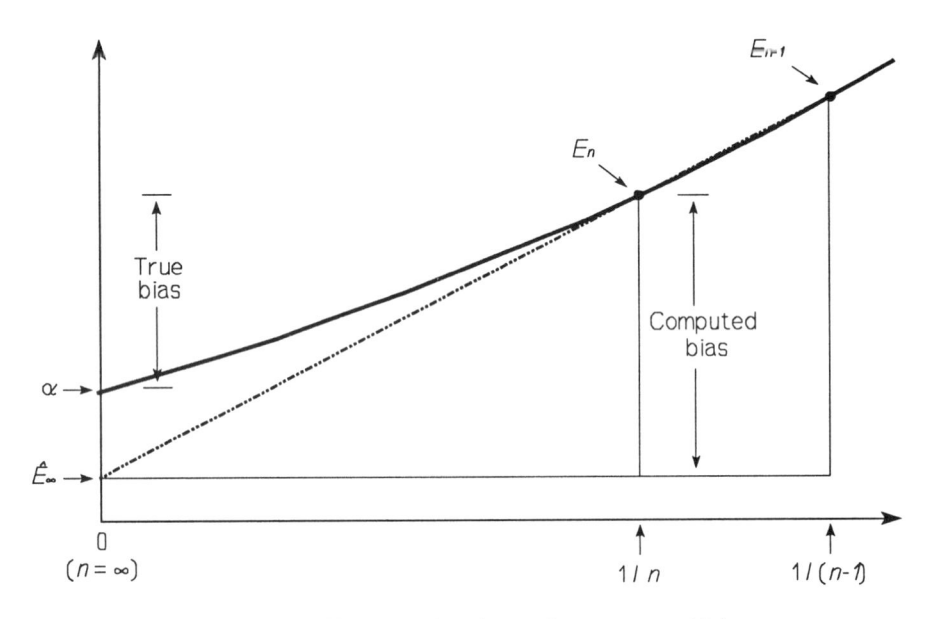

Figure 9.1 Expected value of $\tilde{\alpha}$ versus 1/size.

size and the bias will be cut in half. Another way of saying this is that the bias is approximately linearly related to $1/n$. This situation is graphed in Figure 9.1.

In that figure, the expected value of $\tilde{\alpha}$ is plotted as a function of the reciprocal of the sample size. Notice that the plot has only slight curvature, the usual (but not universal) situation. This curve intersects the vertical axis ($n=\infty$) at α, the true population value of the parameter. The point labeled E_n is the expected value of $\tilde{\alpha}$ when the sample size is some fixed value n. Similarly, E_{n-1} is the expected value when the sample size is $n-1$. If one is willing to assume that the function is perfectly linear, one can extrapolate through those two points to find $\hat{E}_\infty$, the expected value of $\tilde{\alpha}$ when the sample size is infinite. That should, of course, be equal to α, the true value of the parameter. But the slight nonlinearity in the curve has resulted in the extrapolated value of $\hat{E}_\infty$ being somewhat in error. The true bias of an estimate based on a sample size of n is $E_n - \alpha$, but extrapolation gives us a bias of $E_n - \hat{E}_\infty$. We hope that the difference between $\hat{E}_\infty$ and α is less than the difference between E_n and α, or there is no point in extrapolating! Usually this will be the case, although significant nonlinearity is capable of dealing us a cruel blow. I know of no fully general way of detecting such trouble. Life is full of risks, but 90 percent of the battle

The Jackknife and the Bootstrap

is knowing that they exist. In practice, we are nearly always safe in assuming that the nonlinearity is of no serious consequence.

We have just pointed out one potential risk of the jackknife method of estimating bias. Violation of the assumption of linearity can lead to errors. That is not usually a serious problem. The real trouble is that we don't even know the values of E_n and E_{n-1} from which we extrapolate. We must estimate them from the sample. The former is easy. The basic parameter estimate, $\hat{\alpha}$, is obviously an unbiased estimator of E_n. But what about the expected value of the parameter estimate when the sample size is $n-1$? How do we estimate that from the sample? An obvious method is to discard one of the n cases and compute the parameter estimate from the remaining $n-1$ cases. But which one should we discard? The answer is simple: Discard them all, but do it one at a time, and average the results. In other words, temporarily remove the first case and compute the parameter based on the others. Record that parameter estimate. Then replace the first case and remove the second. Compute and record the parameter estimate again. Repeat this procedure n times and find the average. That is what will be used for the estimate of E_{n-1}.

Let us introduce a little more special notation. Let $\hat{\alpha}_{(i)}$ be the parameter estimate when all cases except case i are used. Let $\hat{\alpha}_{(\cdot)}$ be the mean of all n such estimates. These quantities are defined in Equation (9.6).

$$\hat{\alpha}_{(i)} = \hat{\alpha}(x_1, \ldots, x_{i-1}, x_{i+1}, \ldots, x_n)$$
$$\hat{\alpha}_{(\cdot)} = \frac{1}{n} \sum_{i=1}^{n} \hat{\alpha}_{(i)} \tag{9.6}$$

We can now formally derive the jackknife estimate of the bias in the parameter estimator $\hat{\alpha}$. Look at Figure 9.1 and recall from high school geometry the laws for similar triangles. In particular, the ratio of the opposite side to the adjacent side is the same for each triangle. Expressing this in terms of the estimates already described, we have Equation (9.7). Solving for the extrapolated function estimate, which is a hopefully unbiased estimate of α, gives us the top line of Equation (9.8). Subtracting that quantity from $\hat{\alpha}$ gives the estimate of the bias shown in the bottom line of that equation.

$$\frac{\hat{\alpha} - \hat{E}_\infty}{1/n} = \frac{\hat{\alpha}_{(\cdot)} - \hat{E}_\infty}{1/(n-1)} \tag{9.7}$$

$$\hat{E}_\infty = n\,\hat{\alpha} - (n-1)\,\hat{\alpha}_{(\cdot)}$$
$$\beta = (n-1)\,(\hat{\alpha}_{(\cdot)} - \hat{\alpha}) \tag{9.8}$$

It's time for an example. Suppose we are using a neural network to stabilize an industrial process by determining the value of a control variable. The network is provided with assorted sensor responses, and the output of the network controls the feed rate of a critical reactant. At great expense the company collected a dataset consisting of many representative sensor values along with the ideal response (as determined experimentally or by a human expert). The network is trained with this dataset. Then an independent dataset is collected to validate the network. Suppose the nature of the process is such that if the average error is excessive, that condition will be easily detected by a human operator and corrective action can be taken. Furthermore, negative errors have no unusually serious consequences. But large positive errors, those that greatly exceed the average error, are very expensive. The number and magnitude of positive errors that significantly exceed the average must be kept under control. This may inspire us to design a special error measure. For example, we might look at the ninetieth percentile of the sample divided by the median absolute error.

A handful of hard numbers will help the reader to follow the technique. To keep things manageable, let us deal with just ten validation cases. The errors of these cases are (−0.5, 0.1, 2.2, −1.2, 0.5, 1.3, 0.5, −1.7, 0.7, 0.2). The median of this set is the mean of the middle two cases, since there is an even number of cases. This is 0.6. The ninetieth percentile is 1.3, so we get $\hat{\alpha} = 2.167$. Whether this is good or bad depends on the application's specifications. But let's not stop with just the parameter estimate. What about its bias? Eliminate the first case, −0.5. The ninetieth percentile remains the same, but the median rises to 0.7. This gives $\hat{\alpha}_{(1)} = 1.86$. We get the same value if the second case, 0.1, is removed. When the third case, 2.2, is removed, things change a lot. The median drops to 0.5 and the ninetieth percentile drops to 0.7, giving $\tilde{\alpha}_{(3)} = 1.4$. If we continue, removing each of the observations one at a time, we get a mean value of $\tilde{\alpha}_{(\cdot)} = 1.989$. Astute observers will notice that this is considerably less than our previously obtained $\hat{\alpha} = 2.167$. It looks like decreasing the sample size exerts downward pressure on the parameter estimate. Therefore, we would expect that the (hopefully) unbiased value would be larger than what we computed from the full sample. And this is indeed the case. Applying Equation (9.8) gives an estimated bias of –1.60, which, when subtracted from the raw parameter estimate, gives an unbiased estimate of 3.77.

A warning is in order. A small group of well-intentioned, but overly zealous, readers will come to the conclusion that if linear extrapolation is good, quadratic (or, heaven forbid, higher-order) extrapolation will be better. *No!* Remember that nonlinearity is almost always the lesser source of error. The major error comes from using a randomly collected sample to estimate E_n and E_{n-1} from which we extrapolate. Techniques of order higher than linear will magnify this error even more. Better average bias correction may result, but the random error of the bias estimate will be so large that any possible gains will be wiped out.

What about estimating the variance (or standard deviation) of $\hat{\alpha}$? Does the jackknife procedure just discussed help us in that arena? Not only does it do so, but much empirical evidence indicates that the estimated variance is actually more reliable than the estimated bias. This is fortuitous, since the variance usually has more practical utility than the bias.

No detailed derivation of the jackknife variance estimator will be presented. Looked at from one direction, it is almost embarrassingly heuristic. Looked at from the other principal direction, it is far beyond the scope of this text. Therefore, suffice it to say that the jackknife estimator of the variance of $\hat{\alpha}$ is a fixed multiple of the variance of the $\tilde{\alpha}_{(i)}$ values computed with Equation (9.6). That should make good intuitive sense. See what effect omitting individual cases has on the computed $\hat{\alpha}$ and base the variance estimate on that. The constant for multiplying this quantity is chosen so that when α is defined as the distribution's mean, the result is identical to the actual value as shown in Equation (9.5) on page 342. The formula for estimating the standard deviation of $\hat{\alpha}$ is shown in Equation (9.9). The quantities $\tilde{\alpha}_{(i)}$ and $\tilde{\alpha}_{(\cdot)}$ were defined in Equation (9.6).

This discussion of the jackknife estimate of the variance of $\hat{\alpha}$ will be concluded on an optimistic note. The estimated variance (or its more

$$\sigma_{\hat{\alpha}} = \sqrt{\frac{n-1}{n} \sum_{i=1}^{n} (\hat{\alpha}_{(i)} - \hat{\alpha}_{(\cdot)})^2} \qquad (9.9)$$

directly useful square root, $\sigma_{\hat{\alpha}}$) has a strong tendency to be conservative in that its expected value exceeds its true value. Initial instinct may lead us to wonder why this is so good. Wouldn't it be better if it were unbiased? Actually, no. Think about how we use $\sigma_{\hat{\alpha}}$. It indicates how reliable $\hat{\alpha}$ is as an estimator of α. We would be dismayed if we computed a nicely small value of $\sigma_{\hat{\alpha}}$, became very confident in our estimate of the parameter, then later discovered that the true value of $\sigma_{\hat{\alpha}}$ is much higher. (One way in which this might be discovered is by collecting more samples and seeing unexpectedly large variation in the values of $\hat{\alpha}$ computed from each sample.) It is far better to be pleasantly surprised the other way.

Keep in mind that we are not absolutely guaranteed that our computed $\sigma_{\hat{\alpha}}$ exceeds the correct value. There is one major consideration, and one minor picky detail to worry about. The major consideration is that the conservatism is in expectation, not in computed value. We dare not bask in the comfort that things are *definitely* better than they appear. We can only nurture a little warm feeling that, *on the average*, things will be better than they seem. It's better than nothing.

The other consideration is minor indeed, but it is mentioned for the sake of completeness. To be technical, the actual theorem on conservatism of the variance estimate does not directly concern the variance of the parameter estimate derived from the complete sample. Rather, it concerns the variance of the parameter estimate that would be obtained from a sample of size $n-1$. In particular, we compute the variance of $\hat{\alpha}$ as the square of $\sigma_{\hat{\alpha}}$ obtained from Equation (9.9). It can be proved that the expectation of that quantity equals or exceeds $(n-1)/n$ times the true variance of the $\hat{\alpha}$ that would be obtained from a sample of size $n-1$. It is possible to come up with pathological situations in which the expected value of the variance of $\hat{\alpha}$, computed as the square of Equation (9.9), is less than the true variance of that estimator. The result stated in the theorem does not strictly imply the result that we want. However, it comes so close that in practice we may behave as if it did.

Code for the Jackknife

We now present code for the jackknife algorithm. The user must supply a routine that computes the statistic $\tilde{\alpha}$ from a sample. This routine must not tamper with the data. The jackknife routine computes and returns the raw (full sample) function value, along with the estimated bias and variance of that estimator.

```
void jack (
   int n ,                      // Number of data points
   double *data ,               // The data is here
   double *raw ,                // Raw (uncorrected) statistic for all n data
   double *bias ,               // Output of bias (subtract from raw to unbias)
   double *var                  // Output of variance of statistic
   )
{
   int exclude, first ;
   double stat, temp, sum, sumsq ;

   sum = sumsq = 0.0 ;
   exclude = n ;
   first = 1 ;

   while (exclude--) {

      if (first)
         first = 0 ;
      else {                    // If not first trial, swap excluded to end
         temp = data[exclude] ;
         data[exclude] = data[n-1] ;
         data[n-1] = temp ;
         }

      stat = userstat ( n-1 , data ) ;   // $\tilde{\alpha}_{(exclude)}$

      sum += stat ;
      sumsq += stat * stat ;
      }
```

```
  sum /= n ;                        // ã_(•)
  sumsq /= n ;
  sumsq -= sum * sum ;              // Can lose precision in this subtraction!

  *raw = userstat ( n , data ) ;    // ã from full sample
  *bias = (n - 1.0) * (sum - *raw) ; // Equation (9.6)
  *var = (n - 1.0) * sumsq ;        // Equation (9.9) (divided by n above)
}
```

This subroutine is a straightforward implementation of the algorithm previously described. In order that the user's subroutine that computes $\tilde{\alpha}$ does not need to worry about excluding cases, we successively swap the excluded case to the end of the data array. This is quite a bit of overhead, but it is probably small compared to the work performed by userstat. Note that we actually exclude cases starting with the last and working toward the beginning. Thus, for the first pass we do not need to swap anything.

This implementation has one potentially serious problem of which the reader should be aware. Recall that Equation (9.9) subtracts from each $\tilde{\alpha}_{(i)}$ their grand mean, $\tilde{\alpha}_{(\cdot)}$. This is the best (most numerically stable) way of computing a variance. But it has the weakness that each $\tilde{\alpha}_{(i)}$ must be stored until after all have been processed. To avoid a possibly large memory allocation within this subroutine, I have chosen to use the mathematically equivalent but dangerous approach of cumulating the sum of squares directly, then subtracting the squared mean later. If the mean, $\tilde{\alpha}_{(\cdot)}$, happens to be extremely large relative to the standard deviation, $\sigma_{\tilde{\alpha}}$, we will be subtracting two numbers that are large relative to their difference. This is a textbook source of error, as precision is lost in the finite-length floating-point computation. As long as the user avoids designing $\tilde{\alpha}$ in such a way that its value tends to be very large compared to its variation, this implementation should not be a problem. The variance must be quite a few orders of magnitude smaller than the squared mean before problems ensue. But readers who would rather pay the price of a temporary memory allocation in return for guaranteed precision might wish to use Equation (9.9) directly instead.

The Bootstrap

We now present an algorithm that performs nearly the same task as the jackknife algorithm but that does it in a completely different way. The bootstrap is generally more reliable than the jackknife in that its estimates of the bias and variance of $\tilde{\alpha}$ tend to be closer to the true values. However, there is a price to pay. The bootstrap is far more computationally intensive. It usually requires many more evaluations of the user's statistic than does the jackknife. If computation time is of no concern, the bootstrap should always be favored over the jackknife. But I have seen situations in which computation of $\tilde{\alpha}$ for a single sample requires several hours on a fast machine. Sometimes the bootstrap is just not feasible.

Let us briefly review our needs and methods, as some of these concepts will play a large role in the derivation of the bootstrap algorithm. We have a random variable X that follows an unknown distribution G. We want to determine the value of some parameter, $\alpha(G)$. Our method is to collect a random sample of n cases and use those cases to define a discrete approximation, $\hat{G}$, to the true distribution of X. We then compute $\tilde{\alpha} = \alpha(\hat{G})$ as our estimator of α. After having done that, we wish to estimate, based on that same random sample, the bias and variance of $\tilde{\alpha}$.

The fundamental premise of the bootstrap algorithm is elegantly simple. As long as we are relying on the observed $\hat{G}$ to provide us with $\tilde{\alpha}$, we might as well extend that confidence and rely on $\hat{G}$ to tell us more about the sampling distribution of $\tilde{\alpha}$. In other words, treat $\hat{G}$ as if it were a parent distribution itself and collect many samples based on that distribution. For each of those samples, called *bootstrap* samples, compute the value of the parameter, which we shall call $\tilde{\alpha}^\star$. We may then freely analyze the distribution of these computed values, looking at their mean, or at their variance, or in fact at anything else that characterizes them. We *cannot* assume that the distribution of $\tilde{\alpha}^\star$ under $\hat{G}$ is identical to the distribution of $\tilde{\alpha}$ under G, because the procedure is conditioned by the assumption of having obtained a particular sample from G. So we're not entirely immersed in a bowl of cherries. However, we can learn a lot about the distribution of $\tilde{\alpha}$ by studying the distribution of $\tilde{\alpha}^\star$.

We interrupt this presentation for a tiny example that hopefully will make things clear. A rigorous statement of the technique will follow. Suppose we sample five cases, a ridiculously small but tractable sample size. Let these observed values be (3, 5, 2, 1, 7). We compute

$\tilde{\alpha}$ = 2.6 (let us say) from this sample. (The definition of $\tilde{\alpha}$ is irrelevant to this illustration.) What can we infer about the sampling distribution of $\tilde{\alpha}$? Well, let's assume that G is similar to the discrete distribution $\hat{G}$ implied by this sample. We can collect a random sample from $\hat{G}$ by randomly drawing five cases from this sample, obviously with replacement. Crank up the random number generator and select five cases. Perhaps our new sample will be (7, 3, 2, 3, 1). Compute our statistic from this sample. Again, use the superscript $\star$ to indicate that this value of the parameter is computed from a bootstrap sample, as opposed to the original sample. Also use the numeral 1 as a superscript to indicate that this is the first bootstrap sample that has been selected. Let us say that we compute $\tilde{\alpha}^{\star 1}$ = 2.7 from this sample. Then we randomly draw another bootstrap sample. This one might end up as (5, 1, 1, 3, 1). For it we compute $\tilde{\alpha}^{\star 2}$ = 2.9. If we repeat this process many times, we would like to think that whatever *unknown* effect the sampling procedure has on the distribution of $\tilde{\alpha}$ under G, that effect will be reflected in the *observed* distribution of $\tilde{\alpha}^{\star}$ under $\hat{G}$. In fact, that is exactly what the bootstrap method does. It seems almost too simple to work, but the truth of the matter is that it works surprisingly well in a great variety of situations.

A subtle but vitally important point must be emphasized. We are absolutely, positively, *not* asserting that the distribution of $\tilde{\alpha}^{\star}$ under $\hat{G}$ approximates the distribution of $\tilde{\alpha}$ under G. They are probably similar, and they may share some properties. But the fact that the resampling is conditional on an observed sample from G precludes such boldness. Rather, we are saying that the *effect of sampling* on the parameter that we compute can be ascertained by resampling. We want to know what effect sampling has on the distribution of $\tilde{\alpha}$ under G. If validation data were cheap, we could learn a lot by collecting many validation sets and studying the distribution of the parameters computed from each sample. But as we all know, our one validation set may be worth six months of our salary. We cannot get another, so we do the next best thing. We assume that the known $\hat{G}$ is similar enough to G that sampling will have about the same effect under both distributions. We collect many samples under $\hat{G}$ and see what effect sampling has on $\tilde{\alpha}^{\star}$. Whatever effect we observe may be legitimately projected onto the distribution of $\tilde{\alpha}$ under G. Later in this section, when we estimate the bias of $\tilde{\alpha}$, this distinction will be crucial.

We now formalize the bootstrap algorithm. A random sample of n cases is collected. This sample, $(x_1, x_2, ..., x_n)$, defines a discrete distribution function $\hat{G}$ having mass $1/n$ at each of the n sample points.

Compute $\tilde{\alpha} = \alpha(\hat{G})$ as our tentative estimator of $\alpha(G)$. Let $(x_1^\star, x_2^\star, ..., x_n^\star)$ be a bootstrap sample randomly drawn from $(x_1, x_2, ..., x_n)$ with replacement. The distribution of each $x^\star$ in the bootstrap sample is $\hat{G}$. The bootstrap sample itself defines a discrete distribution, $\hat{G}^\star$, having mass k_p/n on x_p, where k_p is the number of times x_p appears in the bootstrap sample. Let $\tilde{\alpha}^\star = \alpha(\hat{G}^\star)$ be the parameter estimate computed from the bootstrap sample. Repeat this random sampling under $\hat{G}$ a total of m times, letting the computed parameter for bootstrap sample i be called $\tilde{\alpha}^{\star i}$. We are free to use this collection of m parameter estimates to make *any* inferences we want about the distribution of $\tilde{\alpha}^\star$ under $\hat{G}$. The beautiful part is that since we *know* $\hat{G}$, we can compute the exact value of the parameter under that distribution as a benchmark for the values computed via resampling. Just think about it. This is real power. We can examine skewness. We can consider fractiles. And the greatest miracle of all is that this truly primitive algorithm actually works! In the majority of practical applications, the bootstrap algorithm is asymptotically correct, and even for small sample sizes it nearly always gives good results.

The most basic application of the bootstrap method is to estimate the variance (or standard deviation) of $\tilde{\alpha}$. This is easy. If resampling under $\hat{G}$ gives a collection of $\tilde{\alpha}^\star$ values whose standard deviation is $\sigma_{\tilde{\alpha}}$, then it is reasonable to assume that random sampling under G will give rise to values of $\tilde{\alpha}$ having practically the same standard deviation. So we use Equation (9.10) to find the mean of the m bootstrap samples, and then we use Equation (9.11) to estimate the standard deviation of $\tilde{\alpha}$ under G.

$$\hat{\alpha}^{\star \cdot} = \frac{1}{m} \sum_{i=1}^{m} \hat{\alpha}^{\star i} \tag{9.10}$$

$$\sigma_{\tilde{\alpha}} = \sqrt{\frac{1}{(m-1)} \sum_{i=1}^{m} (\hat{\alpha}^{\star i} - \hat{\alpha}^{\star \cdot})^2} \tag{9.11}$$

Estimating the bias is even easier, but understanding what's going on is tricky. Look back at the little example on page 351. We computed $\tilde{\alpha} = 2.6$ based on the complete sample. Then we did two bootstrap resamplings and got 2.7 and 2.9 for those. Suppose that we did many more bootstrap resamplings, and the tendency for $\tilde{\alpha}^*$ to exceed $\tilde{\alpha}$ continued. In fact, suppose we average them all and find that $\hat{\alpha}^{*\cdot} = 2.8$. The true value of the parameter under $\hat{G}$ is $\tilde{\alpha}$. Apparently, the random sampling process has induced an upward bias. The actual parameter under $\hat{G}$, which is the source distribution for the resampling, is 2.6, but the average value of the computed parameters for the bootstrap samples is 2.8. There is a bias of 0.2. It is not too much of a leap of faith to suggest that random sampling under G will induce the same upward bias in $\tilde{\alpha}$. So we would be inclined to use 2.6 − 0.2 = 2.4 as a (hopefully) unbiased estimate of α.

We can make this explicit. Compute $\tilde{\alpha} = \alpha(\hat{G})$ for the original sample. Then perform m bootstrap resamplings. The mean of the parameters computed for each bootstrap sample is shown in Equation (9.10). The estimated bias is shown in Equation (9.12). This bias is removed from the original parameter estimate, $\tilde{\alpha}$, by subtracting β. In other words, the statistic $\tilde{\alpha} - \beta$ is a (hopefully) unbiased estimator of α.

$$\beta = \hat{\alpha}^{*\cdot} - \hat{\alpha} \qquad (9.12)$$

One obvious question has been blatantly left unanswered: How many bootstrap resamples are needed? Certainly the more we use, the better our estimates will be. But the point of diminishing returns is reached rapidly. The reason is simply that to use a huge number of resamplings is to chase a quantity that is not worth catching. There are two sources of error in bootstrap estimates: One is randomness in the resampling process. That can be reduced to any arbitrary degree by increasing m. But the other source of error involves the resampling distribution itself. Remember that the resampling is based on $\hat{G}$, which is a random entity defined by the user's validation set. If one is following a stumbling drunk along a narrow precipice, there is no reason to match him step for step. Roughly following behind will do just as well. In the same way, there is no point in evaluating to high accuracy an approximation to a random number! Several hundred resamples are generally recognized as being more than sufficient for virtually all applications. The only exception might be if the validation set contains more than several hundred cases. Then setting m commensurate with the sample size might be justified on the grounds that we might as well strive for the relatively high accuracy that may be attainable. Even then, the need for m exceeding 500 or so is debatable.

Code for the Bootstrap

The bootstrap subroutine is (not surprisingly) similar to the jackknife subroutine, so this discussion will be limited to those aspects that are different. The number of bootstrap resamplings, m, is set to 200 in this implementation. Some readers may wish to pass it as a parameter, but I feel that 200 is such a universally applicable quantity that it is fixed in the code. Disagreement is allowed.

The sum and sum of squares of the resampled statistics, $\tilde{\alpha}^{\star}$, are cumulated just as they were for the jackknife. The same warning about loss of precision due to subtraction of similar quantities applies here.

In the jackknife, the resampled datasets were deterministically found by leaving out one case at a time. For the bootstrap, we randomly select the cases for the sample. Note that to avoid the possibility of array overrun, the random number generator unifrand() must return values that are strictly less than 1.0. A little insurance is included here. Finally, the bias is computed with Equation (9.12) and the variance is computed using Equation (9.11).

```
void boot (
   int n ,                   // Number of data points
   double *data ,            // The data is here
   double *raw ,             // Raw (uncorrected) statistic for all n
   double *bias ,            // Output of bias (subtract from raw)
   double *var               // Output of variance of statistic
   )
{
   int i, rep, sub ;
   int m = 200 ;
   double *x, stat, temp, sum, sumsq ;

   x = (double *) malloc ( n * sizeof(double) ) ;   // Bootstrap resamples go here
   sum = sumsq = 0.0 ;

   for (rep=0 ; rep<m ; rep++) {                    // Do the m resamples
      for (i=0 ; i<n ; i++) {                       // The sample size is n
         sub = (int) (unifrand() * n) ;             // Select this one
         if (sub >= n)                              // In case unifrand returns 1.0
            sub = n-1 ;                             // Keep it in bounds
         x[i] = data[sub] ;                         // Select with replacement
         }
```

```
      stat = userstat ( n , x ) ;           // α̃* for this bootstrap sample
      sum += stat ;                         // Cumulate for Equation (9.10)
      sumsq += stat * stat ;                // Modified Eq (9.11) avoids storage
      }

   sum /= m ;                               // α̃*·
   sumsq /= m ;                             // Modified Equation (9.11)
   sumsq -= sum * sum ;                     // Can lose precision in this subtraction
   *raw = userstat ( n , data ) ;           // α̃
   *bias = sum - *raw ;                     // Equation (9.12)
   *var = sumsq * m / (m - 1.0) ;           // Equation (9.11) (divided by m above)
   free ( x ) ;
}
```

Final Comments on the Jackknife and the Bootstrap

Perhaps there are some readers who have lightly skimmed this chapter and who, at this point, are wondering why so much theoretical nonsense has found its way into a neural network text whose focus is supposed to be practicality. It's pep talk time. These readers must be assured that the jackknife and the bootstrap are *immensely* practical in real-life applications. They just seem obscure because almost nobody in the neural network community uses them. They should. Let's talk about why.

Known data is nearly always rare and expensive to obtain. We want to squeeze as much utility as possible out of our data. Also, as those of us in the neural network community know, the line "Neural networks are not statistics" is heard far too often. One of my personal goals is to banish that sentence forever. The jackknife and the bootstrap are powerful tools to solve both of those problems. Researchers can now be encouraged to custom design specialized performance measures for evaluating network performance. They are no longer limited to mean square error or its relatives. Measures like the probability of errors exceeding preset levels, or ratios of order statistics, or even the occurrence of certain combinations of error conditions, can be freely implemented. Then, the jackknife and the bootstrap can be used to estimate the reliability of the computed performance measures. This is a power that should not be overlooked by serious readers.

The Jackknife and the Bootstrap

Now that the pep talk is over, we should back off and frankly discuss two weaknesses of these methods. The first is their distributional assumptions. They are nonparametric in that they do not hinge on the parent distribution, G. On the other hand, they rely quite heavily on $\hat{G}$ being reasonably representative of G. If the validation set just happens to have focused on one subpopulation of the universe of possibilities, the results of these methods will be valid only within that subpopulation. That, of course, is not a problem of these methods alone. No matter what technique is used to test a neural network, the conclusions can only be as good as the quality of the validation set. The danger is partially psychological. When one has used a sophisticated statistical technique to draw important numerical conclusions, one is likely to place heavy emphasis on those conclusions. One does not wish to entertain the possibility that those conclusions are worthless due to a poor validation set.

The other weakness is also largely psychological in practice, though something to consider. The unfortunate truth is that the jackknife and the bootstrap are in large part based on heuristics and experimental observations. I have tried to restrict the presentation here to those aspects of the methods that are most reliable and universally applicable. For example, the theorem concerning the conservative nature of the jackknife variance estimate, quoted on page 347, is both powerful and rigorously proven. But such niceties are rare. This is not to say these methods are dangerous. They have been studied heavily in a wide variety of practical applications, and their performance generally ranges from good to excellent. Statisticians have to work hard to discover pathological situations in which they fail. But that is little comfort in applications where failure absolutely must be avoided, such as life-support systems. All that can be said is that estimates of the variance from both the jackknife and the bootstrap are quite universally reliable. They are even surprisingly robust against incomplete validation sets, which is saying a lot! Bias estimates are more reliant on the completeness of the validation set, and even under good conditions the random error in the bias estimate can be large enough to make unbiasing the parameter estimate questionable. Nevertheless, just looking at the bias can often be extremely enlightening, even if that quantity is not actually used to unbias the parameter. The bottom line is that these methods are worthy of trust, and their use is strongly encouraged.

Every example so far has been related to validation. A trained network was validated, and the errors of the validation set defined $\hat{G}$. This is the most common use for the jackknife and the bootstrap, but it need not be so. $\hat{G}$ could just as well be based on the training set, and $\tilde{\alpha}$ could be some property of the trained network. Remember that we have nowhere demanded that X be a scalar. The underlying random variable could be training cases randomly selected from the parent population. Naturally, we must be sure that $\alpha(\hat{G})$ is well defined. A stochastic training algorithm that introduces its own source of randomness into $\tilde{\alpha}$ would invalidate the procedure. But there are many examples where the jackknife or the bootstrap could be useful. We might have a probabilistic neural network trained by optimizing one or more weight parameters. It would be interesting to estimate the variability of those optimal parameter estimates. In this situation, the jackknife would be mandatory, because the cross validation used to optimize the weights would be undone by replication in bootstrap samples. Or we might be computing a classification threshold for a Gram-Charlier neural network. We would be very interested in knowing the variance of the optimal threshold. In fact, we might even want to check its bias! In this situation, since replications are innocuous and computation of $\tilde{\alpha}$ is fast, we would favor the bootstrap. We might even be willing to go out on a limb a little for a potentially big payoff. In a multiple-layer feedforward network, the mean across all hidden neurons of the absolute value of the weights leading from some input to those hidden neurons may be seen as a measure of the importance of that input. If we did many training sessions for each training set and selected the minimum error network, we might be willing to cross our fingers and assume that the training method does not introduce randomness into $\tilde{\alpha}$. Before asserting in public that some particular measure of importance has been obtained, we would do well to use the jackknife method to estimate the variance of that measure. The bootstrap would probably be even better, but the time required for multiple training sessions to compute each $\tilde{\alpha}^\star$ would probably preclude its use.

Finally, I would like to express deep gratitude to Bradley Efron of Stanford University for his immensely valuable studies of the jackknife and the bootstrap. The book Efron (1982) is the ultimate reference for those who would like more information on these topics. Much of the material in the preceding sections of this text has been derived from Efron's excellent work.

Economical Error Estimation

When one thinks of validating a neural network, one invariably thinks of using a validation set. Traditionally, the precious collection of known data is divided into two parts. One part is used to train the network, and the other part is painfully held back for use as an independent test set. Sometimes this method is the only practical approach. It is certainly the method most likely to convince illiterate skeptics. Also, some properties of the training algorithm may favor or even demand this method of testing. But in many situations we can do far better. A single collection of known data can serve as both the training set and the validation set, with little or no penalty in prejudiced results. It sounds like magic, and to many it will always remain so. Let the reader be assured that the techniques described in this section are built on a solid mathematical foundation and that they are worthy of trust and acceptance. They are not perfect, but when properly applied, they beat the daylights out of sophisticated traditional statistical tests applied by amateurs to situations that seriously violate the assumptions of those tests.

It must be emphasized from the start that these methods are not universally applicable. They can be applied with full legitimacy only to neural network models whose trained state is well defined by the training set. In other words, if the network were trained twice with exactly the same training set, exactly the same trained network would result. If the training procedure introduces any significant element of randomness into the trained state, these methods cannot be used. The probabilistic neural network, generalized regression neural network, and Gram-Charlier neural network are all well defined. Their trained state is fully described by the training set. (If weight parameters in the PNN or GRNN are optimized as part of training, it is assumed that convergence to the best model is always enforced to reasonable accuracy. As an alternative, we may want to optimize the weights first with the entire training set, then fix them during validation. Strictly speaking, this is cheating and introduces a small optimistic bias into these results.)

Multiple-layer feedforward networks (MLFNs) usually cannot be simultaneously trained and validated with the methods of this section. There are at least two reasons for this. One is practicality. These networks typically require a lot of training time, and the methods of this section require many training sessions. The other problem is that their training almost always involves an element of randomness. In case the reader is in possession of a fast deterministic training algorithm (and a few do exist), then fine. But if not, beware. The only exception is when the network happens to be small, and training time is not an issue. Then it may be feasible to repeat the training many times for each training set and choose the best network. That action *may* reduce the element of randomness sufficiently that it can be ignored (as long as the fingers are firmly crossed behind the back). Good luck on that one.

Population Error, Apparent Error, and Excess Error

Throughout the remainder of this chapter, we will be speaking often of three sorts of error. Their definitions are strongly intuitive (for the most part), so it would almost seem that there is no need to dwell on them. But as is so often the case in mathematics, notation is everything. We will need a lot of special notation, and most of it revolves around one or another of these errors. So here we go.

Apparent error is the easiest to understand. This is what everyone knows as the training set error. If the mean squared error is being reduced as the training goal, and if that is the error measure of interest, then the final training error obtained is the apparent error of the network. More sophisticated users may train the network with one error measure, typically mean square, then evaluate performance with another. In that case, the training set is passed through the trained network, and its score on the alternative error measure is the apparent error. We will not care what this error is; in fact, it doesn't even need to have negative connotations. A measure of quality will do just as well as a measure of error.

In order to remain isolated from the definition of the error, it is useful to introduce an anonymous error measure. Following Bradley Efron (as well as the myriad researchers who also follow him), the letter Q is used to signify error. Let X represent a hypothetical training set randomly selected from the population. When a particular training set is selected, so that we actually have one in hand, it is called x. Note that these terms do not represent a single case or observation. The random variable X (and a particular observed value, x) represent an entire training set. Each case in this training set includes both the network input and the desired output. A trained neural network will be designated as either η_X if it is a hypothetical network being spoken of in the abstract sense, or as η_x if it is a particular network that was trained from a training set actually collected. Let U represent a hypothetical random variable that is suitable as an input to the neural network. An attached subscript indicates that it is a member of a training set. So U_i stands for a network input that is the ith member of a hypothetical training set, while u_i is the ith member of a training that has actually been collected. Similarly, let Y be the desired network output corresponding to the input U, with Y_i being the desired output corresponding to U_i in a hypothetical training set, and y_i being the desired output corresponding to input u_i in the training set in hand. This seems like a lot of notation, but it's really not. Capital letters are used for hypothetical quantities, while lowercase is used for actually observed quantities. U (or u) is an input, and Y (or y) is the corresponding desired output. These are subscripted if they belong to a training set. Otherwise they are assumed to be randomly drawn from some population. And η_X (or η_x) designates a trained neural network. Finally, when we apply an input to a trained neural network, its computed output will be designated $\eta_x(u)$.

Anonymity of error is obtained by letting $Q(y, \eta_x(u))$ represent the error of a known observation (u, y). When working with mean squared error, this quantity is defined as shown in Equation (9.13). When classification is the goal, we usually define the error as the occurrence of misclassification, shown in Equation (9.14).

$$Q(y, \eta_x(u)) = (y - \eta_x(u))^2 \qquad (9.13)$$

$$Q(y, \eta_x(u)) = \begin{cases} 0 & \text{if } y = \eta_x(u) \\ 1 & \text{otherwise} \end{cases} \qquad (9.14)$$

The important point is that we do not care how the error is defined. Those two equations were shown simply to give the reader an idea of what Q means. From now on we will not be concerned with the nature of the error measure.

Several paragraphs ago we started defining the apparent error of a trained neural network. That was said to be the error incurred by the training set. Now that suitable notation has been laid out, the apparent error can be rigorously defined. Let n be the number of cases in the training set. The apparent error of training set x is defined as the mean across the training set of the error due to each case. This is shown in Equation (9.15).

$$\text{App}(x) = \frac{1}{n} \sum_{i=1}^{n} Q(y_i, \eta_x(u_i)) \qquad (9.15)$$

The *population error* is a little trickier to define than was the apparent error. As the reader surely suspects, it is the error that one would expect over the population as a whole, as opposed to the error over just the training set. But there is a subtle point involved in this definition. If any readers are unable to understand the following point, do not be dismayed. It rarely, if ever, has any practical consequences. But for the sake of completeness and reasonable rigor, the point must be made.

Normally, we collect a training set, train the network on the complete set, and then ask how that particular network would do across the entire population. The answer to that question is what most readers would consider to be the population error. Close, but no cigar as far as this chapter is concerned. As will be seen, the methods to follow *never* train the network on the entire training set. They train it on many subsets of the complete training set. So the population error that is estimated is not the expected error based on a *particular* training set. Rather, it is the expected error across the universe of all possible training sets that could be selected from this population. In other words, it is almost as if we are testing the model, the form, of the neural network in the context of the population implied by the training set. In practice, this distinction is of no consequence. Whatever results we get on the variety of subsets can legitimately be projected on the network when it is trained with the complete training set. If anything, performance will slightly improve by virtue of having the entire set to work with. But readers who choose to follow the mathematics of these techniques carefully will be helped if they understand this point right up front.

Earlier in this chapter, we introduced the notation E_G to indicate the expectation of a quantity (its mean, essentially) across a population in which the underlying distribution is G. Let G be the distribution of cases throughout the population of interest. Remember that random variables (cases) sampled under G consist of both an input and a true (desired) output. Without introducing confusion, we will also let G represent the distribution of training sets, X. Strictly speaking, this should not be done, because a training set and an individual case are different entities. But by suffering this small infraction, the need for yet another symbol is avoided. The intended use for G should always be clear from the context.

Suppose we have collected a training set x. Let PE(x) be the expected error under G of η_x, the neural network trained with x. This is the usual intuitive definition of population error, though not the one we will be using in this chapter. PE(x) is the quantity that is estimated when we collect a separate validation set and test the network (which we will *not* be doing here). The definition of this quantity is shown in Equation (9.16).

$$\text{PE}(x) = E_G[Q(Y, \eta_x(U))] \qquad (9.16)$$

The population error is defined (for this chapter) as the expectation under G of PE(X). In other words, it considers the entire universe of possible training sets. This may initially seem inappropriate. However, remember that the methods of this chapter will be using the user's training set as the role model for the parent population. So this definition, expressed in Equation (9.17), is not at all inappropriate.

$$\text{Pop} = E_G[\text{PE}(X)] \qquad (9.17)$$

The final definition, that of *excess error*, is a piece of cake after the previous two. It is just the amount that the population error exceeds the apparent error. It should be obvious that the training set does not provide a fair test of the network. Since performance was tweaked on that set, it is to be expected that the network will do better on that collection of cases than on cases randomly selected from the population. We can think of the excess error in two equivalent ways. We could consider the expectation over G of the apparent error. This is the average value of the training set error across the universe of possible training sets. Subtract that from the expectation of the general error shown in Equation (9.17) and the excess error results. Or we could consider one training set at a time. The training set error is App(x), and the associated error in the general population is PE(x). So the excess error for that particular training set is the difference of these two quantities. The expectation of that difference over G is the excess error. Those two viewpoints are equivalent because expectation is a linear operation. The excess error is defined in Equation (9.18).

$$\begin{aligned} \text{Excess} &= E_G[\text{PE}(X)] - E_G[\text{App}(X)] \\ &= E_G[\text{PE}(X) - \text{App}(X)] \end{aligned} \quad (9.18)$$

Overview of Efficient Error Estimation

A fundamental assumption of the methods presented here is that the collection of known cases is representative of the entire population from which one could draw training cases and in which the neural network will ultimately be used. Algorithms similar to the jackknife and the bootstrap presented earlier in this chapter are used to study the behavior of the neural network when sampling is done under $\hat{G}$, the discrete distribution defined by the complete collection of known cases. This behavior is then assumed to represent the network's behavior under sampling from G. In particular, the observed excess error under $\hat{G}$ is assumed to be equal to the unobservable excess error under G. The user simply adds the computed excess error estimate to the apparent error of the complete training set in order to arrive at an estimate of the population error.

When a trained neural network is put to use, there are two entirely different potential sources of error. One is that the network may be fundamentally unfit for the task. It may be too weak to follow the complexities of the data. It may be too powerful, adapting itself to the idiosyncrasies of the training data rather than modeling only the important general features of the data. Or it may simply be inappropriate, perhaps encompassing one type of nonlinearity when another type of nonlinearity is required. These sorts of errors are what the methods of this chapter are designed to detect.

A more subtle error will be missed by these techniques. If the collection of known cases was selected carelessly, or if plain old bad luck interfered, there will be trouble. Conclusions that are reached based on a given data collection are valid only within the subpopulation represented by that collection. If cases appear later that were not fairly represented in the known collection, anything is possible.

On first thought, this may seem like a serious drawback to these methods. But compared to the alternative, it really is not bad. Suppose a cautious reader reverted to the traditional method of randomly splitting the known collection into two parts, using one part for the training set and the other part for the validation set. Error is still possible. What if the complete collection was obtained from an unrepresentative subset of the population? Conclusions gleaned from the imperfect validation set would still be limited to the sampled subpopulation. The reader is in the same boat that he or she would be in if the entire collection were processed with the efficient methods of this chapter. Do not fall into the trap of thinking that a totally independent validation set is the straight and narrow route to full confidence; it's not. *The key is fair and complete collection of the known dataset.* If that is done, the methods of this chapter will almost always provide *better* inferences than the traditional training/validation set method.

It has already been stated that these methods can be used only when the network can be trained in such a way that its trained state is uniquely determined by the training set. If there is an additional element of randomness, these methods are invalid. There is one more potential problem to be considered. Some (but not all) of these methods will, at some point in their operation, test the trained network on one or more cases that were in the training set. For some neural network models, this should not be done. For example, a probabilistic neural network having narrow Parzen windows may misbehave in areas of low population density. This is because the *unknown* case will encounter its twin in the training set, and excessive optimism will result. This is not a problem if the Parzen windows are wide enough to span the entire training space thoroughly. Users should be wary of using such methods on probabilistic neural networks. Luckily, excellent alternatives exist. Also, parametric networks like the multiple-layer feedforward net and the GCNN do not suffer from this problem. Appropriate comments will be made as each method is described.

Cross Validation

We shall start out with what is probably the most commonly used algorithm for combining training with validation. This method is the fastest of all that will be presented here, and it is also the most intuitive and easy to program and understand. Moreover, it never tests a case that was included in the training set. Therefore, this method is usable for models like the probabilistic neural network that are hampered by duplication. Unfortunately, cross validation suffers from a strong tendency to have relatively large variation in its estimate of excess error. In other words, suppose we have the capability of collecting many independent training sets from the population. If we were to use cross validation as well as the other methods of this chapter to estimate the excess error for each training set, we would probably find that the error estimates provided by cross validation would vary more than those provided by the other methods. Nevertheless, this method is often the only one that is usable because of time or model constraints. Moreover, cross validation plays an integral role in many training algorithms. The most effective known training algorithm for probabilistic neural networks and generalized regression neural networks is based on cross validation. Let us explore this simple but powerful procedure.

Recall that η_x stands for a neural network trained with training set x, and that $\eta_x(u)$ is the output of that neural network in response to input u. Also recall the special notation developed in conjunction with the jackknife procedure to indicate omission of a single case from a dataset. The similar notation $\eta_{x(i)}$ is used here to indicate a neural network that has been trained on the set x with case i omitted from x. Thus, $\eta_{x(i)}(u_i)$ is the output of a neural network that was trained with all cases except case i, in response to an input of case i. In other words, one case has been removed from the training set, the network has been trained on the remaining $n-1$ cases, and the trained network is now being exposed to the case that was omitted. The desired output is y_i. With this in mind, the estimated population and excess error as determined by cross validation are given by Equation (9.19).

$$\text{Pop}_{CV} = \frac{1}{n} \sum_{i=1}^{n} Q(y_i, \eta_{x(i)}(u_i))$$

$$\text{Excess}_{CV} = \text{Pop}_{CV} - \text{App}_{CV}$$

(9.19)

The intuitive simplicity of cross validation should now be apparent. Look at how the population error is estimated. We omit a case, train with the rest, then test the omitted case. Find the mean error across all omitted training cases. That's tough to beat for simplicity. And the procedure does not introduce any statistical bias.

Economical Error Estimation

Each term in the sum is unbiased, since the case being tested is not a member of the training set. So the sum is also unbiased. It must still be remembered that this error estimate is contingent on the training set being representative of the population. But as already stated, that same assumption is made about an independent validation set. So most people consider this error estimator to be as unbiased as any obtainable.

One picky point should be stressed. The procedure just shown bears a striking resemblance to jackknifing. That's all it is, a resemblance. Mathematically speaking, the two are completely different animals. It is common in the literature to use the term jackknifing to describe what is actually cross validation. Even I have been guilty of this crime in the past. With the increasing popularity of these algorithms, there is a strong (and appropriate) movement afoot to correctly distinguish between the two procedures. A method exists for estimating excess error via true jackknifing. However, it is very slow and complicated, and it seems to offer no strong advantage over the other methods presented here. Therefore, it will not appear in this text.

Code for Cross Validation

We now present a subroutine that calculates an estimate for the excess error via cross validation. It also computes the apparent error, so the user may add these two quantities to estimate the population error. The user must provide two subroutines. The first, train (int n , DataClass *data), trains a neural network using the n cases in *data. The second routine, test (int n , DataClass *data), returns the average error of the n test cases in *data.

```
void cv (
    int n ,                 // Number of data points
    DataClass *data ,       // The data is here
    double *app ,           // Apparent error from testing tset
    double *excess          // Excess error (add to app to get pop)
    )
{
    int exclude, first ;
    double errsum ;
    DataClass temp ;
```

```
errsum = 0.0 ;
exclude = n ;
first = 1 ;

while (exclude--) {            // Exclude one case at a time

  if (first)
    first = 0 ;

  else {                       // If not first trial, swap excluded to end
    temp = data[exclude] ;
    data[exclude] = data[n-1] ;
    data[n-1] = temp ;
    }

  train ( n-1 , data ) ;       // Train on first n-1 cases
  errsum += test ( 1 , data+n-1 ) ; // Test last (excluded) case
  }

errsum /= n ;                  // Population error (Eq (9.19))

train ( n , data ) ;           // Apparent error
*app = test ( n , data ) ;     // Is needed to compute excess
*excess = errsum - *app ;
}
```

The preceding code is strikingly similar to the jackknife code seen earlier in this chapter. As was emphasized, though, jackknifing and cross validation are completely different from a mathematical viewpoint. Readers should not look for parallels in the mathematics. The only similarity between these methods is that one case at a time is swapped to the end where it is ignored.

In this code, the network is trained on the n−1 cases at the beginning of the data array. Then the network is tested on the last case. Each case is omitted, and the mean error is found. The apparent error is also computed. The excess error is the difference between these two quantities, as expressed in the bottom line of Equation (9.19).

The Bootstrap Estimate of Excess Error

The bootstrap algorithm described on page 351 may be generalized in such a way that it can be applied to the problem of estimating excess error. The reader is strongly cautioned against trying to understand the generalization on his or her own. It is quite subtle, and attempts to find correspondences between the problem of estimating the bias or variance of a statistic and the problem of estimating excess error will most likely lead to serious confusion. A good text like Efron (1982) is mandatory if the reader is to get it right. The presentation here will be kept as simple and intuitive as possible, while still maintaining mathematical correctness. Of necessity, many vital theoretical details are omitted.

By way of introduction, I will state that the straight bootstrap algorithm is definitely *not* my favorite method of estimating excess error. If the collection of known cases is very large and computation time is of no consequence, then the bootstrap method will probably provide the best (lowest bias and variance) estimates of any method described in this chapter. A tremendous amount of computation is needed, though. And if the data collection is small, empirical evidence indicates that this method exhibits a dangerous downward bias in its estimates. The E0 method of the next section is almost always preferable to the straight bootstrap method. But since this method is occasionally useful, is the motivation for the E0 method, and has significant historical and theoretical credentials, it will be presented.

The development of a bootstrap algorithm starts with the situation in the parent population and then sees if it can be simulated under a bootstrap distribution. There is a parent population that gives rise to cases under a distribution G. A particular collection of these cases defines a training set x. This training set will exhibit a measurable error, App(x). It will also have an unmeasurable error under G, PE(x). By Equation (9.18), the difference of the expectations under G of these quantities is the excess error.

So how do we simulate that situation by means of a bootstrap? Assume that some dataset called x has been collected. That dataset defines a discrete distribution, $\hat{G}$. We can now collect a bootstrap sample under that distribution. Similar to what we did earlier, let us call that bootstrap sample $x^\star$. The apparent error of the bootstrap sample, App($x^\star$), is easily calculated by reclassifying $x^\star$ as shown in Equation (9.15). But what about PE($x^\star$)? That's easy too, because we know the parent population. It's $\hat{G}$. So PE($x^\star$) is the mean across the complete dataset of the errors of the network trained on $x^\star$. These two quantities are made explicit in Equation (9.20). As was done earlier, k_p is the number of times case p appears in the bootstrap sample. Also, $\eta_{x\star}$ is the neural network trained on $x^\star$.

$$\text{PE}(x^\star) = \frac{1}{n} \sum_{i=1}^{n} Q(y_i, \eta_{x\star}(u_i))$$
$$\text{App}(x^\star) = \frac{1}{n} \sum_{i=1}^{n} k_p Q(y_i, \eta_{x\star}(u_i))$$
(9.20)

The excess error for that particular bootstrap sample is the difference $\text{PE}(x^\star) - \text{App}(x^\star)$. Factoring out Q gives Equation (9.21).

$$\text{Excess}(x^\star) = \frac{1}{n} \sum_{i=1}^{n} (1 - k_p) Q(y_i, \eta_{x\star}(u_i)) \quad (9.21)$$

That's about it. Equation (9.21) is the excess error of a single bootstrap sample. To estimate the expected excess error over the population $\hat{G}$, all that needs to be done is to collect many (typically several hundred) such bootstrap samples and find the average excess error. This is shown in Equation (9.22). If we are willing to assume that the same excess error holds true across G, which is, of course, the essence of all bootstrap techniques, then we add the bootstrap excess error to the apparent error of the complete dataset to estimate the population error. This is shown in Equation (9.23).

$$\text{Excess}_{\text{BOOT}} = \frac{1}{m} \sum_{j=1}^{m} \text{Excess}(x_j^\star) \quad (9.22)$$

$$\text{Pop}_{\text{BOOT}} = \text{App}(x) + \text{Excess}_{\text{BOOT}} \quad (9.23)$$

It can be seen why the bootstrap method just described may lead to dangerous negative bias in the estimated excess error. This method regularly tests cases that also appeared in the bootstrap training sets. If the complete training set is large relative to the versatility of the model, this is usually not a significant problem. But it will nearly always be serious for models like the probabilistic neural network that tremendously overperform on duplicates. And if there is any tendency at all toward overfitting, the straight bootstrap algorithm will cultivate false optimism to such a degree that it is almost useless. Trust this method only when the training set is very large relative to the effective number of degrees of freedom in the model. When this constraint is satisfied, this method gives excellent results. Its estimates can have low bias and probably the lowest random error of any method known to me. But great danger lurks here. Be warned.

Code for the Bootstrap Method

This subroutine calculates an estimate for the excess error via the bootstrap algorithm. It also computes the apparent error, so the user may add these two quantities to estimate the population error. The user must provide the same two subroutines that were needed for cross validation. The first, train (int n , DataClass *data), trains a neural network using the n cases in *data. The second routine, test (int n , DataClass *data), returns the average error of the n test cases in *data.

```
void boot (
    int n ,                        // Number of data points
    DataClass *data ,              // The data is here
    double *app ,                  // Apparent error from testing tset
    double *excess                 // Excess error (add to app to get pop)
    )
{
    int i, rep, sub, *count ;
    int m = 200 ;
    double err, errsum ;
    DataClass *x ;

    if (m < n)                     // If the dataset is large
        m = n ;                    // Do enough reps to be thorough

    x = (DataClass *) malloc ( n * sizeof(DataClass) ) ; // Bootstraps here
    count = (int *) malloc ( n * sizeof(int) ) ;         // Count uses in bootstrap

    errsum = 0.0 ;
```

```
for (rep=0 ; rep<m ; rep++) {                         // Bootstrap replications

   memset ( count , 0 , n * sizeof(int) ) ;           // Zero usage counter
   for (i=0 ; i<n ; i++) {                            // Bootstrap sample same size
      sub = unifrand() * n ;                          // Select this case
      if (sub >= n)                                   // Cheap insurance in case
         sub = n-1 ;                                  // unifrand() returns 1
      x[i] = data[sub] ;                              // Get this case
      ++count[sub] ;                                  // Count its use
      }

   train ( n , x ) ;                                  // Train on bootstrap sample
   for (i=0 ; i<n ; i++) {                            // Test all cases
      err = test ( 1 , data+i ) ;                     // Error of this case
      errsum += err * (1 - count[i]) ;                // Equation (9.21)
      }
   }

errsum /= (double) m  *  (double) n ;                 // Grand mean (Eq (9.21) and (9.22))

train ( n , data ) ;                                  // Also return the
*app = test ( n , data ) ;                            // Apparent error
*excess = errsum ;

free ( x ) ;
free ( count ) ;
}
```

This subroutine starts by making sure the number of replications is commensurate with the dataset size if that size is large. This helps to obtain the most accuracy possible. Then memory is allocated to hold the bootstrap samples and the vector that counts usage of the original dataset.

At the beginning of each bootstrap replication, the count vector is zeroed. The bootstrap sample is randomly selected from the original dataset. It is always good programming practice to make sure that array subscripts cannot overrun their array. This is done here. The neural network is trained on the bootstrap sample, and the network is tested on each original case. Equation (9.21) (except for the division by n, which is done later), is used to compute and cumulate the excess error for each bootstrap. When all replications are done, the excess error sum is divided by n to complete Equation (9.21) and by m to average across the replications. Finally, the apparent error is computed for the user's convenience.

Efron's E0 Estimator

When computer time is abundant and the possibility of nasty negative bias due to bootstrap overfitting is a threat, this is my favorite method of estimating excess error. It requires a lot more time than cross validation, but the reward is significantly less random error in the estimate. Also, this method certainly has no negative bias. If anything, on the average it may slightly overestimate the excess error. This makes its results conservative, always welcome as long as it is not taken to an extreme. Finally, it never tests a case that was included in the training set. Thus, it is applicable to probabilistic neural networks and other models for which such duplication is tantamount to cheating.

The philosophy of the E0 method is straightforward. Use the bootstrap method to sample under $\hat{G}$, but test each network on only those members of the complete dataset that are not included in the bootstrap training set. Cumulate the total error across all bootstraps, and divide by the total number of cases tested. That average can be used as an estimate of the population error. Subtract the apparent error to get the excess error.

It's ironic that an algorithm so easy to explain in words is so difficult to express mathematically. To do so, some special notation is necessary. As usual, x is the complete known dataset, and $x^\star$ is a bootstrap sample drawn from x. Let x^v be the set of all cases in x that are not in $x^\star$. Let $\#(x^v)$ be the cardinality of x^v. That is the number of cases in x that are not in $x^\star$. The E0 estimator of the population error is given by Equation (9.24).

$$\text{Pop}_{E0} = \frac{\sum_{j=1}^{m} \sum_{x_j^v} Q(y, \eta_{x_j^\star}(u))}{\sum_{j=1}^{m} \#(x_j^v)} \qquad (9.24)$$

This is really quite a good estimator of the population error. The fact that training cases are never tested makes it usable with any deterministically trained neural network. That fact also eliminates the possibility of negative bias that can lead to undeserved optimism. And the relatively large number of bootstrap samples reduces the amount of random error compared with cross validation. However, there is one slight statistical flaw in this algorithm. Do you see it? (Don't be discouraged if you do not see it. It is subtle.) This flaw will be discussed in a later section, and the E632 method will be introduced to deal with it.

Code for the E0 Estimator

This subroutine calculates the E0 excess error estimator. It also computes the apparent error, so the user may add these two quantities to estimate the population error. The user must provide the usual two subroutines. The first, train (int n , DataClass *data), trains a neural network using the n cases in *data. The second routine, test (int n , DataClass *data), returns the average error of the n test cases in *data.

```
void E0 (
    int n ,                     // Number of data points
    DataClass *data ,           // The data is here
    double *app ,               // Apparent error from testing tset
    double *excess              // Excess error (add to app to get pop)
    )
{
    int i, rep, sub, ntot, *count ;
    int m = 200 ;
    double errsum ;
    DataClass *x ;

    if (m < n)
        m = n ;

    x = (DataClass *) malloc ( n * sizeof(DataClass) ) ;     // Bootstraps here
    count = (int *) malloc ( n * sizeof(int) ) ;             // Count uses in bootstrap

    errsum = 0.0 ;
    ntot = 0 ;
```

Economical Error Estimation

```
for (rep=0 ; rep<m ; rep++) {

    memset ( count , 0 , n * sizeof(int) ) ;      // Zero usage counter

    for (i=0 ; i<n ; i++) {                        // Bootstrap sample same size
        sub = unifrand() * n ;                     // Select this case
        if (sub >= n)                              // Cheap insurance in case
            sub = n-1 ;                            // unifrand() returns 1
        x[i] = data[sub] ;                         // Get this case
        ++count[sub] ;                             // Count its use
    }

    train ( n , x ) ;                              // Train on bootstrap sample

    for (i=0 ; i<n ; i++) {                        // Check all cases
        if (! count[i]) {                          // If not used in training
            errsum += test ( 1 , data+i ) ;        // Find its error
            ++ntot ;                               // Grand test count
        }
    }
}

errsum /= ntot ;                                   // Mean of all tests (Eq (9.24))

train ( n , data ) ;                               // Also need the
*app = test ( n , data ) ;                         // Apparent error
*excess = errsum - *app ;

free ( x ) ;
free ( count ) ;
}
```

This subroutine is very similar to the bootstrap routine listed on page 371. It increases the number of replications if needed, then it allocates work memory. The selection of each bootstrap sample and the training based on that sample are also identical to the bootstrap routine. The difference arises at testing time. Only those cases that were not used in the training set are tested. The error of each such case is cumulated, and a total count is also kept. When all replications have been done, the total error is divided by the total count to get the average population error. Finally, the apparent error is computed, and the excess error is the difference of these quantities.

The E632 Estimator

The E0 estimator is an excellent choice for efficiently estimating the population error of a trained neural network. It is broadly applicable, and it has pessimistic bias and modest variance. However, due to a basic statistical flaw in the algorithm, E0 has somewhat of a tendency to be excessively conservative. Usually we are willing to live with that (or should be); but if it is thought to be a serious problem, we may want at least to consider an alternative. This alternative should be strictly avoided if there is any significant possibility that the model is capable of overfitting the data. That typically happens when the training set is small relative to the effective number of degrees of freedom of the model. Also, this method is not applicable to models like the probabilistic neural network that are incapable of fairly testing a case that is included in the training set. But other models can be tested with the E632 method.

This method is based on an exceedingly simple idea. The apparent error of a neural network is on the average smaller than the actual population error because the test data is *too close* to the training data. Since the test data is the training data itself, the points in data space that comprise the test data lie closer to the training points than would happen if the test cases were drawn from the population in a random and independent manner. (In fact, the test points lie right on top of the training points!) Just the opposite is true in the E0 method. Recall that the $\hat{G}$ distribution is fixed, having been defined by the known dataset. A bootstrap training set is fairly and randomly drawn from that distribution. But the fairness ends when the testing begins. The test cases are fixed by the algorithm to be whatever in $\hat{G}$ is left over after bootstrap selection. Training cases need not apply. As a result, the test cases are *too far* from the training cases. They are likely to have higher average error than would be expected if all of $\hat{G}$ were up for grabs at testing time.

How can we compensate for this effect? A heuristic but apparently effective solution is as follows. The asymptotic probability that any given case in x will be included in a bootstrap sample $x^\star$ is 0.632. So we can simulate sampling test cases fairly by testing members of x^v 63.2 percent of the time, and testing members of $x^\star$ the remaining 36.8 percent of the time. There really is no need to make it that complicated, either. Just compute App(x) and E0 as already described, then use Equation (9.25) to combine these estimates into the less biased E632.

$$\text{Pop}_{E632} = 0.632\, E0 + 0.368\, \text{App} \qquad (9.25)$$

The author questions the utility of this estimator. The mathematics seems reasonable. It is more a philosophical problem. Unbiased statistics have an obvious appeal, so E632 has a claim. On the other hand, I am a staunch conservative when it comes to making inferences based on statistics. It is too easy to be misled. Therefore, the security of an estimator having known pessimistic bias can be comforting. On the other hand, a glance at E632 may be enlightening, if nothing else.

10

Using the PNN Program

- Overview of program capabilities and operation

- Detailed discussion of all commands

- Alphabetical summary of all commands

- Validation suite

PNN is a general-purpose program for training and testing probabilistic neural networks and several close relatives. After training, validation sets may be processed for the purpose of evaluating the network's performance. The trained network may also be executed on unknown data, with the results saved to a disk file. Finally, the trained network may be saved in a compact file format to facilitate reuse at a later date. The format of this file may be found in the module WT_SAVE.CPP on the accompanying code disk.

Interactive operation is possible. The user may enter commands that are executed immediately. However, the more usual mode of control is to prepare in advance an ASCII command file. Each line of this file is a single command, identical to those that might be entered interactively. There are at least two reasons why this method is preferable to interactive control. First, many program runs will require an extended period of time: overnight or even longer. The use of a self-contained command file allows the user to engage in other activities while the program is executing. The other reason is that a command file is self-documenting. The user will have a hard record of the parameters that went into producing the obtained results. The command to read an ASCII command file is the following:

COMMAND FILE = filename

Usually this command is typed by the user to initiate processing of the command file. However, it may also appear in a command file. In other words, recursive processing of command files is allowed.

Every command has one or more components. The mandatory first component is the action to be taken. Many commands will also have auxiliary information. In this case, the action is followed by an equal sign (=), which in turn is followed by the auxiliary information. Blanks may optionally appear before or after the equal sign, and case (upper/lower) is ignored.

Commands may be commented by placing a semicolon (;) after the relevant parts, then following the semicolon with any text. Lines that are only comments are implemented by using a semicolon as the first character on the line.

In order to exit the program and return to the operating system, the command **BYE** must be used. Like all other rules, this may be typed interactively, or it may appear in a command file. A reminder that this is the means of exiting PNN is given to the user at each interactive command prompt.

Output Mode

The probabilistic neural network is intrinsically a classifier. However, several modes of operation are generally available as was discussed earlier in this text. It is convenient for the user if some common interpretations of the outputs are handled internally by the program. For example, PNN provides a CLASSIFICATION mode in which training and testing is implemented by using predefined output values of 1.0 when a case belongs to the class associated with the output neuron, and 0.0 otherwise. Also, PNN provides an AUTO-ASSOCIATION mode in which the inputs are automatically associated with the outputs, saving the user from explicitly specifying outputs. Finally, fully general function mapping is supported with the MAPPING output mode. This mode can be used to implement a wide variety of paradigms. However, the other modes can be very convenient. This section will examine these modes in some detail. The command to activate a given mode is shown below as a section head, and an explanation of the mode follows.

MODE = MAPPING

This mode is the fully general $\Re^n$ to $\Re^m$ function-mapping model (generalized regression). If n is the number of inputs and m is the number of outputs, each training and validation case must consist of $n+m$ numbers.

MODE = AUTOASSOCIATION

AUTOASSOCIATION output mode is similar to the above mode in that general function mapping (generalized regression) is implemented. The difference is that the user does not specify outputs. Rather, the inputs define the outputs. The number of inputs in the network model equals the number of outputs. All training and validation files contain only this one data vector for each case.

MODE = CLASSIFICATION

This mode is different from the others in that the user does not directly specify the output values. Rather, the program itself determines them according to the class of each case. The user specifies the number of outputs as the number of classes that will be used. The class of each case in the training and validation sets is specified by means of the **CLASS** command, which will be described later. For each case, the activation of the output neuron corresponding to the class of that case is defined as 1.0, and the activations of all other neurons are defined as 0.0. This is the original probabilistic neural network paradigm.

Network Model

Several variations on the PNN and its relatives are available. The details of these models were discussed in depth in Chapters four through six. Only brief summaries, with appropriate references, will be given here. The model is selected with the following command:

NETWORK MODEL = Model

The models that are available are shown below as section heads, and an explanation of each follows.

NETWORK MODEL = BASIC

This is the simplest probabilistic neural network. Exactly one sigma is used to cover all variables (and all classes in CLASSIFICATION mode). Training is the fastest of all PNN models, but quality is usually lowest. It is particularly important that the scaling of all variables reflects their relative importance when this model is used.

NETWORK MODEL = SEPVAR

This middle-of-the-road PNN model is usually the best compromise between power and training speed. A separate sigma is used for each variable, but these are shared among all classes in CLASSIFICATION mode. (In other modes this is not an issue, as there are no separate classes). When in doubt as to which PNN model to use, this is a good choice. Remember that during the initial training phase, this model is, in effect, identical to the BASIC (single-sigma) model. Thus, for a given training time, you have nothing to lose and possibly a lot to gain relative to the BASIC model.

NETWORK MODEL = SEPCLASS

This is the most general model. Not only does it use a different sigma for each variable, but it also uses separate sigma vectors for each class. This implies that the SEPCLASS model can be used only in CLASSIFICATION output mode. Training can be very slow for this model, and the increased possibility of accidental overfitting makes validation especially important when this model is used.

NETWORK MODEL = GCNN

This is the traditional Gram-Charlier neural network. By default, the maximum moment used is 3. This can be changed by the command MAX MOMENT = n, where n ranges from 3 through 8. The relative position of the NETWORK MODEL = GCNN command and the MAX MOMENT = n command (if used) is not important. Either may precede or follow the other.

NETWORK MODEL = GCNN_EW

This is Edgeworth's modification of the Gram-Charlier neural network. By default, the maximum moment used is 3. This can be changed by the command MAX MOMENT = n, where n ranges from 3 through 5. The relative position of the NETWORK MODEL = GCNN_EW command and the MAX MOMENT = n command (if used) is not important. Either may precede or follow the other.

Kernel Functions

For probabilistic neural networks, the kernel function can be specified with the following command:

KERNEL = Kernel

The kernel functions that are available are now listed, along with a brief explanation for each.

KERNEL = GAUSS

This is by far the most common kernel. The Gaussian function is widely accepted as being well behaved and reliable. Unless there is strong reason to use another, choose this one. If NETWORK MODEL=SEPVAR or SEPCLASS, the GAUSS kernel is mandatory.

KERNEL = RECIPROCAL

The kernel function described on page 169 (Equation (4.10)) is an alternative that has much heavier tails than the GAUSS kernel. Distant cases in the training set exert relatively more influence in processing a case than they do for the GAUSS kernel. This kernel is valid only for NETWORK MODEL=BASIC.

Building the Training Set

Before learning can commence, a training set must be in place. The training set is created by reading one or more disk files containing the training cases. Each time a file is read, any existing training set is preserved. The new data is appended to the old data. If the user wishes to start all over with a totally new training set, the following command may be used:

ERASE TRAINING SET

All PNN data files share the same format. This includes the training set files currently under discussion, as well as validation and test files that will be described later. They are standard ASCII files that may be read and written by nearly any text editor. Each case occupies exactly one line in the file. That line contains as many numbers as are needed to define the case. In CLASSIFICATION and AUTOASSOCIATION modes, that will be the number of inputs. (Class membership, which is not in the data file, is discussed later in this section.) In MAPPING mode, the quantity of numbers will be the number of inputs plus the number of outputs, with the inputs appearing before the outputs on each line. Each number is separated from the other numbers by one or more spaces. A sign and a decimal point are optional. A training data file is read by means of the following command:

CUMULATE TRAINING SET = filename

Note that this command does not initiate any learning. It causes the named file to be read and appended to any existing training set. A path and extension may optionally appear as part of the filename.

For classification, the class membership information is not included in the data file. It is specified *before* the **CUMULATE TRAINING SET** command appears. This command is

CLASS = integer

The integer is the class number, from one through the number of classes. It may not exceed the number of outputs in the model. Once this command appears, cases in all subsequent **CUMULATE TRAINING SET** commands will be considered to be in the specified class. The **CLASS** command does not need to be repeated for each training file unless the class membership changes.

Prior probabilities for class membership can be specified. This is done with the following command:

PRIOR = number

The specified number must be positive, and may optionally contain a decimal point. The prior probabilities need not sum to one, as they are treated in a relative way only. Internally, they will be added, and each will be divided by their sum. This automatic normalization frees the user from the burden of specifying normalized values.

As an alternative option, the user may issue the following command:

PRIOR = N

In the above command, the letter N indicates that the user wants the priors to be determined by the number of cases in each class. Thus, it is assumed that the makeup of the training set reflects the makeup of the general population.

If no prior probabilities are specified, then equal priors will be assumed. The effect of an unequal number of cases in each class will be removed.

It is the responsibility of the user to be consistent. If a PRIOR statement appears for at least one class during training set cumulation, then a PRIOR statement should appear for all. Similarly, mixing PRIOR = number and PRIOR = N statements should be avoided.

Learning

Once the necessary parameters have been set, learning can commence. This is done with the following command:

COMPUTE WEIGHTS

In CLASSIFICATION output mode, whatever prior probabilities were in effect during cumulation of the training set (including the equal priors implied by no PRIOR statements) will be taken into account in learning weights. The error criterion that is optimized is computed based on the priors.

There are several parameters related to the learning process that apply to many or to all of the learning methods. Once set, they will remain in effect for all COMPUTE WEIGHTS commands until explicitly reset. These commands, which relate to termination of learning, are now described.

ALLOWABLE ERROR = number can be used to specify a stopping criterion. If the learning progresses to the point that the error becomes this small, it is halted. Usually, we would set this parameter equal to zero, then press ESCape to halt training when patience expires. But setting it to larger, realistic values can be useful when running multiple experiments in a command file.

TOLERANCE = number specifies a very advanced criterion related to the numerical optimization algorithm. It is strongly suggested that this number remain at the default unless the user has carefully studied the source code and is an expert in numerical optimization.

SIGMA LOW = number suggests a minimum value of sigma for the BASIC, SEPVAR, and SEPCLASS models. Initial global scanning for a rough starting point will not try values below this number unless the error criterion is at a minimum here. In that case the search will continue to as low a value as is needed.

SIGMA HIGH = number is similar to SIGMA LOW except that it specifies the maximum value of sigma for the initial search.

SIGMA TRIES = number is the number of sigma values ranging from SIGMA LOW to SIGMA HIGH that will be tried in the initial search. The minimum of three insures that the initial search will be completed as quickly as possible, without wasting time trying unproductive areas. However, using only three points makes it likely that the global minimum will be missed. At least five points should really be tried unless the user is convinced that the SIGMA LOW to SIGMA HIGH range is narrow and correct. If the user is completely in the dark and has specified a wide initial sigma range, ten or more tries would not be unreasonable. Multiple minima in the initial search range are not uncommon.

Confusion Matrices

One standard method for testing a classifier, neural or otherwise, is with the aid of a confusion matrix. This matrix portrays the patterns of misclassification that are obtained from a validation set. There is one row for each class, and as many columns as there are classes, plus one additional column to accommodate the reject category. The element in row a and column b is the number of cases that are truly members of class a but that have been classified into class b. The element in the last column of row a contains the number of cases in class a whose activation did not attain the minimum threshold and so were tossed into the reject category. Ideally, we would want the last column to be entirely zero, and the rest of the matrix should be strictly diagonal. Off-diagonal quantities represent error.

PNN evaluates and displays the confusion matrix one row at a time. It is the user's responsibility to keep track of the true class memberships and to assemble the rows into a matrix. Before computing a row of the confusion matrix, the user should issue the following command to zero the counters in all columns of the row that will be computed:

ZERO CONFUSION ROW

If desired, the user may also set the classification threshold. The command to do this is

ACTIVATION THRESHOLD FOR CONFUSION = number

The number is a percent (0–100) of full activation, with prior probabilities taken into account. When the threshold is set, it will remain at that value unless it is set with this command again. The default may be found in DEFAULTS.CPP, but it is highly recommended that the user explicitly set it. This threshold controls the ease with which cases are banished to the reject category. Larger values will force more marginal cases to land in the reject heap. Using a threshold of zero will let all cases be classified, so that the reject column will be entirely zero.

A single row of the confusion matrix is computed by means of one or more of the following commands:

CLASSIFY WITH INPUT = filename

The named data file has the same format as training files. The user may even want to use the training file to compute a confusion error measure to complement the reported error. Each case in the file is given to the network. The activation level of the maximally activated output neuron is compared to the confusion threshold. If the activation equals or exceeds the threshold, the corresponding element of the confusion row will be incremented. If it is less than the threshold, the reject counter that appears in the last column will be incremented.

The most recently computed row of the confusion matrix can be given to the user in one or both of two ways. The row can be printed on the screen, or it may be appended to the end of an ASCII text file. The named file will be created if it does not exist at the time this command is issued. These two commands are the following:

LIST CONFUSION ROW
WRITE CONFUSION ROW TO FILE = filename

Testing in AUTOASSOCIATION and MAPPING Modes

The previous section discussed a straightforward method for testing when in CLASSIFICATION mode. This section covers the other two modes. The following command reads a data file and computes the mean squared error and RMS error for those cases.

TEST NETWORK WITH INPUT = filename

The format of the named data file is identical to that of training files. It is an ASCII text file having one line per case. If in AUTOASSOCIATION mode, each line contains as many numbers, with optional sign and decimal point, as there are network inputs. If in MAPPING mode, the lines also contain the desired outputs. The outputs follow the inputs, just as in a training file. Each case will be presented to the network, and the resulting outputs will be computed. Those outputs are compared to the target outputs (which are the inputs in AUTO mode), and the mean of the squared error (MSE) is computed. This is the sum of squared errors divided by both the number of cases and the number of output neurons. The square root of this figure is the RMS error. The RMS error is divided by the standard deviation of the target output (with all output variables pooled) to give the relative error. Finally, the R^2 statistic is reported. Great care should be used in interpreting that figure, as it often overestimates the ability of the network by ignoring multiplicative and offset errors!

The primary use for the TEST NETWORK WITH INPUT function is to test a validation set that is independent of the training set. In this way we can evaluate the performance of the network in an unbiased manner.

Saving Weights and Execution Results

We often want to preserve the weights of a trained network, particularly if the training required a long period of time. We may want to perform additional training starting with a weight set that is already good. Or we may simply want to use the network to perform some useful task. The PNN program saves the network in a compact internal format. This format is documented in the module WT_SAVE.CPP that can be found on the accompanying code disk. The weights are saved to and restored from a disk file with the following commands:

SAVE NETWORK = filename
RESTORE NETWORK = filename

The PNN program also provides a simple facility for actually using the trained network to perform tasks. It can read a file containing test cases, compute the activations attained in response to those cases, and write the results to a file. Two steps are required. The first step is to tell PNN the name of the file to which outputs will be written. Outputs will be appended to that file if it exists. If it does not exist, it will be created when the first outputs are about to be written. The file is named with the following command:

RUN OUTPUT = filename

Then, the user issues one or more commands to read input data. The command to do this is:

RUN NETWORK WITH INPUT = filename

In response to that command, all cases in the named file will be processed. This input file contains as many numbers as there are network inputs, one line per case. The generated output file will also contain one line per case, and it will have as many numbers as there are network outputs.

Alphabetical Glossary of Commands

ACTIVATION THRESHOLD FOR CONFUSION = number — This is used in conjunction with computing confusion in CLASSIFICATION mode. It is the minimum percent activation (0–100) that the maximally activated output must attain to avoid that case being tossed into the reject category.

ALLOWABLE ERROR = number — When the error falls this low during learning, stop trying to improve it.

Alphabetical Glossary of Commands

BYE — Quit the PNN program.

CLASS = integer — This sets the class number for subsequent CUMULATE TRAINING SET commands. This command is valid only in CLASSIFICATION mode.

CLASSIFY WITH INPUT = filename — After a network has been trained in CLASSIFICATION mode, this reads an ASCII text file of input data and cumulates a row of the confusion matrix.

COMMAND FILE = filename — This processes an ASCII text file of commands.

COMPUTE WEIGHTS — Train the network.

CUMULATE TRAINING SET = filename — This is the command used to build a training set. It reads an ASCII text file of training data. If a training set already exists, the new data will be appended.

ERASE TRAINING SET — Erase the entire training set. This frees memory, so it should be done when the training set is no longer needed.

ERASE NETWORK — Erase learned weights.

INPUTS = integer — This is the number of inputs.

KERNEL = GAUSS — This, the default, is by far the most common kernel. Unless there is strong reason to use another, choose this one. If NETWORK MODEL = SEPVAR or SEPCLASS, the GAUSS kernel is mandatory.

KERNEL = RECIPROCAL — The kernel function described on page 169 is an alternative that has much heavier tails than the GAUSS kernel. Distant cases in the training set exert relatively more influence in processing a case than they do for the GAUSS kernel. This kernel is valid only for NETWORK MODEL = BASIC. Expect the unexpected if this kernel is used.

LIST CONFUSION ROW — Write the most recently computed confusion row on the computer screen.

MAX MOMENT = integer — Specify the maximum moment used in the GCNN and GCNN_EW models. The minimum value is 3, and the maximum is 8 for the GCNN and 5 for the GCNN_EW.

MODE = AUTOASSOCIATION — Set the mode to AUTOASSOCIATION.

MODE = CLASSIFICATION — Set the mode to CLASSIFICATION.

MODE = MAPPING — Set the mode to general function mapping.

NETWORK MODEL = BASIC — The BASIC probabilistic neural network model is used. This employs one sigma for all variables in all classes.

NETWORK MODEL = GCNN — The traditional Gram-Charlier neural network is used.

NETWORK MODEL = GCNN_EW — Edgeworth's modification of the GCNN is used.

NETWORK MODEL = SEPCLASS — The probabilistic neural network used has a separate sigma for each variable and class. This is valid for CLASSIFICATION mode only.

NETWORK MODEL = SEPVAR — The probabilistic neural network used has a separate sigma for each variable. In CLASSIFICATION mode, all classes share the same sigma vector.

OUTPUTS = integer — This is the number of outputs.

PRIOR = N — This indicates that the user wants to let the number of training cases in each class determine the prior probabilities.

PRIOR = number — This specifies the prior probability that will be assumed for all subsequent classes (until another PRIOR statement occurs).

Alphabetical Glossary of Commands

RESTORE NETWORK = filename — This restores a trained network that was saved to a disk file. It sets the weights and fundamental structure items. Learning parameters are not restored. (In fact, they weren't even saved.)

RUN NETWORK WITH INPUT = filename — This lets the user actually use the network to perform a task. It causes a file of input data to be read, and it writes the network's outputs to the current output file (as set by RUN OUTPUT).

RUN OUTPUT = filename — This names the ASCII text file to which subsequent RUN NETWORK WITH INPUT commands will write results.

SAVE NETWORK = filename — This saves a trained network to a disk file. The parameters that controlled the training of the network are not saved.

SIGMA HIGH = number suggests a maximum value of sigma for the BASIC, SEPVAR, and SEPCLASS models. Initial global scanning for a rough starting point will not try values above this number unless the error criterion is at a minimum here. In that case the search will continue to as high a value as is needed.

SIGMA LOW = number is similar to SIGMA HIGH except that it specifies the minimum value of sigma for the initial search.

SIGMA TRIES = number is the number of sigma values ranging from SIGMA LOW to SIGMA HIGH that will be tried in the initial search. The minimum is three, but values of ten or more are usually reasonable to ensure that the global minimum is located.

TEST NETWORK WITH INPUT = filename — This reads a validation set (or the training set, if desired) and computes several error measures. This command is valid only in AUTO-ASSOCIATION and MAPPING modes.

TOLERANCE = number specifies a very advanced criterion related to the numerical optimization algorithm. It is strongly suggested that this number remain at the default unless the user has carefully studied the source code and is an expert in numerical optimization.

WRITE CONFUSION ROW TO FILE = filename — This appends to an ASCII disk file the most recently computed row of confusion.

ZERO CONFUSION ROW — This zeros all elements in the confusion row.

Verification of Program Operation

This section lists a few test files for exercising PNN. There are two purposes for this presentation. The first purpose is to aid the user in understanding the program by including some examples of realistic command files. A secondary purpose is to serve as a testing tool for readers who recompile the PNN source code for their own system. Although these tests are not utterly exhaustive, they do provide a fairly rigorous test of most aspects of program operation.

All of the command control files use two or three short data files. These files, which are listed below, are designed to be applicable to all three output modes.

TEST1.DAT
1.0 1.2 1.0 0.0
1.1 1.1 1.0 0.0
1.2 1.2 1.0 0.0
1.3 1.2 1.0 0.0

TEST2.DAT
1.5 1.5 0.0 1.0
1.32 1.4 0.0 1.0
1.45 1.2 0.0 1.0
1.23 1.3 0.0 1.0

TEST3.DAT
1.6 1.7 0.0 1.0
1.55 1.5 0.0 1.0
1.65 1.6 0.0 1.0
1.7 1.6 0.0 1.0

Verification of Program Operation

The first command control file, VALID1.CON, tests the BASIC model. It trains, tests, and saves networks in each of the three output modes. Then the networks are restored and retested. The test results should be identical to those obtained before saving. Finally, each network is trained again, picking up where the original training left off. Since the original training was exhaustive, this subsequent training should converge quickly and produce results that are almost identical to those before retraining. The ASCII file VALID1.ASC produced by this test suite enables the user to examine results to verify that they are as expected. VALID1.CON is now listed.

```
; This tests all three output modes of the BASIC model

NETWORK MODEL = BASIC
KERNEL = GAUSS
RUN OUTPUT = valid1.asc

; Start out in MAPPING mode.  Train to the limit and save network.

MODE = MAPPING

INPUTS = 2
OUTPUTS = 2

CUMULATE TRAINING SET = test1.dat
CUMULATE TRAINING SET = test2.dat

ALLOWABLE ERROR = 0.0
SIGMA LOW = 0.003
SIGMA HIGH = 5.0
SIGMA TRIES = 5
COMPUTE WEIGHTS

TEST NETWORK WITH INPUT = test1.dat
TEST NETWORK WITH INPUT = test2.dat
RUN NETWORK WITH INPUT = test1.dat
RUN NETWORK WITH INPUT = test2.dat
SAVE NETWORK = valid1a.wts
ERASE NETWORK
ERASE TRAINING SET
```

; Now switch to AUTOASSOCIATION mode

MODE = AUTOASSOCIATION

INPUTS = 4
OUTPUTS = 4

CUMULATE TRAINING SET = test1.dat
CUMULATE TRAINING SET = test2.dat

COMPUTE WEIGHTS

TEST NETWORK WITH INPUT = test1.dat
TEST NETWORK WITH INPUT = test2.dat
RUN NETWORK WITH INPUT = test1.dat
RUN NETWORK WITH INPUT = test2.dat
SAVE NETWORK = valid1b.wts
ERASE NETWORK
ERASE TRAINING SET

; Finally, go to CLASSIFICATION mode

MODE = CLASSIFICATION

INPUTS = 2
OUTPUTS = 2

CLASS = 1
CUMULATE TRAINING SET = test1.dat

CLASS = 2
CUMULATE TRAINING SET = test2.dat

COMPUTE WEIGHTS

ZERO CONFUSION ROW
CLASSIFY WITH INPUT = test1.dat
LIST CONFUSION ROW
ZERO CONFUSION ROW
CLASSIFY WITH INPUT = test2.dat
LIST CONFUSION ROW

Verification of Program Operation

```
RUN NETWORK WITH INPUT = test1.dat
RUN NETWORK WITH INPUT = test2.dat
SAVE NETWORK = valid1c.wts
ERASE NETWORK
ERASE TRAINING SET

; Networks in all three modes have been trained and saved.
; Read back the MAPPING network.  Test it to verify identical results,
; then train again.  Nothing significant should change, as we already
; trained it to the limit.  Test it to verify that.

RESTORE NETWORK = valid1a.wts

TEST NETWORK WITH INPUT = test1.dat
TEST NETWORK WITH INPUT = test2.dat
RUN NETWORK WITH INPUT = test1.dat
RUN NETWORK WITH INPUT = test2.dat

CUMULATE TRAINING SET = test1.dat
CUMULATE TRAINING SET = test2.dat

COMPUTE WEIGHTS

TEST NETWORK WITH INPUT = test1.dat
TEST NETWORK WITH INPUT = test2.dat
RUN NETWORK WITH INPUT = test1.dat
RUN NETWORK WITH INPUT = test2.dat
ERASE NETWORK
ERASE TRAINING SET

; Now do the same for the AUTOASSOCIATION network

RESTORE NETWORK = valid1b.wts

TEST NETWORK WITH INPUT = test1.dat
TEST NETWORK WITH INPUT = test2.dat
RUN NETWORK WITH INPUT = test1.dat
RUN NETWORK WITH INPUT = test2.dat

CUMULATE TRAINING SET = test1.dat
CUMULATE TRAINING SET = test2.dat
```

COMPUTE WEIGHTS

TEST NETWORK WITH INPUT = test1.dat
TEST NETWORK WITH INPUT = test2.dat
RUN NETWORK WITH INPUT = test1.dat
RUN NETWORK WITH INPUT = test2.dat
ERASE NETWORK
ERASE TRAINING SET

; Finally, do the CLASSIFICATION network

RESTORE NETWORK = valid1c.wts

RUN NETWORK WITH INPUT = test1.dat
RUN NETWORK WITH INPUT = test2.dat

CLASS = 1
CUMULATE TRAINING SET = test1.dat

CLASS = 2
CUMULATE TRAINING SET = test2.dat

COMPUTE WEIGHTS

ZERO CONFUSION ROW
CLASSIFY WITH INPUT = test1.dat
LIST CONFUSION ROW
ZERO CONFUSION ROW
CLASSIFY WITH INPUT = test2.dat
LIST CONFUSION ROW
RUN NETWORK WITH INPUT = test1.dat
RUN NETWORK WITH INPUT = test2.dat
ERASE NETWORK
ERASE TRAINING SET
BYE

The second command control file, VALID2.CON, is not listed here, but it is on the accompanying program disk. This file is identical to VALID1.CON except that it uses the SEPVAR model instead of the BASIC model.

Verification of Program Operation

The third command control file, VALID3.CON, is also similar to the first two files. However, since it tests the SEPCLASS model, only CLASSIFICATION output mode is used. Also, it uses three classes instead of the two classes used previously. This file is now listed.

```
;  This tests the SEPCLASS model

NETWORK MODEL = SEPCLASS
KERNEL = GAUSS
MODE = CLASSIFICATION
RUN OUTPUT = valid3.asc

INPUTS = 2
OUTPUTS = 3

CLASS = 1
CUMULATE TRAINING SET = test1.dat

CLASS = 2
CUMULATE TRAINING SET = test2.dat

CLASS = 3
CUMULATE TRAINING SET = test3.dat

COMPUTE WEIGHTS

ZERO CONFUSION ROW
CLASSIFY WITH INPUT = test1.dat
LIST CONFUSION ROW
ZERO CONFUSION ROW
CLASSIFY WITH INPUT = test2.dat
LIST CONFUSION ROW
ZERO CONFUSION ROW
CLASSIFY WITH INPUT = test3.dat
LIST CONFUSION ROW
RUN NETWORK WITH INPUT = test1.dat
RUN NETWORK WITH INPUT = test2.dat
RUN NETWORK WITH INPUT = test3.dat
SAVE NETWORK = valid3.wts
ERASE NETWORK
ERASE TRAINING SET
```

```
RESTORE NETWORK = valid3.wts

RUN NETWORK WITH INPUT = test1.dat
RUN NETWORK WITH INPUT = test2.dat
RUN NETWORK WITH INPUT = test3.dat

CLASS = 1
CUMULATE TRAINING SET = test1.dat

CLASS = 2
CUMULATE TRAINING SET = test2.dat

CLASS = 3
CUMULATE TRAINING SET = test3.dat

COMPUTE WEIGHTS

ZERO CONFUSION ROW
CLASSIFY WITH INPUT = test1.dat
LIST CONFUSION ROW
ZERO CONFUSION ROW
CLASSIFY WITH INPUT = test2.dat
LIST CONFUSION ROW
ZERO CONFUSION ROW
CLASSIFY WITH INPUT = test3.dat
LIST CONFUSION ROW
RUN NETWORK WITH INPUT = test1.dat
RUN NETWORK WITH INPUT = test2.dat
RUN NETWORK WITH INPUT = test3.dat
ERASE NETWORK
ERASE TRAINING SET
BYE
```

The final command control file, VALID4.CON, tests all versions of the Gram-Charlier neural network. It is listed below. Since it is extremely repetitive in that many values of MAX MOMENT are tried, several middle sections are omitted, and each omitted section is replaced with a vertical ellipsis. Only one network of the GCNN model and one of the GCNN_EW model are saved and restored. There would be no point in testing SAVE and RESTORE for all versions.

Verification of Program Operation

```
; This tests the GCNN and GCNN_EW models

RUN OUTPUT = valid4.asc
NETWORK MODEL = GCNN
MODE = CLASSIFICATION

INPUTS = 2
OUTPUTS = 2

CLASS = 1
CUMULATE TRAINING SET = test1.dat

CLASS = 2
CUMULATE TRAINING SET = test2.dat

MAX MOMENT = 3
COMPUTE WEIGHTS

ZERO CONFUSION ROW
CLASSIFY WITH INPUT = test1.dat
LIST CONFUSION ROW
ZERO CONFUSION ROW
CLASSIFY WITH INPUT = test2.dat
LIST CONFUSION ROW
RUN NETWORK WITH INPUT = test1.dat
RUN NETWORK WITH INPUT = test2.dat
ERASE NETWORK
        •
        •
        •
MAX MOMENT = 6
COMPUTE WEIGHTS

ZERO CONFUSION ROW
CLASSIFY WITH INPUT = test1.dat
LIST CONFUSION ROW
ZERO CONFUSION ROW
CLASSIFY WITH INPUT = test2.dat
LIST CONFUSION ROW
RUN NETWORK WITH INPUT = test1.dat
RUN NETWORK WITH INPUT = test2.dat
```

```
SAVE NETWORK = valid4a.wts
ERASE NETWORK
    •
    •
    •

NETWORK MODEL = GCNN_EW

    •
    •
    •

MAX MOMENT = 4
COMPUTE WEIGHTS

ZERO CONFUSION ROW
CLASSIFY WITH INPUT = test1.dat
LIST CONFUSION ROW
ZERO CONFUSION ROW
CLASSIFY WITH INPUT = test2.dat
LIST CONFUSION ROW
RUN NETWORK WITH INPUT = test1.dat
RUN NETWORK WITH INPUT = test2.dat
SAVE NETWORK = valid4b.wts
ERASE NETWORK
    •
    •
    •

RESTORE NETWORK = valid4a.wts
RUN NETWORK WITH INPUT = test1.dat
RUN NETWORK WITH INPUT = test2.dat
ERASE NETWORK

RESTORE NETWORK = valid4b.wts
RUN NETWORK WITH INPUT = test1.dat
RUN NETWORK WITH INPUT = test2.dat
ERASE NETWORK
BYE
```

Appendix

This appendix contains information concerning the files supplied on the accompanying disk. The most important code listed in the text is included on this disk so that the reader does not need to type it in manually. The disk also contains the complete source code and executable of a probabilistic neural network program as well as an updated version of the MLFN program included with *Signal and Image Processing with Neural Networks*.

Disk Contents

The enclosed diskette contains an installation program that loads fully functioning versions of the PNN and MLFN2 neural network programs along with all source files required to compile them. The C++ source files included in the PNN and MLFN2 directories should be able to be compiled using any ANSI C++ compiler. The author has tested them with Borland C++ 4.02 and Symantec C++ 6.1.

Included in a directory called PNN\VALIDATE are three data files and four sample validation command files that can be used to test the PNN program. Refer to Chapter 10 for information on how to construct a command file and run the validation suite.

The MISC directory contains a variety of programs that are listed in the text but that are not directly related to the PNN and MLFN2 programs. These include subroutines for the Gram-Charlier neural network, data reduction, and validation algorithms. The following is a listing of files included on the disk:

\PNN

PNN.EXE	BRENTMIN.CPP	GCNN.CPP
PNNF.EXE	CONFUSE.CPP	GLOB_MIN.CPP
CLASSES.H	CONTROL.CPP	MEM.CPP.CPP
CONST.H	DEFAULTS.CPP	MESSAGES.CPP
FUNCDEFS.H	DERMIN.CPP	PARSDUBL.CPP
PNN.CPP	DOTPROD.CPP	PNNET.CPP
BASIC.CPP	EXECUTE.CPP	PROCESS.CPP

PROG_WIN.CPP
SEPCLASS.CPP
SEPVAR.CPP

TEST.CPP
TRAIN.CPP
VECLEN.CPP

WT_SAVE.CPP
READ.ME

\MLFN2

MLFN2.EXE
MLFN2F.EXE
CLASSES.H
CONST.H
FUNCDEFS.H
ACTIVITY.CPP
ACT_FUNC.CPP
AN1.CPP
AN2.CPP
ANNEAL1.CPP
ANNEAL2.CPP
ANX_DD.CPP
CONFUSE.CPPC
ONJGRAD.CPP

CONTROL.CPP
DIRECMIN.CPP
DOTPROD.CPP
DOTPRODC.CPP
EXECUTE.CPP
FLRAND.CPP
GRADIENT.CPP
LAYERNET.CPP
LEV_MARQ.CPP
LIMIT.CPP
LM_CORE.CPP
MEM.CPP
MESSAGES.CPP
MLFN2.CPP

PARSDUBL.CPP
PERTURB.CPP
RANDOM.CPP
REGRESS.CPP
REGRS_DD.CPP
SHAKE.CPP
SSG.CPP
SVDCMP.CPP
TEST.CPP
TRAIN.CPP
VECLEN.CPP
WT_SAVE.CPP
READ.ME

\PNN\VALIDATE

TEST1.DAT
TEST2.DAT
TEST3.DAT
VALID1.CON
VALID2.CON
VALID3.CON
VALID4.CON

\MISC

EIGEN.CPP
ERROR.CPP
GCNN.CPP
JACKBOOT.CPP

Appendix

Hardware and Software Requirements

The PNN and MLFN2 programs included on disk can be run on any standard IBM-compatible computer having an 80386 or higher processor. A math coprocessor is strongly recommended, but it is not mandatory. An ANSI C++ compiler is required if the user wishes to recompile the program.

Making a Backup Copy

Before using the enclosed diskette, make a backup copy of the original. This backup is for personal use and will only be required in case of damage to the original. Any other use of the diskette violates copyright law. Assuming the floppy drive you will be using is drive A, please do the following:

1. Insert the original diskette included with the book in drive A.

2. At the A:> prompt, type DISKCOPY A: A: and press Return. You will be prompted to place the source diskette into drive A.

3. Press return and wait until you are prompted to place the target diskette in drive A.

4. Remove the original diskette and replace it with your blank backup diskette. Press return.

Continue to alternately insert the original (source) and backup (target) diskettes as prompted until the message COPY COMPLETE appears.

Installing the Disk

The installation program included on the diskette contains 82 files in compressed format. The default installation settings will create a directory called MASTERS and the three subdirectories PNN, MLFN2, and MISC. To install the files, please do the following:

1. Assuming you will be using drive A as the floppy drive for your diskette, at the A:> prompt type INSTALL.

2. Follow the instructions displayed by the installation program. At the end of the process you will be given the opportunity to review the READ.ME file for more information about the diskette.

Bibliography

Aarts, E., and van Laarhoven, P. (1987). *Simulated Annealing: Theory and Practice*. John Wiley & Sons, New York.

Abe, S., Kayama, M., Takenaga, H., and Kitamura, T. (1992). "Neural Networks as a Tool to Generate Pattern Classification Algorithms." *International Joint Conference on Neural Networks*, Baltimore, MD.

Acton, Forman S. (1959). *Analysis of Straight-Line Data*. Dover Publications, New York.

Acton, Forman S. (1970). *Numerical Methods That Work*. Harper & Row, New York.

Anderson, James, and Rosenfeld, Edward, eds. (1988). *Neurocomputing: Foundations of Research*. MIT Press, Cambridge, MA.

Anderson, T. W. (1958). *An Introduction to Multivariate Statistical Analysis*. John Wiley & Sons, New York.

Austin, Scott (1990). "Genetic Solutions to XOR Problems." *AI Expert* (December), 52–57.

Avitzur, Ron (1992). "Your Own Handprinting Recognition Engine." *Dr. Dobb's Journal* (April), 32–37.

Azencott, R., ed. (1992). *Simulated Annealing: Parallelization Techniques*. John Wiley & Sons, New York.

Baba, Norio (1989). "A New Approach for Finding the Global Minimum of Error Function of Neural Networks." *Neural Networks*, **2**(5): 367–373.

Baba, N., and Kozaki, M. (1992). "An Intelligent Forecasting System of Stock Price Using Neural Networks." *International Joint Conference on Neural Networks*, Baltimore, MD.

Barmann, Frank, and Biegler-Konig, Friedrich (1992). "On a Class of Efficient Learning Algorithms for Neural Networks." *Neural Networks*, **5**: 139–144.

Barnard, Etienne, and Casasent, David (1990). "Shift Invariance and the Neocognitron." *Neural Networks*, **3**: 403–410.

Barr, Avron, Cohen, Paul R., and Feigenbaum, Edward A., eds. (vol. I, 1981; vol. II, 1982; vol. III, 1982; vol. IV, 1989). *The Handbook of Artificial Intelligence*. Addison-Wesley, Reading, MA.

Bartlett, E. B. (1991). "Chaotic Time-series Prediction Using Artificial Neural Networks." *Abstracts from 2nd Government Neural Network Applications Workshop* (September), Session III.

Barton, D. E., and Dennis, K. E. (1952). "The Conditions Under Which Gram-Charlier and Edgeworth Curves Are Positive Definite and Unimodal." *Biometrika*, **39**: 425.

Battiti, R., and Colla, M. (1994). "Democracy in Neural Nets: Voting Schemes for Classification." *Neural Networks*, **7**: 691–707.

Birx, D., and Pipenberg, S. (1992). "Chaotic Oscillators and Complex-Mapping Feedforward Networks for Signal Detection in Noisy Environments." *International Joint Conference on Neural Networks*, Baltimore, MD.

Birx, D., and Pipenberg, S. (1993). "A Complex Mapping Network for Phase-Sensitive Classification." *IEEE Transactions on Neural Networks*, **4**(1): 127-135.

Blum, A. L., and Rivest, R. L. (1992). "Training a 3-Node Neural Network Is NP-Complete." *Neural Networks*, **5**(1): 117–127.

Blum, Edward, and Li, Leong (1991). "Approximation Theory and Feedforward Networks." *Neural Networks*, **4**: 511–515.

Booker, L. B., Goldberg, D. E., and Holland, J. H. (1989). "Classifier Systems and Genetic Algorithms." *Artificial Intelligence*, **40**: 235–282.

Box, George, and Jenkins, Gwilym (1976). *Time-series Analysis, Forecasting and Control.* Prentice Hall, Englewood Cliffs, NJ.

Bracewell, Ronald N. (1986). *The Fourier Transform and Its Applications.* McGraw-Hill, New York.

Brent, Richard (1973). *Algorithms for Minimization without Derivatives.* Prentice-Hall, Englewood Cliffs, NJ.

Brillinger, David R. (1975). *Time Series, Data Analysis and Theory.* Holt, Rinehart and Winston, New York.

Burgin, George (1992). "Using Cerebellar Arithmetic Computers." *AI Expert* (June), 32–41.

Cacoullos, T. (1966). "Estimation of a Multivariate Density." *Annals of the Institute of Statistical Mathematics* (Tokyo), **18**(2): 179–189.

Cardaliaguet, Pierre, and Euvrard, Guillaume (1992). "Approximation of a Function and its Derivative with a Neural Network." *Neural Networks*, **5**(2): 207–220.

Carpenter, Gail A., and Grossberg, Stephen (1987). "A Massively Parallel Architecture for a Self-Organizing Neural Pattern Recognition Machine." Academic Press *(Computer Vision, Graphics, and Image Processing)*, **37**: 54–115.

Carpenter, Gail A., Grossberg, Stephen, and Reynolds, John H. (1991). "ARTMAP: Supervised Real-Time Learning and Classification of Nonstationary Data by a Self-Organizing Neural Network." *Neural Networks*, **4**: 565–588.

Caruana, R. A., and Schaffer, J. D. (1988). "Representation and Hidden Bias: Gray vs. Binary Coding for Genetic Algorithms," in Laird, J. (ed.), *Proceedings of the Fifth International Congress on Machine Learning*. Morgan Kaufmann, San Mateo, CA.

Caudill, Maureen (1988). "Neural Networks Primer, Part IV—The Kohonen Model." *AI Expert* (August).

Caudill, Maureen (1990). "Using Neural Nets: Fuzzy Decisions." *AI Expert* (April), 59–64.

Chambers, J. M. (1967). "An Extension of the Edgeworth Expansion to the Multivariate Case." *Biometrika*, **54**: 367–383.

Chin, Daniel (1994). "A More Efficient Global Optimization Algorithm Based on Styblinski and Tang." *Neural Networks*, **7**: 573.

Chui, C. (1992). *An Introduction to Wavelets*. Academic Press, New York.

Cooley, William, and Lohnes, Paul (1971). *Multivariate Data Analysis*. John Wiley & Sons, New York.

Cotter, Neil E., and Guillerm, Thierry J. (1992). "The CMAC and a Theorem of Kolmogorov." *Neural Networks*, **5**: 221–228.

Cottrell, G., Munro, P., and Zipser, D. (1987). "Image Compression by Backpropagation: An Example of Extensional Programming." *ICS Report 8702*, University of California at San Diego.

Cox, Earl (1992). "Solving Problems with Fuzzy Logic." *AI Expert* (March), 28–37.

Cox, Earl (1992). "Integrating Fuzzy Logic into Neural Nets." *AI Expert* (June), 43–47.

Cramer, Harald (1926). "On Some Classes of Series Used in Mathematical Statistics." *Skandinaviske Mathematikercongres*, Copenhagen.

Cramer, Harald (1946). *Mathematical Methods of Statistics*. Princeton University Press, Princeton, NJ.

Crooks, Ted (1992). "Care and Feeding of Neural Networks." *AI Expert* (July), 36–41.

Daubechies, Ingrid (1990). "The Wavelet Transform, Time-Frequency Localization, and Signal Analysis." *IEEE Transactions on Information Theory*, **36**(5): 961–1005.

Davis, D. T., and Hwang, J. N. (1992). "Attentional Focus Training by Boundary Region Data Selection." *International Joint Conference on Neural Networks*, Baltimore, MD.

Davis, Lawrence (1991). *Handbook of Genetic Algorithms*. Van Nostrand Reinhold, New York.

Devroye, L. (1986). *Non-Uniform Random Number Generation*. Springer-Verlag, New York.

Dracopoulos, D., and Jones, A. (1993). "Modeling Dynamic Systems." *World Congress on Neural Networks*, Portland, OR.

Draper, N. R., and Smith, H. (1966). *Applied Regression Analysis*. John Wiley & Sons, New York.

Duffin, R. J., and Schaeffer, A. C. (1952). "A Class of Nonharmonic Fourier Series." *Transactions of the American Mathematical Society*, **72**: 341-366.

Eberhart, Russell C., and Dobbins, Roy W., eds. (1990). *Neural Network PC Tools, A Practical Guide*. Academic Press, San Diego, CA.

Efron, Bradley (1982). *The Jackknife, the Bootstrap, and Other Resampling Plans*. Society for Industrial and Applied Mathematics, Philadelphia, PA.

Fahlmann, Scott E. (1988). "An Empirical Study of Learning Speed in Backpropagation Networks." *CMU Technical Report CMU-CS–88–162* (June 1988).

Fakhr, W., Kamel, M., and Elmasry, M. I. (1992). "Probability of Error, Maximum Mutual Information, and Size Minimization of Neural Networks." *International Joint Conference on Neural Networks*, Baltimore, MD.

Finkbeiner, Daniel T., II (1972). *Elements of Linear Algebra*. W. H. Freeman, San Francisco, CA.

Foley, James D., van Dam, Andries, Feiner, Steven K., and Hughes, John F. (1990). *Computer Graphics: Principles and Practice (Second Edition)*. Addison-Wesley, Reading, MA.

Forsythe, George E., Malcolm, Michael A., and Moler, Cleve B. (1977). *Computer Methods for Mathematical Computations*. Prentice-Hall, Englewood Cliffs, NJ.

Freeman, James A., and Skapura, David M. (1992). *Neural Networks: Algorithms, Applications, and Programming Techniques*. Addison-Wesley, Reading, MA.

Fu, K. S., ed. (1971). *Pattern Recognition and Machine Learning*. Plenum Press, New York.

Fukunaga, Keinosuke (1972). *Introduction to Statistical Pattern Recognition*. Academic Press, Orlando, FL.

Fukunaga, Keinosuke. (1987). "Bayes Error Estimation Using Parzen and k-NN Procedures." *IEEE Transactions on Pattern Analysis and Machine Intelligence*, **9**: 634–643.

Fukushima, Kunihiko (1987). "Neural Network Model for Selective Attention in Visual Pattern Recognition and Associative Recall." *Applied Optics* (December), **26**: 23.

Fukushima, Kunihiko (1989). "Analysis of the Process of Visual Pattern Recognition by the Neocognitron." *Neural Networks*, **2**: 413–420.

Gallant, Ronald, and White, Halbert (1992). "On Learning the Derivatives of an Unknown Mapping with Multilayer Feedforward Networks." *Neural Networks*, **2**: 129–138.

Gallinari, P., Thiria, S., Badran, F., and Fogelman-Soulie, F. (1991). "On the Relations between Discriminant Analysis and Multilayer Perceptrons." *Neural Networks*, **4**(3): 349–360.

Garson, David G. (1991). "Interpreting Neural-Network Connection Weights." *AI Expert* (April), 47–51.

Georgiou, G. (1993). "The Multivalued and Continuous Perceptrons." *World Congress on Neural Networks*, Portland, OR.

Gill, Philip E., Murray, Walter, and Wright, Margaret H. (1981). *Practical Optimization*. Academic Press, San Diego, CA.

Glassner, Andrew S., ed. (1990). *Graphics Gems*. Academic Press, San Diego, CA.

Goldberg, David E. (1989). *Genetic Algorithms in Search, Optimization and Machine Learning*. Addison-Wesley, Reading, MA.

Golub, Gene, and Van Loan, Charles (1989). *Matrix Computations*. Johns Hopkins University Press. Baltimore, MD.

Gori, M., and Tesi, A. (1990). "Some Examples of Local Minima during Learning with Back-Propagation." *Third Italian Workshop on Parallel Architectures and Neural Networks (E. R. Caianiello, ed.)*. World Scientific Publishing.

Gorlen, Keith E., Orlow, Sanford M., and Plexico, Perry S. (1990). *Data Abstraction and Object-Oriented Programming in C++*. John Wiley & Sons, Chichester, England.

Grossberg, Stephen (1988). *Neural Networks and Natural Intelligence.* MIT Press, Cambridge, MA.

Guiver, John P., and Klimasauskas, Casimir, C. (1991). "Applying Neural Networks, Part IV: Improving Performance." *PC AI* (July/August).

Hald, A. (1952). *Statistical Theory with Engineering Applications.* John Wiley & Sons, New York.

Hansen, L., and Salamon, P. (1990). "Neural Network Ensembles." *IEEE Transactions on Pattern Analysis and Machine Intelligence,* **12**: 993–1000.

Haralick, R. M. (1979). "Statistical and Structural Approaches to Texture." *Proceedings of the IEEE,* **67**: 786-804.

Harrington, Steven (1987). *Computer Graphics, A Programming Approach* (Second Edition). McGraw-Hill, New York.

Hashem, M. (1992). "Sensitivity Analysis for Feedforward Neural Networks with Differentiable Activation Functions." *International Joint Conference on Neural Networks,* Baltimore, MD.

Hastings, Cecil, Jr. (1955). *Approximations for Digital Computers.* Princeton University Press, Princeton, NJ.

Hecht-Nielsen, Robert (1987). "Nearest Matched Filter Classification of Spatiotemporal Patterns." *Applied Optics* (May 15), **26**(10).

Hecht-Nielsen, Robert (1991). *Neurocomputing.* Addison-Wesley, Reading, MA.

Hecht-Nielsen, Robert (1992). "Theory of the Backpropagation Network." *Neural Networks for Perception, vol. 2 (Harry Wechsler, ed.),* Academic Press, New York.

Hirose, A. (1992). "Proposal of Fully Complex-Valued Neural Networks." *International Joint Conference on Neural Networks,* Baltimore, MD.

Hirose, A. (1993). "Simultaneous Learning of Multiple Oscillations of Recurrent Complex-Valued Neural Networks." *World Congress on Neural Networks*, Portland, OR.

Hirose, Yoshio, Yamashita, Koichi, and Hijiya, Shimpei (1991). "Back-Propagation Algorithm Which Varies the Number of Hidden Units." *Neural Networks*, **4**(1): 61–66.

Ho, T. K., Hull, J. J., and Srihari, S. N. (1994). "Decision Combination in Multiple Classifier Systems." *IEEE Transactions on Pattern Analysis and Machine Intelligence*, **16**: 66–75.

Hornik, Kurt, Stinchcombe, Maxwell, and White, Halbert (1989). "Multilayer Feedforward Networks are Universal Approximators." *Neural Networks*, **2**(5): 359–366.

Hornik, Kurt (1991). "Approximation Capabilities of Multilayer Feedforward Networks." *Neural Networks*, **4**(2): 251–257.

Howell, Jim (1990). "Inside a Neural Network." *AI Expert* (November), 29–33.

Hu, M. K. (1962). "Visual Pattern Recognition By Moment Invariants." *IRE Transactions on Information Theory*, **8**(2):179–187.

IEEE Digital Signal Processing Committee, eds. (1979). *Programs for Digital Signal Processing*. IEEE Press, New York.

Ito, Y. (1991a). "Representation of Functions by Superpositions of a Step or Sigmoid Function and Their Applications to Neural Network Theory." *Neural Networks*, **4**(3): 385–394.

Ito, Y. (1991b). "Approximation of Functions on a Compact Set by Finite Sums of a Sigmoid Function without Scaling." *Neural Networks*, **4**(6): 817–826.

Ito, Y. (1992). "Approximation of Continuous Functions on $\mathbf{R}^d$ by Linear Combinations of Shifted Rotations of a Sigmoid Function with and without Scaling." *Neural Networks*, **5**(1): 105–115.

Jain, A. K., Dubes, R. C., and Chen, C. C. (1987). "Bootstrap Techniques for Error Estimation." *IEEE Transactions on Pattern Analysis and Machine Intelligence*, **9**: 628–633.

Kalman, B. L., and Kwasny, S. C. (1991). "A Superior Error Function for Training Neural Networks." *International Joint Conference on Neural Networks*, Seattle, WA.

Kalman, B. L., and Kwasny, S. C. (1992). "Why Tanh? Choosing a Sigmoidal Function." *International Joint Conference on Neural Networks*, Baltimore, MD.

Karr, Chuck (1991). "Genetic Algorithms for Fuzzy Controllers." *AI Expert* (February), 26–33.

Karr, Chuck (1991). "Applying Genetics to Fuzzy Logic." *AI Expert* (March), 39–43.

Kendall, M., and Stuart, A. (vol. I, 1969; vol. II, 1973; vol. III, 1976). *The Advanced Theory of Statistics*. Hafner, New York.

Kenue, S. K. (1991). "Efficient Activation Functions for the Back-Propagation Neural Network." *SPIE, Proceedings from Intelligent Robots and Computer Vision X: Neural, Biological, and 3-D Methods* (November).

Kim, M. W., and Arozullah, M. (1992a). "Generalized Probabilistic Neural Network-Based Classifiers." *International Joint Conference on Neural Networks*, Baltimore, MD.

Kim, M. W., and Arozullah, M. (1992b). "Neural Network Based Optimum Radar Target Detection in Non-Gaussian Noise." *International Joint Conference on Neural Networks*, Baltimore, MD.

Kim, M. W. (1993). "Handwritten Digit Recognition Using Gram-Charlier and Generalized Probabilistic Neural Networks." *World Conference on Neural Networks*, Portland, OR.

Klimasauskas, Casimir C. (1987). *The 1987 Annotated Neuro-Computing Bibliography*. NeuroConnection, Sewickley, PA.

Klimasauskas, Casimir C. (1992a). "Making Fuzzy Logic 'Clear.'" *Advanced Technology for Developers*, 1 (May), 8–12.

Klimasauskas, Casimir C. (1992b). "Hybrid Technologies: More Power for the Future." *Advanced Technology for Developers*, 1 (August), 17–20.

Klir, George J., and Folger, Tina A. (1988). *Fuzzy Sets, Uncertainty, and Information*. Prentice Hall, Englewood Cliffs, NJ.

Knuth, Donald (1981). *Seminumerical Algorithms*. Addison-Wesley, Reading, MA.

Kohonen, Teuvo (1982). "Self-Organized Formation of Topologically Correct Feature Maps." *Biological Cybernetics*, **43**: 59–69.

Kohonen, Teuvo (1989). *Self-organization and Associative Memory*. Springer-Verlag, New York.

Kosko, Bart (1987). "Fuzziness vs. Probability." *Air Force Office of Scientific Research (AFOSR F49620-86-C-0070) and Advanced Research Projects Agency (ARPA Order No. 5794)*, (July).

Kosko, Bart (1988a). "Bidirectional Associative Memories." *IEEE Transactions on Systems, Man, and Cybernetics* (Jan./Feb.), **18**:1.

Kosko, Bart (1988b). "Hidden Patterns in Combined and Adaptive Knowledge Networks." *International Journal of Approximate Reasoning*, vol. 1.

Kosko, Bart (1992). *Neural Networks and Fuzzy Systems*. Prentice Hall, Englewood Cliffs, NJ.

Kotz, Samuel, and Johnson, Norman, eds. (1982). *Encyclopedia of Statistical Sciences*. John Wiley & Sons, New York.

Kreinovich, Vladik Ya. (1991). "Arbitrary Nonlinearity Is Sufficient to Represent All Functions by Neural Networks: A Theorem." *Neural Networks*, **4**(3): 381–383.

Kuhl, Frank, Reeves, Anthony, and Taylor, Russell (1986). "Shape Identification with Moments and Fourier Descriptors." *Proceedings of the 1986 ACSM-ASPRS Convention* (March), 159–168.

Kurkova, Vera (1992). "Kolmogorov's Theorem and Multilayer Neural Networks." *Neural Networks*, **5**(3): 501–506.

Lawton, George (1992). "Genetic Algorithms for Schedule Optimization." *AI Expert* (May), 23–27.

Levin, A. (1993). "Predicting with Feedforward Networks." *World Congress on Neural Networks*, Portland, OR.

Lim, Jae S. (1990). *Two-Dimensional Signal and Image Processing*. Prentice Hall, Englewood Cliffs, NJ.

Lo, Zhen-Ping, Yu, Yaoqi, and Bavarian, Behnam (1993). "Analysis of the Convergence Properties of Topology-Preserving Neural Networks." *IEEE Transactions on Neural Networks*, **4**(2): 207–220.

Lu, C. N., Wu, H. T., and Vemuri, S. (1992). "Neural Network Based Short-Term Load Forecasting." *IEEE/PES 1992 Winter Meeting, New York* (92 WM 125-5 PWRS).

Maren, Alianna, Harston, Craig, and Pap, Robert (1990). *Handbook of Neural Computing Applications*. Academic Press, New York.

Masters, Timothy (1993). *Practical Neural Network Recipes in C++*. Academic Press, New York.

Masters, Timothy (1994). *Signal and Image Processing with Neural Networks*. John Wiley & Sons, New York.

Matsuba, I., Masui, H., and Hebishima, S. (1992). "Optimizing Multilayer Neural Networks Using Fractal Dimensions of Time-Series Data." *International Joint Conference on Neural Networks*, Baltimore, MD.

McClelland, James, and Rumelhart, David (1988). *Explorations in Parallel Distributed Processing*. MIT Press, Cambridge, MA.

Meisel, W. (1972). *Computer-Oriented Approaches to Pattern Recognition*. Academic Press, New York.

Miller, J., Goodman, R., and Smyth, P. (1991). "Objective Functions for Probability Estimation." *International Joint Conference on Neural Networks*, Seattle, WA.

Minsky, Marvin, and Papert, Seymour (1969). *Perceptrons*. MIT Press, Cambridge, MA.

Mougeot, M., Azencott, R., and Angeniol, B. (1991). "Image Compression with Back Propagation: Improvement of the Visual Restoration Using Different Cost Functions." *Neural Networks*, **4**(4): 467–476.

Mucciardi, A., and Gose, E. (1970). "An Algorithm for Automatic Clustering in N-Dimensional Spaces Using Hyperellipsoidal Cells." *IEEE Sys. Sci. Cybernetics Conference*, Pittsburgh, PA.

Musavi, M., Kalantri, K., and Ahmed, W. (1992). "Improving the Performance of Probabilistic Neural Networks." *International Joint Conference on Neural Networks*, Baltimore, MD.

Musavi, M., Kalantri, K., Ahmed, W., and Chan, K. (1993). "A Minimum Error Neural Network (MNN)." *Neural Networks*, **6**: 397–407.

Negoita, Constantin V., and Ralescu, Dan (1987). *Simulation, Knowledge-Based Computing, and Fuzzy Statistics*. Van Nostrand Reinhold, New York.

Nitta, T. (1993). "Three-Dimensional Backpropagation." *World Congress on Neural Networks*, Portland, OR.

Nitta, T. (1993). "A Complex-Numbered Version of the Back-propagation Algorithm." *World Congress on Neural Networks*, Portland, OR.

Pao, Yoh-Han (1989). *Adaptive Pattern Recognition and Neural Networks*. Addison-Wesley, Reading, MA.

Parzen, E. (1962). "On Estimation of a Probability Density Function and Mode." *Annals of Mathematical Statistics*, **33**: 1065–1076.

Pethel, S. D., Bowden, C. M., and Sung, C. C. (1991). "Applications of Neural Net Algorithms to Nonlinear Time Series." *Abstracts from 2nd Government Neural Network Applications Workshop* (September), Session III.

Polak, E. (1971). *Computational Methods in Optimization*. Academic Press, New York.

Polzleitner, Wolfgang, and Wechsler, Harry (1990). "Selective and Focused Invariant Recognition Using Distributed Associative Memories (DAM)." *IEEE Transactions on Pattern Analysis and Machine Intelligence* (August), **12**(8).

Pratt, William K. (1991). *Digital Image Processing*. John Wiley & Sons, New York.

Press, William H., Flannery, B., Teukolsky, S., and Vetterling, W. (1992). *Numerical Recipes in C*. Cambridge University Press, New York.

Raudys, Sarunas J., and Jain, Anil K. (1991). "Small Sample Size Effects in Statistical Pattern Recognition: Recommendations for Practitioners." *IEEE Transactions on Pattern Analysis and Machine Intelligence* (March), **13**(3).

Reed, R., Oh, S., and Marks, R. J. (1992). "Regularization Using Jittered Training Data." *International Joint Conference on Neural Networks*, Baltimore, MD.

Reeves, A., Prokop, R., Andrews, S., and Kuhl, F. (1988). "Three-Dimensional Shape Analysis Using Moments and Fourier Descriptors." *IEEE Transactions on Pattern Analysis and Machine Intelligence* (November), **10**: 937–943.

Rich, Elaine (1983). *Artificial Intelligence*. McGraw-Hill, New York.

Rosenblatt, Frank (1958). "The Perceptron: A Probabilistic Model for Information Storage and Organization in the Brain." *Psychological Review*, **65**: 386–408.

Rosenfeld, A., and Kak, A. (1982). *Digital Picture Processing*. Academic Press, New York.

Rumelhart, David, McClelland, James, and the PDP Research Group (1986). *Parallel Distributed Processing*. MIT Press, Cambridge, MA.

Sabourin, M., and Mitiche, A. (1992). "Optical Character Recognition by a Neural Network." *Neural Networks*, **5**: 843–852.

Samad, Tariq (1988). "Backpropagation Is Significantly Faster if the Expected Value of the Source Unit Is Used for Update." *1988 Conference of the International Neural Network Society*.

Samad, Tariq (1991). "Back Propagation with Expected Source Values." *Neural Networks*, **4**(5): 615–618.

Schioler, H., and Hartmann, U. (1992). "Mapping Neural Network Derived from the Parzen Window Estimator." *Neural Networks*, **5**(6): 903–909.

Schwartz, Tom J. (1991). "Fuzzy Tools for Expert Systems." *AI Expert* (February), 34–41.

Sedgewick, Robert (1988). *Algorithms*. Addison-Wesley, Reading, MA.

Shapiro, Stuart C., ed. (1990). *Encyclopedia of Artificial Intelligence*. John Wiley & Sons, New York.

Siegel, Sidney (1956). *Nonparametric Statistics for the Behavioral Sciences*. McGraw-Hill, New York.

Soulie, Francoise Fogelman, Robert, Yves, and Tchuente, Maurice, eds. (1987). *Automata Networks in Computer Science*. Princeton University Press, Princeton, NJ.

Specht, Donald (1967). "Generation of Polynomial Discriminant Functions for Pattern Recognition." *IEEE Transactions on Electronic Computers*, **3**: 308–319.

Specht, Donald (1988). "Probabilistic Neural Networks for Classification, Mapping, or Associative Memory." *IEEE International Conference on Neural Networks*, San Diego, CA.

Specht, Donald (1990a). "Probabilistic Neural Networks." *Neural Networks*, **3**: 109–118.

Specht, Donald (1990b). "Probabilistic Neural Networks and the Polynomial Adeline as Complementary Techniques for Classification." *IEEE Transactions on Neural Networks*, **1**(1): 111–121.

Specht, Donald (1991). "A General Regression Neural Network." *IEEE Transactions on Neural Networks*, **2**(6): 568–576.

Specht, Donald (1992). "Enhancements to Probabilistic Neural Networks." *International Joint Conference on Neural Networks*, Baltimore, MD.

Specht, Donald F., and Shapiro, Philip D. (1991). "Generalization Accuracy of Probabilistic Neural Networks Compared with Back-Propagation Networks." *Lockheed Missiles & Space Co., Inc. Independent Research Project RDD 360*, I-887-I-892.

Spillman, Richard (1990). "Managing Uncertainty with Belief Functions." *AI Expert* (May), 44–49.

Stork, David G. (1989). "Self-Organization, Pattern Recognition, and Adaptive Resonance Networks." *Journal of Neural Network Computing* (Summer).

Strand, E. M., and Jones, W. T. (1992). "An Adaptive Pattern Set Strategy for Enhancing Generalization While Improving Backpropagation Training Efficiency." *International Joint Conference on Neural Networks*, Baltimore, MD.

Styblinski, M. A., and Tang, T.-S. (1990). "Experiments in Nonconvex Optimization: Stochastic Approximation with Function Smoothing and Simulated Annealing." *Neural Networks*, **3**: 467–483.

Sudharsanan, Subramania I., and Sundareshan, Malur K. (1991). "Exponential Stability and a Systematic Synthesis of a Neural Network for Quadratic Minimization." *Neural Networks*, **4**: 599–613.

Sultan, A. F., Swift, G. W., and Fedirchuk, D. J. (1992). "Detection of High Impedance Arcing Faults Using a Multi-Layer Perceptron." *IEEE/PES 1992 Winter Meeting, New York* (92 WM 207-1 PWRD).

Sussmann, Hector J. (1992). "Uniqueness of the Weights for Minimal Feedforward Nets with a Given Input-Output Map." *Neural Networks*, **5**(4): 589–593.

Szu, Harold (1986). "Fast Simulated Annealing." *AIP Conference Proceedings 151: Neural Networks for Computing*, Snowbird, UT.

Szu, Harold (1987). "Nonconvex Optimization by Fast Simulated Annealing." *Proceedings of the IEEE*, **75**(11): 1538–1540.

Tanimoto, Steven L. (1987). *The Elements of Artificial Intelligence.* Computer Science Press, Rockville, MD.

Taylor, Russell, Reeves, Anthony, and Kuhl, Frank (1992). "Methods for Identifying Object Class, Type, and Orientation, in the Presence of Uncertainty." *Remote Sensing Reviews*, **6**(1): 183–206.

Ulmer, Richard, Jr., and Gorman, John (1989). "Partial Shape Recognition Using Simulated Annealing." *IEEE Proceedings, 1989 Southeastcon.*

Unnikrishnan, K. P., and Venugopal, K. P. (1992). "Learning in Connectionist Networks Using the Alopex Algorithm." *International Joint Conference on Neural Networks*, Baltimore, MD.

van Ooyen, A., and Nienhuis, B. (1992). "Improving the Convergence of the Back-Propagation Algorithm." *Neural Networks*, **5**(3): 465–471.

von Mises, Richard (1964). *Mathematical Theory of Probability and Statistics*. Academic Press, New York.

Wallace, Timothy P., and Wintz, Paul A. (1980). "An Efficient Three-Dimensional Aircraft Recognition Algorithm Using Normalized Fourier Descriptors." *Computer Graphics and Image Processing*, **13**: 99-126.

Wang, Kaitsong, Gorman, John, and Kuhl, Frank (1992). "Spherical Harmonics and Moments for Recognition of Three-Dimensional Objects." *Remote Sensing Reviews*, **6**(1): 229–250.

Wayner, Peter (1991). "Genetic Algorithms." *BYTE* (January), 361–368.

Webb, Andrew R., and Lowe, David (1990). "The Optimized Internal Representation of Multilayer Classifier Networks Performs Nonlinear Discriminant Analysis." *Neural Networks*, **3**(4): 367–375.

Wenskay, Donald (1990). "Intellectual Property Protection for Neural Networks." *Neural Networks*, **3**(2): 229–236.

Weymaere, Nico and Martens, Jean-Pierre (1991). "A Fast and Robust Learning Algorithm for Feedforward Neural Networks." *Neural Networks*, **4**(3): 361–369.

White, Halbert (1989). "Neural-Network Learning and Statistics." *AI Expert* (December), 48–52.

Wiggins, Ralphe (1992). "Docking a Truck: A Genetic Fuzzy Approach." *AI Expert* (May), 29–35.

Wirth, Niklaus (1976). *Algorithms + Data Structures = Programs*. Prentice-Hall, Englewood Cliffs, NJ.

Wolpert, David H. (1992). "Stacked Generalization." *Neural Networks*, **5**: 241–259.

Yau, Hung-Chun, and Manry, Michael T. (1991). "Iterative Improvement of a Nearest Neighbor Classifier." *Neural Networks*, **4**: 517–524.

Zadeh, Lotfi A. (1992). "The Calculus of Fuzzy If/Then Rules." *AI Expert* (March), 23–27.

Zeidenberg, Matthew (1990). *Neural Network Models in Artificial Intelligence*. Ellis Horwood, New York.

Zhang, Y., Chen, G. P., Malik, O. P., and Hope, G. S. (1992). "An Artificial Neural Network-Based Adaptive Power System Stabilizer." *IEEE/PES 1992 Winter Meeting, New York* (92 WM 018-2 EC).

Zhou, Yi-Tong, and Chellappa (1992). *Artificial Neural Networks for Computer Vision*. Springer-Verlag, New York.

Zornetzer, Steven, Davis, Joel, and Lau, Clifford, eds. (1990). *An Introduction to Neural and Electronic Networks*. Academic Press, New York.

Index

A

acceptance:
    criterion, 88
    rate, 89
ACTIVATION THRESHOLD (PNN), 388
ALLOWABLE ERROR (PNN), 386
alternation, 136
among-class variance, 317
anneal1 (subroutine), 79
anneal2 (subroutine), 96
anx_cj (subroutine), 137
apparent error, 360, 361
AUTOASSOCIATION (PNN), 381, 389

B

backpropagation, 2
BASIC (PNN), 382
Bayes classification, 162
Bayesian confidence, 192
between-class variance, 317
bias of an estimator, 337, 353
binary data, 176, 191
boot (subroutine), 371
bootstrap, 343, 351, 369
Box-Muller algorithm, 126
brentmin (subroutine), 19
BYE (PNN), 380

C

cauchy (subroutine), 132
Cauchy distribution, 102
central moment, 264
centroid, 316
cheby (subroutine), 233
Chebyshev polynomial, 231
class:
    Discrim, 323
    EWnet, 279
    GCnet, 267
    PrincoData, 303
CLASS (PNN), 385
classification, 158
CLASSIFICATION (PNN), 381
CLASSIFY WITH INPUT (PNN), 388
clustering, 191
COMMAND FILE (PNN), 380
comment, 380
COMPUTE WEIGHTS (PNN), 386
confusion matrix (PNN), 387
conjugate gradient method, 31
correlation matrix, 302
cost of misclassification, 162
cross validation, 182, 365
cumulant, 276
CUMULATE TRAINING (PNN), 385
cv (subroutine), 367

D

delta function, 198
density (subroutine), 269
density estimation, 163
dependent variable, 224
derivative, 201
dermin (subroutine), 37
deterministic algorithm, 2
Discrim (class), 323
discriminant function, 319
distance computation, 190, 196

E

E0 (subroutine), 374
Edgeworth's expansion, 273
efficiency, 272
eigenvalue, 299
ERASE TRAINING SET (PNN), 384
error:
    apparent, 360, 361
    excess, 363
    population, 362
error criterion, 197, 201
    derivative, 201
Euclidean distance, 196
EWnet (class), 279
excess error, 363
expectation, 339

F

factors (subroutine), 309, 330
fast cooling, 93
find_new_dir (subroutine), 46
flrand (subroutine), 124

G

gamma (subroutine), 46
GAUSS (PNN), 384, 391
Gaussian function, 168
GCnet (class), 267
GCNN (PNN), 383
GCNN_EW (PNN), 383
general linear models, 198
generalized regression, 234, 381
    architecture, 239
glob_min (subroutine), 11
glossary, 390
gold_min (subroutine), 186

gradient:
    GRNN, 240
    PNN, 201, 207
Gram-Charlier neural network, 383

H

Hermite polynomial, 259
Hessian, 50
histogram bin, 168

I

independent variable, 224

J

jack (subroutine), 349
jackknife, 343
jacobi (subroutine), 311

K

kernel, 163
    multivariate, 170
KERNEL (PNN), 383, 384

L

learning (PNN), 386
lev_marq (subroutine), 58
Levenberg-Marquardt method, 47
line minimization, 8
linear congruential algorithm, 117
linear discriminant function, 319

Index

linear regression, 226
LIST CONFUSION ROW (PNN), 388
lm_core_real (subroutine), 65

M

MAPPING (PNN), 381, 389
minimization:
    backpropagation, 2
    conjugate gradient, 31
    deterministic, 2
    Levenberg-Marquardt, 47
    line, 8
    steepest descent, 4
    stochastic, 74
misclassification cost, 162
MODE (PNN), 381
moment, 264
momentum, 5
multiple regression, 227
multivariate:
    GCNN, 289
    kernel, 170

N

NETWORK MODEL (PNN), 382, 383
normal random numbers, 125
normal_pair (subroutine), 127

O

optimization:
    backpropagation, 2
    conjugate gradient, 31
    deterministic, 2
    Levenberg-Marquardt, 47
    steepest descent, 4
    stochastic, 74
outliers, 161
output mode (PNN), 381

P

Parzen's method, 163
perturb (subroutine), 113
perturbation, 88, 112
polynomial:
    Chebyshev, 231
    regression, 230
population error, 362
potential function, 163
principal components, 191, 295
PrincoData (class), 303
PRIOR (PNN), 385
prior probability, 162, 204
probability distribution, 338
process_real (subroutine), 67

R

rand1s (subroutine), 121
random numbers:
    beta, 129
    Cauchy, 127
    gamma, 130
    normal, 125
    spherical, 131
    uniform, 116
RECIPROCAL (PNN), 384, 391
regression, 198
    generalized, 234
    linear, 226
    multiple, 227
    ordinary, 224
    polynomial, 230
RESTORE NETWORK (PNN), 390
RUN NETWORK (PNN), 390
RUN OUTPUT (PNN), 390

S

SAVE NETWORK (PNN), 390
saving weights (PNN), 389
scaling parameter, 164, 180
scaling principal components, 300
SEPCLASS (PNN), 383
SEPVAR (PNN), 382
shuffling, 120
sigma, 164
    separate classes, 212
    separate variables, 194
SIGMA HIGH (PNN), 387
SIGMA LOW (PNN), 387
SIGMA TRIES (PNN), 387
simulated annealing, 74
singular value decomposition, 229
starting temperature, 78
statistic, 338
steepest descent, 8
stochastic:
    algorithm, 2, 74
    smoothing, 103
stopping temperature, 78
subroutine:
    anneal1, 79
    anneal2, 96
    anx_cj, 137
    boot, 371
    brentmin, 19
    cauchy, 132
    cheby, 233
    cv, 367
    density, 269
    dermin, 37
    E0, 374
    factors, 309, 330
    find_new_dir, 46
    flrand, 124
    gamma, 46
    glob_min, 11
    gold_min, 186
    GRNN gradient, 244
    jack, 349
    jacobi, 311
    lev_marq, 58
    lm_core_real, 64
    normal_pair, 127
    perturb, 113
    PNN gradient, 210, 216
    process_real, 67
    rand1s, 121
    unifrand, 125

T

temperature:
    reduction, 78
    starting, 78
    stopping, 78
TEST NETWORK (PNN), 389
TOLERANCE (PNN), 386, 393
training set, 162
TRAINING SET (PNN), 384

U

uniform random numbers, 116
unifrand (subroutine), 125

V

validation set, 336
variance 353:
    among-class, 317
    between-class, 317
    of an estimator, 337
    within-class, 316

W

weight function, 163, 167
within-class variance, 316
WRITE CONFUSION ROW (PNN), 388

Z

ZERO CONFUSION ROW (PNN), 388